T0312100

How Reform Worked in China

How Reform Worked in China

The Transition from Plan to Market

Yingyi Qian

The MIT Press
Cambridge, Massachusetts
London, England

This book was set in Palatino LT Std by Toppan Best-set Premedia Limited.

Library of Congress Cataloging-in-Publication Data

Names: Qian, Yingyi, 1956- author.
Title: How reform worked in China : the transition from plan to market / Yingyi Qian.
Description: Cambridge, MA : MIT Press, [2017] | Includes bibliographical references and index.
Identifiers: LCCN 2017007623 | ISBN 9780262534246 (pbk. : alk. paper)
Subjects: LCSH: China--Economic policy--2000- | Central planning--China. | Central-local government relations--China. | Federal government--China. | Decentralization in government--China. | Mixed economy--China.
Classification: LCC HC427.95 .Q2526 2017 | DDC 338.951--dc23 LC record available at https://lccn.loc.gov/2017007623

For my parents

Contents

Acknowledgments

I am most grateful to my coauthors of the publications included in this book, both for giving me the opportunity to work with them and for allowing me to include these articles in the book. I thank Jiahua Che, Hehui Jin, Lawrence J. Lau, Eric Maskin, Gabriella Montinola, Gérard Roland, Barry R. Weingast, and Chenggang Xu for their intellectual inspiration and input in our joint works, and for their valuable comments and suggestions for other articles included in this book.

During the course of research on these projects, I benefited enormously from helpful comments and suggestions from many distinguished colleagues and scholars, especially Philippe Aghion, Alberto Alesina, Takeshi Amemiya, Masahiko Aoki, Kenneth Arrow, Chong-En Bai, Abhijit Banerjee, Pranab Bardhan, Erik Berglof, Patrick Bolton, Bill Evans, Ronald Findlay, Roger Gordon, Avner Greif, Peter Hammond, Oliver Hart, Bengt Holmstrom, Athar Hussain, D. Gale Johnson, Lawrence Katz, Anjini Kochar, Michael Kremer, Anne Krueger, Carla Kruger, Paul Krugman, Jean-Jacques Laffont, Nicholas Lardy, David D. Li, Wei Li, John Litwack, Ronald McKinnon, John McMillan, Dilip Mookherjee, Jonathan Morduch, Peter Murrell, Ramon Myers, Barry Naughton, Roger Noll, Douglass North, Jean Oi, Albert Park, Dwight Perkins, Louis Putterman, Thomas Rawski, Dani Rodrik, Sherwin Rosen, Seth Sanders, Robert Schwab, Anna Seleny, Susan Shirk, William Simon, Pablo Spiller, T. N. Srinivasan, Jan Svejnar, Yijiang Wang, Shang-Jin Wei, Martin Weitzman, David Wildasin, Oliver Williamson, Frank Wolak, Jinglian Wu, Alwyn Young, and Heng-fu Zou.

My interest in China's economic reform started in 1983 when I first met Professor Jinglian Wu at Yale when he was a visiting scholar and I was a graduate student. After I enrolled in the PhD program in economics at Harvard, my academic interest in China's reform deepened. I benefited from several academic mentors during my graduate studies at Harvard; among them, Janos Kornai gave me insights on reform in Eastern European and the Soviet Union, Dwight Perkins guided me toward learning about China from a historical perspective, and Eric Maskin taught me how to use modern economic tools such as game theory to analyze reform problems.

Since 1990, when I joined the economics faculty at Stanford, research on China's reform has become my professional pursuit. Almost all of the articles contained in this book were completed or initiated when I was at Stanford. I am most grateful to my Stanford colleagues Masahiko Aoki, Lawrence J. Lau, Ronald McKinnon, Paul Milgrom, and Joseph Stiglitz for their consistent encouragement and support for my research on China. Outside of Stanford, many gave me intellectual stimulation and support for my research, and I am especially grateful to Oliver Hart, Janos Kornai, Jean-Jacques Laffont, Eric Maskin, Douglass North, Dani Rodrik, Andrei Shleifer, and Oliver Williamson. They may disagree with each other, and we may have different opinions, but they are never short of intellectual depth and challenges.

I have been fortunate to be a faculty member of three universities—Stanford University, the University of Maryland, and the University of California at Berkeley—that provided excellent academic environments as well as financial support for the research on the chapters in this book. I am also grateful to the School of Economics and Management at Tsinghua University in Beijing, where I am currently a faculty member and the dean.

Finally, I would like to thank the dedicated team at the MIT Press, starting with John S. Covell and after his retirement continuing with Jane A. Macdonald and Emily Taber in the acquisitions department and Virginia Crossman in the editorial department, for their dedicated work in making this book possible.

Introduction: A New Perspective on Reform

1. The Success of China's Economic Reform

Starting in 1979, China embarked on a profound economic reform that led to a transformation of the country from a centrally planned economy to a market economy. Over the next 37 years, China produced one of the most spectacular growth records in human history. According to the World Bank, in 2015 the nominal GDP of China was nearly $11 trillion, surpassing 60 percent of U.S. nominal GDP. In comparison, China's nominal GDP in 1978 was only $148 billion, merely 6 percent of that of the U.S. If measured by Purchasing Power Parity (PPP), in 2015 China's GDP was $19 trillion, larger than the $18 trillion GDP of the U.S., the world's largest economy in the last 100 years.[1] The global market took note of the rise of the Chinese economy and in 2015 witnessed two symbolic events: the significant impact of China's exchange rate movements on U.S. markets in August, and the notable effects of the U.S. interest rate rise on Chinese capital flows in December. For China and the world, 2015 was a year to remember.

At least one economist had actually predicted such an outcome twenty years earlier. Angus Maddison (1998) predicted in the late 1990s that China would overtake the U.S. in total GDP by 2015, as measured by PPP. Written in 2000, my article "How Reform Worked in China" (chapter 1 in this book) contains the following simple condition under which Maddison's prediction would make sense: China needed to grow 4 percentage points faster than the U.S. annually from 1995 to 2015 (see chapter 1, note 1). This is exactly what happened. Although this outcome was not a surprise to Maddison, it exceeded the expectations of most economists.

Of course, China's per capita GDP is still not high. In 2015, China's per capita GDP was $7,925 on the nominal term, about 1/7 that of the

U.S. It was $14,239 as measured by PPP, or one quarter of that of the U.S.[2] With that level of per capita GDP, China has become a solid middle-income country for its population of over 1.3 billion. At the same time, the structure of the Chinese economy has also changed dramatically. The share of agriculture in GDP fell from 27.2 percent in 1978 to 9.0 percent in 2015, while the share of people living in cities increased from 18 percent to 56 percent during the same period.[3]

2015 also marked the slowdown of Chinese economic growth when, for the first time since 1991, China's growth rate fell below 7 percent. The year was a turning point, not only because China reached 60 percent of U.S. GDP in the nominal term and overtook the U.S. as the largest economy in the PPP term, but also because China's economic growth was entering a new era. In the coming decades, China faces new challenges, partly due to the nature of its new middle-income status: China is a lot richer than it was before. It is also partly due to the costs China has paid to achieve such rapid growth, including negative effects on the environment, an increase in inequality, wasteful investment, excess capacity, high leverages, unfunded social mandates, and its financial risks. On top of that, its demography has shifted and its population is getting older. In 2014, the share of the population aged 60 or older stood at 15.53 percent, while the population aged 65 or older was 10.06 percent. The share of the population aged 15–59 (i.e., those in the labor force) has been declining in absolute number since 2012.

The Chinese call this situation the "New Normal." The challenges China faces in the next 35 years are unprecedented. The Decision of the Third Plenum of the 18th Congress of the Chinese Communist Party listed over 300 reform items necessary to improve the economy, including fiscal, monetary, social security, health care, and environmental items, as well as State-Owned Enterprises (SOEs), just to name a few. The ambitious goal of these reforms is to develop China into a "moderately prosperous economy" by 2021, the centennial anniversary of the founding of the Chinese Communist Party, and further into a "moderately developed country" by 2049, the centennial of the founding of the People's Republic of China.

Looking backward, it is now a historical fact that China has successfully grown from a poor, agricultural, closed, and centrally planned economy to a middle-income, industrial, open, and large emerging market economy. Looking forward, it is still an open question as to whether China's growth can be sustained (necessarily at a lower rate) as it continues to advance from a middle-income economy to a high-income economy. The next 35 years will answer that question.[4]

2. Two Perspectives on China's Economic Reform

Economists try to understand economic growth through a "growth accounting" approach, which estimates the direct sources contributing to growth—capital accumulation, labor expansion (through realloca-tion from agriculture to industry and services), human capital (through educational attainment), technological progress, and so on. Because of the common factors that contribute to growth over time and across countries, growth accounting helps economists understand the common and direct reasons for the economic growth of all countries during all time periods. The approach is particularly useful for understanding how the "residual," the so-called total factor productivity, contributes to growth. Productivity is considered anything other than the resources already measured as inputs, and its sources include technological pro-gress and institutional changes.[5]

In addition to growth accounting, economists also want to under-stand the role of reform in economic development, and, in particular, the institutional changes behind the scenes and the mechanisms bring-ing about these changes. Economists all agree that China's fast growth in the past 37 years has critically depended on market-oriented reform, but there is less agreement on the main factors of reform that have contributed to the success of China's economy.

To begin with, all unreformed economies have good growth poten-tial because of the slack created by enormous economic distortions, and these economies operate deep inside the production possibility frontier. Additionally, less developed economies can take advantage of the tech-nological achievements of more advanced countries. Closed economies can also benefit from opening by accessing foreign markets, talent pools, and technologies. But all these conditions for growth were present in China before 1979 and in other poor countries, as well. It was the reforms that made the difference.

Economists have tried to understand and interpret China's eco-nomic reform ever since it began. Most of the interpretations fall into one of two schools of thought—the first, I call the "School of Universal Principles," and the second, the "School of Chinese Characteristics."

Those adhering to the School of Universal Principles believe that the success of China's economic reform is due to the universal reasons underlying all economic success around the globe. These are: letting the government get out of way; letting the market work; providing private incentives; and opening up to the global market. Therefore, market liberalization, private incentives, and opening up, plus a stable macroeconomic environment, explain the success of China's reform. All of them are well-summarized in the Washington Consensus. The key to China's success for these economists is its adoption of free market policies. Therefore, China's story offers nothing new to our understanding of reform, other than proof of the fundamental principles of the market.

Adherents to the School of Chinese Characteristics believe just the opposite—that the success of China's economic reform disproves standard economic theory. Thus, China's reform is successful precisely because it did not follow the Washington Consensus: China did not privatize all enterprises at once, nor did it liberalize the market overnight. China's government played a crucial role in the economy through ownership, control, and regulation, as well as industrial policies, and these economists believe that China's success is because of, not in spite of, the strong governmental role in the reform. They hold that these Chinese characteristics explain China's success, not the conventional universal principles. On a deeper level, the School of Chinese Characteristics also provides an alternative principle: the mistrust of market, private ownership, and globalization.

Both schools contain elements of truth, but both are only partially right.

The School of Universal Principles correctly emphasizes that it is ultimately the market that provides the driving force for growth. This argument is most relevant when one compares pre- and post-reform China. The institutions of the Party and the state are common to both but there are critical differences in the liberalization of the market, the expansion of private ownership, and the opening up of the economy. Further, over time China has seen more and more of these "universally working" elements. One cannot rule out the possibility that, over the long run, China is developing a market economy more or less in the same way that advanced countries have, despite various short-term anomalies.

The additional advantage of the School of Universal Principles is its normative implications. It offers a clear goal for transition to a market economy and a target for eventual convergence. It also provides a benchmark for measuring the "distance" between transition economies and the "best practices" seen in advanced countries. The School of Universal Principles provides the reformers in China and also in other countries with much needed economic principles as well as arguments against non-reformers.

However, the School of Universal Principles is incomplete both in explaining China's reform and in providing guidance for reform. As a positive theory, it cannot adequately explain the details of China's reform path. It tends to ignore the complexity and sophistication of the reform and does not explain its underlying mechanisms. As a normative theory, it is often too abstract and generic to be useful in practice. The general principles usually have linear implications from plan to market: the more market, the better; the less government, the better; and the faster the reform, the better. Such universal principles are useful benchmarks in theory, yet they are usually not implementable in practice. They generally cannot be operational guides for reform in a realistic context.

The School of Chinese Characteristics correctly highlights some salient features of Chinese reform that are apparently special to China and inconsistent with the best practices advocated by the School of Universal Principles. These Chinese characteristics include: the strong role of government in the form of state ownership, mixed ownership involving government, dual-track liberalization, industrial policies, gradualism, capital control, and so on. Of course, not all of these elements are unique to China. Twenty years ago, a similar debate on the "East Asia miracle" involved some of these elements in the contexts of the East Asian economies of such countries as Japan, South Korea, and Singapore. But China's case involves an even greater role of government. In addition, because China's population is three times larger than all high-performing East Asian economies combined, the Chinese characteristics argument seems even more compelling as a positive theory.

The School of Chinese Characteristics also has strong normative implications, at two different levels. At the tactical level, it provides a reform guide that is not usually the one recommended by expert economists trained in the West or by international organizations such as the World Bank and the International Monetary Fund. It refuses to follow common recommendations on the grounds that these "universally applicable" reform measures do not fit into China's reality. At the more general level, it points to the eventual deviation from the best practices of the advanced market economies in the long run, and redefines the market economy with a stronger role of government. At either level, both non-reformers and reformers make use of this type of argument. Non-reformers are against the goal of market-oriented reform entirely. Reformers are either against a particular method of implementing the reform or they have some doubts that the best practices seen in advanced countries are truly the best solutions.

However, despite its correct observations regarding Chinese reform, the School of Chinese Characteristics can be both superficial and mis-leading. From a positive perspective, it does not delve deep enough to see what role these Chinese characteristics really play. It is not clear how Chinese characteristics served as necessary stepping-stones in the reform, nor is it clear how they became essential elements of the reform. As a result, this school does not rule out the possibility that without certain characteristics China could actually do better, perhaps not in terms of a faster growth, but in terms of lower costs. Furthermore, when the analysis of China's success depends too much on unique features of Chinese characteristics, then China's case becomes too special and the arguments lose generality.

From a normative perspective, the School of Chinese Characteristics can be misleading because it can be used as an excuse to delay market-oriented reform or to reject such reform altogether. This is seen clearly in China, especially after the 2008 global financial crisis. The world economy, and specifically the developed economies of the U.S., the European Union, and Japan, suffered greatly during the crisis and to this date still have not recovered fully. This gives ammunition to adher-ents to the School of Chinese Characteristics to reject the "universal principles," not so much on the grounds that China is doing particu-larly well, but on the grounds that the advanced countries are not. Non-reformers use the ideas from the School of Chinese Characteristics to further their goals of advocating alternative ways to permanently and fundamentally deviate from market-oriented reform. This is wor-risome because it goes beyond the debate of different reform methods and rejects market-oriented reform altogether.

3. The Third Perspective on China's Economic Reform

Those in the School of Universal Principles believe their principles should be universally applied, regardless of location, time, and specific country conditions. Those in the School of Chinese Characteristics are proud of what China has achieved and reject the universal principles altogether based on limited observations. However, because we are dealing with complicated institutional changes on such a large scale without the analytical and experimental tools of the natural sciences, we especially need modesty and humility.

In this book, I propose a new, third perspective through which to understand China's economic reform. This perspective takes certain elements from each school of thought, but it is not simply a middle road between the two. Fundamentally, this perspective is less about why reform worked and more about how reform worked. If the former is science, the latter is applied science and engineering. As in engineering, the possibility for implementation is the key.

This perspective uses the universal principles as a starting point and benchmark for comparison. It also takes elements from the School of Chinese Characteristics, but goes deeper to figure out the mechanisms underneath the surface. It is less about the goal of reform than the reform process itself.

To understand any reform, it is essential to focus on how to get things done. From a practitioner's point of view, it is more useful to find a feasible reform path than the best way. This may be, and usually is, the "second-best" way or even the "third-best" way because implementation and execution are key. This is the engineering of reform.

In this perspective, economics as a science is the same everywhere, but economic reform processes are different. The differences depend on two elements: first, the initial historical conditions, and second, the contemporary constraints.

The essential elements of this perspective can be summarized in four observations. First, the universal principles of economics work in China just as they work elsewhere. Second, the Chinese economy has at this point converged more or less to the standard form of the market economy and will continue to do so. Third, the Chinese approach to reform worked because it was a constrained optimization. Fourth, understanding the initial historical conditions and contemporary constraints and how reform designs respond to such conditions and constraints is the key to understanding how reform has worked in China. Both of the former two observations are consistent with the thought in the School of Universal Principles, but are only the starting point. The latter two observations share some views with the School of Chinese Characteristics, but the analyses are different.

All countries have different initial historical conditions and face different contemporary constraints. The good news is that preexisting distortions can often provide enormous potential for improvement and growth. One important initial condition in China was its strong Party and state. On the outside, the strength of the Party and state could be considered disadvantageous for market-oriented reform. How to provide private incentives and overcome vested interest to liberate the market is not at all obvious at the inception of the reform. This book looks at the details of this particular context.

The universal principles and Chinese characteristics can be interpreted in terms of function and form, respectively. In terms of function, the principles are simple, standard, and universal. The reform works by getting the incentives right, making the market work, and opening up to the outside world. On the other hand, the specific forms or mechanisms of the reform can be complicated and it may use nonstandard methods to perform a given function, as it needs to respond to initial conditions and contemporary constraints.

Best-practice institutions (for example, private property protected by the rule of law), which are derived from the universal principles in the context of advanced economies, serve these economies well today, although this has not necessarily been true throughout the history of these countries. The best practices do not need to take a unique form, nor should they necessarily be the reform choice for other economies. However, best-practice institutions are still very useful as a benchmark and also as an eventual goal to which to aspire.

From the perspective of best practices, reform often adopts the form of "flawed" institutions. But not all flawed institutions are the same. In fact, most of them are so flawed that they do not work. What we need instead are *appropriate* and *adequate* institutions. For appropriateness, they have to be suitable to local conditions and satisfy all constraints, including political ones. For adequateness, they have to be sufficiently effective to unleash the standard forces of the market and incentives—that is, to relax the binding constraints for the market and incentives to work. When both conditions are satisfied, the institutions are not only feasible but also good enough to facilitate economic growth. They are effective in the short run, and will also evolve further and be replaced by other institutions in the long run.[6]

The following two examples concerning ownership of firms demonstrate the dynamic evolution of appropriate and adequate forms of institutional change in China.

The first example shows the dynamics of ownership in domestic firms. Figure 0.1 illustrates the shares of industrial output from state-

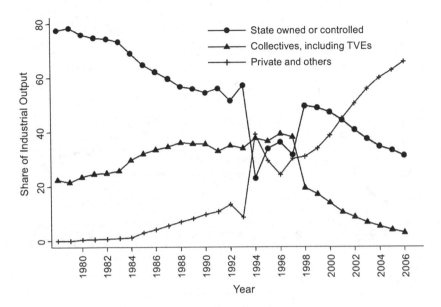

Figure 0.1
The Shares of Industrial Output: State, Collective, and Private Firms (1978–2006).
Source: China Statistical Yearbook, various years.

owned or controlled firms, collective firms (i.e., firms with local government control), and others (mostly private firms) over time. The
dynamic is interesting, especially in terms of the rise and fall of collective firms, which include Township-Village Enterprises (TVEs). TVEs
are an example of a "flawed" ownership form, but they were known
to work during the first two decades of China's reform. First, they satisfied the appropriateness condition: they had the advantage at the time
of political and economic discrimination against private ownership.
Second, they satisfied the adequateness condition: they provided an
immediate entry into high-profit-margin businesses when inefficient
state-owned firms failed to deliver. As the economy developed,
however, the relative advantage of collective firms declined and their
share in the economy fell.

The second example demonstrates the dynamics of ownership
in foreign direct investment. Figure 0.2 shows the shares of wholly
foreign-owned firms, equity joint venture firms, and contractual joint
venture firms over time. The relationships in figure 0.2 are also interesting, especially the rise and fall of the equity joint venture firms. In
these firms, foreigners have control but the government has a stake in
ownership. First, they satisfied the appropriateness condition: foreign

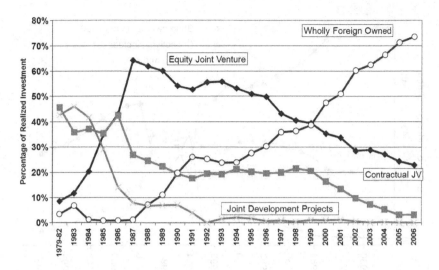

Figure 0.2
Ownership Forms of Foreign Direct Investment (1979–2006).
Source: China Statistical Yearbook, various years.

firms needed help from the local government, and the government's
incentive came from its stake in ownership. Second, they satisfied the
adequateness condition: foreign control provided better management.
But, as the market condition improved, the relative advantage of equity
joint venture firms declined, so their share in the economy also fell.

Therefore, in the third perspective, prescribing a standard menu of
best-practice institutions (as is often done by the School of Universal
Principles) is easy and attractive, but may not work well in a specific
country at a specific time. Alternatively, devising institutions that are
both appropriate and adequate to local conditions is challenging and
often requires innovation. Recognizing that institutions matter is only
the beginning; the deeper and more relevant issue is to understand how
reform in institutions works.

This approach can be used to reconcile the apparent tension about
China's economy in what Loren Brandt and Thomas Rawski (2008)
describe as "a remarkable combination of high-speed growth and
deeply flawed institutions." Indeed, China's institutions are flawed,
and sometimes deeply flawed, as compared with the best-practice institutions prescribed by the universal principles. But these imperfect
institutions reflect not only the country's level of economic development
but also its contexts of transition and reform. They can achieve the
goals of improving efficiency and generating growth when the economy

has a lot of slack due to preexisting distortions. This book answers the question of what mechanisms in which imperfect institutions can work to support good economic performance.

The third perspective pursued in this book parallels Dani Rodrik's approach to economic reform as shown in his 2007 book *One Economics, Many Recipes*. "One economics" means there are universal principles that apply to all countries. However, because each country has specific local contexts, the reform recipe is often different from country to country. Whereas Rodrik studies many different countries, I focus only on China—the most dynamic and important, yet difficult-to-understand case.

4. Chapters in the Book

The twelve chapters of this book consist of a collection of my articles, many of which were jointly written with my collaborators.

The first chapter carries the same title as the main title of the book. Written 15 years ago, it examines how reform worked in China through the lens of "transitional institutions." The transitional institutions are those institutions that respond to local conditions to increase economic efficiency while satisfying constraints. They are usually not fully efficient and are therefore "second-best institutions." However, they are "incentive compatible" for stakeholders, and especially for the government, because the government finds implementing them to be in its interest. At the same time, these institutions are good enough to reduce distortions and provide adequate efficiency improvement.

The rest of the book is organized in four parts, the first three dealing with three types of institutions underlying the economy: markets, firms, and government, respectively. The last part explicitly addresses an important initial condition: the organization of government. The chapters in each part feature concrete examples to demonstrate the central theme of the book, the necessity of the third perspective to understand how China's reform worked, with detailed theoretical and empirical analysis.

Part I concerns market liberalization with Chinese characteristics— the dual-track approach. Chapter 2 provides a partial equilibrium analysis of dual-track market liberalization and chapter 3 provides a general equilibrium analysis. Dual-track market liberalization is the simplest case in which transition from plan to market can be implemented in such a way that it is not only efficiency improving (and sometimes achieves full efficiency) but also, at the same time, Pareto improving—that is, nobody is worse off. It is also unorthodox from the perspective of the universal principles, which would advocate for freeing all the prices at once. The feature of everybody being better off is desirable in reform, and dual-track market liberalization can be implemented in practice, provided the state enforces the planned track—the initial condition that China satisfied with its strong state institution.

Part II analyzes ownership of firms. The three chapters in this part each have a different focus: chapter 4 is descriptive and narrative, providing a full detailed account of the rural industrial sector with a variety of enterprise ownership forms. Chapter 5 develops a theoretical model of ownership by taking into account a very important institutional feature in a transition economy—the lack of security of property rights. In this context, it compares three types of firm ownership: state-owned, privately owned, and community government owned. It derives conditions under which each is more productive than the other two. This model not only explains township-village enterprises (an example of community government owned firms) in the first two decades of the reform, but also sheds light on enterprises with mixed ownership involving government (including public-private partnership) in the last two decades. Chapter 6 is an empirical study that tests some of the implications of the theoretical model developed in chapter 5 using data from rural China. The evidence supports the model's predictions.

Part III discusses the decentralization of government and its implications for economic reform. Fiscal federalism is a topic in public finance that usually focuses on the efficiency of providing public goods through competition among localities when people vote by foot to match their preferences. China is not a federal state *de jure* but during the reform it implemented a decentralized fiscal system to provide local governments with fiscal incentives to develop their local economies. Chapter 7 includes observations about China's regional decentralization during the reform and links it with local economic development. In this context, it proposes to use the framework of "federalism, Chinese style" to study the relationship between local government and economic development. Chapter 8 explores the idea that federalism or, more precisely, government decentralization is a useful reform to expand market incentives. This approach to market-oriented reform is unusual because the standard approach is to get government out of the way. It acknowledges Chinese characteristics but evokes the universal principle of the necessity of incentives. Chapter 9 is an empirical study to test the hypotheses developed in the previous two chapters. Local government's fiscal incentives, as measured by the marginal revenue retention rate, were greatly strengthened in the early stage of reforms, which in turn provided the incentives for local governments to support more productive firms such as non-state enterprises, including private firms and local government firms, rather than central government firms.

Part IV concerns a specific form of initial conditions—regional-based organization of central planning in China as opposed to functional- or industrial-based organization of central planning in the Soviet Union. Alternative ways to organize central planning have significant implications for economic transition to the market and run parallel to the alternative ways of organizing corporations in a market economy. Chapter 10 represents the first paper to draw attention to the distinction between alternative organizations of central planning and to connect them to the pioneering work of Alfred Chandler (1966) and Oliver Williamson (1975), which compared M-form (multi-divisional form) and U-form (unitary form) corporate organization. It also further studies the implications of government organization on market-oriented reform. Chapter 11 focuses on the incentive issues in M-form and U-form organizations by examining the theoretical implications for the use of local information in the economy. It then utilizes data from China to test the validity of the model. Chapter 12 studies the coordination issue in M-form and U-form organizations, where the distinctive feature of the former is the relatively low cost for coordinating local experiments when each region is self-contained. Indeed, reform through experimentation was a distinct feature throughout Chinese reform, but it was rarely seen in the former Soviet Union or Eastern Europe. This chapter provides a reason for this difference: the initial condition of central planning organization.

The four parts together demonstrate the central theme of the book: that examining how reform worked in China requires detailed analysis based on universal principles and taking into account the specific initial conditions and contemporary constraints in order to explain observed Chinese characteristics. The process of analysis demonstrates the benefits and costs of the reform and reveals the second-best nature of the institutional change. Therefore, by analyzing the underlying mechanisms of how reform worked, we better understand the process and outcome of reform.

5. Concluding Remarks

As China's economy is already the largest in the world as measured in PPP terms, is the second largest on the nominal term, and will probably become the largest on the nominal term in the next 15 years, understanding China's reform is a worthwhile venture in itself. In addition, the general ideas and analytical approaches presented in this book may also provide lessons for reforms in other countries.

The general lessons from this book are that for a reform to be successful, it is important to use the universal principles, even if they alone are not enough, and that it is equally important to find specific ways to implement the reform by fully incorporating the initial historical conditions as well as contemporary constraints. With large slack in the economy, appropriate and adequate institutions in the form of second-best institutions can go a long way toward successful economic reform—China's experiences have shown that it can be done. But the lesson from the study of China also shows that simply copying the "China model," if there is one, is not useful. Nevertheless, the perspective of reform provided by this book's analysis on China's case is valuable precisely because it emphasizes that for reform to succeed, it is not enough to understand why reform works; we must also understand how reform works.

When Lawrence Summers speculated in 1992 that the revolutionary change in China might be the most significant event of the late twentieth century, many people did not take his statement seriously. But he was right. If China's economic reform is the most significant event of the late twentieth century, then the rise of the Chinese economy to the world stage may be the most significant event of the early twenty-first century.

Notes

1. "List of countries by GDP (nominal)," https://en.wikipedia.org/wiki/List_of_countries_by_GDP_(nominal); and "List of countries by GDP (PPP)," https://en.wikipedia.org/wiki/List_of_countries_by_GDP_(PPP). Accessed on August 4, 2016.

2. "List of countries by GDP (nominal) per capita," https://en.wikipedia.org/wiki/List_of_countries_by_GDP_(nominal)_per_capita; and "List of countries by GDP (PPP) per capita," https://en.wikipedia.org/wiki/List_of_countries_by_GDP_(PPP)_per_capita. Accessed on August 4, 2016.

3. Data are all from *China Statistical Yearbook 2016*, unless noted.

4. The larger question is about political transition. Even with a large, open, middle-income economy deeply integrated with the rest of the world, China has a political system that is much the same today as it was 37 years ago. The interaction between economic development and political modernization is a very important topic but it is beyond the scope of this book.

5. See Dwight Perkins and Thomas Rawski (2008) for a growth accounting study of China between 1952 and 2005.

6. These ideas were first presented in my Lian Huang Memorial Lecture "China's Economic Transformation in Perspective," delivered at the Stanford Institute of Economic Policy Research on February 27, 2008.

References

Brandt, Loren, and Thomas Rawski. 2008. China's Great Economic Transformation. In *China's Great Economic Transformation*, edited by Loren Brandt and Thomas Rawski, pp. 1–26. Cambridge, UK: Cambridge University Press.

Chandler, Alfred, Jr. 1966. *Strategy and Structure*. New York: Doubleday & Company, Inc.

China Statistical Yearbook 2016. 2016. National Bureau of Statistics of China, Beijing: China Statistics Press.

Maddison, Angus. 1998. *Chinese Economic Performance in an International Perspective*. Paris: OECD.

Perkins, Dwight, and Thomas Rawski. 2008. Forecasting China's Economic Growth to 2025. In *China's Great Economic Transformation*, edited by Loren Brandt and Thomas Rawski, pp. 829–886. Cambridge, UK: Cambridge University Press.

Rodrik, Dani. 2007. *One Economics, Many Recipes: Globalization, Institutions, and Economic Growth*. Princeton, NJ: Princeton University Press.

Summers, Lawrence. 1992. The Rise of China. *Transition* (World Bank) 3 (6): 7.

Williamson, Oliver. 1975. *Markets and Hierarchies*. New York: Free Press.

1 How Reform Worked in China

1. A Puzzling Reform That Worked

In the last twenty-two years of the 20th century, China has transformed itself from a poor, centrally planned economy to a lower-middle-income, emerging market economy. With total gross domestic product (GDP) growing at an average annual rate of about 9 percent, China's per capita GDP more than quadrupled during this period. The benefits of growth were also shared by the people on a broad basis: the number of people living in absolute poverty was substantially reduced from over 250 million to about 50 million, a decline from a third to a twenty-fifth of its population; and life expectancy has increased from 64 in the 1970s to over 70 in the late 1990s. Both the formal statistics and casual tourist impressions tell the same story: China's growth is real. Two decades ago, few economists would have bet on the outcome in China today. At the time, coming out of the disastrous decade of the Cultural Revolution, China was poor, overpopulated, short of human capital and natural resources, and constrained by the ideology hostile toward markets and opposed to radical reform. Growth of this kind under such initial conditions is a surprise.

China's phenomenal growth is not just another successful growth story because China is not a "typical" country, although in cross-country regressions China can only represent one data point, the same as Singapore or Ireland or Botswana. China is the largest transition and developing economy. As an economy in transition from plan to market, China has a population three times greater than all other transition economies combined, including the 15 former Soviet Republics. In 2000, its $1 trillion economy was already bigger than all other transition economies combined. As a developing economy, China has a

---

Originally published in Dani Rodrik, editor, *In Search of Prosperity: Analytic Narratives on Economic Growth*, Princeton University Press, 2003, pp. 297–333.

population almost three times that of all eight high-performing East Asian economies of Japan, South Korea, Taiwan, Hong Kong, Singapore, Malaysia, Thailand, and Indonesia. It has managed to match the growth record of these economies during their heyday, but with a much larger population. The cumulative effects of the two decades' growth are significant when comparing China with its two largest neighbors: in total GDP terms, in 1988 China was less than half of Russia, but ten years later Russia was less than half of China. On per capita basis, two decades ago China and India were about equal, but now China is about twice as rich as India.

China's growth is unlikely to end any time soon. In the first half of 2001, China's economy ignored the global slowdown and continued to grow at an annual rate of about 8 percent. Defying the perception that China has reached a plateau of growth, more and more economists are starting to believe that the best part of China's growth has not come yet. With entry into the World Trade Organization (WTO), they suspect that China's economy is on the verge of the next boom.

According to Maddison's (1998) calculation, China might overtake the United States in total GDP in terms of "purchasing power parity" by 2015.[1] If Maddison is right, China would be the only economy, excluding the European Union, capable of surpassing the U.S. economy (in purchasing power parity) within the next two decades. And this would make China the largest economy in the world, regaining the historical position that it lost in the middle of the nineteenth century. No wonder Lawrence Summers speculated in the early 1990s: "It may be that when the history of the late 20th century is written in a hundred years the most significant event will be the revolutionary change in China" (Summers 1992).

On the ground of economic growth and improving living standards, there is no question that China's reform has worked. But this reform is puzzling. In the early 1990s, the economics profession and policymakers reached a striking degree of unanimity on the recipe for transition from plan to market. Simply put, it calls for stabilization, liberalization, and privatization, following political democratization. Although many economists may not consider this recipe sufficient, few would question its necessity. Theoretically, it is difficult to imagine how a reform would work without these essential ingredients. Empirically, the fresh memory of the frustrated reform experience in Hungary, Poland, and the former Soviet Union prior to 1990 suggests that a reform will fail if it does not follow these recommendations.

The Chinese path of reform and its associated rapid growth is puzzling because it seems to defy this conventional wisdom. Although China has adopted many of the policies advocated by economists—such as being open to trade and foreign investment and sensitive to macroeconomic stability—violations of the standard prescriptions are striking. For the most part of the past two decades, China's reform succeeded without complete liberalization, without privatization, and without democratization. One might have reasoned that coexistence of the planning mechanism with partial liberalization would only cause more distortion and become a source of disruption, not growth. Without privatization and secure private property rights, how could there be genuine market incentives? Without democracy, economic reform lacks a political basis and commitment to a market and thus is vulnerable. The actual performance of the Chinese reform provides a striking contrast to these expectations. Why has China grown so fast, ask Blanchard and Fischer (1993), when conditions thought to be necessary for growth were absent?

It is not surprising that China's reform has been viewed as an anomaly and thus has been unappreciated by mainstream economists. For example, *From Plan to Market: World Development Report 1996* on transition economies (World Bank 1996) gave China short shrift because it couldn't figure out where to put China on the various measurement parameters. China simply does not fit into the general description of the report.

Those who do not find China's reform puzzling often misunderstand it. Two types of misperceptions of China's economic success are common. The first is to regard foreign direct investment (FDI) and exports as the driving force for China's success. In this connection the roles of overseas Chinese and of Hong Kong and Taiwan are often emphasized. The simplicity of the argument adds to its power, and the tacit message—it is the foreigners and foreign markets that made China grow—finds an appreciative audience outside China. However, the argument loses its plausibility as soon as one considers a parallel experience in Germany. If Hong Kong or Taiwan could play such a powerful role on mainland China, West Germany should have been even more effective in East Germany, given that West Germany is much larger and stronger than Taiwan and Hong Kong combined, and East Germany is much smaller than mainland China.

The role of FDI in China is vastly overstated in the press. In the 1980s, FDI in China was tiny. FDI only started to increase substantially in 1993, and at its peak it accounted for about 10 percent of total investment.

On per capita basis, China's FDI was not high by international standards. It is true that China's exports expanded very quickly, but that cannot be the main story. The direct contribution of foreign trade and investment to large countries cannot be quantitatively as important as to those small countries.

Like FDI, China's exports were very concentrated in coastal provinces. However, contrary to a popular perception, China's growth was not just a phenomenon of coastal provinces—it is across the board, both coastal and inland. Inland provinces are growing fast, though coastal provinces are growing faster. Anyone who has traveled to inland cities such as Xi'an or Guiyang cannot fail to notice their vibrant local economies. Indeed, if each of China's provinces is counted as a distinct economy, about 20 of the top 30 growth regions in the world in the past two decades would be provinces in China—many of which did not receive much foreign investment and did not depend on exports. Table 1.1 shows GDP growth by province in China and refutes the perception that growth in China is only coastal.

If focusing on FDI and foreign trade tends to downplay the entire reform process and of the role of indigenous institutions, then a simple-minded view on trade and foreign investment creates obstacles to the

Table 1.1
GDP Growth Rates by Province (percent)

Provinces	1978–90	1978–95	Provinces	1978–90	1978–95
Beijing	9.0	9.8	Henan	12.6	10.9
Tianjin	7.7	8.9	Hubei	9.4	10.5
Hebei	8.5	10.2	Hunan	7.7	8.7
Shanxi	8.2	8.8	Guangdong	12.3	14.2
Inner Mongolia	9.8	13.0	Guangxi	7.2	9.9
Liaoning	8.1	8.8	Hainan	10.1	12.3
Jilin	8.9	9.5	Sichuan	8.6	9.5
Heilongjiang	4.9	4.8	Guizhou	9.2	9.1
Shanghai	7.4	9.1	Yunan	9.7	9.9
Jiangsu	11.0	12.8	Tibet	7.7	8.3
Zhejiang	11.7	13.8	Shaanxi	9.0	9.1
Anhui	9.3	10.7	Gansu	8.2	8.6
Fujian	11.5	13.7	Qinghai	6.5	6.8
Jiangxi	9.0	10.4	Ningxia	9.2	8.9
Shangdong	10.0	11.9	Xinjiang	10.8	11.1

Source: China Statistical Yearbook.

understanding of growth in any country. This is because the effect of openness has to work through corresponding internal changes. Russia became very open after reform, more so than China, but neither higher growth nor more FDI ensued. Even in small East Asian countries, an export-oriented policy worked through domestic changes in investment and human capital accumulation. Therefore, it could well be the case that it is not exports that drive growth, but that the same forces of domestic change drive both exports and domestic growth.

The second common misperception about China's success is to attribute it exclusively to the agricultural reform in the early 1980s. To be sure, China's agricultural reform was a huge success. And the reason for it is pretty much a standard story of family farming plus market liberalization, although research has shown that the story is more complicated than that. For example, there seemed to be significant contributions from the rural R&D and infrastructure investments made in the 1970s toward the agriculture productivity growth in the 1980s (Huang and Rozelle 1996); and the state institutions for marketing also played important roles in rural development (Rozelle 1996). Nevertheless, economists are generally comfortable with the Chinese agriculture reform because it fits their models of the world.

This way of thinking becomes a myth when one regards agricultural reform as the only successful reform in China. Often it carries two implicit messages: China did not do well in nonagricultural sectors because it did not follow the conventional advice, and China did well in agriculture reform because it was—and still is—a poor, agricultural country. The truth is that the agricultural reform was the first reform success in China, but its bigger achievements lie elsewhere. At the outset of reform in the late 1970s, over 70 percent of China's labor force was employed in agriculture. By 2000, China's agriculture labor force had already declined to below the 50 percent mark, which is impossible without successful development outside the agriculture sector. In the late 1990s, the agricultural share of China's GDP was as 16 percent, about the same level as in Poland and the Soviet Union in the early 1980s. Table 1.2 provides evidence showing that most of China's growth came from the non-agricultural sector—the industrial and tertiary sectors.

The agricultural sector can have important indirect effects on nonagricultural sectors. For example, successful agricultural reform provides sources of savings and labor to boost industrialization. But in

Table 1.2
Growth Rates of GDP and GDP Components (percent)

Year	GDP	Agriculture	Industry	Tertiary
1979	7.6	6.1	8.2	7.8
1980	7.8	-1.5	13.6	5.9
1981	5.5	7.0	1.9	10.4
1982	9.1	11.5	5.6	13.0
1983	10.9	8.3	10.4	15.2
1984	15.2	12.9	14.5	19.4
1985	13.5	1.8	18.6	18.3
1986	8.8	3.3	10.2	12.1
1987	11.6	4.7	13.7	14.4
1988	11.3	2.5	14.5	13.2
1989	4.1	3.1	3.8	5.4
1990	3.8	7.3	3.2	2.3
1991	9.2	2.4	13.9	8.8
1992	14.2	4.7	21.2	12.4
1993	13.5	4.7	19.9	10.7
1994	12.6	4.0	18.4	9.6
1995	10.5	5.0	14.1	8.0

Notes: Data on industry includes construction.
Source: China Statistical Yearbook.

order for this mechanism to work, reforms of the nonagricultural sector are necessary. The fact that today China is no longer a poor, agricultural country demonstrates that the main success of China's reform lies outside agriculture.

One cannot understand China's growth without understanding how its reform worked in the domestic, nonagricultural sector, which is the focus of this paper.

2. Perspectives on Institutions

In their standard way of thinking, economists consider labor, physical capital, human capital, and productivity as the proximate determinants of growth. But factor accumulation and productivity changes are endogenous, depending on improvement in technology, allocative efficiency, and incentives, which in turn are shaped by institutions. The advocates of new institutional economics (Coase 1992; North 1997; and Williamson 1994) recognize that a good market economy requires not only "getting prices right," but also "getting property rights right" and "getting institutions right." This is because property rights, and institutions in general, set the rules that affect the behavior of economic agents.

The institutional economists thus regard the conventional wisdom of transition focusing on stabilization, liberalization, and privatization as inadequate, because it misses the important institutional dimension. To these economists, a set of institutions is critical for sustained growth, including secure private property rights protected by the rule of law, impartial enforcement of contracts through an independent judiciary, appropriate government regulations to foster market competition, effective corporate governance, transparent financial systems, and so on. The fact that all of them can be readily found in developed economies, especially in the United States, implies that they are "best-practice" institutions.

Economists then use these institutions as a benchmark to judge transition and developing economies, and often find huge institutional gaps. These findings then serve three purposes. First, they generate a diagnosis of the deficiency of institutions in developing and transition economies. Second, they are used to explain why these economies perform poorly, confirming the central hypothesis that institutions matter. Third, they lead to recommendations for institution building: If the economy has weak property rights, clarify them. A weak financial system? Strengthen it. A bad law? Change it. A corrupt legal system? Clean it up.

This "menu perspective" on institutions is useful in providing a benchmark of best-practice institutions with which today's most developed economies have pushed the development frontier. But this perspective does not provide enough intellectual power for investigations of how reform worked (or did not work) in many developing and transition economies. Compare China with Russia for the last decade. Neither of them had rule of law, secure private property rights, effective corporate governance, or a strong financial system. But the two exhibited a huge difference in performance, which obviously cannot be attributed to the presence or absence of the best-practice institutions.

The same kind of problem arises from the cross-country regressions incorporating institutional development indices. For example, the World Bank study *Beyond Washington Consensus: Institutions Matter* (Burki and Perry 1998) gets serious on institutions. It compiles a "composite institutional development index" for each country, using a menu of institutions that include the rule of law, financial institutions, ownership, public administration, and so on. The study carries out cross-country growth regressions using this index to find positive associations between economic growth and institutional development. While the cross-country regressions are useful in estimating the magnitudes of the effects of explanatory variables on growth, they only do this right when the latter are correctly measured and truly exogenous. Otherwise they lead to biased estimations or leave large residuals unexplained. Indeed, China, together with Taiwan and Chile, is an outlier in the regression showing the relationship between institutional development and economic growth (Figure 1.1.a, Burki and Perry 1998). China is again an outlier in the more refined regression of the "true" partial coefficient between institutional development and growth (Figure 1.1.b, Burki and Perry 1998), together with Thailand, Indonesia, and South Korea. In all these cross-country regressions, China's performance is too high relative to its index value of institutional development. This is not surprising because the measurement of the institutional development index is imprecise and the underlying variable is likely not exogenous.

Recognizing the importance of institutions is only a beginning. A major problem in the study of reform in developing and transition economies is not that there is a neglect of, or even lack of attention paid to, institutions. Not anymore. The problem is the naive perspective on institutions. The naive perspective often confuses the goal (i.e., where to finish) with the process (i.e., how to get there) and thus tends to ignore the intriguing issues of transition paths connecting the starting point and the goal. It is like neglecting the "transition equations" (or "equations of motion") and the "initial conditions" in dynamic programming. Although building best-practice institutions is a desirable goal, getting institutions right is a process involving incessant changes interacting with initial conditions. The difference between China and Russia is not at all that China has established best-practice institutions and that Russia did not. The difference lies in the institutions in transition.

To understand how reforms work in developing and transition economies, we need to broaden our perspective on institutions. It is not enough to study the forms of institutions found in the most developed economies as a desirable goal; it is also essential to study the variety of unfamiliar forms of institutions in transition. The distinction between the conventional, best-practice institutions and the transitional institutions is important. Gerschenkron (1962) made a crucial point in his studies of economic development of latecomers such as Germany in the nineteenth century: the latecomers need to make special arrangements to compensate for their backwardness, and they can find ways to do so. In parallel, the broadened perspective on institutions takes a dynamic, not static, view on institutions. It recognizes that the real challenge of reform facing transition and developing countries is not so much knowing where to end up, but searching for a feasible path toward the goal. Therefore, it focuses on transitional institutions, not best-practice institutions. To use the analogy of mountain climbing, although the peak of a mountain offers the best view, mountaineers enjoy a better and better view along the path toward the peak. For mountaineers, the most challenging job is not the study of the peak, but the search for a feasible path toward it. Like Shleifer and Triesman's (1999) study of the Russian transition, our study of China's transition is not about what is desirable, but about what is feasible.

Compared to the developed economies, the backwardness resulting from the initial institutional conditions in transition and developing economies can be both disadvantageous and advantageous for growth. On the one hand, the immediate effects of the initial institutional conditions are generally not hospitable to growth in most transition and developing economies. Although these countries can take advantage of being latecomers to shorten the time of change, they may not be able to complete all the changes in a short period of time. This is disadvantageous for growth. On the other hand, because the adverse initial institutions created myriad distortions, these economies usually enjoy great growth potential once institutions are changed to remove these distortions. In this regard the most striking examples are former centrally planned economies. These economies started reform from an extremely inefficient status quo. They operated not only far away from the Pareto frontier due to the enormous allocative distortions, but also deep inside the production possibility set because of poor incentives. Huge room existed for efficiency which might generate great growth opportunity not seen in the developed economies. Thus the central question for many transition and developing countries is how to make institutional changes to realize the great growth potential when the initial condition has multiple distortions.

Underlying China's reform is a series of institutional changes in the novel form of transitional institutions. These institutions work because they achieve two objectives at the same time—they improve economic efficiency on the one hand, and make the reform compatible with the interest of those in power on the other. They also take into consideration China's specific initial conditions. At one level, one could argue that China's transitional institutions merely unleashed the standard forces of incentives, hard budget constraints, and competition. This is true, but such an economic rationale is not enough. The transitional institutions are not created solely for increasing the size of a pie, but also to reflect the distributional concerns of how the enlarged pie is divided and the political concerns of how the interests of those in power are served. Rudimentary political logic readily predicts the existence of inefficiency, but it has difficulties in explaining why inefficient institutions are replaced by more efficient ones. China's reform shows that when the growth potential is large, with intelligence and will, reformers can devise efficiency-improving institutional reforms to benefit all, especially including those in power. There is apparently more room than we thought for institutional innovations to address both economic and political concerns, that is, for reforms to improve efficiency while remaining compatible with the interests of those in power.

The general principle of efficiency-improving and interest-compatible institutional change is simple, but the specific forms and mechanisms of transitional institutions often are not. Successful institutional reforms usually are not a straightforward copy of best-practice institutions. They need not be and sometimes should not be. They need not be because room exists for efficiency improvement that does not require fine-tuning at the beginning. They should not be because many dimensions of the initial conditions are country- and context-specific, requiring special arrangements to accommodate. Therefore, inevitably, transitional institutions display a variety of nonstandard forms. Furthermore, because these institutions are often responses to the initial institutional distortions, the mechanisms of their functioning can be intricate. Understanding these mechanisms sometimes needs to appeal to the counter-intuitive "second-best argument," which states that removing one distortion may be counter productive in the presence of another distortion. For all these reasons, studying institutions in transition requires careful, and sometimes imaginative, analysis.

In this chapter I study the general principle and the specific mechanisms underlying China's transitional institutions through the analysis of four successful reforms and one failure. Together, these five examples cover a broad spectrum of institutional reforms of the market, firms, and the government.

The first example is market liberalization through the so-called dual-track approach under which prices were liberalized at the margin while inframarginal plan prices and quotas were maintained. This reform is unconventional but shows in the simplest way of how a reform can simultaneously improve efficiency and protect existing rents. The dual track reveals both the economic and political rationale, and also illustrates how a market-oriented reform can utilize existing institutions designed for central planning.

The second example concerns an innovative form of ownership of firms—local government ownership in general and rural township-village enterprises (TVEs) in particular. This form is not standard, neither private nor state (i.e., national government) ownership. Yet TVEs were China's growth engine until the mid-1990s. The nonstandard ownership form worked to improve efficiency in an adverse environment characterized by insecure private property rights. At the same time, the equity stake of local governments served the interests both of local and national governments by giving them a higher share of revenue relative to the standard private ownership form.

The third example is one of making fiscal federalism productive. China's fiscal contracting between the central and local governments has worked to provide the incentives for local governments to pursue economic prosperity. By granting high marginal retention rates, this innovative arrangement aligned the interests of local governments with local business, and played a fundamental role in turning local governments into "helping hands" of local business. Local governments responded to incentives by supporting productive non-state enterprises and reforming non-productive state enterprises.

The fourth example is about how to constrain the government in order to protect private incentives in the absence of rule of law. The institution of anonymous banking is not only unconventional but also contrary to the principle of transparency. But it has an economic logic: when other institutional means is not working, it limits government predation by reducing the amount of information available to it.

The government accepts such a constraint because it benefits from the revenue out of the banking system through its control over interest rates and capital flow. Although such a practice of financial repression is against the usual policy recommendations, it plays a crucial role in inducing the government to give up discretionary taxes on individuals.

Not all China's reforms worked. One miserable failure is the reform of large-scaled state-owned enterprises (SOEs). After many experiments, no reforms on SOEs have been found to improve economic efficiency in a fashion compatible with the interests of those in power. The institution of Party appointment of top managers is a key obstacle. This failed reform is very costly to China, but fortunately it is not fatal, as SOEs now account for less than one-quarter of the entire economy, and their role is diminishing.

3. Creating the Market: A Dual-Track Approach to Liberalization

The simplest way to demonstrate how China's reform worked is through an illustration of the dual-track approach to market liberalization (Lau, Qian, and Roland 2000). It highlights the general principle underlying this innovative, transitional institution: reform must improve efficiency and yet be compatible with important interests. It also shows that initial conditions, including existing institutions, play a role in implementing the reform.

It is well known that the essential building block of a market system is allocating resource according to free market prices. An essential ingredient of any market-oriented reform involves price liberalization. The eastern European experience has shown two alternative approaches. In the first approach, practiced in Hungary for example, after its 1968 reform, bureaucrats set prices administratively, supposedly in accordance with market supply and demand. But in reality, prices were set through bureaucratic bargaining, often to serve the political objectives of bureaucrats, such as keeping state firms afloat (Kornai 1986). Such reform satisfies bureaucrats' interests, but does not improve efficiency in any significant way because prices are not really determined by the market. This approach proved a failure. After 1990, eastern European countries have adopted a standard approach: prices are freed in one stroke and determined solely by the market.

China adopted a third, unconventional approach to market liberalization known as the dual-track approach. Its basic principle is as follows. On one track, economic agents are assigned rights to, and obligations for, fixed quantities of goods at fixed planned prices as specified in the pre-existing plan. At the same time, a market track is introduced under which economic agents participate in the market at free market prices, provided that they fulfill their obligations under the pre-existing plan. In essence, prices were liberalized at the margin while inframarginal plan prices and quotas were maintained for some time before being phased out. Clearly this approach differed from the two approaches experienced by the eastern European countries: it differs from their experience prior to 1990 because real market prices and markets as a resource allocation institution were created immediately. It was also different from their experience after 1990 because of the continued plan track.

The first implication of the dual-track approach is political: it represents a mechanism for the implementation of a reform without creating losers. The introduction of the market track provides the opportunity for economic agents who participate in it to be better off, whereas the maintenance of the plan track provides implicit transfers to compensate potential losers from the market liberalization by protecting the status quo rents under the pre-existing plan. This can be seen easily from the special case of efficient rationing and efficient planned supply; that is, the planned output is allocated to users with the highest willingness to pay and the planned supply is delivered by suppliers with the lowest marginal costs. Dual-track liberalization means that planned quantity continues to be delivered at the planned price, but any additional quantity can be sold freely in the market. With the dual track, the surpluses of the rationed users and the planned suppliers remain exactly the same. At the same time the new users and suppliers outside the plan are together better off. In comparison, the single-track approach to liberalization in general has distributional consequences that cannot guarantee an outcome without losers.

The second implication of the dual-track approach is economical: it always improves efficiency. Moreover, as the compensatory transfers are inframarginal, the dual-track approach may achieve allocative efficiency too. This can be seen most obviously in the special case of efficient rationing and efficient planned supply. In this case, because there is no inefficiency under the planned track by assumption, the efficient market track matching the residual demand and supply then implies the efficiency of the overall allocation. In a more general case of inefficient rationing and/or inefficient planned supply, the kind of market liberalization as described above cannot achieve efficiency although it always improves efficiency. However, efficiency can still be achieved under full market liberalization under which market resales of plan-allocated goods and market purchases by planned suppliers for fulfilling planned delivery quotas are permitted after the fulfillment of the obligations of planned suppliers and rationed users under the plan (Lau, Qian, and Roland 2000). This type of transactions take many common forms in practice, for example, subcontracting by inefficient planned suppliers to more efficient non-planned suppliers, and labor reallocation when workers in inefficient enterprises keep housing while taking a new job in more efficient firms. In both examples, after fulfilling the obligations under the plan (planned delivery of supply and welfare support through housing subsidies, respectively), the market track functions to undo the inefficiency of the plan track.

The dual-track approach to market liberalization is an example of reform making best use of existing institutions. First, it efficiently utilizes the existing information embedded in the original plan (i.e., existing rents distribution) and thus its implementation does not require additional information. Second, it also enforces the plan through the existing plan institutions and does not need additional institutions. Enforcement of the plan track is crucial for preserving the pre-existing rents. However, contrary to common understanding of the relationship between state power and reform, state enforcement power is needed here not to implement an unpopular reform, but to carry out one that creates only winners, and no losers.

Agricultural market liberalization followed the dual-track approach. The commune (and later households) was assigned the obligation to sell a fixed quantity of output to the state procurement agency as previously mandated under the plan at predetermined plan prices and to pay a fixed tax to the government. It also had the right to receive a fixed quantity of inputs, principally chemical fertilizers, from state-owned suppliers at predetermined plan prices. Subject to fulfilling these conditions, the commune was free to produce and sell whatever it considered profitable, and to retain any profit. Moreover, the commune and households could purchase grain (or other) outputs from the market for resale to the state to fulfill its responsibility. As Table 1.3 shows, under the dual track, the state procurement of domestically produced grains between 1978 and 1988 remained essentially fixed, with 47.8 million tons in 1978 and 50.5 million tons in 1988, while

Table 1.3
Dual-Track Market Liberalization

Grain (million tons)

	1978	1988
State procurement at plan price	47.8	50.5
State procurement at market price	near 0	43.8
Total domestic production	304.8	394.1

Steel (million tons)

	1981	1990
Plan quota	13.91	15.58
Domestic production	26.70	51.53
Plan/production	0.52	0.30

Labor (million)

	1978	1994
State permanent employees	74.51	83.61
State contract employees	0	28.53
Non-state employees	48.9	204.85
State permanent/total	0.60	0.26

Source: Lau, Qian, and Roland (2000).

total domestic grain production increased from 304.8 million tons to 394.1 million tons, almost a one-third increase.

Industrial market liberalization also shows how markets could grow out of plans (Byrd 1991; Naughton 1995). For coal, China's principal energy source, the planned delivery was increased somewhat from 329 million tons in 1981 to 427 million tons in 1989 (mainly because new state coal mines were opened), but the market track increased dramatically from 293 million tons to 628 million tons in the same period. The increases came mainly from small rural coal mines run by individuals and TVEs. For steel, another one of China's major industrial materials, the plan track was quite stable in absolute terms, but the share of plan allocation fell from 52 percent in 1981 to 30 percent in 1990. Unlike coal, the supply response in steel came mainly from large SOEs rather than small non-state firms. In the cases of both coal and steel, because the plan track was basically "frozen," the economy was able to grow out of the plan on the basis of the market-track expansion by state or non-state firms.

Labor market development follows a similar pattern. Table 1.3 shows that employment in the non-state sector increased from 48.9 million to

204.9 million in 1994. In contrast, total employment in the state sector, including civil servants in government agencies and non-profit organizations, increased only from 74.5 million to 112.1 million. Furthermore, within the state sector, there are two tracks as well. Beginning in 1980, while pre-existing employees maintained their permanent employment status, most new hires in the state sector were made under the more flexible contract system. Employment in the plan track has been virtually stationary—it went from 74.51 million in 1978 to 83.61 million in 1994.

4. Developing Firms: Non-Conventional Ownership Form of Township-Village Enterprises

Ownership reform of firms is a central issue in the transition to a market economy. The eastern European experience in ownership transformation has the following pattern. In the earlier reforms (prior to 1990), there was a lack of development of non-state enterprises and a lack of privatization of state-owned enterprises, both were thought responsible for the reform failure. In the post-1990 transition, mass privatization of state enterprises became the cornerstone of the reform, and in many cases, it was a political mandate. Evidence shows that new entry private firms, rather than privatized state firms, have been the driving force for recovery and growth.

New entry firms have been also the driving force of China's growth. But China differs from Eastern Europe and most other developing economies in an important aspect: in the first fifteen years of reform between 1979 and 1993, most new entry Chinese firms were neither private firms nor state firms (i.e., national government firms), but local government firms. As Table 1.4 shows, private enterprises played

Table 1.4
Industrial Output Share by Ownership (percent of total)

	1978	1993
State firms	78%	43%
Non-state firms of which:	22%	57%
of which:		
Local government firms	22%	42%
Private and other types firms	0%	15%

Source: China Statistical Yearbook.

only a minor role: in 1993 they contributed less than 15 percent of the national industrial output. In contrast, in the same year, local government firms contributed to 42 percent of the national industrial output (Table 1.4).

The most important segment of local government firms are township-village enterprises (TVEs) in rural areas, which numbered 1.5 million with employment of 52 million in 1993. The TVE shares of output and employment in rural industry were 72 percent and 58 percent respectively, the rest being private shares. Although TVEs were being privatized and private firms became the engine of growth in the late 1990s, China's reform performance would look very different without the early contributions of TVEs. Thus, in order to understand how reform worked in China, one has to understand TVEs.

The crucial feature of TVEs is the local community (i.e., township or village) government control of firms, in contrast with private or national government control (Chang and Wang 1994; Li 1996; and Che and Qian 1998a). Given the obvious costs associated with government intervention, what are the comparative advantages of community government ownership over private ownership?

One of the most salient institutional features in China (and in many developing countries as well) is the absence of rule of law to protect private property rights. Along with a strong anti-private property ideology inherited from the central planning era, private property rights, both cash flow and control over assets, are not secure. Indeed, the state has attacked private enterprises during several general political crackdowns after the reform, which include the "anti-spiritual-pollution campaign" of 1983, the "anti-bourgeois-liberalization campaign" of 1987, and most recently, after the Tiananmen Square demonstrations of 1989. Therefore it is not surprising that private firms were under-developed because of the absence of legal protection of private property rights.

In such an institutional environment the property rights of local government-owned firms, such as TVEs, can be more secure than those of private enterprises because of the protection of community governments. In some countries the national government relies on local governments for votes. The political support provided by the local governments makes them useful to the national government, which can use them as the basis of its power. But under China's political system rural community governments do not vote or elect the national government. Their support for the national government takes a different form—providing local public goods, such as maintaining order, building roads, providing water and irrigation system, and implementing family planning. These local public goods have both political and economic dimensions. For example, maintaining order provides political support to the national government; at the same time it is also conducive to local business development.

Because the local community government provides local public goods, the interests of the national government are potentially more aligned with those of the local governments than with those of owners of private enterprises. Indeed, when the local government controls TVEs, it will become more useful to the national government than private owners. The following arguments show that, as a result, the national government may be friendlier toward TVEs than private enterprises and therefore, property rights of TVEs become endogenously more secure than those of private enterprises in the absence of rule of law (Che and Qian 1998b).

Ownership of firms provides owners with control over firms' books and accounts, which allows the owner to hide a portion of revenues. This provides the owner with incentives when revenue-based contracts are credible in the absence of rule of law. In the case of private ownership it is the manager who has the control rights and receives unobservable revenue. Worrying about the possibility of government predation, private owners rationally hide excessive revenue by choosing short-term or liquid projects. This provides incentives to managers but also incurs revenue-hiding costs. When the manager has control rights over firms, the local government loses control. Then the local government would not have the incentives to provide local public goods because it cannot be sure it can reap the future benefits.

In the case of local government ownership it is the local government that has control rights and receives unobservable revenue. When the local government runs a business, ownership and control rights interact with government activities and generate two effects that are absent under private ownership. First, the local government has higher incentives in providing local public goods because its ownership rights give it access to the future revenue in a credible way. Second, anticipating this, the national government would leave a bigger budget to the local government and thus optimally prey less on TVEs than on private enterprises. This in turn makes the local government less worried about revenue confiscation and reduces TVE revenue hiding. Both effects improve efficiency.

Both economic and political rationales work in the ownership form of TVEs. TVEs not only contribute to growth, but also serve the interests of national and local governments. The crucial linkage is the role of local government in providing local public goods. There is evidence suggesting such a linkage. The national government has stipulated that the TVE after-tax profits should be used essentially for two purposes: reinvestment and provision of local public goods. Nationwide in 1985 about 46 percent of the after-tax profits of TVEs were reinvested, and 49 percent were used for local public expenditure. In 1992, 59 percent of the after-tax profits of TVEs were reinvested and 40 percent were used for local public expenditure (*A Statistical Survey of China* 1992; 1993).

Does TVE ownership, relative to private ownership, better serve the interests of the national and local community governments in terms of tax revenue? From the panel data of 28 provinces between 1986 and 1993, the relationship between ownership forms and fiscal revenues of local and national governments has been estimated (Jin and Qian 1998). The main findings are that, in rural China, the share of TVEs relative to private enterprises in a province has a positive association with the revenue shares of the national, and especially the township and village, government, after controlling for the level of per capita income and other geographic variables. Specifically, a 10 percentage point increase in the share of TVEs relative to private enterprises in total rural non-agriculture employment (i.e., TVEs plus private enterprises) is associated with a 1.1 percentage point increase in the revenue share to the national government. Considering that the mean of the national share is 7.3 percent, the national government benefits significantly from TVE ownership in terms of fiscal revenue. Moreover, a 10 percentage point increase in the share of TVEs is associated with a 2.4 percentage point increase in the revenue share to township and village governments. This is an even more significant effect, given that the mean of the township and village government revenue share is 8.2 percent. These results indicate that local government ownership not only provides higher revenues to both the national and township and village governments, but also makes proportionally more revenue stay in rural areas.

From the perspective of fiscal institutions, the above results reveal other interesting implications of TVE ownership. One of the common institutional problems in developing and transition countries is an inadequate system for generating tax revenue for the government and a good fiscal system for using it. On the revenue side, all transitional economies have been experiencing sharp government revenue short-falls because of the erosion of monopoly profits from SOEs and the greater difficulty in taxing new private firms. In a centrally planned economy, taxation is simple: the government uses distorted prices to concentrate most surpluses to the final industrial sectors and extracts revenues from them. After the liberalization of prices and ownership, profits are more equally distributed among different sectors and the government loses revenue bases, especially in enterprises it does not control (McKinnon 1993). The fiscal collapse is one of the major reasons behind the recent Russian crisis. On the expenditure side, the govern-ments in developing countries often bias the use of revenue toward certain groups in urban areas for political reasons (Bates 1987). After revenue is collected, the government is often unable to spend it on local public goods in rural areas because of political lobbying from the urban elites.

Both problems hurt rural industrialization and development. Local government ownership of TVEs can mitigate both problems. With the ownership and control rights over firms, the local gov-ernment has a less costly way to extract revenues from these firms than from private firms because the latter control their own finan-cial accounts. For the same reason, when local governments control firms, it is harder for the central government to extract revenue from them, and thus revenue is more likely to stay in the local areas. The above evidence shows that the role of TVE ownership to some extent substitutes for the problematic fiscal system: on the revenue side, it allows for some revenue extraction despite the lack of an effec-tive taxation system at the time of general tax revenue decline; on the expenditure side, it keeps a large proportion of revenue in rural areas, avoiding redistribution by the national government to the urban areas.

TVEs are an example of how existing institutions can be modified to serve the new purpose of development. The root of TVE organiza-tion is the agricultural commune system initiated in 1958. The commune system was a huge failure in agricultural production, responsible for more than 20 million deaths in the early 1960s. The same organiza-tional structure of the commune also bred the commune and brigade enterprises, the predecessor of TVEs. They were the driving force for the first wave of rural industrialization in 1958, but were no success in themselves. Operating on the fringe of the central planning, they were a moderate success in the second wave of rural industrialization in the 1970s. Commune and brigade enterprises were renamed as TVEs in the 1980s and became the engine of growth and the driving force for market-oriented reform. This illustrates the complexity of institutional development. Local government ownership became something phenomenal only under particular circumstances, with complementary changes elsewhere in the economy. The fact that TVEs were being privatized in the 1990s is another reminder that one should not take a static view of institutional reforms. There is no foolproof way of designing a particular institution.

5. Reforming the Government: Productive Fiscal Federalism

Economists working on transition used to focus on the trilogy of stabilization, liberalization, and privatization. But they increasingly realized that the government was an important missing component in this menu. Even in an economy that has been stabilized, liberalized, and privatized, there is no guarantee that growth will ensue. A crucial determinant of growth is the behavior of government, especially that of local governments which often have direct regulatory authority over new, small enterprises. In one way, local governments can be a "grabbing hand" vis-à-vis private enterprises; in another way, they can be a "helping hand" (Shleifer 1997). To some extent, whether local governments act as "grabbing hands" or "helping hands" depends on their incentives. The incentives of local government officials can be structured in many ways. One aspect that has important bearing on the incentives of local governments is their fiscal relationships with higher-level government.

A comparison between China and Russia is relevant. Both are large countries, and thus the central-local relationship is an important issue for reform, which is quite different from smaller transition countries like Poland and Hungary. Arguably, Russia has implemented more reforms in the areas of price and trade liberalization and privatization than China. Nevertheless, local governments in Russia are often obstacles to local development. In contrast, local governments in China have been very enthusiastic in supporting local development and helping local businesses. Why the difference? The difference cannot be attributed to China's better rule of law. One plausible explanation is the local government's fiscal incentives.

An important innovation in China has been a fiscal reform of central-local relations, beginning as early as 1980. Before the reform, the shares of local government expenditure in total government expenditure were 46 percent during 1971–75 and 50 percent during 1976–80. After the reform, the shares were 51 percent during 1981–85 and 60 percent during 1986–90. After excluding price subsidies during 1986–90 to make the data comparable to previous periods, the shares of local spending came down to about 50 percent. Therefore, the aggregate local-central spending ratio has been basically the same before and after the reform. However, the share of local government expenditure itself does not capture the important elements of reform and decentralization in China for two reasons. First, prior to the reforms, local governments had no authority over the structure of their expenditures. After the reforms, local governments acquired authority over expenditures within a broad set of guidelines set by the central government. Provinces also gained the authority to decide on the fiscal arrangements with the sub-provincial governments within them.

Second, China's decentralization involved more than just the devolution of government authority. It also involved changes introduced between 1980 and 1993 in the fiscal incentives for local governments through the so-called "fiscal contracting system." Government revenue in China falls into three categories: budgetary funds, extra-budgetary funds, and off-budget funds. The off-budget funds are not recorded, so little can be said about them. Extra-budgetary revenue consists of tax surcharges and user fees levied by the central and local government's agencies as well as earnings from SOEs. The extra-budgetary local revenues are not subject to sharing with the central government, but the budgetary revenues are. Up to 1994, all budgetary revenues except customs duties were collected by local governments. In 1980, reforms put into place the new fiscal system known by the nickname "eating from separate kitchens." This system represents a dramatic departure from the previous system of "unified revenue collection and unified spending," that is "eating from one big pot."

Under the new system, the central and provincial budgetary revenue and expenditures were determined in the following way (Wong 1997). First, central fixed revenue was defined to include customs duties, direct taxes or profit remittances from the central-government-supervised SOEs and some other taxes. All other revenue falls under the heading of "local revenue." Second, local revenue was divided between the central and provincial governments according to pre-determined sharing schemes. In one such scheme, for example, between 1980 and 1987, Guangdong province would remit a fixed amount of 1 billion yuan per year; and between 1988 and 1993, it would remit a fixed amount per year, which increased by 9 percent per year. Guizhou province would receive fixed subsidies that increased by 10 percent per year. On the other hand, Jiangsu province would remit a fixed share of revenue to the central government. Over time, many provincial governments retained 100 percent of the total local revenue at the margin, which effectively made them residual claimants. Figure 1.1 displays the average of the provincial marginal revenue retention rates and the share of provinces with 100 percent marginal retention rates.

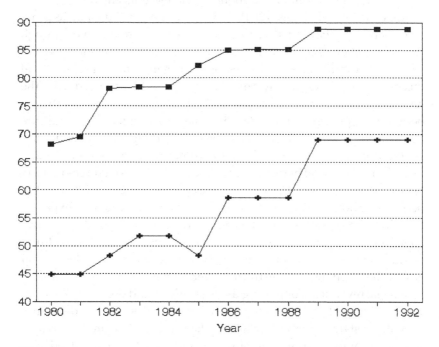

Figure 1.1
Provincial Marginal Revenue Retention Rates (1980–92). Notes: The upper line is the average of marginal retention rates. The lower line is the share of the provinces with 100 percent marginal retention rates.
Source: Jin, Qian, and Weingast (2001).

It shows that in the early 1990s, provinces retained nearly 90 percent of local revenues on average and about 70 percent of provinces became "residual claimants" because they retained 100 percent of local revenue at the margin.

What are the motivations for introducing the fiscal contracting system? There are two stated purposes (Oksenberg and Tong 1991). First, the central government intended to guarantee itself a certain flow of revenue from provincial governments. Second, the central government also wanted to provide provincial governments with incentives to build up local economies and their own revenue bases. High fixed remission amounts and high marginal local revenue retention rates apparently serve both purposes.

Two issues are relevant in examining how this reform worked in practice. First, to what extent had the provincial governments' fiscal incentives been strengthened as the result of this reform? Second, how did provincial governments respond to the fiscal incentives?

Jin, Qian, and Weingast (2001) have used the panel data of 28 provinces between 1982 and 1992 to answer these two questions. Through the examination of the correlation between local governments' revenue generated and their expenditures one can gauge the marginal fiscal incentives of provincial governments. As Table 1.5 shows, during the reform period between 1982 and 1991, the correlation coefficient between the provincial budgetary revenue and budgetary expenditure is, on average, 0.75, and that for the extra-budgetary revenue and expenditure is as high as 0.97. These numbers imply that a one yuan increase in provincial budgetary revenue results in about three-quarters of a yuan of provincial budgetary expenditure, and the relationship becomes almost one to one for extra-budgetary revenue and expenditure. In comparison, during the pre-reform 1970–79 period, the corresponding coefficient between the budgetary revenue and expenditure is, on average, 0.17. It indicates that prior to the reform the central government, on average, extracted over 80 percent of any increase in provincial revenues. Comparing the post-reform and pre-reform results, we find that the fiscal contracting system represents a drastic departure from the past by allowing provinces to keep the lion's share of increases in revenue at the margin. Therefore, the new fiscal system indeed substantially enhanced the fiscal incentives for local governments.

A comparison of these findings with parallel investigations in Russia is also revealing. Zhuravskaya (2000) examined the fiscal incentives of city governments in the region-city fiscal relationship in post-reform

Table 1.5
The Correlations between Local Revenue and Expenditure

	1982–91		1970–79	
	β	R^2	β	R^2
Fixed Effect				
(1) Budgetary expenditure on budgetary revenue	0.752 (19.73)	0.968	0.172 (6.172)	0.930
(2) Extra-budgetary expenditure on extra-budgetary revenue	0.971 (32.25)	0.991		

Notes: (1) Each regression includes a full set of year dummies.
(2) Huber-White robust t-statistics are in parentheses.
Source: Jin, Qian, and Weingast (2001).

Russia (city is one level below region, which in turn is one level below the federal government). Using the data of 35 cities for the period 1992–1997, and by regressing the change in "shared revenues" between local and regional governments on the change of "own revenue," she found that the coefficient was -0.90. This estimation means that increases in a city's own revenue are almost entirely offset by decreases in shared revenues from the region to the city. The resulting near-zero incentives in post-reform Russia looks similar to pre-reform China but stands in sharp contrast to post-reform China.

The incentive theory tells us that if the central government takes away all the locally generated revenue, the local government has no incentive to support productive local businesses because it cannot benefit from such an effort. Conversely, if local governments' expenditures are closely linked to the revenue they generate, local governments are more likely to support productive local businesses as they benefit directly from their efforts. The empirical evidence found by Jin, Qian, and Weingast (2001) reveals that such incentive effects do exist and are significant. An increase in the marginal fiscal revenue retention rate in a province by 10 percentage points is associated with an increase of 1 percentage point in the growth rate of employment by non-state enterprises in that province. This result holds when "non-state enterprises" are measured by rural enterprises only and by all non-agriculture-non-state enterprises, rural and urban. Quantitatively these numbers are quite significant because the mean of the growth rates of rural enterprise employment is 6 percent and that of all non-agriculture-non-state employment is 9 percent. Similar results are found for some reform measurements in state-owned enterprises. A 10 percentage point increase in the marginal revenue retention rate in a province is associated with a 0.5 percentage point increase in the share of contract workers (as opposed to permanent workers) where the mean is 9 percent. As for the change of the share of bonuses in total employee wages, a 10 percentage point increase in the marginal revenue retention rate is associated with a 0.15 percentage point increase in the share of contract workers where the mean is 15 percent. These results imply that local fiscal incentives are an important inducement for local economic development and reform, more so for the former.

6. Constraining the Government without Reducing Its Revenue

One of the fundamental institutional obstacles to economic development, according to economic historians such as North, is the lack of institutional constraint on the powerful, discretionary state. When the state is not constrained, it faces a fundamental commitment problem, that is, how to credibly commit not to prey on private gains or intrude on private economic activities despite the great temptation to do so. The lack of such commitment often results in an excessive discretionary marginal tax rates that is detrimental to private incentives. Moreover, the state itself also suffers from its lack of commitment: when the discretionary marginal tax rate is too high, the state is only able to grab little revenue because it is on the downward-sloping part of the Laffer curve. While the rule of law is an effective way of constraining the state in developed countries, China does not yet have it.

But there are other institutional arrangements that perform the similar function of constraining the government to protect private incentives. It may be possible to reduce the effectiveness of state power by reducing the information available to it. Bai, Li, Qian, and Wang (1999) suggest that reducing information available to the state has played an important role in constraining the government in China. These practices of concealment include anonymous business transactions through the use of cash and anonymous financial assets through the use of anonymous bank deposits.

In China there was very tight control over the use of cash for business transactions before the reform. Any transaction of more than 30 yuan (about U.S.$20) had to go through a state bank. During the reform, government controls were relaxed. The ratio of cash in circulation to GDP was less than 6 percent at the eve of reform in 1978, but increased to more than 13 percent in the 1990s. When a transaction is conducted in cash rather than through a state bank, the state obtains no information about the actual income earned through business transactions.

Cash is not only useful for anonymous transactions but also for storing value in an anonymous way. Yet there is a more efficient way of accumulating wealth anonymously: the use of anonymous household bank deposits. In China, individuals making bank deposits need not present personal IDs or register their real names. As a result, the state banks cannot in any way find out which deposits belong to whom. As such, the state does not have the information about an individual's financial wealth in the forms of cash and bank deposits.

The use of anonymous transactions and financial assets leads to a combination of income and wealth hiding, which in turn sets credible limits to government taxation and thus preserves private incentives. The theoretical argument goes as follows. Consider first the benchmark case of information centralization under which the state observes all the income generated in the economy. For the ease of making argument, suppose an extreme case prevails in which the state cannot make any credible commitment in the absence of the rule of law. Then, the discretionary *ex post* marginal tax rate of 100 percent will be imposed on all individuals' income because the state has perfect information. When individuals anticipate that the state is going to undertake such discretionary taxation, and given that all revenues are observable to the state, individuals will have no private incentives to work or invest. The result is a very low-efficiency equilibrium.

In contrast, under the regime of anonymous transaction and anonymous bank deposits as described above, the state does not observe individual incomes or savings but only aggregate savings deposits. This implies that the state cannot target particular individuals and thus can only levy a flat tax on savings deposits. Consider that even an autocratic government faces at least one constraint—the fear of rebellion by the poor and needy, and the government maximizes revenue minus the cost associated with probable revolt. However, the fear of rebellion itself is not sufficient to constrain the state under good information, because the state can still avoid rebellion from the poor by taxing at 100 percent marginal rate only on the rich. With anonymous

transactions and financial assets, the state is forced to tax the rich and
the poor and needy at the same flat rate. Then there is a maximum
amount the state can levy beyond which the needy may starve and
revolt. As a result, anonymous transaction and financial assets would
impose an upper bound of taxation on savings deposits. In this way,
even in the absence of any institution to explicitly constrain government power, limiting the information about an individual's transactions and savings can credibly limit government predation. This
mechanism can enhance secure private property rights that would
otherwise not possible.

The above analysis shows how reducing information available to the
state improves economic efficiency. It is clear that this is in the interest
of private entrepreneurs, but less clear how this is also in the interest
of the state. Conceivably it could be against the interest of the state if the
state cannot tax anything. The government could benefit from anonymous transactions and financial assets by controlling international
capital flow and imposing restrictions on domestic interest rates. Then
the government is able to collect "quasi-fiscal" revenues from the state
banking system, despite the fact that it may well lose fiscal revenue in
terms of income taxes. Through this type of financial repression, the
government also benefits from information opaqueness.

In summary, opaqueness of information, together with financial
repression, achieves two goals at the same time: improved efficiency
and compatibility with interests. Foremost, it credibly limits government predation by imposing upper bounds on explicit taxation on
outputs and implicit taxation on bank deposits. This fosters private
incentives. Second, it also implies that the lower bound on the implicit
taxation on bank deposits is greater than zero so that the government
can collect some revenues from the state banking system. This suits the
government's own interests. Together, the institution of anonymous
transactions and financial assets, together with a mild financial repression, can limit government predation without reducing its revenue.
While it does not reduce government revenue in absolute amounts, it
does reduce the average tax rate because of the expansion of the pie of
the economy as a result of improved private incentives.

Evidence from China reveals a general trend of fiscal decline together
with financial deepening after the reform. The total (consolidated) government budgetary revenue as a percentage of GDP declined sharply
from 31 percent in 1978 to only 11 percent in 1996. If one includes
extra-budgetary revenue and off-budgetary revenue, then the total

government fiscal revenue as percentage of GDP declined from about 40 percent in 1978 to 17 percent in 1996. Notice, however, that the absolute amount of fiscal revenue has been rising in real terms because of the fast growth of the economy. More precisely, real government budgetary revenue almost doubled in 20 years when the economy expanded by almost five-fold. An important reason for the decline of the government's fiscal revenue as a percentage of GDP is not the formal reduction of tax rates, but rather the inability of the government to collect taxes, which is mainly due to hiding private revenue from government observation.

However, government's fiscal revenue is only a partial story, because the government has another important "quasi-fiscal" revenue source from the state banking system. Accompanying the fiscal decline, there was an impressive financial deepening in China when individuals voluntarily held cash and deposited money in the state banking system. The ratio of household bank deposits to GDP was merely 6 percent in 1978. It went up to 56 percent in 1996 and further to more than 65 percent in 1998. This impressive financial build-up benefitted the government in two ways: it collected revenue from both currency seigniorage and from implicit taxes on savings deposits when interest rates were set below the market rate. According to Table 1.6, between 1986 and 1994 currency seigniorage averaged about 3 percent of GDP each year, where about 1.2 percent was inflationary but 1.8 percent was due to the expansion of real money balance. Implicit taxes on bank deposits were about 2 percent of GDP each year on average, assuming a zero interest rate as the opportunity cost of capital. Then total quasi-fiscal revenue from the state banking system (the central bank and state commercial banks) was over 5 percent of GDP each year. Combining the fiscal and the quasi-fiscal revenues, total government revenue would be more than 22 percent of GDP in the mid-1990s. This may well be substantially less than that in the pre-reform period, but does not represent a collapse of government revenue.

It is interesting to compare China again with Russia in this regard. In both countries, government fiscal revenue as shares of GDP declined dramatically, even more so in China than in Russia. In both countries individual economic agents engaged in revenue hiding, but in Russia individuals engaged in barter transactions, while in China cash transactions were more common. In Russia, there was high inflation, and the government collected only a low level of seigniorage. In fact, because of the extensive use of U.S. dollars and free international

Table 1.6
Currency Seigniorage and Implicit Taxation on Bank Deposits (percent of GDP)

	Currency Seigniorage			Implicit Tax on Bank Deposits
	(1) Inflation Tax	(2) Real Expansion	(3) Currency Seigniorage	(4) Implicit Tax on Bank Deposits
1986	0.7	1.5	2.2	1.33
1987	1.1	0.7	1.8	3.07
1988	0.9	3.9	4.8	1.12
1989	0.8	0.5	1.3	-0.09
1990	0.7	-0.7	-0.0	-1.11
1991	1.0	1.5	2.5	0.70
1992	1.7	3.0	4.7	5.61
1993	2.0	3.6	5.6	4.40
1994	1.9	3.3	5.2	4.43
Average 1986–94	1.2	1.8	3.0	2.10

Notes: Column (3): Equal to sum of Columns (1) and (2).
Column (4): A zero real interest rate is assumed as opportunity cost of capital. Inflation compensation for household term deposits maturing in over three years is not taken in to account.
Source: Bai, Li, Qian, and Wang (1999).

capital flow, the seigniorage in Russia went into the Treasury Department in Washington and capital flew to Swiss banks. In contrast, the Chinese government was able to control inflation at a modest level and collected sizeable seigniorage revenue through capital control and interest rate control.

Anonymous household bank deposits existed even before the reform. It is not so much that a new institution is created, but that an existing institution finds a new use in a new environment. Because private economic activities were prohibited before the reform, private savings were very low and the role of anonymous bank deposits in protecting private incentives was limited at best. Anonymous bank deposits became an important institution to protect private interests only after the reform when the ban on private businesses was lifted and the use of cash for business transaction became legal. In fact, China learned about anonymous bank deposits from the Soviet Union. But unlike China, Russia abandoned them after the reform in order to follow international "common practice." As a result, the mafia, colluding with the banks, was able to obtain information about the depositors' wealth. This is an important difference between China's local government, which does not have information about depositors, and Russia's mafia, which has this information.

7. From Transitional Institutions to Best-Practice Institutions

During the transition from central planning to a market economy, markets need to be created and expanded, firms need to be developed, and the government needs to be transformed. The previous four sections have provided four examples from China's experience showing how innovative institutional reforms improve efficiency, benefit major decision makers, and complement existing institutions. In the dual-track market liberalization, efficiency improves because market prices play a role of resource allocation and reform is interest-compatible because existing rents are protected by the planned track. In the example of TVEs, efficiency improves because of more secure property rights for local government owned firms and local governments have more incentives to provide more local public goods. Both the national and local governments' interests are better served because TVEs provide more revenue, as compared with private enterprises, to both. Under the fiscal contracting system, the closer link between local revenue generated and local government expenditures enhances the incentives of local governments, which in turn helps the development of local non-state enterprises and the reform of state-owned enterprises. In the final example, in the absence of the rule of law, anonymous transactions and financial assets improve efficiency because they credibly constrain the state's discretionary behavior to better protect private incentives. The state itself also benefits from the improved private incentives when it is able to extract quasi-fiscal revenues from the state banking system through a mild financial repression.

However, the institutional forms in all the above four examples are better understood as transitional institutions. They are transitional because they incur higher costs and generate lower benefits than some alternative institutions if other complementary institutions are in place. The costs of the dual-track liberalization include the cost of enforcing the planned track, the consequence of failed enforcement such as supply diversion, and the possibility of ratcheting up the scope of the planned track. The weak managerial incentives, together with costly government intervention in TVEs, make them uncompetitive in the market place in the long run. The fiscal contracting system suffers from the renegotiation problem and perhaps makes macroeconomic stability more difficult to achieve. The information opaqueness resulting from anonymous transactions and banking often facilitates corruption, detrimental to corporate governance, and make it harder to introduce modern taxation. Therefore, these institutions should not be viewed as permanent and should eventually be replaced by the more conventional, best-practice institutions when the underlying environment improves.

The fact that best-practice institutions are more efficient than transitional institutions does not imply that the former should always prevail. To the contrary, theoretical arguments and empirical evidence from other countries show the opposite. Specifically, vested interests who benefitted from transitional institutions may block further their replacement, leading to a possible "partial reform trap." Hellman (1998) emphasized this possibility and provided some evidence from Eastern Europe and Russia showing that it was the interim winners, not the losers, of partial reform who blocked further reform. However this is only one of two possibilities. Dewatripont and Roland (1992, 1995) and Wei (1997) demonstrated another, more optimistic possibility in which a sequential reform strategy has important advantages of building constituencies as well as momentum, at the interim stage of reform, for further reform. China's experience has demonstrated that this latter possibility can hold and the new vested interests do not necessarily block further reforms. Three factors seem to facilitate the effects of building up constituencies and momentum: the nature of early reforms, the potential gains from further reforms, and the compensation schemes for potential losers. In what follows we examine each of the four examples above.

Since the early 1990s, the planned track of the dual track in product markets was gradually phased out. By 1996, the plan track was reduced to 16.6 percent in agricultural goods, 14.7 percent in industrial producer goods, and only 7.2 percent in total retail sales of consumer goods. These numbers became even smaller in the late 1990s and the planned track in those markets almost ceased to exist. On January 1, 1994, planned allocation of foreign exchange was completely abolished, and the planned track and the market track were merged into a single market track. Two direct factors have contributed to the smooth transition to a single track market.

First, because of the fast growth of the market track, the planned track becomes less significant as compared to the market track. For example, Table 1.3 shows that steel production under planned track dropped to 30 percent in 1990 from the level of 52 percent in 1981. Similarly, in 1978, 97 percent of total retail sales were under the planned track, but only 31 percent in 1989. In the foreign exchange markets, at the time when planned track of the foreign exchange was finally abolished in January 1994, the share of centrally allocated foreign exchange had already fallen to less than 20 percent of the total. With rapid growth, the plan track becomes a matter of little consequence to most potential losers, which in turn reduces the cost required for compensating them.

Second, when the plan track was abolished, potential losers were explicitly compensated. For example, although consumers have been able to buy foodstuffs in the market since 1980, urban food coupons (for purchasing grain, meat, oil, etc.) were finally removed only in the early 1990s. Guangzhou completed the removal of the above coupons in 1992 and spent on average 103 yuan in 1988, 113 yuan in 1990, and 43 yuan in 1992 per urban resident for compensation (*Guangzhou Statistical Yearbook*). Beijing also spent 182 yuan in 1990, 185 yuan in 1991, and 123 yuan in 1994 per head before eliminating the coupons (*Beijing Statistical Yearbook*). At the time of abolishment of the central allocation of foreign exchange in 1994, annual lump-sum subsidies sufficient to enable the purchase of the pre-reform allocation of foreign exchange, were offered for a period of three years for those organizations which used to receive cheap foreign exchange.

After reaching the peak in the early 1990s, TVEs were being privatized throughout the 1990s. Privatization of TVEs accelerated in 1998 after the Chinese Constitution was amended to regard the private sector as "an important component" of the economy. Wuxi in southern Jiangxu Province was often regarded as the model for TVEs for the whole country, and it was the subject of almost all major studies on TVEs, including the important one by the World Bank (Byrd and Lin 1990). Until the mid-1990s, TVEs were dominant in Wuxi and private enterprises were almost non-existent. Correspondingly, the income from TVEs was the chief revenue source for the township and village governments there. However, throughout the late 1990s, TVEs were being privatized in all the three counties in Wuxi, and by the year 2000 over 90 percent of TVEs had been privatized (author's interview, March, 2001).

Three changes have played significant roles in increasing the gains from privatization of TVEs or the costs for the local government to continue to run TVEs. First, an important benefit of TVE ownership is the political protection of local government against adverse environment in order to secure property rights. In the late 1990s, private ownership of enterprises gained more legitimacy, as evidenced by the aforementioned constitutional amendment and the increased share of the private sector in the economy. Therefore, the benefit of TVEs in terms of more secure property rights decreased. Second, the cost of TVE ownership, mainly the lack of managerial incentives, became more important as the economy became increasingly marketized and both product and labor market competition intensified. In the product market, fast entry of firms changed the previous seller's market to a buyer's market, eroding the profit margins TVEs enjoyed in the 1980s as early starters. Indeed, in the 1990s, the profitability of many TVEs deteriorated, while private enterprises started to boom in the same location. In the labor market, TVEs also started to lose good managers to foreign and joint venture firms when the latter gave the managers high salaries or even company shares. Third, the reforms in the monetary and banking systems made local bank branches more independent of local governments. TVEs found more difficulty in obtaining credit from the banking system.

The potential social gains from privatization will not automatically lead to privatization unless local governments have the incentives to do it. As shown above, the significant benefits of TVE ownership to local governments are the tax revenues they extract from TVEs. After privatization, the township and village governments were able to keep all the privatization revenue. They were also able to continue to levy fees on all local private firms, usually 1.5 percent of total sales. This "local tax" is not shared with the higher level government; instead, township and village governments usually pay a fixed amount. Therefore, local governments support, rather than oppose, privatization out of their own interests.

China's fiscal contracting system had played a positive role of providing fiscal incentives for local governments. But the fiscal contracting was an ad hoc arrangement and was not rule-based. On January 1, 1994, China introduced major tax and fiscal reforms that are more aligned with international best practices. Previously, China had never had a national tax bureau; there was no need because all taxes were collected by local governments and shared with the central government. The 1994 reform established formal fiscal federalism by introducing a clear distinction between national and local taxes and by establishing a national tax bureau and local tax bureaus, each responsible for its own tax collection. The reform also set up fixed rules between the national and local governments. For example, under the new system, the value-added tax is shared by the national and local government at a fixed ratio of 75:25.

Although the new tax and fiscal institutions are more in line with international best practice, they might potentially hurt the interests of some local governments, which kept larger marginal shares of revenue under the previous fiscal contracting system. Why did the local governments accept such a change? Although some local governments (such as Guangdong province) benefitted tremendously from the earlier fiscal contracting system, they also recognized that the ad hoc nature of the contracting system created many uncertainties and that the political pressures from other provinces had increased. The potential gain by moving to a rule-based tax system instead of insisting on the ad hoc contracting system is in their long-term interests. Moreover, the central government compensated the local governments for their potential revenue losses in the short run in the following way: local government expenditures in the subsequent three years would be guaranteed to stay at the 1993 levels. This is why in the fourth quarter of 1993 local expenditure exploded because local governments wanted to increase the base for the compensation. The move from the fiscal contracting system to fiscal federalism turned out to be quite successful.

On April 1, 2000, China introduced "real name" household deposits under which all bank deposits require a depositor's ID. This is an important step in moving from anonymous banking to real-name banking, an international practice. Like in South Korea, this change was not so much about increasing tax revenue, but to reduce political corruption by making the flow of money transparent. What is interesting is the particular way China introduced real-name banking: It followed a dual-track approach. The real name policy only applies to new deposits made after April 1, 2000. Withdrawls from existing deposits, which amounted to about 6 trillion yuan (or more than 60 percent of China's GDP), continued to be anonymous. This drastically reduced opposition to this reform. By following the dual-track approach, the existing bank deposits were "grandfathered in" and thus protected, and only new deposits were required to follow the new rule.

The Chinese experience of institutional changes shows the possibility that transitional institutions can be superseded by conventional
best-practice institutions when more development and reform take
place. Transitional institutions do not necessarily lead to a partial
reform trap, and incremental reforms do not always create obstacles to
block further reforms. However, China's experience also shows that
this will not develop automatically. It depends on the nature of early
reforms, future gains, and especially, compensation schemes.

8.   An Example of Failure: Reform of Large State-Owned
Enterprises

The above sections analyzed how reforms worked in China through
four examples of success. These reforms worked precisely because they
found ways to improve economic efficiency and, at the same time, to
divide the pie to benefit all, especially those in power. In one notable
area reform has not worked in China. This is the reform of large-scaled
state-owned enterprises. In this section, we examine the troubled
path of this reform, showing how efficiency-improving and interest-
compatible solutions failed to emerge.

Reforming state-owned enterprises has always been a priority in
China. In fact, SOE reform started in Sichuan province in October 1978,
even before agriculture reform, in an experiment of expanding enterprise autonomy and introducing profit retention. But the most successful SOE reforms to date are perhaps privatization of small-sized SOEs
and layoffs of redundant employees in the mid-1990s. Privatization of
small-sized SOEs was started by local governments as experiments,
first in a few provinces such as Shandong, Guangdong, and Sichuan as
early as 1992 (Cao, Qian, and Weingast 1999). Later, the central government endorsed it under the policy of "grasping the large and releasing
the small." Since 1995, millions of redundant SOE workers have also
been laid off. After reaching a peak in 1995, the total state employment
in China (including both civil servants and SOE employees) started to
shrink. By the late 1990s, it dropped to below 100 million, the level of
the late 1980s.

However, the core of the SOE sector—the large-scaled state-owned
enterprises—remains a problem spot. Many reforms were implemented, but they did not work well, or at all. In the 1980s, the "managerial contract responsibility system" was introduced to provide
profit incentives for managers. It had limited success by some

measurements, for example, in increasing productivity (Groves, Hong, McMillan, and Naughton 1994). But the financial performance (i.e., profitability) of these enterprises continued to decline. On average, profits and taxes per unit of net capital stock and working capital in state industrial enterprises fell from 24.2 percent in 1978 to 12.4 percent in 1990 and further down to 6.5 percent in 1996 (*China Statistical Yearbook* 1997). In the late 1990s, more than one-third of SOEs were in the red.

In the 1990s, the focus of SOE reform shifted to ownership and governance issues, but it still saw no breakthroughs. Several failed attempts in the late 1990s were quite revealing. Some large SOEs were corporatized, including those already listed on China's two stock exchanges. But they often suffered from the conflict between the so-called "three old committees" (i.e., the Party committee, the employee representative committee, and the workers union) and the "three new meetings" (i.e., the meeting of shareholders, the meeting of board of directors, and the meeting of the supervisory committee). In some cases, the conflict between the Party secretary and the CEO was so severe that it interfered with an enterprise's normal operation. In response, some enterprises opted to place the same person in both positions. But this leads to another problem: insider's control. To address this problem, starting in 1998, hundreds of external "special inspectors" were sent by the central government to large SOEs to supervise their operations. However, these inspectors were mostly retired high-level bureaucrats who had no knowledge about business operation and financial accounting. Not surprisingly, they could not play any constructive role in addressing the corporate governance problem. Then the government came up another solution by setting up a "Large Enterprise Working Committee" within the Party's Central Committee to be responsible for making appointments of top managers in large SOEs directly instead of going through different levels of bureaucracy.

So what is the problem? The key problem is the Party's control over the appointment of SOE managers (Qian 1996). Although the past SOE reform adopted various reform policies, the fundamental principle of the so-called "Party control personnel" remained unchallenged. It is not uncommon for the Party to make political appointments for administrative posts. But the Party in China not only appoints cadres to administrative posts, but also all the managers of state-owned enterprises. The Party has exercised its control over the selection and dismissal of SOE managers through its organization departments at different levels. For example, the Central Party Organization Department has the authority to appoint the top managers of very large SOEs (the level of minister or deputy minister), as the Provincial or Municipality Party Organization Department does for most large and medium-sized SOEs (the level of bureau chief or deputy bureau chief). This authority applies to joint-stock companies as long as the state has the majority share, even if they are listed on the stock market or are located in the special economic zones. The appointment and dismissal process represents the most important channel of political influence over enterprises by the Party.

Under the Party control personnel system, SOE managers, like mayors, ministers, and Politburo members, are political appointees of the Party. This political process of managerial appointments has serious problems. First, besides being politicized, the appointment process is secretive and complicated. When the Party selects both managers and politicians at the same time, it may not choose the people who are the right managers. Second, selection and evaluation methods are based on information obtained through bureaucratic rather than market channels, such as the stock market, rating companies, and investment banks. Third, the Party bureaucrats have neither the ability nor the incentives to make the right decisions on managerial selection according to business criteria because they are mainly politically motivated. It is interesting to compare SOEs with TVEs in this regard. Although TVE managers are appointed by township or village governments, they do not go through the higher level Party apparatus because they are not "state cadres." Therefore, they are not subject to the same political process as SOE managers.

With the Party acting as a "super owner," corporate governance is hard to establish. Corporate governance is a set of institutional arrangements governing the relationships among investors (shareholders and creditors), managers, and workers. The structure of corporate governance concerns (1) how control rights are allocated and exercised; (2) how boards of directors and top managers are selected and monitored; and (3) how incentives are designed and enforced. In other developed economies, major issues of corporate governance concern legal rules limiting the agency problems, protecting shareholders and creditors, and providing room for managerial initiatives. The same problems arise in China, but with a special concern about the role of the state as a large stakeholder. Unless the state, institutional investors, and individual investors are put on an equal footing, political intervention by the powerful government and the Party will continue to plague the performance of these firms.

The SOE sector in China now accounts for about one-quarter of industrial output, but more in such services as wholesale commerce, transportation, communication, and banking. Large-scaled SOEs still constitute the backbone of the economy. The state sector continues to place a disproportionally large claim on economic resources. For instance, SOEs' share of bank lending remained at near 60 percent by the end of 1998. Although SOEs remain the main revenue source for the government (they account for more than one half of total government revenue), they also represent a big financial burden. The poor financial performance of SOEs is responsible for China's banking sector problem. Total non-performing loans may have reached as high as 50 percent of GDP in 1999 before some of them were removed from the banks' balance sheets to the newly created "assets management companies."

Fortunately for China, the vibrant non-state sector has grown so fast that the problem of the state sector becomes less critical. Things would be different twenty years ago when the state sector constituted about 80 percent of total national industrial output. But will China's reform of large-scaled SOEs (including privatizing them) eventually work? The most recent government policy on SOE reform adopted in September of 1999 intended to jump start the stalled reform (*China Daily*, September 27, 1999). The first, and perhaps most important, new policy is "readjustment of the layout of the state economy" to narrow down its scope dramatically. SOEs are operating in almost all sectors of the economy, ranging from fighter plane production to hotel operation, from book selling to toymaking. Committing the government to withdrawing from most industrial and service sectors is a significant and encouraging step forward in transforming the state sector in the economy. The second new policy calls for the diversification of ownership structure for those enterprises over which the state still wants to maintain control. Except for a few enterprises in which the state intends to retain 100 percent ownership, all other enterprises will become joint stock companies with multiple owners. These new owners can be either domestic private investors or foreign investors, and the companies can be listed on the domestic or foreign stock markets. Examples include PetroChina, listed on the New York Stock Exchange, and China Telecom (Hong Kong), listed on the Hong Kong Stock Exchange.

Will the reform work this time? As for the Party's role in corporate governance, the recent policy on SOE reform sent out a mixed signal. On the one hand, the government intends to follow the international common practice in hiring, empowering, and rewarding top managers for its enterprises, including giving them stocks. On the other hand, the policy reiterated the fundamental principle of "Party control personnel," although it also mentioned that the "control method" will improve. Party control gives the enterprise Party committee extraordinary power in making strategic decisions, and thus presents a fundamental problem in corporate governance. In the coming years we will not be surprised to see frustrating contradictions at every turn of corporate governance reforms.

9. Concluding Remarks

This chapter has demonstrated how novel transitional institutions of market, firms, and government worked in China. The institutional reforms achieved two objectives at the same time: they are both efficiency-enhancing and interest-compatible. The real challenge of reform facing transition and developing countries is not so much about knowing where to end up, but finding a feasible path toward the goal. To understand how reform works in a country, it is not enough to study the best-practice institutions as a desirable goal. One should also study how feasible, imperfect institutions fit the economic and political reality and function as stepping stones in the transition toward the goal. The good news is that in these economies a large room usually exists for efficiency improvement (that is why they need reforms in the first place). China's experience has shown that there will be a time period in which impressive growth does not require perfect institutions, and imperfect but sensible institutions can perform. On the other hand, China's success in unconventional institutions does not constitute an argument against fostering best-practice institutions such as rule of law, private ownership of firms, and transparent government. It is an argument against simplistic and naive views on institutional reform.

As a whole, China's reform experience is unique among developing and transition economies. However, each component of China's reform may find analogues in other countries. For instance, all schemes involving various forms of "grandfathering" resemble the Chinese dual-track approach. The two-tier wage system with lower wages for newly hired employees and higher wages for existing employees has been used in some industries such as the U.S. airline industry. The dual-track also worked in the export zones in Mauritius, as documented by Rodrik (1999). Although the huge scale of TVEs is unique to China, successful firms in developing and transition economies in which the government holds equity stakes are not unusual. Moscow firms controlled by its mayor or Indonesian firms in which the Suharto family holds substantial shares all enjoyed the comparative advantage of political protection. Giving equity stakes to the government does not guarantee growth, but it does align the interests of the government with growth and sometimes helps growth in an environment that lacks rule of law. Anonymous banking is not unique to China. South Korea, and even some developed countries in Europe such as Austria, had it for a long time, not to mention Switzerland, where the entire banking industry is built upon it.

The thrust of the arguments in this chapter—that is, institutional development needs to fit initial conditions and to be made compatible with the interests of the ruling groups—also finds parallels in other successful experiences, such as Botswana. In contrast to most African countries where institutions were imported and were significantly at odds with the indigenous political culture and the political ambitions of the most powerful people, Botswana's imported institutions were largely consistent with the political ambitions of the powerful. The success of Botswana is to a great extent due to the fact that good economics was also good politics (see Acemoglu, Johnson, and Robinson 2003). This is the common ground between China and Botswana, despite the huge differences between the two successful growth experiences.

The single-country study of China's growth experience highlights the context-specificity of what worked and what not, which may not be exposed in cross-country regressions. It allows us to use a richer set of information to bring out the diverse paths of good transition and development. China's path of reform is filled with seemingly frustrating contradictions. Starting from misaligned prices, unproductive firms, and an overreaching government, the inefficient economy had a large scope for improvement. Unconventional solutions applicable to developing and transition economies usually come from the people who have a stake in the economy and have the information about its own initial conditions and history.

Our study does not predict the eventual success of China's transition, but it does question the prognosis that China's reform is doomed to fail because it did not follow the conventional wisdom. Whether China's present short march to a market economy muddles through or ends like Indonesia of the late 1990s is still unknown. But nothing on this scale and within such short a time period has ever been attempted in the history of the world.

Note

1. In terms of purchasing power parity, China's per capita GDP in 1995 was about 11% of that of the U.S. Because China had the population approximately 4.5 times as large as the U.S., China's total GDP, in terms of purchasing power parity, was about one-half of that of the U.S. in 1995. If China continues to grow 4 percentage points faster than the U.S. annually, then China's total GDP will be larger than that of the U.S. in 20 years.

References

Acemoglu, Daron, Simon Johnson, and James A. Robinson. "An African Success Story: Botswana," in Dani Rodrik (eds.) *In Search of Prosperity: Analytical Narratives on Economic Growth.*" Princeton University Press, forthcoming.

Bai, Chong-En, David D. Li, and Yingyi Qian, Yijiang Wang. "Anonymous Banking and Financial Repression: How Does China's Reform Limit Government Predation without Reducing Its Revenue?" Mimeo, Stanford University, 1999.

Bates, Robert, *Essays on the Political Economy of Rural Africa*, Berkeley: University of California Press, 1987. *Beijing Statistical Yearbook.* Various years. Beijing: China Statistical Publishing House.

Blanchard, Olivier; and Stanley Fischer. Editorial, *NBER Macroeconomics Annual* 1993, National Bureau for Economic Research, 1993.

Burki, Shahid Javed; and Guillermo E. Perry. *Beyond the Washington Consensus: Institutions Matter.* World Bank Latin American and Caribbean Studies, The World Bank, Washington DC, 1998.

Byrd, William. *The Market Mechanism and Economic Reforms in China.* New York: M. E. Sharpe, 1991.

Byrd, William and Qingsong Lin (eds.), *China's Rural Industry: Structure, Development, and Reform*, Oxford University Press, 1990.

Cao, Yuanzheng; Yingyi Qian; and Barry R. Weingast. "From Federalism, Chinese Style, to Privatization, Chinese Style." *Economics of Transition*, March 1999, 7(1), pp. 103–131.

Chang, Chun; and Yijiang Wang. "The Nature of the Township Enterprises." *Journal of Comparative Economics*, 1994, 19, pp. 434–452.

Che, Jiahua; and Yingyi Qian. "Institutional Environment, Community Government, and Corporate Governance: Understanding China's Township-Village Enterprises." *Journal of Law, Economics, and Organization*, April 1998a, *14*(1), pp. 1–23.

Che, Jiahua; and Yingyi Qian. "Insecure Property Rights and Government Ownership of Firms." *Quarterly Journal of Economics*, May 1998b, *113*(2), pp. 467–496.

China Statistical Yearbook. Beijing: China Statistical Publishing House, various years.

Coase, Ronald. "The Institutional Structure of Production." *American Economic Review*, September 1992, *82*, pp. 713–719.

Dewatripont, Mathias; and Gérard Roland. "Economic Reform and Dynamic Political Constraints," *Review of Economic Studies*, 1992, *59*, pp. 703–730.

Dewatripont, Mathias; and Gérard Roland. "The Design of Reform Packages under Uncertainty," *American Economic Review*. December 1995, *83*(5), pp. 1207–1223.

Gerschenkron, Alexander. *Economic Backwardness in Historical Perspective: A Book of Essays*, Cambridge, MA: Harvard University Press, 1962.

Groves, Theodore, Yongmiao Hong, John McMillan, and Barry Naughton. "Autonomy and Incentives in Chinese State Enterprises," *Quarterly Journal of Economics*, 1994, *109*(1), pp. 183–209.

Guangzhou Statistical Yearbook. Various years. Beijing: China Statistical Publishing House.

Hellman, Joel S. "Winners Take All: The Politics of Partial Reform in Postcommunist Transitions." *World Politics*, January 1998, *50*, pp. 203–34.

Huang, Jikun; and Scott Rozelle. "Technological Change: Rediscovery of the Engine of Productivity Growth in China's Rural Economy," *Journal of Development Economics*, July 1996, *49*, pp. 337–369.

Jin, Hehui; and Yingyi Qian. "Public vs. Private Ownership of Firms: Evidence from Rural China." *Quarterly Journal of Economics*, August 1998, *113*(3), pp. 773–808.

Jin, Hehui; Yingyi Qian; and Barry R. Weingast. "Regional Decentralization and Fiscal Incentives: Federalism, Chinese Style." Mimeo, Stanford University, 2001.

Kornai, Janos. "The Hungarian Reform Process: Visions, Hopes, and Reality." *Journal of Economic Literature*, December 1986, 24, pp. 1687–1737.

Lau, Lawrence; Yingyi Qian; and Gérard Roland. "Reform without Losers: An Interpretation of China's Dual-Track Approach to Transition." *Journal of Political Economy*, February 2000, *108*(1), pp. 120–143.

Li, David D. "A Theory of Ambiguous Property Rights in Transition Economies: The Case of the Chinese Non-State Sector." *Journal of Comparative Economics*, August 1996, 23(1), pp. 1–19.

Maddison, Angus. *Chinese Economic Performance in the Long Run*. Paris: OECD Development Centre, 1998.

McKinnon, Ronald. *The Order of Economic Liberalization: Financial Control in the Transition to a Market Economy*. Baltimore and London: The Johns Hopkins University Press, 2nd edition, 1993.

Naughton, Barry. *Growing Out of the Plan*. Cambridge University Press, 1995.

North, Douglass. "The Contribution of the New Institutional Economics to an Understanding of the Transition Problem." *WIDER Annual Lectures*, March 1997.

Oksenberg, Michel, and Tong, James. "The Evolution of Central-Provincial Fiscal Relations in China, 1971-1984: The Formal System." *China Quarterly*, March 1991.

Qian, Yingyi. "Enterprise Reform in China: Agency Problems and Political Control." *Economics of Transition*, 1996, 4(2), pp. 427–447.

Rodrik, Dani. "Institutions for High-Quality Growth: What They Are and How to Acquire Them." mimeo, Harvard University, 1999.

Rozelle, Scott. "Gradual Reform and Institutional Development: The Keys to Success of China's Rural Reforms," in John McMillan and Barry Naughton (eds.), *Reforming Asian Socialism: The Growth of Market Institutions*. Ann Arbor, MI: The University of Michigan Press, 1996.

Shleifer, Andrei. "Government in Transition." *European Economic Review*, April 1997, pp. 385–410.

Shleifer, Andrei; and Daniel Triesman. *Without a Map: Political Tactics and Economic Reform in Russia*, Cambridge, MA: The MIT Press, 1999.

Summers, Lawrence. "The Rise of China." *Transition Newsletter*, Volume 3, number 6, p. 7, The World Bank, 1992.

Wei, Shang-Jin. "Gradualism versus Big Bang: Speed and Sustainability of Reforms." *Canadian Journal of Economics*, November 1997, 30(4), pp. 1234–47.

Williamson, Oliver. "Institutions and Economic Organization: The Governance Perspective." Annual Bank Conference on Development Economics. The World Bank, 1994.

Wong, Christine P. W. (eds.). *Financing Local Government in the People's Republic of China*. Hong Kong: Oxford University Press, 1997.

World Bank. *From Plan to Market: World Development Report 1996*. Oxford University Press, 1996.

Zhuravskaya, Ekaterina V. "Incentives to Provide Local Public Goods: Fiscal Federalism, Russian Style." *Journal of Public Economics*, June 2000, 76(3), pp. 337–68.

I DUAL-TRACK MARKET LIBERALIZATION

2 Reform without Losers: An Interpretation of China's Dual-Track Approach to Transition

1. Introduction

Efficiency-enhancing economic reform should potentially allow winners to compensate losers, thereby making the reform Pareto-improving. However, in practice, it seems very difficult to find mechanisms that make economic reform Pareto-improving, and even more difficult for reform to be simultaneously Pareto-improving and efficient, due to distortionary costs of compensation or to lack of credibility of its implementation. We demonstrate in this paper that a simple mechanism of a "dual-track" approach, as used in China's economic reform, can serve to implement efficient Pareto-improving economic reform. The basic principle of the dual-track approach is as follows. Under the plan track, economic agents are assigned rights to and obligations for fixed quantities of goods at fixed plan prices as specified in the preexisting plan. In addition, a market track is introduced under which economic agents participate in the market at free market prices, provided that they fulfill their obligations under the preexisting plan.

We distinguish between two types of market liberalization in this context. We refer to "limited market liberalization" if market resales of plan-allocated goods and market purchases by planned suppliers for fulfilling plan-mandated delivery quotas are not permitted. Thus, under limited market liberalization, planned suppliers must physically produce all plan-mandated output deliveries and physically use all plan-allocated inputs themselves, even though it might have been cheaper to sell the inputs on the market track and purchase the same output from the market track for redelivery. In contrast, we refer to "full market liberalization" if market resales and market purchases for

With Lawrence J. Lau and Gérard Roland; originally published in *Journal of Political Economy*, February 2000, 108(1), pp. 120–143.

redelivery are all allowed by a planned supplier or a rationed user, as long as its obligations under the plan are all fulfilled.

Within the conventional supply and demand framework, we analyze various distributional and efficiency aspects of the dual-track mechanism.[1] We show that, independently of the initial conditions concerning supply and demand, as long as the preexisting feasible plan continues to be enforced appropriately, the dual-track approach to market liberalization is always Pareto-improving. In addition, it also achieves efficiency under full market liberalization and other usual conditions such as profit maximization and perfect competition.

The idea that the dual-track approach can provide a concrete mechanism for the implementation of efficient Pareto-improving reform is both simple and subtle. The introduction of the market track provides the opportunity for economic agents who participate in it to be better off, whereas the maintenance of the plan track provides implicit transfers to compensate potential losers from the market liberalization by protecting the status quo rents under the preexisting plan. Thus, the dual-track approach is, by design, Pareto-improving. Moreover, as the compensatory transfers are inframarginal and thus lump-sum[2] in nature, the dual-track approach can be efficient too. One desirable feature of the dual-track approach is its minimal *additional* informational and institutional requirements: it utilizes the existing information contained in the original plan and enforces the plan through existing planning institutions. No new information and no new institutions are needed.

While the "single-track" (or "big-bang") full market liberalization will lead to efficiency under the usual conditions such as profit maximization and perfect competition, Pareto-improvement cannot in general be assured. In contrast, the dual-track full market liberalization provides a useful way to implement a reform without creating losers while simultaneously achieving efficiency under the same conditions. In transition economies under both democratic and nondemocratic systems, there is a need to buy off bureaucrats, government employees, workers, and consumers accustomed to receiving implicit subsidies, and to prevent reform reversal being pushed by coalitions hurt by the reform. Due to its Pareto-improving property, the dual-track approach minimizes political opposition to reform *ex ante* and maximizes political opposition to reversal of reform *ex post*. Enforcement of the plan track is crucial for preserving the preexisting rents. Sufficient state enforcement power is needed here *not* to implement an unpopular reform, but to carry out a reform that creates no losers, only winners.

An implicit guiding principle underlying China's economic reform strategy since 1979 has been that reform should proceed without creating losers, and the dual-track approach has been a concrete mechanism to achieve that objective.[3] The agricultural market liberalization illustrates that the dual-track approach can be both Pareto-improving and efficient. The commune (and later households) is assigned the responsibility to sell a fixed quantity of output to the state procurement agency as previously mandated under the plan at predetermined plan prices and to pay a fixed tax (often in kind) to the Government. It also has the right (and obligation) to receive a fixed quantity of inputs, principally chemical fertilizers, from state-owned suppliers at predetermined plan prices. Subject to fulfilling these conditions, the commune is free to produce and sell whatever it considers profitable, and retain any profit. Moreover, the commune can purchase from the market grain (or other) output for resale to the state in fulfillment of its responsibility. There is thus full market liberalization.

Beyond the Chinese experience, schemes involving various forms of "grandfathering" in the West have a resemblance to the dual-track approach. For example, the two-tier wage system with lower wages for newly hired personnel and higher wages for existing personnel has been used in some industries such as the U.S. airline industry. Discussions of pension reform involving the transition from "pay as you go" to funded pension schemes also feature similar considerations.

The rest of the paper is organized as follows. We present a theoretical analysis of the dual-track liberalization in Section 2. In Section 3, we discuss the conditions for the success of the dual-track approach. In Section 4, we examine to what extent these conditions were fulfilled in China and provide examples of its dual-track experience in product and labor markets. Section 5 concludes.

2. The Theoretical Analysis

In order to understand fully the dual-track mechanism, we consider a variety of possible market situations concerning demand and supply. Since the plan price and quantity are fixed by the state, they need not bear any particular relationship to the market equilibrium price and quantity, and can be either below or above the market price and quantity respectively. The plan prices of most normal producer and consumer goods are likely to be below the market prices; however, the preexisting total compensation (wage plus housing, health and pension benefits) of workers in state-owned enterprises (SOEs) under the plan may well be above the market wage rate. Similarly, while high-quality goods are often in short supply under the plan, the plan production of low-quality and unwanted goods may be greater than the total demand under full market liberalization. Furthermore, in general, there is no reason to assume that the planned output is allocated to users with the highest willingness to pay (efficient rationing) or that the planned supply is delivered by suppliers with the lowest marginal costs (efficient planned supply). In what follows, we denote by P^M and P^E (respectively, Q^M and Q^E) as market equilibrium prices (respectively, quantities) under limited and full market liberalization. We use Q^P to denote plan quantity and P^P_i ($i=1,2$) to denote possible plan prices with P^P_1 below P^E and P^P_2 above P^E.

A. The Plan Quantity Is Less than the Fully Liberalized Market Equilibrium Quantity

We begin with the special case of efficient rationing and efficient planned supply. Rationed demand and planned supply are therefore the top and bottom segments of the willingness to pay curve and the marginal cost curve respectively (see Figure 2.1). Under the assumption of atomistic profit and utility maximization, the willingness to pay and marginal cost curves turn out to be precisely the market supply and demand curves. Dual-track liberalization means that Q^P continues to be delivered at plan price P^P_i but that any additional quantity can be sold freely in the market. The market track will thus provide an additional supply ($Q^E - Q^P$) at price P^E. The allocative outcome under dual-track liberalization is just as efficient as that under single-track liberalization. The difference between the two is entirely distributional.

Suppose first the plan price is P^P_1, below P^E. Under the plan, the rationed users have a surplus given by the area bounded by $ABCG$; the planned suppliers have a planned profit/loss equal to area $GCDF$. With the dual track, the surpluses of the rationed users and the planned suppliers remain exactly the same by design. Compared to the outcome of the single-track liberalization, there is an implicit lump sum transfer equal to ($P^E - P^P_1)Q^P$ from the planned suppliers to the rationed users so that the latter and the former are both no worse off than before.[4] However, the new users and suppliers outside the plan are together

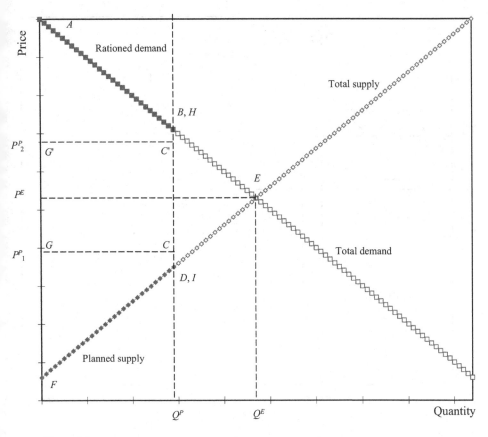

Figure 2.1
Efficient Rationed Demand and Efficient Planned Supply

better off by the area of the triangle *BED*. The analysis is similar if the plan price is P^P_2, above P^E.

Note that in this special case of efficient rationing and efficient planned supply the introduction of the market track achieves efficiency even under limited market liberalization. This is because the most deserving users and the most efficient suppliers are already under the plan track and they would have been the first users and suppliers in a fully liberalized market in any case.

We next consider the general case in which Q^P is not necessarily allocated to users with the highest willingness to pay and some of the planned suppliers may have higher marginal costs than other potential suppliers. In Figure 2.2, we represent the willingness to pay curve of

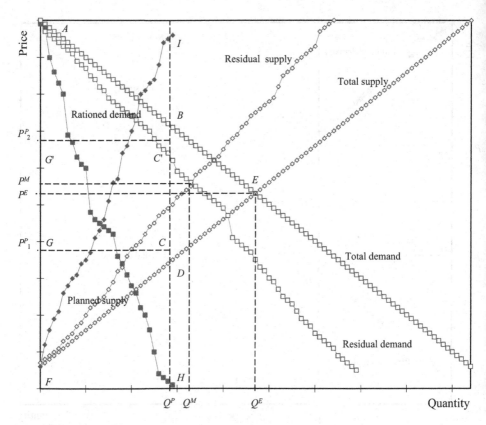

Figure 2.2
Inefficient Rationed Demand and Inefficient Planned Supply: Planned Quantity Is Less Than the Fully Liberalized Market Equilibrium Quantity

the rationed users by a generic curve *AH* and the marginal cost curve of the planned supply by a generic curve *FI*.

Unlike the special case above, the allocative outcome now depends on whether there is limited or full liberalization of the market track. Under limited liberalization, the plan track and the market track are completely segregated, therefore in our partial equilibrium framework the market track consists of only the *residual* demand and supply, that is, total demand and supply reduced respectively by the rationed demand and planned supply. Their intersection represents the limited market liberalization equilibrium. While under limited liberalization the dual-track approach is Pareto-improving, it cannot achieve efficiency in general, because one cannot rule out the possibility that a rationed user may have a willingness to pay below P^E, or a planned supplier may have its marginal cost above P^E. In fact, the following proposition shows that limited liberalization of the market track always leads to inefficiency in the form of overproduction relative to the fully liberalized market equilibrium.

Proposition 1. If the plan quantity is less than the fully liberalized market equilibrium quantity, then,

(1) the combined output of the plan and market tracks under limited liberalization of the market track is greater than or equal to the fully liberalized market equilibrium quantity; and
(2) the market equilibrium price under limited liberalization is greater (respectively, less) than or equal to the market equilibrium price under full liberalization of the market track if planned supply (respectively, rationed demand) is efficient.

Proof: If $P^M \leq P^E$, then every potential user with a willingness to pay greater than or equal to P^E will be an actual user; moreover, since rationing is not necessarily efficient, there may also be actual users of planned supplies whose willingness to pay is below P^E. Thus, total actual demand, $Q^P + Q^M$, must be greater than or equal to Q^E. If $P^M \geq P^E$, then every potential supplier with a marginal cost less than or equal to P^E will be an actual supplier; moreover, since supply planning is not necessarily efficient, there may also be one or more actual suppliers whose marginal costs are above P^E. Thus, total actual supply, $Q^P + Q^M$, must also be greater or equal to Q^E.

  If there is efficient planned supply, the residual supply curve is the top segment of the total supply curve. Since the total supply curve is monotonically increasing, then $Q^P + Q^M \geq Q^E$ implies that $P^M \geq P^E$. Similarly, if there is efficient rationing, the residual demand curve is the bottom segment of the total demand curve. Since the total demand curve is monotonically decreasing, $Q^P + Q^M \geq Q^E$ implies $P^M \leq P^E$. Q.E.D.

  We now analyze full liberalization of the market track. Rationed users are now allowed to resell rationed goods in the market as long as Q^P is delivered to and accepted by them at plan price P^P_i. Similarly, planned suppliers are allowed to purchase the goods in the market to fulfill their delivery obligations at plan price P^P_i instead of producing the goods themselves. Thus, the market consists of the total demand and supply.

Suppose the plan price $P^P{}_1$ is below P^E. Under the plan, the rationed users have a surplus given by the area under the rationed demand curve AH less the rectangle $P^P{}_1.Q^P$; the planned suppliers have a planned profit/loss equal to the difference between $P^P{}_1.Q^P$ and the area under the planned supply curve FI. Compared to the outcome of the single-track liberalization, the dual-track liberalization entails an implicit lump sum transfer equal to the rectangle $(P^E - P^P{}_1).Q^P$ from the planned suppliers to the rationed users. As a result, a rationed user whose willingness to pay is greater than or equal to P^E and a planned supplier whose marginal cost is less than or equal to P^E will have their pre-reform rents unchanged. A rationed user whose willingness to pay is less than P^E will still accept delivery from planned suppliers at the plan price, but will resell the plan-allocated inputs on the market at price P^E, thereby obtaining a surplus equal to $(P^E - P^P{}_1)$. This corresponds to the common practice of "resale" of rationed goods. A planned supplier whose marginal cost is above P^E will still deliver to its rationed users their plan-mandated supplies at the plan price, but, instead of producing them, he will try to purchase them on the market at price P^E for redelivery, thereby limiting his loss to only $(P^E - P^P{}_1)$. This corresponds to the common practice of "subcontracting" by inefficient planned suppliers to more efficient suppliers. Clearly, the rationed users and the planned suppliers are no worse off than before, and at least some of them are even better off. Thus, Pareto improvement and efficiency are simultaneously attained.

A similar argument can be made for $P^P{}_2$ above P^E, as, for example, in the context of a labor market. Under the dual-track approach, an enterprise whose marginal product of labor exceeds or equals P^E will also have its pre-reform rents unchanged. An enterprise whose marginal product of labor is below P^E will still pay the plan wage, but will "resell" its labor on the market for P^E, thereby limiting its loss to the difference between $P^P{}_2$ and P^E. This corresponds to the common practice of "labor reallocation." Reallocated workers preserve their preexisting rents because they continue to receive a total compensation equal to the plan rather than the market wage rate. Similarly, those workers whose reservation wages are less than or equal to P^E will also have their pre-reform rents unchanged. Those workers whose reservation wages are above P^E will receive $P^P{}_2 - P^E$ and be replaced by workers whose reservation wage is below or equal to P^E at market wage P^E. This corresponds to the common practice of "labor substitution," which can take different forms. For example, a worker may be persuaded to take an early retirement package, or a worker may resign in exchange for a job for his or her child or relative who may have a lower reservation wage. The rents received by existing workers under the plan are preserved in the form of (implicit) lump sum transfers from the SOEs to the existing workers.

The above discussion is summarized by

Proposition 2. If the plan quantity is less than the fully liberalized market equilibrium quantity, then, independently of the initial conditions concerning the plan price and the degree of efficiency of rationed demand and planned supply, then

(1) the dual-track approach with either limited or full liberalization of the market track is Pareto-improving; and
(2) the dual-track approach with full liberalization of the market track achieves efficiency.

Now consider sequential dual-track liberalization of the market in the following fashion: in a first stage limited market liberalization is implemented, and then in a second stage full market liberalization is implemented. By Proposition 1, the first stage limited market liberalization leads to inefficient overproduction, and by Proposition 2, the second stage full market liberalization implies efficiency and thus there must be production contraction. Furthermore, in the first stage, going from a centrally planned economy to limited market liberalization, Pareto improvement is clearly attained, but efficiency cannot be guaranteed. In the second stage when full liberalization is introduced, compared with the terminal point of the first stage, the reform is still Pareto-improving for agents within the plan, but is not necessarily Pareto-improving for agents outside the plan, although efficiency is attained.[5] Therefore, the sequential dual-track liberalization may result in some opposition to further reforms (from some agents outside the plan) after the first and before the second stage, while the dual-track full market liberalization implemented in one-stroke will not. Nevertheless, it is also clear that even under the sequential dual-track liberalization, there are no losers at the end of the second stage relative to the status quo before the reform.

It is useful to compare our results with the related literature. Murphy, Shleifer, and Vishny (1992) study a "partial reform" scheme in a similar partial equilibrium model where (a) suppliers are free to sell to all users (no quota delivery enforcement) and (b) private firms can freely purchase inputs at any price, but state-owned firms (which are covered by the plan) are not allowed to purchase inputs above the plan price. They show that such a partial reform may lead to inefficient supply diversion, compared to the efficiency of the single-track liberalization. In their model, there is no assurance that the partial reform is Pareto-improving, since suppliers are freed from any prior delivery obligations. Moreover, inefficiency of the plan (e.g., inefficient planned supply) may persist under the partial reform. Our definition of dual-track liberalization differs from that of their partial reform in two important respects: not only are plan delivery quotas enforced under the dual-track approach, but also SOEs, like private firms, in all sectors are allowed to buy and sell any inputs (and outputs) freely at the market price. In our model, the dual-track liberalization is Pareto-improving, and with full liberalization of the market track, it also achieves efficiency even if the original plan is inefficient.

Sachs and Woo (1994) observe that, in Eastern Europe and the former Soviet Union, too high a subsidized wage rate prevents employees of SOEs from moving to the more efficient non-SOEs which pay the lower market rate of total compensation. They therefore argue that it is necessary to cut subsidies and close down state-owned enterprises in order to achieve an efficient labor reallocation. This is a situation of inefficient rationing in the labor market with the plan wage rate above the fully liberalized market equilibrium. Our results show that the dual-track approach with full liberalization can provide a mechanism for achieving an efficient labor reallocation in a Pareto-improving way. For example, workers who benefit from subsidized wages in inefficient state-owned enterprises can be allowed to keep the housing provided by their enterprise while taking a new job in the more efficient but lower-paying non-state sector. Under this scheme, workers should have the incentive to leave the SOEs and accept the lower market wage rate because they would not be made worse off.

B. The Plan Quantity Is Greater than the Fully Liberalized Market Equilibrium Quantity

This case applies to the overproduction of goods such as tanks and other low-quality unwanted goods or to the overemployment of labor. The generic rationed demand and planned supply curves are depicted in Figure 2.3. Under limited market liberalization, the plan track and the market track are completely segregated. By assumption, $Q^P \geq Q^E$. What is notable is that, generically, there is still positive demand and

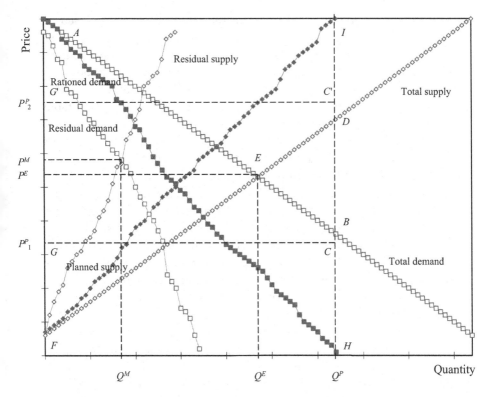

Figure 2.3
Inefficient Rationed Demand and Inefficient Planned Supply: Planned Quantity Is
Greater Than the Fully Liberalized Market Equilibrium Quantity

supply in the market track, because among the residual users and
suppliers there are still those with high willingness to pay and low
marginal costs. Thus, once again, $Q^P + Q^M \geq Q^E$. Clearly, the dual-track
approach is Pareto-improving but cannot achieve efficiency since the
total quantity for the entire economy is greater than Q^E, the efficient
quantity.

Under full liberalization, the market consists of the total demand
and supply. The important difference to the above case is that the
physical fulfillment of the plan production target is incompatible
with efficiency. However, Pareto improvement and efficiency can be
achieved if the enforcement of the plan is in terms of the rents that
it generates rather than the physical output targets. With $P^P_1 < P^E$, a
planned supplier can buy back from the market, at equilibrium, delivery obligations (which may be interpreted as "call options" exercisable

at P^P_1, held by the rationed users) in the good that it is supposed to deliver under the plan, at $P^E - P^P_1$, thus reducing or even eliminating the necessity of making physical deliveries (and actual production). A rationed user should be indifferent between accepting physical delivery or selling his delivery rights ("call options"), at a price ($P^E - P^P_1$), since it is always possible to buy at the market price P^E. Profitable market exchanges of rights and obligations are possible because of the inefficiencies caused by the plan. Under this scenario, the net output of the good will be equal to Q^E and yet there will be no complaints about the non-fulfillment of plan obligations from anyone. Indeed, the planned suppliers and rationed users have all received or given value for their plan rights and obligations and, in fact, are at their optimized levels of profits and utilities. Hence, we conclude that even when the plan quantity is greater than the market equilibrium quantity, the dual-track approach with full market liberalization still results in the simultaneous attainment of Pareto improvement and efficiency as long as plan enforcement is in terms of the rents that they generate but not in terms of physical production.[6]

The case of P^P_2 above P^E can be similarly analyzed. A rationed user can buy back from the market acceptance obligations (which may be interpreted as "put options" exercisable at P^P_2, held by the planned suppliers) at price $P^P_2 - P^E$ in the good that it is supposed to receive under the plan. For the labor market, under full market liberalization, enterprises allocated labor under the plan will "resell" labor at a loss of $P^P_2 - P^E$ per unit if its marginal product falls below P^E. This is equivalent to a subsidy scheme at the rate of $P^P_2 - P^E$ provided by the enterprise. Workers within the plan whose reservation wage is higher than P^E accept the subsidy and quit the job. Thus, all enterprises will actually employ labor up to the point at which the value of the marginal product is equal to P^E. Any worker with a reservation wage below or equal to P^E will be actually employed. Efficiency is thus achieved. Moreover, the allocation is Pareto-improving. Before the reform, the workers within the plan have a surplus equal to $P^P_2.Q^P$ less the area under the reservation wage curve FI. The enterprises within the plan have a surplus equal to the area under the curve AH less $P^P_2.Q^P$. After the reform, all workers within the plan with a reservation wage above P^E are clearly better off, since they no longer have to work at P^E and in addition receive a subsidy $P^P_2 - P^E$. All enterprises with marginal products of labor below P^E are also clearly better off, since they only have to overpay their plan-allocated workers by at most $P^P_2 - P^E$. The remaining workers and enterprises within the plan are no worse off than before. Workers and enterprises outside the plan are also clearly better off due to the new opportunities offered by the market track.

The following proposition summarizes the above discussion:

Proposition 3. If the plan quantity is greater than the fully liberalized market equilibrium quantity, then independently of the initial conditions concerning the plan prices and the degree of efficiency of rationed demand and planned supply,

(1) the dual-track approach with limited or full liberalization is always Pareto-improving; and
(2) the dual-track approach with full liberalization achieves efficiency if the rights and obligations under the plan are enforced in terms of the rents.

3. Discussions on the Conditions for Pareto Improvement and Efficiency

A. Condition for Pareto Improvement: Enforcement of the Plan Track

The Pareto improvement property of the dual track requires enforcement of the rights and obligations under the plan track. Such enforcement, together with incremental autonomy on the market track, is also sufficient for Pareto improvement. No other conditions such as profit maximization or perfect competition or full liberalization are needed. By definition, enforcement of the plan track preserves existing rents while autonomy on the market track allows agents to exploit opportunities for trade. This also implies that enforcement of the plan track alone prevents any decline in aggregate output. This argument applies to the models which explain the output declines in Central and Eastern Europe by the disruption effects from the single-track liberalization under some types of market imperfection (Blanchard and Kremer 1997; Roland and Verdier 1999; and Li 1999).

While Pareto improvement is always qualitatively valid under the enforcement of plan track, how much scope for such improvement is there under limited market liberalization? It depends on how many slack resources are available. As argued by Kornai (1980), there was always coexistence of shortages and slack in the planned economy. Furthermore, due to the very poor incentives of economic agents in the planned economy, the production was often organized deep inside the production possibility frontier. Therefore, even if the plan seemed taut, once some incentives are provided, new resources can be released for production and the scope for Pareto improvement can be substantial.

There are several reasons that make enforcement of the plan track possible. First, even if incentives to evade quotas may be stronger under reform than under central planning, these incentives would be the same in regard to the fulfillment of *ex post* unprofitable contracts in a conventional market economy. In either case, the government will have the responsibility for contract enforcement. Moreover, in a previously centrally planned economy such enforcement can be implemented by utilizing the existing institutions and no new institutions need to be created.

Second, enforcing the preexisting plan is informationally much less demanding for the government than drawing up a new plan. Under central planning, the information requirement for drawing up a plan is huge because the market is not used. Enforcing a preexisting plan is different. In fact, the dual-track approach uses minimal additional information as compared with other possible compensation schemes that may be used with other approaches to reform.

Third, under the dual track, the focus of plan enforcement shifts to the plan-mandated inter-enterprise deliveries as opposed to total enterprise productions. Under central planning, when an enterprise fulfills the production target, it will also fulfill the plan-mandated deliveries because there is no real incentive to do otherwise. In contrast, under the dual-track approach, an enterprise can fulfill its production target and yet at the same time fail to make or accept any planned deliveries (e.g., by selling the entire production or buying inputs on the market track). Therefore, the focus of enforcement must be shifted from physical production to deliveries, with the consequence that complaints from planned delivery recipients and planned suppliers become the most important source of information on plan compliance. Typically, enforcement actions will be undertaken only in response to complaints from the plan-mandated recipients or suppliers of the planned output deliveries.

Fourth, the rents of the economic agents under the preexisting plan can be protected without the enforcement of *physical* deliveries. Physical deliveries are also difficult to enforce, unless the state actively monitors the inter-enterprise material flows of the plan individually. Under the reform, the state needs only to react when delivery disputes arise, taking into account that there will be cases when it is in the joint interests of the planned suppliers and the rationed users to evade the plan. In practice, the enforcement of the rights and obligations under the plan by the state is likely to be only in terms of the rents that they generate. The plan-allocated delivery quotas can be viewed as the combination of a (put) option on the part of the planned suppliers to sell at price $P^P{}_1$ to the rationed users, and of a (call) option on the part of the rationed users to buy from the planned suppliers also at price $P^P{}_1$.[7] Under full market liberalization, enforcement of the rights and obligations under the plan amounts to enforcement of these options.

However, there are also reasons that may make enforcement of the plan track difficult. First, it is difficult, if not impossible, to enforce the allocation of consumer goods, especially when the plan price is above the market price. For example, low-quality consumer goods may become unwanted once the market is open to non-planned suppliers. According to the logic of the dual-track approach, the rationed users who no longer purchase planned quantities at the plan price must compensate the planned suppliers to maintain the latter's rents. This is clearly more difficult to enforce if the rationed users are individual consumers rather than enterprises.

Second, compliance with the plan by economic agents depends on their expectations of the credibility of state enforcement. If state enforcement is not credible, then the economic agents will have no incentive to fulfill their plan obligations. If anyone thinks that the plan-mandated deliveries at plan prices are not going to be received by him or her, he or she will not make the plan-mandated sales at the fixed plan prices either. In that case, dual-track liberalization degenerates to single-track liberalization. In general, multiple (self-fulfilling) equilibria (outcomes) are possible under a dual-track approach, depending on the expectations of the credibility of state enforcement.

B. Conditions for Efficiency

Additional conditions of profit and utility maximization, perfect competition, and full liberalization of the market track are required for efficiency of the dual-track liberalization. But these conditions are also necessary for the efficiency of single-track liberalization too.

Our market supply and demand curves are assumed to reflect the marginal costs of suppliers and the willingness to pay of users. Behind these supply and demand curves, the enterprises are assumed to be atomistic (which implies perfect competition) and profit-maximizing, and the households are assumed to be utility-maximizing. Because the planned track represents lump sum transfers, profit maximization at the margin would be the same as total profit maximization. The assumptions of utility and profit maximization at the margin ensure that enterprises and households will have the right incentives. The efficiency of the dual-track approach relies on those incentives, which may depend on ownership and governance structure.[8]

As we have shown, efficiency requires full market liberalization under which market resales, subcontracting, and market purchases for redelivery are all allowed. Indeed, our distinction between limited and full market liberalization is a major difference between our model and those of Byrd (1991) and others on the dual-track approach.

4.   The Chinese Experience with Dual-Track Liberalization

A.   Applicability of the Model to China
To what extent are the conditions laid out in Section 3 fulfilled in China's implementation of dual-track liberalization?

First, the credibility of continued enforcement of the rights and obligations under the plan seems not to be an issue in China.[9] Evidence of the credibility of continued enforcement is provided by the actual volume of transactions at plan prices, which, as we shall show below, remains large in absolute terms after a decade of reform. Moreover, it is also clear that until recently, SOEs in China cannot lay off their preexisting workers, nor can their preexisting workers leave the enterprises without permission, which provides another example of the effective enforcement of the plan. With regard to consumer goods in the plan, it turns out that for China, almost all of them (cloth, grain, meat, oil, housing, etc.) were in excess demand at the beginning of the reform, and thus were not subject to the problem of plan quantity being greater than the fully liberalized market quantity.

Second, the validity of the profit-maximization condition depends on circumstances. In the agricultural reform, the dual-track approach was introduced simultaneously with the household responsibility system, which essentially made farm households residual claimants (Lin 1992). Therefore, the assumption of profit maximization is valid. In urban state owned industrial enterprises, a "contract responsibility system" was introduced to expand autonomy and grant profit retention to enterprises. This reform also improved enterprise incentives and performance (Groves, Hong, McMillan, and Naughton 1994). However, unlike the agricultural reform, the contract responsibility system in industrial enterprises is not a good substitute for ownership reform. Indeed, the incentives of SOEs are much weaker than those of non-state enterprises.

Third, the Chinese experience in the product market liberalization is close to the case of full market liberalization because resales, subcontracting, and purchases for redelivery were not prohibited. For example, farm households have been permitted to purchase grain or other output on the market to be redelivered to the state procurement agencies in fulfillment of their planned delivery quota since 1979. However, in the 1980s, there was only limited liberalization of the market track in the labor market. Employers with plan-allocated workers were obliged to retain them at their preexisting wage rates, and the market track applied only to new employment with the market wage rate set by the equilibrium of the residual labor supply and demand. It is only in the mid-1990s that China has begun to deal with the problems of labor reallocation and layoffs on a significant scale.

B. Dual-Track Liberalization in Product Markets

The agricultural reform undertaken in 1979 is the first successful application of the dual-track approach. Table 2.1 shows that the state procurement of domestically produced grains has remained essentially fixed over time, despite an almost one-third increase in grain output over the decade 1978–1988.[10] The data also demonstrate sufficiently effective enforcement by the state of the planned delivery obligations.

Table 2.2 shows that between 1978 and 1985, the share of transactions at plan prices in agricultural goods fell from 94% to 37%. Unfortunately, the absolute values of these transactions are not available. However, we do know that, between 1978 and 1990, the agricultural output of China doubled. Table 2.2, therefore, provides evidence of the huge supply response to the introduction of the market track in agriculture.

The most noticeable and often cited application of the dual-track approach concerns industrial goods. The first incidence of use of dual pricing in industry was for crude oil in 1981, when the government allowed the export of above-quota crude oil at a higher price. In 1984 the government permitted the market track for all industrial goods but restricted the market price range within 20% of planned prices,

Table 2.1
The Dual Tracks in Grain (million tons)

	1978	1979	1980	1981	1982	1983	1984	1985	1986	1987	1988
State procurement at plan price	47.8	54.0	50.2	52.1	56.2	91.2	102.4	59.6	53.3	56.9	50.5
State procurement at market price				10.6	17.5	7.6	9.3	19.6	32.3	42.3	43.8
Total domestic production	304.8	332.1	320.6	325.0	354.5	387.3	407.3	379.1	391.5	403.0	394.1
Plan procurement / domestic production	0.16	0.16	0.16	0.16	0.16	0.24	0.25	0.16	0.14	0.14	0.13

Sources: Historic Materials for Grain Works in Contemporary China, pp. 1800–1805, 1838–1839. Domestic production: *China Statistical Yearbook*, various issues.

Table 2.2
The Dual Tracks in Agricultural Goods (% of output value)

	1978	1985	1986	1987	1988	1989	1990
Transactions at plan prices	94.4	37.0	35.0	29.4	24.0	35.5	31.0
Transactions at market prices	5.6	63.0	65.0	70.6	76.0	64.5	69.0

Note: Transactions at market prices include transactions at so-called "guide prices," which are government-set prices but with reference to market supply and demand.
Source: China Reform and Development Report (1992–93), p. 54.

and this restriction was removed in early 1985 (Wu and Zhao 1987). As a result, the share of transactions at plan prices, in terms of output value, fell from 100% before the reform to 64% in 1985 and further to 45% in 1990 (China Reform and Development Report (1992–93), p. 54, and Xu 1988, p. 292). This provides evidence of the decline of the plan track relative to the market track, but also of the relatively effective enforcement by the state of the plan delivery obligations (otherwise the share would have declined to zero).

Table 2.3 presents the cases of coal and steel, two of the most important industrial commodities which were also the most tightly controlled under central planning. For coal, China's principal energy source, the planned delivery had some slight increases in absolute terms during the 1980s, but the market track increased much more. The increments came mainly from small rural non-state coal mines run by individuals and township and village enterprises. As a result, the share of the plan allocation declined from 53% in 1981 to 42% in 1990.[11] For steel, the plan track in absolute terms was quite stable (with a slight decline after 1987), but the share of plan allocation fell from 52% in 1981 to 30% in 1990. Unlike coal, the supply response in steel came mainly from large SOEs rather than small non-state firms (Byrd 1991).[12] In both the cases of coal and steel, because the plan track is essentially frozen, the economy is able to "grow out of the plan" on the basis of the market track expansion by state or non-state firms (Naughton 1995).

As for consumer goods, urban residents continued to have the right to purchase grain, meat, electricity and housing at the same pre-reform prices and within the limits of the pre-reform rationed quantities. But at the same time, they were also free to buy consumer goods from the free market at generally higher prices. Because we do not have data on the total retail sales of goods covered by the plan, we present in

Table 2.3
The Dual Tracks in Industrial Goods (million tons)

	1981	1983	1985	1987	1988	1989	1990
Coal							
Plan quota	328.94	365.31	400.25	402.58	407.98	426.66	455.19
Domestic production	621.64	714.53	872.28	928.08	979.88	1055.14	1079.88
Plan/production	0.53	0.51	0.46	0.43	0.42	0.40	0.42
Steel							
Plan quota	13.91	17.85	18.81	18.96	17.84	16.56	15.58
Domestic production	26.70	30.72	36.93	43.86	46.89	48.59	51.53
Plan/production	0.52	0.58	0.51	0.43	0.38	0.34	0.30

Source: China Statistical Yearbook (1991), p. 482.

Table 2.4
The Dual Tracks in Retail Sales (% of sales)

	1978	1985	1986	1987	1988	1989	1990
Transactions at plan prices	97.0	47.0	35.0	33.7	28.9	31.3	30.0
Transactions at market prices	3.0	53.0	65.0	66.3	71.1	69.7	70.0

Note: Transactions at market prices include transactions at so-called "guide prices," which are government-set prices but with reference to market supply and demand.
Source: China Reform and Development Report (1992–93), p. 54.

Table 2.4 the available data on the share of transactions at plan prices in such retail sales. It shows that the proportion of transactions at plan prices declined from 97% in 1978 to only 30% in 1990. It has continued to decline since 1990.

C. Dual-Track Liberalization in the Labor Market
China's labor market reform started with limited market liberalization. China's high saving (investment) rate provides the potential for the rapid creation of new jobs in the market track without privatization of the SOEs.[13] Table 2.5 shows that between 1978 and 1994, employment in the non-state sector increased by 318.8% (with the urban non-state sector increasing by 171.4% and the rural non-state sector by 426.4%), while employment in the state sector (including civil servants in government agencies and non-profit organizations) increased by only 50.5%. But within the state sector, there are two tracks. Beginning in

Table 2.5
The Dual Tracks in Non-Agricultural Employment (million employees)

	1978	1983	1985	1988	1989	1990	1991	1992	1993	1994
State	74.51	87.71	89.90	99.84	101.08	103.46	106.64	108.89	109.20	112.14
Permanent	74.51	87.14	86.58	89.76	89.18	89.74	90.75	88.31	85.24	83.61
Contract	0.00	0.57	3.32	10.08	11.90	13.72	15.89	20.58	23.96	28.53
Non-State	48.90	62.10	107.97	138.28	136.49	152.53	159.49	172.28	195.87	204.85
Urban	20.63	29.75	38.18	42.83	42.82	43.84	46.04	47.41	50.45	56.01
Rural	28.27	32.35	69.79	95.45	93.67	108.69	113.45	124.87	145.42	148.84
State permanent/total	0.60	0.58	0.44	0.38	0.38	0.35	0.34	0.31	0.28	0.26

Source: China Statistical Yearbook (1994), pp. 84–85; and 1995, p. 99.

1980, while preexisting employees maintained their permanent employment status, most new hires in the state sector were made under the more flexible contract system and often at lower wage rates. Table 2.5 shows that employment in the plan track has been virtually stationary—it went from 87.14 million in 1983, the eve of the introduction of economic reform in industry, to 83.61 million in 1994.[14]

A similar dual-track scheme is applied to senior government bureaucrats. In the early 1980s, the old revolutionaries who joined the government in 1949 were allowed to keep their benefits and ranks and were not forced to retire. But for all new appointments in the government, there have been strict age limits—65 for ministers or provincial governors, 60 for vice ministers or vice provincial governors, and 55 for bureau directors. There are also term limits as well—two 3- or 5-year terms. Mandatory retirement has also been imposed.

As Proposition 1 implies, limited labor market liberalization has led to overemployment as compared with the full market liberalization outcome. Mass labor furloughing and reallocation by SOEs have become a major nationwide phenomenon since 1994. In 1996, approximately 10 million factory workers lost their jobs (*China Daily*, April 5, 1997), but these furloughed workers are compensated. Two schemes used for protecting workers' preexisting rents are *xiagang* ("stepping down from one's post") and *zaijiuye* ("reemployment"). *Xiagang* workers continue to receive a partial salary, housing, health care, and other benefits from their enterprises. Many furloughed workers were retrained through *zaijiuye* projects and later found jobs in the non-state sector. By the end of 1996, out of the 8.91 million *xiagang* workers, 3.57 million had found jobs, 2.34 million had decided to stay home, and 3 million were still looking for jobs (Cao, Qian, and Weingast 1999).[15]

5. Concluding Remarks

The tables in section 4 show the gradually declining trend of the plan track throughout the 1980s, providing evidence that, *ex post*, there is no "ratcheting up" of the plan. Moreover, recent data reveal that the plan track in product markets has been largely "phased out" in the 1990s, and this phasing out of the plan track was generally accompanied by explicit compensation. By 1996, the plan track was reduced to 16.6% in agricultural goods, 14.7% in industrial producer goods, and only 7.2% in total retail sales of consumer goods (*People's Daily*,

August 22, 1997). Why was the implicit commitment on the part of the state to no ratcheting-up or no phasing-out without compensation credible? Without credible commitment, either the property of Pareto-improvement is lost or economic agents would have diminished incentives to participate in the market track. Industrial enterprises may have found the commitment not to ratchet up credible because of the earlier, successful experience of dual-track reform in agriculture. Moreover, with rapid growth, the plan track becomes, in no time, a matter of little consequence to most potential losers, which in turn reduces the cost required to compensate them. The questions of credibility are beyond the scope of our paper because our model is essentially static and does not address the issues of investment and capacity expansion both within and outside of the plan. They will be pursued in future research.

Notes

* Lau and Qian gratefully acknowledge financial support from the Smith-Richardson Foundation and Roland thanks the Center for Advanced Studies in the Behavioral Sciences in Stanford where he was a fellow in 1998–99 when the revision was completed. The authors wish to thank Masahiko Aoki, Kenneth Arrow, Coit Blacker, Ronald Findlay, Peter Hammond, Anne Krueger, Paul Krugman, Jean-Jacques Laffont, David D. Li, Ronald McKinnon, Roger Noll, John Riley, Dani Rodrik, Sherwin Rosen, T. N. Srinivasan, Ross Starr, Shang-Jin Wei, Ho-Mou Wu and seminar participants at DELTA, the National Bureau of Economic Research, Stanford University, and the University of Michigan for helpful comments and discussions, and Shu-Cheng Liu and Li-An Zhou for excellent research assistance.

1. See Lau, Qian, and Roland (1997) for a general equilibrium analysis.

2. The term "lump-sum transfers" used here simply means that the transfers are independent of the actions of individual economic agents. The values of such transfers may depend on market prices.

3. The principle of reform without losers has been perceived as common wisdom in the Chinese economic reform literature. Although economists inside China (e.g., Wu and Zhao 1987, Lin, Cai, and Li 1996, and Zhang and Yi 1995) and experts on the Chinese economy outside China (e.g., McMillan and Naughton 1992, Naughton 1995) have made informal discussions on the issue, they have not presented formal analysis and systematic evidence. The only exceptions are Sicular (1988) and Byrd (1991), who analyzed the dual-track pricing in China's agricultural and industrial reforms respectively.

4. Note that in a general equilibrium framework, an equilibrium under a fully liberalized dual-track approach is generally not the same as that under a single-track approach because of differences in the distribution of income (see Lau, Qian, and Roland 1997). However, efficiency holds in either case.

5. By the same argument, if there are black marketeers before the reform, they are likely to be made worse off by full market liberalization.

6. Another way to look at this case is to take into account the possibility of the "recycling" of goods through the market. If the plan period, say a year, is subdivided into a sufficiently large number of sub-periods, say 365, then in each sub-period a planned supplier should produce $Q^P_i/365$ as planned output and be required to deliver $Q^P_i/365$ to rationed users. The planned supplier can meet his physical delivery obligations as follows. He produces and physically delivers $Q^P_i/365$ for the first sub-period at the plan price and then simultaneously repurchases from the market any available quantity at the market price P^E, from rationed users whose willingness to pay is below P^E. In the second sub-period, the planned supplier produces to the point that his marginal cost is equal to P^E, say $Q^*_i/365$, which he delivers together with his market purchases made in the previous sub-period, and just sufficient additional new current production is necessary so that his physical delivery obligations of $Q^P_i/365$ are fulfilled (Q^*_i can be zero). But simultaneously he repurchases from the market a quantity equal to $(Q^P_i - Q^*_i)/365$ at the market price P^E, from rationed users whose willingness to pay is below P^E. Every period, he continues this pattern of partial production *cum* purchases and resales until the end of the year. He would have produced approximately Q^*_i which can be significantly less than the planned supply of Q^P_i, but he would have physically delivered exactly Q^P_i, as required by the plan. Thus, total net production under full market liberalization will not exceed Q^E, but physical delivery is "fulfilled."

7. The values of these options are precisely the "lump-sum transfers." Of course, the two options cannot simultaneously have positive value since they are exercisable at the same price.

8. We do not consider the incentive problem resulting from the soft budget constraint. The soft budget constraints have the greatest impact on dynamic decisions concerning new investment, which are beyond the scope of this paper.

9. In contrast, the collapse of the Council for Mutual Economic Assistance (CMEA) and the breakup of the Soviet Union made the cross-country planned deliveries in Eastern Europe and the former Soviet Union under the original plans unenforceable.

10. The years 1983 and 1984 were anomalies as there were bumper harvests and the state made additional purchases over and above the mandatory delivery quotas, partly because the market price was below the plan procurement price.

11. Outside the planned delivery, some local state-owned mines might be subject to the local plan. However, according to Byrd (1991), of the total incremental output between 1978 and 1984, 21.2% were from "unified allocation coal mines" (most of them were under central plan), 8.4% from local state-owned mines, and 70.4% from nonstate mines which were under the market track. Similarly, Naughton (1995) figured that of the total increment between 1983 and 1987, the central government mines accounted for 27%, local state-owned mines contributed 1%, and the nonstate mines contributed 72%. Therefore, the picture will not change even if we don't know exactly how local state-owned mines allocated coal.

12. There might be some local government planned delivery outside the planned delivery figures here. We have data on enterprise-direct sales of steel between 1987 and 1990, which are 9.53, 13.18, 14.57, and 18.23 million tons respectively (*China Statistical Yearbook* 1988: p. 461; 1989: p. 379; 1990: p. 512; and 1991: p. 478). If the difference between domestic production and plan quota together with enterprise-direct sales is the local government planned delivery, then they represent 15.37, 16.31, 17.46, and 17.72 million tons respectively between 1987 and 1990, which are quite stable. Almost all increases in these years came from the market track.

13. The experience in Taiwan and South Korea showed a similar pattern (Lau and Song 1992).

14. If, in addition, we exclude civil servants in government agencies, employment in the plan track would not have risen at all.

15. Although the interests of furloughed and laid-off workers in the SOEs are protected, workers outside the state sector, say, migrant workers from rural areas, may suffer as a result of fully liberalizing the market track because the market equilibrium wage rate is lowered.

References

Blanchard, Olivier; and Kremer, Michael. "Disorganization." *Quarterly Journal of Economics*, 112, no. 4 (November 1997): 1091–1126.

Byrd, William A. *The Market Mechanism and Economic Reforms in China*. Armonk, NY: M. E. Sharpe, Inc., 1991.

Cao, Yuanzheng; Qian, Yingyi; and Weingast, Barry. "From Federalism, Chinese Style, to Privatization, Chinese Style." *Economics of Transition*, 7, no. 1 (March 1999): 103–131.

China Reform and Development Report (1992–93). Beijing: China Far East Publishing House, 1994.

China Statistical Yearbook, Beijing: China Statistical Press, various years.

Groves, Theodore; Hong, Yongmiao; McMillan, John; and Naughton, Barry. "Autonomy and Incentives in Chinese State Enterprises." *Quarterly Journal of Economics*, 109, no. 1 (February 1994): 183–209.

Historic Materials for Grain Works in Contemporary China. Beijing: China Agriculture Press, 1989.

Kornai, Janos. *Economics of Shortage*. Amsterdam: North Holland, 1980.

Lau, Lawrence J.; Qian, Yingyi; and Roland, Gérard. "Pareto-Improving Economic Reforms through Dual-Track Liberalization," *Economics Letters*, 55, no. 2 (1997): 285–292.

Lau, Lawrence J.; and Song, Dae-Hee. "Growth versus Privatization--An Alternative Strategy to Reduce the Public Enterprise Sector: The Experience of Taiwan and South Korea," Manuscript. Stanford, CA: Department of Economics, Stanford University, 1992.

Li, Wei. "A Tale of Two Reforms." *RAND Journal of Economics*, 30, no. 1, (Spring 1999): 120–136.

Lin, Justin Yifu. "Rural Reforms and Agricultural Growth in China." *American Economic Review*. 82, no. 1 (March 1992): 34–51.

Lin, Justin Yifu; Cai, Fang; and Li, Zhou. "The Lessons of China's Transition to a Market Economy." *Cato Journal*, 16, no. 2 (Fall, 1996): 201–31.

McMillan, John; and Naughton, Barry. "How to Reform a Planned Economy: Lessons from China." *Oxford Review of Economic Policy*, 8, no. 1 (Spring 1992): 130–143.

Murphy, Kevin M.; Shleifer, Andrei; and Vishny, Robert W. "The Transition to a Market Economy: Pitfalls of Partial Reform." *Quarterly Journal of Economics*, 107, no. 3 (August 1992): 887–906.

Naughton, Barry. *Growing Out of the Plan*. Cambridge: Cambridge University Press, 1995.

Roland, Gérard; and Verdier, Thierry. "Transition and the Output Fall." *Economics of Transition*, 7, no. 1 (March 1999): 1–28.

Sachs, Jeffrey; and Woo, Wing Thye. "Structural Factors in the Economic Reforms of China, Eastern Europe, and the Former Soviet Union." *Economic Policy*, 19 (Spring 1994): 101–145.

Sicular, Terry. "Plan and Market in China's Agricultural Commerce." *Journal of Political Economy*. 96, no. 2 (April 1988): 283–307.

Wu, Jinglian, and Zhao, Renwei. "The Dual Pricing System in China's Industry." *Journal of Comparative Economics*. 11, no. 3 (September 1987): 309–318.

Xu, Qingfei. *China's Economic System Reform*. Beijing: China Fiscal and Economic Publishing House, 1988.

Zhang, Weiying; and Yi, Gang. "China's Gradual Reform: A Historical Perspective." Manuscript. Peking University, 1995.

3 Pareto-Improving Economic Reforms through Dual-Track Liberalization

1. Introduction

Our purpose is to show that, in a competitive general equilibrium context, the "dual-track" strategy for liberalization not only attains full economic efficiency as the "big-bang" strategy but also simultaneously enables a Pareto-improving transition, that is, a transition without losers, from a centrally planned to a market economy. A dual-track strategy may be defined as follows: (1) in one track, the "plan track," the existing (often inefficient) central economic plan, and the distribution of rents under it, are left intact; and (2) in the other track, the "market track," liberalization is carried out *at the margin*, that is, economic agents have both the right and the incentive to participate in the free market provided that the obligations under the original plan are fulfilled. In particular, market resales of plan-allocated inputs and consumption goods, and market purchases of outputs for re-delivery are allowed.

The dual-track strategy is appealing for two reasons. First, liberalization at the margin achieves, or at a minimum increases, economic efficiency. This is because all markets are open under dual-track liberalization (as under big-bang liberalization) and thus any rent transfers are inframarginal. Second, it is Pareto-improving, that is, no one is made worse off and at least someone is made strictly better off. This is because, by maintaining the pre-existing distribution of rents under the original plan, the dual-track strategy implicitly implements lump-sum transfers to compensate any losers under the reforms.

The efficiency property of the dual-track approach can be shown in a straightforward way under the assumption that all markets are open under the economic reform. The Pareto-improving property of the dual-track approach is by construction. Thus, in contrast with the

With Lawrence J. Lau and Gérard Roland; originally published in *Economics Letters*, February, 1997, 55(2), pp. 285–292.

big-bang approach, under which liberalization is carried out with no attempt to preserve the original central plan or distributions of rent, the dual-track approach has significant distributional and political advantages: it minimizes political opposition to reforms *ex ante* and maximizes political opposition to reversal of reforms *ex post* (because of the new vested interests created). It is interesting to note that both advocates (e.g., Byrd 1987, 1989; McMillan and Naughton 1992) and opponents (e.g., Murphy et al. 1992; Sachs and Woo 1994) of the dual-track approach have not emphasized this crucial "Pareto-improving" dimension.

The efficiency and Pareto-improving properties of the dual-track approach depend on two crucial conditions in addition to the standard assumptions necessary to ensure the efficiency of a big-bang competitive equilibrium: (1) the original plan must be feasible; and (2) the state must have the capacity (and credibility) to fully enforce such a plan. The first condition may be reasonably assumed to hold generally. The second condition requires state power during the process of economic reform, but essentially no more than that necessary for contract enforcement in a market economy.

We documented elsewhere (Lau et al. 1996) the Chinese experience with the dual-track strategy for liberalization. The success of the Chinese economic reforms has demonstrated that the dual-track strategy works in practice.

The rest of the paper is organized as follows. The model is introduced in Section 2. The efficiency property of a dual-track competitive equilibrium is demonstrated in Section 3, whereas the Pareto-improving property is demonstrated in Section 4. Brief remarks on the significance of state enforcement of the original plan are made in Section 5.

2. The Model

Consider an economy consisting of l goods (indexed by h), m producers (indexed by i), and n consumers (indexed by j). Producer i has a production set Y_i with elements $y_i \in R^l$. Consumer j has a consumption set X_j with elements $x_j \in R^l$. The lth good is leisure, denoted by x_{jl}. Consumer endowment is $\omega = (\omega_1, \ldots, \omega_n)$, where $\omega_j = (0, \ldots 0, x_{jl}) \in R^l$, that is, consumers have only leisure endowment. We adopt the following sign conventions: for producers, outputs are positive and inputs are negative; for consumers, consumption goods (including leisure) are positive.

The Status Quo (prior to reform): The economy is characterized by central planning in the following sense. There exists a national production plan $v = (v_1, ..., v_m)$ where $v_i \, \varepsilon \, R^l$ for each producer i, and a national consumption plan $c = (c_1, ..., c_n)$ where $c_j \, \varepsilon \, R^l$ for each consumer j. Let $q=(q_1, ..., q_l)$ be the plan price, with q_l normalized at unity. Producer i produces exactly v_i with planned profit (loss) $\pi_i^q=qv_i$, which is allocated to each consumer in the fixed proportion θ_{ij}. Consumer j receives income equal to $q_l(\underline{x}_{jl} - c_{jl}) + \Sigma_i \theta_{ij} \pi_i^q$ and consumes c_j with utility $u_j(c_j)$. This is the extreme version of central planning, under which there is no discretion and no market at all. An economy under central planning is characterized by (v, c, q, θ). We assume that the original plan is feasible, which requires:

(1) $v_i \, \varepsilon \, Y_i$ for all i (The production plan for each producer is feasible);
(2) $c_j \, \varepsilon \, X_j$ for all j (The consumption plan for each consumer is feasible, in particular, $c_{jl} \leq \underline{x}_{jl}$);
(3) $\Sigma_i \, v_i = \Sigma_j \, c_j$ (Material balance holds for the economy as a whole); and
(4) $qc_j \leq q_l \cdot \underline{x}_{jl} + \Sigma_i \theta_{ij} \pi_i^q$ for all j (The consumption plan for each consumer is affordable at the plan prices).[1]

The Big-Bang Strategy: Under the big-bang strategy of economic reform, the central plan is abolished and all markets are instantaneously open. Producers are completely free to plan their production so as to maximize profits subject to their production sets and consumers are completely free to maximize their utility functions given their initial endowments.

The Dual-Track Strategy: Under the dual-track strategy:

(1) The original central plan (v, c, q, θ) remains intact in the following sense. The rights and obligations of the producers and the consumers under the plan to receive and to deliver at plan price q continue to be fully enforced by the state.
(2) All markets are instantaneously open. Market resales of plan-allocated goods and purchases of goods for redelivery are allowed. Each good now carries two prices: in addition to the plan price q, there is a market price $p=(p_1, ..., p_l)$.
(3) Producers are permitted to retain all incremental profits, provided that all the quota obligations to deliver and to receive are fulfilled. Otherwise, it is free to plan its production and trading activities, in particular, to sell, or offer to sell, expected input quota deliveries.

(4) All consumers are completely free to maximize their utility functions given their initial endowments, including reselling plan-allocated consumption goods on the market.

Producer Behavior: Producer i makes production decision $y_i \in Y_i$ and trading decision s_i and t_i to maximize profits, subject to the fulfillment of delivery obligations v_i, where s_i and t_i are, respectively, the sale and purchase (both taken to be non-negative) of goods by producer i at market prices.[2] Thus, the maximized profit of the producer is given by:

$$\pi_i = \max \{ qv_i + ps_i - pt_i \mid y_i \in Y_i, v_i + s_i = y_i + t_i \},$$

that is, planned deliveries (and receipts if negative) of goods plus sales to the market must be equal to its own production plus purchases from the market. Substituting $s_i - t_i = y_i - v_i$, we obtain:

$$\pi_i = \max \{ qv_i + p(y_i - v_i) \mid y_i \in Y_i \} = \max \{ py_i \mid y_i \in Y_i \} - (p-q)v_i.$$

We note that since v_i, p and q are given, whatever maximizes $\{ py_i \mid y_i \in Y_i \}$, unconstrained, also maximizes profit under the quota fulfillment constraints. The production behavior of the producers is hence identical under the big-bang and the dual-track reforms. The difference is only in the trading behavior. Under big-bang equilibrium, there are no quota deliveries and no pure trading is required. Under dual-track equilibrium, if $y_{ih} < v_{ih}$, $s_{ih} - t_{ih}$ will be negative, implying net purchases of good h from the market to meet the delivery quota, and if $v_{ih} < y_{ih}$, $s_{ih} - t_{ih}$ will be positive, implying net sales of good h to the market from own production. Trading outputs and inputs to fulfill plan quotas may involve a "wash sale," that is, a simultaneous sale and purchase of the same good, possibly for different quantities and transacting with different parties. This enables producers to undo the quota constraints.

However, quotas still have effects on the distribution of incomes through the redistribution of the profits of the producers and more directly through the planned allocations of consumer goods. We note that $\pi_i = (\pi_i - \pi_i^q) + \pi_i^q$, where π_i^q is the pre-existing pre-reform planned profit of producer i and $(\pi_i - \pi_i^q)$ is the incremental post-reform profit (which must be positive, otherwise the producer would have remained at the status quo). The pre-reform planned profits continue to be distributed in accordance with θ whereas the incremental post-reform profits are taken to be distributed in accordance with θ^*, not necessarily equal to θ. Both the efficiency and the Pareto-improving properties of the dual-track strategy are independent of how the profits of the producers are distributed either before or after the reform.

Consumer Behavior: Consumer j maximizes utility subject to budget constraints:

$$\max \{ u_j(x_j) \mid p(x_j - c_j) + qc_j \leq q_l \cdot \underline{x}_{jl} + \Sigma_i \theta_{ij} \pi_i^q + \Sigma_i \theta^*_{ij}(\pi_i - \pi_i^q), x_{jl} \leq \underline{x}_{jl} \}$$

$$= \max \{ u_j(x_j) \mid px_j \leq (p-q)c_j + q_l \cdot \underline{x}_{jl} + \Sigma_i \theta_{ij} \pi_i^q + \Sigma_i \theta^*_{ij}(\pi_i - \pi_i^q), x_{jl} \leq \underline{x}_{jl} \}.$$

Here quotas also have effects on the distribution of incomes and hence on aggregate consumer demands. Consumers are permitted to sell, at market prices, the plan-allocated consumption goods.

Definition: $(p, y, x, s - t, \theta^*, \omega, q, v, c, \theta)$ is a dual-track competitive equilibrium if:

(1) Each producer maximizes profits subject to fulfilling all obligations under the plan;
(2) Each consumer maximizes utility subject to budget constraints; and
(3) $\Sigma_i y_i \geq \Sigma_j x_j$, that is, aggregate market net final supply is greater than or equal to aggregate market net final demand.

3. Efficiency of a Dual-Track Equilibrium

We assume the same conditions that otherwise also assure full economic efficiency of a big-bang competitive equilibrium, that is, free disposal, non-satiation of consumers, absence of non-convexities in either the production or the consumption sets, price-taking behavior, and zero transactions costs. We have (Arrow and Hahn 1971):

Proposition 1. Under the standard assumptions on Y_i, X_j and preferences, there exists a competitive dual-track equilibrium with $p > 0$.

Proposition 2. Every dual-track competitive equilibrium with $p > 0$ is efficient.

Note that a dual-track competitive equilibrium defined in Section 2 above is simply a competitive equilibrium with a modified set of initial endowments: positive endowments of the plan-allocated inputs and consumer goods and negative endowments of the plan-mandated outputs and labor-hours. Thus, existence and efficiency of a competitive equilibrium are guaranteed under the standard conditions.

The dual-track competitive equilibrium is realized with the enforcement of the rights and obligations under the plan by the state. However, the enforcement is in terms of the transfers of the market values of the quota deliveries. For example, at a dual-track competitive equilibrium, it is possible for producer i to fulfill its obligation by simply paying the planned recipient(s) of its quota output of the first good $(p_1\text{-}q_1)v_{i1}$ without physically delivering the good. In principle, the planned recipient(s) can then purchase the good in the market at price p_1 (the planned recipients are also obligated to pay q_1 for the quota deliveries). It is also possible for the producer to purchase all or part of its delivery obligations from the market at p_1 and then redeliver the goods to planned recipient(s) at q_1. Thus, the plan-allocated delivery quotas can be viewed as the combination of a (put) option on the part of the planned producer(s) to sell at price q to the planned recipients and a (call) option on the part of the planned recipients to take from the planned producer(s) also at price q. These options on the underlying goods are freely transferable on the market at price p - q. Because they both have the same strike price q, at equilibrium, only one of the two options has a positive market value. They in turn entitle their holders to sell or purchase the underlying goods at price q. Similarly, the plan-allocated consumption goods quotas can be viewed as ration coupons that are also freely transferable on the market.[3]

There is thus nothing to prevent a producer from buying back from the market, at equilibrium, delivery obligations (call options) in the good that it is supposed to deliver under the plan, thus reducing or even eliminating the necessity of making physical delivery (and actual production). Under this scenario, it is possible that the equilibrium aggregate gross output of a good may be less than the planned aggregate gross output, in which case full *physical delivery* of the planned aggregate gross output becomes impossible and technically the plan is not fulfilled, at least not in physical terms. And yet there will be no complaints about the non-fulfillment of plan obligations from anyone because the producers and consumers have all received or given value for their rights and obligations under the plan and in fact are at their optimized levels of profits and utilities.

Physical delivery will not be possible for good h if $\Sigma_i\, y^+_{ih} < \Sigma_i\, v^+_{ih}$, where y^+_{ih} and v^+_{ih} are the positive components of the equilibrium and planned production of good h by producer i. If the state planning commission insists on actual physical delivery of the planned production, even though the producers and consumers do not demand it, then a dual-track competitive equilibrium as described above may not be able to satisfy it. This leads to the question of "physical implementability"—whether a given dual-track competitive equilibrium can be implemented if physical delivery of quotas is required.

Definition: A dual-track competitive equilibrium is physically implementable if $\Sigma_i y^+_i \geq \Sigma_i v^+_i$.

Physical delivery requires that the equilibrium aggregate gross output be no less than the planned aggregate gross output. If this condition is satisfied, the plan quotas can be *physically* fulfilled at equilibrium. Our concept of physical implementability may be contrasted to the constraints introduced by Byrd (1989) that $y^+_i \geq v^+_i$ and $y^-_i \leq v^-_i$, where y^-_i and v^-_i are the negative components of, respectively, the equilibrium and planned production of producer i, on the producers' behavior. Byrd's constraints rule out the purchase of outputs for redelivery and the resale of plan-allocated inputs (however, Byrd does not indicate how such prohibitions can be actually enforced). Our dual-track strategy does not impose such conditions. Our physical implementability condition introduced here is strictly weaker than Byrd's conditions because ours is implied by Byrd's but not vice versa.

Is physical implementability likely to be a serious problem in practice? The fact that most consumption goods are rationed under central planning precisely indicates that these goods are in short supply and the response to dual-track liberalization should in all likelihood be a rise, rather than a fall, in the equilibrium aggregate production of the goods. The growth of the economy will also increase both the intermediate and the final demands, and hence equilibrium aggregate gross output. It is therefore reasonable to assume that physical implementability can be satisfied in the process of transition.

Moreover, the failure of physical implementation can also be effectively circumvented in practice. The general equilibrium model considered above is essentially a timeless one in which all transactions take place simultaneously at equilibrium. In real life, a plan is typically executed over a period, say a year. If the plan period is subdivided into a sufficiently large number of sub-periods, say 365, then in each sub-period producer i will produce $y_i/365$ and be required to deliver $v_i/365$. For simplicity, suppose there is only a single producer of good 1, producer 1, both under the plan and in equilibrium. Suppose further that the equilibrium y_{11} is only one-half of v_{11}. Thus, physical implementability apparently fails. However, producer 1 can meet his physical delivery obligations as follows. He produces and physically delivers $v_{11}/365$ for the first period at the plan price and then simultaneously repurchases half of it from the market at the market price. In the second sub-period, producer 1 produces $(1/2)v_{11}/365$ and delivers it together with the other half repurchased in the first sub-period, thus fulfilling again his physical delivery obligations, but then also simultaneously repurchases an amount equal to half of his deliveries from the market. He continues this pattern of production *cum* recycling until the end of the year. He would have produced $(1/2)(366/365)v_{11}$ or $1/365$ more than the equilibrium gross output $(1/2)v_{11}$. He would have physically delivered exactly v_{11}, as required by the plan. His profits would have been reduced by $(1/2)p_1v_{11}/365$, a small amount compared to the total. Hence, we conclude that physical implementability is not in practice a real problem.

4. The Pareto-Superiority of a Dual-Track Equilibrium

Pareto-improving economic reforms, that is, reforms with no losers and at least one winner, are obviously politically appealing. The problem is that in most situations there is no readily available strategy to implement Pareto-improving economic reforms because of the lack of information. The dual-track strategy makes use of existing information and hence can be readily executed.

Proposition 3. The strategy of dual-track liberalization is Pareto-improving.

The dual-track approach is Pareto-improving by construction. The key is initial feasibility. Since all producers and consumers have the same delivery quotas and plan-allocated inputs, both before and after the reform, and in addition, they have both the incentive and the autonomy to act on the margin, they cannot be worse off (in particular, they can elect to do nothing more than under the plan, which remains feasible under dual-track reform). Thus, the potential difference between a dual-track competitive equilibrium and a big-bang competitive equilibrium is not in efficiency, but in the distribution of income. However, precisely because the distribution of income will be different, a dual-track competitive equilibrium can be expected to be different from a big-bang competitive equilibrium, even though both equilibria will be efficient under the standard assumptions.

The fundamental insight here is that the dual-track strategy provides implicitly a set of feasible lump-sum transfers (transfers that are independent of the actions of the individual economic agents) to compensate the losers of the economic reforms. One of the problems of the big-bang strategy is that it may be too costly to organize explicit transfers to compensate such losers, even though in principle the gains outweigh the losses. First, finding a set of feasible lump-sum transfers to make everyone better off, or at least as well off as before, is informationally difficult, if not impossible. The dual-track strategy simply utilizes the information contained in the original plan, whereas the big-bang strategy disregards such information. Note that with the dual-track strategy, it is not even necessary to know, either *ex ante* or *ex post*, who the potential losers of the economic reforms may be. Second, establishing new institutions to carry out the transfers may also be costly. The dual-track strategy implements the lump-sum transfers by simply enforcing the original plan through existing institutions. No new institutions such as tax authorities or welfare agencies need to be established. Thus, the dual-track strategy is able to solve both informational and institutional problems at relatively low costs by making efficient use of existing information (the plan) and existing institutions (the state planning commission).

5. State Enforcement of the Original Plan

In order for the dual-track strategy to work, the state must be able to enforce the original plan. Without state enforcement, there is no incentive for the economic agents to honor the obligations under the plan, and the dual-track approach degenerates into the big-bang approach.

Our model differs from the model of Murphy, Shleifer and Vishny (1992) in both the definition of dual-track and the implications of state enforcement of the original plan. In their model, the market track is not open to everyone. The state firms are bound by planned prices and are not allowed to buy or sell freely at the market prices. Thus inefficient input diversion may occur, and that diversion can only be stopped by state enforcement of quotas. Thus, state enforcement of quota is essential for increasing efficiency. By contrast, in our model, the market track is assumed to be fully liberalized, that is, everyone, including state firms, has the right to transact at the market prices; therefore efficiency is guaranteed regardless of state enforcement of the original plan. State enforcement is required in our model not for efficiency, but to ensure the Pareto-improving property.

Notes

* Financial support from the Smith-Richardson Foundation for Lau and Qian is gratefully acknowledged. The authors wish to thank Professors Masahiko Aoki, Kenneth Arrow, Coit Blacker, Peter Hammond, Paul Krugman, Jean-Jacques Laffont, David Li, Ross Starr and Ho-Mou Wu for helpful comments and discussions.

1. The excess money balances of the consumers, as well as the planned profits of the producers, if any, in this centrally planned economy are of no consequence because they cannot be used.

2. We introduce both gross sales and purchases, s_i and t_i, rather than simply net sales at market prices for the purpose of making explicit the possibility of simultaneous purchase and resale of the same good.

3. There is also a put element here. The planned producer can require the planned consumers to take their quota delivery at price q.

References

Arrow, Kenneth J., and Frank H. Hahn, *General Competitive Analysis*, San Francisco: Holden-Day, 1971.

Byrd, William A., "The Impact of the Two-Tier Plan/Market System in Chinese Industry," *Journal of Comparative Economics*, 11, 295–308, 1987.

Byrd, William A., "Plan and Market in the Chinese Economy: A Simple General Equilibrium Model," *Journal of Comparative Economics*, 13, 177–204, 1989.

Lau, Lawrence J., Yingyi Qian, and Gerard Roland, "Gain without Pain: An Interpretation of China's Dual-Track Approach to Transition," mimeo, Stanford University, 1996.

McMillan, John and Barry Naughton, "How to Reform a Planned Economy: Lessons from China," *Oxford Review of Economic Policy*, 8, Spring, 1992.

Murphy, Kevin, Andrei Shleifer, and Robert W. Vishny, "The Transition to a Market Economy: Pitfalls of Partial Reform," *Quarterly Journal of Economics*, August, 1992.

Sachs, Jeffrey, and Wing Thye Woo, "Structural Factors in the Economic Reforms of China, Eastern Europe, and the Former Soviet Union," *Economic Policy*, Spring, 1994.

II UNCONVENTIONAL OWNERSHIP OF FIRMS

4   Institutional Environment, Community Government, and Corporate Governance: Understanding China's Township-Village Enterprises

1. Introduction

The remarkable development of the non-state sector has changed the landscape of China's industries (Table 4.1). In 1978, 78% of national industrial output came from state-owned enterprises (SOEs); by 1993, that percentage had sunk to a 43% level, with non-state enterprises providing 57% of total production. The most dynamic segment in the non-state sector is rural enterprises (*xiangzhen qiye*), which accounted for 36% of the national industrial output in 1993, up from 9% in 1978. Within the rural sector, the township and village enterprises (*xiangcun qiye*), or TVEs, account for about three-quarters of rural industrial output, or more than one-quarter of the national total.[1]

What are TVEs? A TVE refers to a (typically industrial) business unit that belongs to all residents of a rural community where it is also usually located. A rural community can be either a township (about 3,500 households) or a village (about 200 households), with each community usually having a number of such enterprises. TVEs are neither SOEs (which are national public firms owned by the central government), cooperatives (such as labor-managed firms in Yugoslavia and worker cooperatives in Mondragon, Spain), nor private enterprises. We will argue that TVEs are best characterized as community enterprises with a governance structure in which the community government has control. The central focus of our paper is what roles the community government plays in the corporate governance of TVEs and how these roles are shaped by the imperfect environments of both state and market.

We start our analysis by viewing the collection of TVEs in a community as one firm, because most strategic control rights are exercised

With Jiahua Che; originally published in *Journal of Law, Economics, and Organization*, April 1998, 14(1), pp. 1–23.

Table 4.1
China: Shares of Industrial Output Value by Ownership (1978–1993)

	1978	1993	Changes between 1978 and 1993
STATE-OWNED ENTERPRISES (SOEs)	77.63%	43.13%	-34.50%
NON-STATE OWNED ENTERPRISES	22.37%	56.87%	34.50%
Urban non-state enterprises	13.28%	10.42%	-2.86%
a. Urban collectives	13.28%	9.72%	-3.56%
b. Urban individuals	0.00%	0.70%	0.70%
Rural enterprises	9.09%	36.29%	27.20%
a. Township enterprises	5.05%*	14.23%	9.18%
b. Village enterprises	4.04%*	12.25%	8.21%
c. Household groups	0.00%	2.21%	2.21%
d. Individual households	0.00%	7.60%	7.60%
Others (large private, foreign, joint ventures, stockcompanies, etc.)	0.00%	10.16%	10.16%
Total	100%	100%	0%

Note: * Estimated.
Source: Statistical Yearbook of China 1994, p. 373, and p. 375.

by the community governments rather than the enterprises themselves, according to extensive evidence in legal regulation and from practice. From this perspective, it is natural to regard community residents as major beneficiaries of the firm, community government as the board of directors and management at the headquarters of the firm, and individual TVEs as divisions, branches, or subsidiaries within the firm. Such a three-tier structure resembles that of conventional, publicly-held multi-divisional corporations in the West.

This perspective allows us to establish a theoretical framework that focuses on the role of the community government in TVE governance and the institutional environments that shape these roles. We characterize the community government with two basic features concerning its scope of authority. First, the community government has full autonomy over both government and business activities within its community; and second, as the lowest level of government in the rural area, the community government's power is limited in dealing with state financial institutions such as state banks. We analyze how the community government's involvement in TVE governance interacts with the imperfect state and market institutions in the processes of transition from a planned to a market economy and development from an agrarian to an industrial economy. We address three major issues in this analysis.

First, because of a lack of institutions that protect property rights, private enterprises are vulnerable to state predation, which distorts private investment incentives. We argue that, because community governments also provide productive local public goods, which increase future revenues for higher levels of government, community government-controlled TVEs are better at preventing higher government predation and thus bring about fewer incentive distortions. The cost of TVEs is the lower incentives provided for managers.

Second, start-up private enterprises also have difficulty in raising capital to finance their investments in imperfect capital markets due to well-known problems such as moral hazard and adverse selection. We explain that, by involving the community government as an intermediary, the governance of TVEs helps facilitate financial contracting because of the community government's better endowed physical capital (which can be used as equity investment) and human capital (which can be used for monitoring managers). However, the benefits of TVEs are counterbalanced by two major costs of TVEs—the government's monitoring cost and the cost of preventing the government from diverting funds for private benefits.

Finally, there is an intriguing question as to why TVEs and SOEs, which are both government-controlled, might differ. One fundamental difference is the degree of softness of budget constraints these enterprises face. SOEs suffer from a soft budget constraint problem (Kornai 1980). Since government controls both SOEs and banks, it can order a bank to refinance projects, if it seems necessary. In the case of TVEs, however, although the community government controls enterprises, it does not control banks. Thus the community government can only influence or bargain with a bank, but it cannot order it to provide refinancing. This separation of control over enterprises and banks may allow banks to refuse refinancing when the benefits of refinancing are small (Dewatripont and Maskin 1995). In this way, community governments and TVEs face harder budget constraints.

Our analysis furthers the existing literature on TVEs. Although most studies of TVEs acknowledge some of the positive roles community governments play, they do not substantiate how such roles come about in the particular institutional environment. For example, community government is considered to be capable of economizing transaction costs for TVEs (Nee 1992), providing critical inputs (such as credit) for TVEs (Chang and Wang 1994), and protecting TVEs in adverse political circumstance (Li 1996). However, it remains unclear why the community government has such capabilities. Without understanding these mechanisms, it also becomes difficult for analysts to assess the limits of the community government's roles. In this paper, we intend to fill this gap by sorting out the mechanisms underlying such roles. In addition, we address some crucial differences between TVEs and SOEs.

The paper is organized as follows. Section 2 presents empirical evidence on the governance of TVEs and the role of community government in TVEs. Section 3 provides a theoretical framework by characterizing TVE governance, the institutional environment in which TVEs operate, and the community government which plays a central role in that governance. Sections 4 and 5 analyze the costs and benefits of TVE governance compared with those of start-up private enterprises in the contexts of security of property rights and financing of investments, respectively. Section 6 explains why TVEs have harder budget constraints than SOEs. Section 7 concludes with two general lessons drawn from the TVE experience. The Appendix describes the evolutionary process of TVEs.

2. Empirical Evidence on the Governance of TVEs and the Role of Community Government

What makes TVEs special is a governance structure in which the community government plays an active role. In this section we provide empirical evidence concerning TVE governance and the role of community government from the points of view of both legal regulation and actual practice.

Legal Regulation on the Governance of TVEs

The central government has issued nationwide regulations regarding TVEs that are intended to delineate distributions of control rights and benefits among township and village enterprises, community residents, and community governments. One of the most comprehensive legal regulations to date is *the Regulation on Township and Village Collective Enterprises of the People's Republic of China*, issued in 1990 (Ministry of Agriculture, China 1990). This regulation spells out, among other things, ownership rights of a TVE's assets, allocation of control rights, and rules concerning distribution of after-tax profits.

First, the regulation specifies the nature of community ownership of the assets of TVEs as follows: "Assets (of a TVE) are owned collectively by the whole of rural residents of the township or village who run the enterprise; the ownership rights over the enterprise assets shall be exercised by the rural residents' meeting (or congress) or a collective economic organization that represents the whole of rural residents of the township or village. The ownership rights of the enterprise assets will not change when the enterprise is under a managerial contract responsibility system, leasing, or joint operations with enterprises of other types of ownership" (Article 18, Chapter 3, Ministry of Agriculture, China 1990; p. 81). Therefore, TVE assets legally belong to the residents of the township or village, not to enterprise employees or residents outside the community.

Second, the regulation specifies the allocation of control rights: "The owner of a TVE, according to the law, determines the direction and formats of its business operations, selects managers or determines the method of such selection, determines the specific distribution ratios of after-tax profits between the owner and the enterprise, and has the rights over the enterprise concerning its spin-off, merger, relocation, stop-operation, close-down, application for bankruptcy, etc." (Article 19, Chapter 3, Ministry of Agriculture, China 1990; p. 84). Thus the owner has the control rights. While the owner can delegate such rights to an agency, according to the previous paragraph, the agency must represent the whole of the community rather than a particular enterprise. Typically, this agency is called the "Economic Commission" or the "General Corporation for Development" of the community government.

Third, the regulation also stipulates rules for the distribution of after-tax profits of TVEs: "The part retained by the enterprise should be no less than 60% of the total and should be arranged under the enterprise's autonomous decision. The retained after-tax profits for the enterprise should be mainly used for the increase of the funds for production development in technological transformation and expansion of reproduction, and also for the appropriate increase of welfare funds and bonus funds." And "the part remitted to the owner of the enterprise should be used mainly for the support of construction of agricultural infrastructures, agriculture technology services, rural public welfare, renewal and transformation of enterprises, or development of new enterprises" (Article 32, Chapter 5, Ministry of Agriculture, China 1990;

p. 137). As is evident, this regulation restricts the use of revenue by community residents and government to essentially two purposes: reinvestment and local public goods.

The Role of Community Government in TVEs in Practice

Below we present empirical evidence from field studies about actual practice concerning the role of community government in exercising control rights over TVEs. We use two studies: one from the World Bank (Byrd and Lin 1990), and another from Oi (1994). The World Bank study was conducted in the late 1980s in collaboration with the Chinese Academy of Social Sciences. It covered four counties in China (Jieshou of Anhui province, Nanhai of Guangdong province, Shangrao of Jiangxi province, and Wuxi of Jiangsu province). Oi's study took place mainly in Zouping county of Shandong province in the early 1990s. Both studies found that, although most TVEs enjoy a considerable degree of enterprise autonomy, this autonomy is largely restricted to daily operation decisions or management. In particular, the community government makes three types of strategic decisions in the areas of (i) investment and finance, (ii) selection of managers, and (iii) the use of after-tax profits for public expenditure, as detailed below.[2]

Investment and Finance.   Both studies found that most projects set up by TVEs have to be approved by community governments. The community governments initiate internal fund raising, either from collective accumulation or from individual contributions. The community governments are also pivotal in securing loans from either the Agriculture Bank of China (ABC) or Rural Credit Cooperatives (RCCs), two major external sources of financing. The field studies show that the community government provides several levels of service. First, when TVE loans come from the county branches of the ABC, the township and village governments initiate the process of bargaining and borrowing. Second, township and village enterprises can use the community assets (which could be assets of other enterprises in the same community) as equity or collateral. Third, township and village governments may provide loan guarantees. In such a case, community governments assume the final responsibility for repayment if the borrowing TVE cannot pay it back. Community governments manage to repay bad loans through their fiscal budgets, or from after-tax profit remittances, or by arranging for other TVEs to repay them.[3] Without the community government's involvement, it is usually very difficult, if not impossible, for TVEs to obtain loans directly from either the ABC or RCCs.

Selection and Rewarding of TVE Managers. Managers are often employed under some form of managerial contract that specifies tenure and compensation schemes. However, the community government represents the owner of TVEs in negotiating the form of contracts (e.g., fixed-wage, profit-sharing, or leasing contracts) and signs the contract with the managers.[4]

Use of After-Tax Profits for Public Expenditure. The community government has direct control over two parts of after-tax profits from TVEs. The first part is that portion remitted directly to the community government and known as "management fees." The second part is the profits retained by TVEs but earmarked for public expenditures. The community government decides on the use of those funds for support-ing agriculture and providing community welfare, that is, for schools, roads, health care, pensions, etc. In addition, the community govern-ment also has significant influence on the remaining after-tax profits, which are used for reinvestment through, for example, controlling investment as described above. At the national level, in 1985, about 46% of TVEs' after-tax profits was reinvested and 49% was used for local public expenditure, including 12% for welfare. In 1992, 59% of TVEs' after-tax profits was reinvested and 40% was used for local public expenditure, including 9% used for welfare (*A Statistical Survey of China 1992*, p. 67; *A Statistical Survey of China 1993*, p. 67).

3. A Theoretical Framework

In this section, we establish a theoretical framework upon which the rest of the analysis will be built. We first characterize the gover-nance of TVEs by drawing a parallel with the governance of a con-ventional, multi-divisional corporation in the West. We then specify the institutional environments of the state and market in which TVEs are operating. Finally, we delineate two basic features of the community government which are essential in our subsequent analy-sis of the central roles of the community government in the gover-nance of TVEs.

Characteristics of the Governance of TVEs

As the above empirical evidence demonstrates, the governance of TVEs, from both legal and practical points of view, has the following three properties:

(i) all community enterprises within one community are owned collectively by the residents of that community;
(ii) the decisions of managers of these enterprises are restricted mostly to daily operations; and
(iii) the community government exercises strategic control rights over these enterprises on behalf of the community residents.

Therefore, we interpret the collection of all community enterprises within a particular community as the bottom tier of a three-tier structure, in which the middle tier is the community government which exercises strategic controls over these enterprises, and the top tier consists of the residents. With this perspective, we view the entire three-tier structure as a firm, which can appropriately be called a "community corporation."

This perspective provides valuable insights into TVEs.[5] Indeed the three-tier structure of TVEs resembles a publicly-held, multi-divisional corporation or a holding company in the West (Byrd 1990 and Oi 1992).[6] As is well known, a publicly-held corporation has many owners who grant control rights to the board of directors and the top executives of the firm. Inside a multi-divisional corporation, headquarters centralizes strategic decisions involving finance, investment, and selection and evaluation of managers, while delegating daily management to divisions (Chandler 1966; Williamson 1975). In the parallel situation of TVEs, community residents are the major beneficiaries of the firm, the community government serves as both the board of directors and management at the firm's headquarters, and individual TVEs are separate divisions, branches, or subsidiaries within the firm.[7]

As in corporations, the three-tier structure of TVEs entails agency costs, such as those associated with the separation of beneficiaries and control, and those associated with the managers of community enterprises. These agency costs may be exacerbated further in TVEs for the following reasons. First, it is the community government rather than business managers that exercises strategic control of the firm, and this setup may give rise to (additional) political costs. Second, the rights of community residents as beneficiaries of TVEs are restricted. Community residents generally cannot sell their implicit "shares" to other people, and they do not have the formal right to elect and dismiss the community government's officials and to vote on strategic decisions.

Considering these agency costs, it would appear that private enterprises, which have a much simpler organizational structure and are less prone to the internal agency problem, should have advantages over TVEs.[8] In order to explain the success of TVEs, we need to investigate the potential benefits of their three-tier structure. The key to understanding TVEs' potential benefits lies in the roles of the community government and the institutional environment that shapes these roles.

The Imperfect Institutional Environment

The roles of the community government in TVEs are shaped by the institutional environment in which they operate. We take the view that during economic development and transitions to market both state and market institutions are imperfect and will take time to evolve. We consider three types of imperfections and their potential adverse consequences on economic development and transition to markets.

First, state institutions are imperfect, particularly, due to a lack of the rule of law and institutions that constrain the state from arbitrary revenue expropriation.[9] In China, there is no independent judiciary system: the parliament, executive branch, and courts are all under the control of the Party. Therefore, there is no law- or institution-based commitment to bind the state to a fixed schedule of taxes; the state has the ultimate authority for determining taxes and can arbitrarily set and change tax schemes for enterprises and lower level governments. This creates serious commitment problems which can distort investment incentives.

Second, the capital market is also imperfect, due to the well-known adverse selection and moral hazard problems. As an investor may not be sure whether an entrepreneur's idea is good and the investor may also be unable to force the entrepreneur to take an appropriate action, entrepreneurs find it difficult to raise capital, and many investment opportunities pass by without financing. These problems are even more profound in developing and transition economies such as China because start-up entrepreneurs do not generally have much wealth.

Third, China lacks a competitive banking system. Until recently, all banks in China were state-owned. The central government controls

SOEs, state banks, and the central bank. Clearly, the central government can order a state bank to provide funds to a state enterprise and
to order the central bank to print money whenever it appears necessary.[10] The combination of state ownership of industrial firms with
control over financial institutions may cause another serious commitment problem, that is, the state often has difficulty refusing to bail out
inefficient SOEs once investments are sunk (Dewatripont and Maskin
1995). Anticipating relaxed financial discipline, SOE managers may
then make irresponsible business decisions, which can lead to inefficiencies. This is known as the "soft budget constraint" problem (Kornai
1980).

It is in this imperfect institutional environment that we see the
potential benefits of involving the community government in TVE
governance. These benefits come about as a result of some of the
particular features of community governments in rural China.

The Basic Features of the Community Government

The governmental hierarchy in China has six layers: central, provincial,
prefecture, county, township, and village (a municipality is assigned a
level of provincial, prefecture, or county depending on size). The community governments of townships and villages (formerly communes
and brigades) have the following two basic features, which, as we will
show, underscore the crucial differences between TVEs and private
enterprises on the one hand, and between TVEs and SOEs on the other.

The first basic feature concerns the community government's scope
of authorities:

(G1) The community government has full autonomy over both government and business activities within its community.

China's economy was more decentralized than most other centrally
planned economies even before reforms began. Since 1980, reforms
have focused on further decentralization of the government (Qian and
Weingast 1996; Qian and Xu 1993; Wong 1992). As a result, community
governments have obtained full autonomy over activities such as community development and welfare.

As the governing body, the community government carries out a
wide variety of government activities, ranging from maintaining social
order to providing basic living conditions (e.g., sanitary facilities), from
building local infrastructure (e.g., roads) to implementing family planning policy. In addition to these traditional government functions, the
community governments in China are engaged in organizing local

business as well. This central involvement in business activities originated in the commune system, when community governments were responsible for agricultural production. Later, it evolved into the management of industrial activities (see Appendix).

This comprehensive scope of the community government's authority in China distinguishes it from local governments in many other countries, whose authority is usually confined to government activities. On the other hand, it also distinguishes the community government-run business from businesses operated by private entrepreneurs, because the latter do not have responsibility for government activities.

The second basic feature concerns the limits of the community government's authorities:

(G2) As the lowest level of government in rural areas, the community government's power is limited in dealing with state financial institutions (such as state banks).

In China, the rural sector has not been incorporated into the state industrial system (Byrd and Lin 1990; Ma et al. 1994); furthermore, the authority of the community government has not been extended to the state banking system. The ABC and RCCs are the two major potential sources of external finance for both TVEs and private enterprises. Although the community government controls TVEs, it does not control these state banks. Therefore, the community government cannot order a bank to provide funds; instead, it has to negotiate the terms of financing with these banks.

We will argue in the next three sections that these two basic features play important roles for TVEs in dealing with the unsympathetic environment described above. In particular, the community government's first basic feature (G1) helps TVEs reduce state predation and raise capital in an imperfect capital market. Both factors give TVEs advantages relative to private enterprises. Furthermore, the second basic feature (G2) causes harder budget constraints for TVEs than for SOEs.

4. Security of Property Rights

Evidence shows that property rights are better secured in TVEs than in private enterprises. First, the state's regulations have been less hostile to TVEs than to private enterprises. Collective enterprises such as TVEs always have been legally allowed to operate. As early as the mid-1970s, during the wave of "agriculture mechanization," many rural areas began to launch commune-brigade enterprises (the predecessor of TVEs) despite the fact that they were regarded as the "tail of capitalism" and faced all kinds of attacks (Byrd and Lin 1990, p. 10). Starting in 1978, the central government declared that commune-brigade enterprises should strive for greater development, and it encouraged provincial, city, and county governments to adopt "a policy of allowing tax breaks or tax exemptions for commune and brigade enterprises in the light of their situation."[11] In comparison, the central government did not allow private enterprises to operate until 1981 and limited their hiring to no more than eight employees per enterprise (a restriction that was removed in 1984).

Second, security of private property rights is not guaranteed even if legislation or regulations exist on paper. The state has attacked private enterprises during each of the general political crackdowns, which includes the "anti-spiritual pollution campaign" of 1983, the "anti-bourgeois liberalization campaign" of 1987, and most recently, after the Tiananmen incident of 1989. In August 1989, the state attacked "individual and private entrepreneurs who use illegal methods to seek huge profits and thereby create great social disparity and contribute to discontent among the public" and launched a series of investigations into the taxation of individual and private firms.[12] In comparison, no such attack on TVEs was reported during this same time period.

Facing such uncertainties, private enterprises have been concerned—understandably—about the adverse consequences of political crackdowns and they have reacted by withholding investment or seeking protection. Based on her interviews in Wenzhou in 1991, Whiting (1995) reports that private entrepreneurs were very worried about possible "policy changes" toward private enterprises and the great "psychological pressure" felt by private enterprise owners. A study by the Economic Policy Research Center of the Ministry of Agriculture reports significant reduction of investment in private enterprises from 1989 to 1990 because of these perceived policy changes. According to this study, the registered capital of private enterprises in Wenzhou declined by 5% in 1989; in several cases, private entrepreneurs liquidated their assets and took them abroad.[13] Some private enterprises sought protection by converting their firms into TVEs. The authors' interviews in Wenzhou in 1992 and 1994 found that several private enterprises were converted into TVEs in the wake of the retrenchment between 1989 and 1991.

Still the question remains: why are the property rights of TVEs better secured than those of private enterprises? We will argue that the first basic feature of the community government (**G1**) provides an advantage to TVEs when there is a lack of credible commitment from the state. The idea is that, when the community government engages in both providing productive local public goods and controlling TVEs, it becomes more useful than private entrepreneurs to the higher government. At equilibrium, the higher level government may optimally prey less on TVEs than on private enterprises, and the community government may be less worried about revenue confiscation by the higher government. As a result, more efficient projects may be implemented.

To elaborate on this idea, we consider a two-period model with three players—an entrepreneur, a community government, and a county government. The objective of the county government is maximization of the sum of the two-period revenues collected. In order to capture the institutional imperfections of the state, we assume that nothing binds the county government from arbitrarily taking away observable revenues from either private enterprises or community governments. This implies that no revenue-based contracts are feasible.

In each period, a project generates some observable revenues as well as some unobservable private benefits. There are two projects, referred to as project 1 and project 2. In the first period, for any given effort level of the entrepreneur, project 2 yields higher sums of the observable revenue and the unobservable private benefit than project 1. However, the unobservable private benefit from project 1 is higher than from project 2. One could think that project 1 involves more revenue hiding than project 2, at the cost of a lesser amount of total returns (such as choosing projects whose profits can be easily concealed). In the second period, the technologies of generating the observable revenues and unobservable benefits are the same between project 1 and project 2, with both dependent on effective government services described below. Overall, project 2 is more efficient (in terms of the net sums of the observable revenues and the unobservable private benefits in two periods) than project 1.

The community government provides productive local public goods, which help increase both project revenues and the private benefits of projects in the second period. For example, a stable social environment reduces business uncertainties, infrastructure investment helps reduce the costs of production, and basic living conditions improve workers' productivity. However, because of the free rider problem, entrepreneurs individually have no incentives to provide an efficient level of local public goods. On the other hand, because these services increase observable revenues in the second period, the county government has an interest in seeing that these services are adequate. Whether or not the community government provides such services, however, depends on its incentives. We assume that effective government service depends on both the level of effort (low or high) from the community government (with some private cost) and the revenue that remains with it from the first period. One can think of that portion of the revenue as the working budget for the community government in the second period. To capture the complementarity between the community government's budget and efforts, we also assume that the marginal productivity of the community government's budget is high (or low) if the community government exerts high (or low) effort.

In the case of private enterprises, an entrepreneur chooses the project type and receives unobservable private benefits. Because private benefits accrue to the entrepreneur and the second period's observable revenues are always taken away by the county government, the community government has no share in the second period payoffs, either observable or unobservable. Consequently the community government will provide low effort in providing its services. Thus, according to our assumption of low marginal productivity with a community government's low effort, the county government will provide only the minimum working budget for the community government in the second period. Anticipating this, the entrepreneur maximizes the first period private benefits by choosing the less efficient project 1. In the end, because project 1 entails costly revenue hiding, and because there are few effective community government services, the total amount of observable revenues collected by the county government is also small. This is clearly an inefficient equilibrium, and is a direct result of the lack of credible commitment on the part of the county government.

Can TVEs do better? With TVEs, it is the community government that selects the project type (as is evident in Section 2) and receives unobservable private benefits. Because all the private benefits accrue to the community government, it now has an incentive to exert a high effort in providing government services. As a result, the marginal productivity of its working budget becomes high. Instead of leaving a minimum amount of observable revenues to the community government, the county government may now appear more "generous" and leave a larger amount for the community government's working budget, because this may increase the observable revenues in the second period. This amounts to "keeping hens for more eggs," an old Chinese saying. As long as the higher second period observable revenues from the increased productivity of the community government's budget outweighs the costs of sacrificing the first period's revenue, the county government will provide, out of its own interest, a larger budget to the community government.

Moreover, realizing that a larger amount of first period observable revenues will be left to its discretion, the community government may have an incentive to choose project 2 over project 1. For although the community government's first period private benefits are reduced, the first period observable revenues increase, which may raise its working budget for the second period. This in turn may enhance its second period private benefits.

Therefore, it is possible that, with TVEs, the more efficient project 2 will be chosen, a larger amount of revenue will be left with the community government, more community government services are provided, and more revenues are also collected by the county government. At equilibrium, the county government will (optimally) prey less on TVEs than on private enterprises. Evidently, the main drawback of TVEs is the low incentives provided to the entrepreneur, who now becomes the manager of TVEs and is deprived of receiving unobservable private benefits.

In essence, TVE governance may reduce the efficiency loss resulting from state predation because the community government integrates government and business activities. Two effects can be identified. The first is the incentive effect. Controlling business activities allows the community government to receive private benefits, so that it will benefit from the fruits of exerting much effort in conducting government activities when contracts are not enforceable. Then the county government is willing to leave more revenues with the community government. The second effect is the less-revenue-hiding effect. When the community government integrates the two activities, it partially internalizes the costs of inefficient project choices. Hence, given the incentives provided by the ownership, the community government may choose more efficient projects, and the county government appears even more "generous" toward TVEs than to private enterprises. In summary, the community government's involvement in TVEs can be interpreted as an organizational response to the commitment problem under imperfect state institutions.

These theoretical results are consistent with the evidence presented at the beginning of this section. They are also consistent with the evidence presented in Section 2 that a large portion of after-tax revenue of TVEs is actually used for public expenditure. In addition, in their econometric work using provincial data between 1986 and 1993, Jin and Qian (1997) found that the share of TVEs in the rural non-farm economy increases both the state and community shares of rural income (and reduces the household share), after controlling for the level of per capita income. This evidence not only supports our above results, but also shows that it is in the interests of both the state and community governments to have more TVEs than private enterprises.

5. Financing of Investment

Evidence also shows that TVEs receive larger loans, invest in larger-scale projects, and engage in more capital-intensive industries than do private enterprises. In a 1989 sample from Zhejiang and Sichuan provinces, the median size of loans extended to township enterprises, village enterprises, and private enterprises was 123,700 yuan, 43,000 yuan, and 18,000 yuan, respectively, and the mean size of such loans was 299,649 yuan, 218,873 yuan, and 58,996 yuan, respectively. The capital : labor ratio was 11,323 yuan per township enterprise, 7,458 yuan per village enterprise, and 6,447 yuan per private enterprise.[14] At the national level, about one-half of TVE industrial output comes from heavy industries, which are generally more capital-intensive industries. For example, in 1985, 49.9% of industrial output came from heavy industries (of which 78.5% was from manufacturing, 13.6% from material processing, and 15.4% from mining), and in 1991, 45.6% of industrial output came from heavy industries (of which 66.4% came from manufacturing, 21.0% from material processing, and 12.6% from mining) (Ministry of Agriculture, China 1992b; p. 50).

What explains the different pattern of financing investments between TVEs and private enterprises? It is not hard to understand that start-up private enterprises entail high agency costs in terms of borrowing funds for investment, because of the problems of adverse selection and moral hazard as well as their limited wealth (Holmstrom 1995). In the case of TVEs, the first basic feature of community government (G1) helps to explain the advantage of TVEs in financing investment.

As indicated by the evidence in Section 3, when a TVE needs funds for its investment, the community government borrows a loan from a bank and provides the funds to the entrepreneur, now the TVE manager. Because community governments have been engaged in both government and business activities for some time, they already had substantial physical and financial resources at the beginning of economic reform. For example, in 1980, rural per capita household savings deposits were only 14.7 yuan (*Almanac of China's Finance and Banking* 1993). In contrast, rural per capita collective fixed assets were 126.94 yuan (Ministry of Agriculture, China 1986). In addition, as we demonstrated above, the integration of these two activities provides a safeguard for the autonomous control of these assets. As a result, the community government can utilize these assets to act as an intermediary for financing TVEs in an imperfect capital market.

The involvement of the community government, however, adds at least two types of agency costs. First, separating management and control entails costly government monitoring. Second, the government may have incentives to divert funds away from investment as well (to serve its own political agenda for example). Therefore TVE governance has a trade-off between different types of agency costs in intermediating investment finance.

To formalize these ideas, we again consider a model with three players—an entrepreneur, a community government, and a state bank, which has capital. The cost of capital is r, which represents the safe rate of return. The entrepreneur has an idea about an investment project that requires one unit of capital; however, he has very limited wealth (less than one unit of capital). If the entrepreneur does not divert the investment funds he borrows from the bank, the project generates the safe return a, which is higher than r. But the entrepreneur may divert some funds for certain private benefits b. If he does that, the project becomes risky: It succeeds and generates the return a with some probability π less than 1; otherwise the project fails and yields zero return. We assume that the expected return plus the private benefits will be lower than the safe rate of return (i.e., $a\pi+b < r$), therefore the bank will not finance the project if the entrepreneur diverts the funds. We assume now that loan contracts are feasible but there is a usual limited liability constraint on the part of the entrepreneur.

When the entrepreneur has no wealth to invest as equity, he has a strong incentive to divert the funds because he is the sole claimant of the private benefits, whereas he is entitled to (at most) part of the project's returns. Nevertheless, when the entrepreneur does have some wealth to invest, his propensity to divert investment funds for private benefits will depend on the amount of his own wealth that is invested in the project. A higher amount of his own investment increases his stake in the project and therefore helps internalize the costs of diverting investment funds. Consequently, there will be a threshold of wealth for an individual entrepreneur such that the bank is (not) willing to finance his investment if his wealth is greater (less) than the threshold.[15] Because an entrepreneur's wealth is generally low at the start of reform and development, his investment usually cannot be financed.

Under TVE governance, the community government borrows from the bank and provides the funds to the entrepreneur, now the manager of a TVE. To capture the possible advantages of the TVE, we assume that community wealth is larger than private wealth, and that, with some monitoring cost c, the government can ensure that no funds will be diverted by the manager. However, the community government itself is also subject to incentive problems. For simplicity, we assume that the government can divert funds only if it is engaged in monitoring managers.[16] When the community government monitors the manager but diverts the funds for itself, it receives the same amount of private benefits and brings on the same project riskiness as when funds are diverted by the entrepreneur.

Clearly both the community government's stake in the project and the return from the investment must be sufficiently high that the cost of fund diversion can be internalized on the one hand, and the monitoring cost will be covered on the other hand. This implies that there will be a community wealth threshold for the TVE at least as high as the private wealth threshold is for entrepreneurs.[17] The investment by the TVE will be financed only if the community government invests an amount of the community wealth that is beyond the threshold. Thus the community government can facilitate financial contracting between the bank and the TVE when it controls a large amount of community assets.

This model indicates two counter-balancing effects in TVE governance: On the one hand, the greater the amount of physical and financial assets endowed by the community government, the lesser the external agency costs; on the other hand, community government involvement in TVE governance inflicts higher internal agency costs. And the TVE is more efficient only if the reduction of external agency costs is sufficient to compensate for the increases in internal agency costs.

Some comparative statics results also can be derived. First, when the entrepreneur's wealth is large, the external agency cost is small; thus there is unlikely any role for the community government as an intermediary. Second, the larger the monitoring costs and the greater the private benefits from diverting investment funds, the more costly for the community government's involvement. These results imply that TVEs are more likely to disappear when the government experiences an increase in monitoring costs or an increase in private benefits (say, from pursuing its political agenda) and when the entrepreneur has more wealth. Conversely, TVEs are more likely to crop up in regions where the community government is better endowed in terms of human capital, enjoys close ties with local entrepreneurs, and controls a considerable portion of the community's assets.

In the above-cited econometric work, Jin and Qian (1997) reported that the share of TVEs in rural industrial output in a province is positively related to per capita community assets at the beginning of reform in 1980, but negatively related to private financial activities (measured by the ratio of rural private financial savings to rural GDP). They also found that the share of TVEs is positively related to the state supply of credit to rural enterprises (measured by credit per rural enterprise employee). These empirical findings support the above results.

6.   Why Do TVEs Have Harder Budget Constraints Than SOEs?

A natural question arises as to why TVEs and SOEs differ, although both are government-controlled. Product market competition is often cited as a reason. It is true that TVEs are operating in competitive product markets. However, unlike SOEs in Eastern Europe and the former Soviet Union, most SOEs in China, except in a few monopoly industries, do not have much monopoly power either. Indeed, they are typically small in size and dispersed across many regions (Qian and Xu 1993). While product market competition is necessary for achieving efficiency, it is not sufficient. We see a more fundamental difference between TVEs and SOEs in the varying degrees of hardness of budget constraints these enterprises face. Indeed, even if product markets are perfectly competitive, an inefficient firm can still survive as long as it faces soft budget constraints.

The following evidence suggests that TVEs generally have harder budget constraints than SOEs. First, TVEs have been receiving proportionally fewer loans than SOEs and were hit badly during the retrenchment period. During the late 1980s and early 1990s, the total size of SOE industrial output was about twice that of TVEs. However, for each year between 1986 and 1992, loans to rural enterprises (mainly TVEs) accounted for only about 8% of all non-agricultural loans, while loans to SOEs accounted for about 86%. Due to the retrenchment, new loans to rural enterprises fell from 15.85 billion yuan in 1988 to 12.9 billion yuan in 1989, but new loans to SOEs increased from 128.43 billion yuan in 1988 to 172.49 billion yuan in 1989. Thus, the share of new loans to rural enterprises in total non-agricultural areas declined from 10.2% in 1988 to 6.8% in 1989, and the share of new loans to SOEs increased from 82.9% in 1988 to 90.5% in 1989 (*Almanac of China's Finance and Banking* 1993: p. 356). Second, TVEs are less likely to incur losses than SOEs. Total losses from all TVEs were 4.7 billion yuan in 1990 and 4.3 billion yuan in 1991 (*Statistical Survey of China* 1992: p. 67), while the total losses from industrial SOEs alone were 34.9 billion yuan in 1990 and 36.7 billion yuan in 1991 (*China Statistical Yearbook* 1994: p. 399). Third, TVEs are more likely to reduce employment in response to a government's austerity program than SOEs. Total TVE employment fell from 48.9 million in 1988 to 47.2 million in 1989 and further to 45.9 million in 1990, while employment in the state-sector actually increased (*China Statistical Yearbook* 1992). In fact, until 1993, SOEs almost never laid off workers and loss-making SOEs never went bankrupt.

This leads to an interesting question: why do TVEs have harder budget constraint than SOEs? We argue that the second basic feature of the community government (**G2**) may provide an answer. The soft budget constraint problem arises because of the difficulty that those (the state banks here) who bail out bad projects have in effectuating termination once investment costs are sunk (Dewatripont and Maskin 1995). Because of differences in the structures of control rights and information allocation in the cases of TVEs and SOEs, the net benefits from refinancing projects for TVEs and SOEs differ. Thus the state bank's incentives for refinancing after sunk investments differ as well.

In order to explain how allocation of control rights affects the degree of softness of budget constraints, we follow the logic in the argument put forward by Dewatripont and Maskin (1995) and modify slightly the model in the previous section. Suppose that a project takes two periods rather than one to complete. If no funds are diverted in the first period, the project will be carried out smoothly throughout the two periods and will yield the higher return a. However, if funds are diverted in the first period, the fate of the project will depend on refinancing in the second period. Without refinancing, the project generates no returns and negative private benefits (reflecting the private costs of implementing a project). With refinancing, if no funds are diverted in the second period, the project generates the higher return a along with some private benefits b accruing to the manager (as a result of fund diversion in the first period). Otherwise the refinanced project becomes a risky one, generating the higher return a with probability π less than 1, along with a larger amount of private benefits $2b$ accruing to the manager (as a result of repeated fund diversion in both periods). For simplicity we exclude the possibility of fund diversion by the community government that was assumed previously (including such a possibility only strengthens our results).

We assume that no monitoring is possible in the first period and that with some monitoring costs, the owner of an enterprise can ensure that the manager will not divert the funds in the second period. Then it is evident that a manager will not have an incentive to divert funds in the first period if the project is unlikely to be refinanced when it stumbles. On the other hand, the manager will divert funds if he expects the project to be refinanced, as private benefits b is positive.

Whether a project will be refinanced or not depends on the control structure of the firm and the bank. In the case of an SOE, the government controls both the enterprise and the bank and receives the entire return from refinancing; hence it internalizes the costs of monitoring. Given the sunk investment, the incentives for refinancing are high, despite the fact that the government does not like refinancing before the first period because managers tend to behave opportunistically. This internalization of the monitoring costs by maintaining control over both an enterprise and the bank is *ex post* efficient, but *ex ante* inefficient.

In the case of a TVE, the community government controls TVEs, but not the state bank. Let us suppose that the funds are diverted in the first period and hence the project needs refinancing in the second period. By assumption, in order for refinancing to be profitable for the bank, the community government needs to monitor the manager in the second period. When controls over the enterprise and over the bank are separate, the community government needs to be motivated for monitoring managers. Consequently, in order to induce the community government to monitor, some amount of incentive rents have to be paid out of project returns to the community government. This reduces the project returns to the bank. Accordingly, from the point of view of the bank, refinancing a TVE is more expensive than refinancing an SOE. It follows that the bank is more inclined to refuse refinancing when a TVE's project stumbles in the first period. This in turn reduces the manager's incentives to divert funds in the first period.

Essentially, with TVEs, because the community government does not control banks, there is a separation of control over information (i.e., through monitoring managers) and control over funds: the community government has control over information but not funds, while banks have control over funds but not information. This implies that some rents have to be transferred from the bank to the community government, thereby reducing the bank's incentives for *ex post* refinancing. This in turn increases *ex ante* efficiency. In such a manner, this separation of power serves as a commitment device that is used to achieve harder budget constraints.[18]

7. Conclusions

We have analyzed the phenomenon of China's township-village enterprises from an organizational perspective and with a focus on governance. Unlike most of the literature on TVEs that identifies the boundaries of the firm at the individual enterprise level, we view the boundaries of the firm at the community level. We draw important parallels and highlight crucial differences in governance structures between TVEs and conventional, publicly-held multi-divisional corporations in the West. From this perspective, we analyze the central role that community governments play in TVE governance as an organizational response to the imperfect institutional environment of both state and market. What underlies these roles, we argue, is the fact that community governments in rural China are appropriately empowered (**G1**) and constrained (**G2**).

Two general lessons can be drawn from China's TVE experience. First, in transition and developing economies, the ownership of firms

and corporate governance should consider the institutional environments of both the state and market. The distinct feature of transition
and developing economies is the underdevelopment of institutions
that constrain the state and support markets. Unfortunately, in many
transition and developing economies, perhaps too much faith is placed
in idealized state and market institutions without enough attention
paid to the reality of the existing institutional environment. In China,
however, the organizational innovation of TVEs as a "community corporation" emerged and succeeded at the time when both the state and
privately owned enterprises were experiencing difficulties with growth.
In our analysis, TVE governance is perceived as an organizational
response to imperfect institutions in China. Although this new organizational structure differs from, and appears less efficient than, those
found in mature market economies, it functions better given the institutional reality.[19]

Second, local governments can be a driving force in economic
transition and development, provided that they are both appropriately
empowered and constrained. The TVE experience as a transition and
development model differs considerably from those in Eastern Europe
and the former Soviet Union and many other developing countries
where local governments have played a much less significant role.
One plausible reason may be that China's community governments
have full autonomy over a range of community activities, including both government and business activities (**G1**). This may help
explain why other transition and developing countries have not
developed business organizations similar to TVEs, despite similarly
imperfect institutional environments. In sum, the success of TVEs
in China demonstrates that there is no standard model of transition
from plan to market, nor does there exist such a model for economic
development.

Appendix: The Evolution of TVEs

Prior to 1979: The primitive stage of TVEs can be traced back to 1958,
the time of the Great Leap Forward and the inception of the commune
system. Many small-scale industrial enterprises (e.g., steel mills) were
set up by communes, and all of them failed shortly thereafter. These
failed experiments were the first attempt at rural industrialization in
which community governments played an essential role.

During the nationwide agricultural mechanization drive of the early 1970s, rural small-scale industrial enterprises rapidly re-emerged (Wong 1991). Most of these enterprises started as agricultural machine repair shops and food processing mills, and many of them soon became subcontractors of SOEs in nearby urban areas. These community enterprises were known as "commune and brigade enterprises," the predecessor to the TVEs. The total output value of commune and brigade enterprises increased from 9.25 billion yuan in 1970 to 27.2 billion yuan in 1976, with an average annual real growth rate of 25.7% (Byrd and Lin 1990, p. 10). By 1978, there were about 1.5 million such enterprises with a total output value of 49.3 billion yuan (*China Statistical Yearbook* 1992: pp. 389–390), of which 38.5 billion yuan was for industrial output, which accounted for 9% of the national industrial output (*Ministry of Agriculture, China* 1992a: p. 1).

1979–1993: Since 1979 when economic reform took place, the TVEs have become the most dynamic sector in the economy, especially after 1985. As the household responsibility system replaced the commune production scheme in agriculture, the community government shifted their focus to rural industrialization. In 1984, with the abolishment of the commune system, the central government renamed commune and brigade enterprises as township and village enterprises. At the end of 1992, China had 48,200 townships and 806,000 villages. On average, each township with a population of about 18,000 has 8.2 township enterprises with 66 employees per enterprise, and each village with a population of about 1,000 has 1.4 village enterprises with 23 employees per enterprise (*China Statistical Yearbook* 1993: p. 15 and p. 395). Between 1978 and 1993, the share of industrial output of TVEs as a national total increased from 9% to 27% (Table 4.1).

During this period, the central government's attitude toward TVEs changed from tolerance to encouragement. It issued several internal documents that promoted TVEs in the 1980s, and released the public and national legal regulations on TVEs in 1990 (see Section 2). The only central government agency responsible for TVEs is the small "Township and Village Enterprises Bureau" under the Ministry of Agriculture. Supervision of TVEs was carried out by the county governments.

Since 1994: Several new developments concerning TVEs have emerged since 1994. One is the rise of the mixed corporate form known as "joint-stock cooperatives" (*gufen hezuozhi*). Under this form, shares of TVEs are sold or distributed to TVE employees and managers or community residents in the form of both "collective shares" ("one person, one vote") and conventional individual shares ("one share, one vote"). Another development is the privatization of TVEs, mainly in the form of sales of control rights to managers and employees or to foreign investors. After the privatization, the community government continues to play a role in rural industrialization by concentrating its attention on investment in infrastructure (e.g., power supplies, roads and harbors), coordination and urban planning, and other conventional public works. In some cases, the community governments continue to hold a minority stake in the partially privatized former TVEs.

Another significant development is the direct election of village leaders by community residents. By 1995, about one-third of the villages had already formulated "village self-governing charters," more than one-half of the villages had established "village resident congresses," and more than 90% of village residents had participated in elections. It is also reported that to promote direct election in villages, China has established model villages in 63 counties, in 3,917 townships, and in 82,266 villages (*People's Daily*, November 15, 1995).

Notes

* The authors are grateful to Masahiko Aoki, Pranab Bardhan, Erik Berglof, Ronald McKinnon, Paul Milgrom, Ramon Myers, Dwight Perkins, Thomas Rawski, William Simon, Yijiang Wang, Barry Weingast, two referees, and especially Pablo Spiller for helpful discussions and comments. The paper was written when Che was a graduate student at Stanford University and Qian was a National Fellow at the Hoover Institution at Stanford. Financial support from the Center for Economic Policy Research (CEPR) at Stanford is gratefully acknowledged.

1. Chinese statistics classify rural enterprises into four categories in terms of ownership: townships (*xiangban*), villages (*cunban*), groups of households (*lianhu*, including cooperatives and partnerships), and individual households (*geti*, i.e., a sole proprietorship employing less than eight employees). TVEs refer to the first two categories. Although each village is under the jurisdiction of a township, a village enterprise differs from a township enterprise; the former is run by the village government and the latter by the township government. In 1992, 39% of rural industrial output originated from enterprises run by townships, 34% by villages, 7% by groups of households, and 20% by individual households (*Statistical Material of Township Enterprises* 1992, p. 17).

2. These conclusions are confirmed by other studies from Chinese sources, see, for example, Ma, et al. (1994), which contains 32 case studies of TVEs in three provinces of Shandong, Jiangsu and Gansu.

3. Byrd (1990) observed: "The community government's ability to absorb risk by varying its public expenditure may be limited, but it can spread risk across its enterprises to increase the flexibility and ability to absorb losses of any one firm." Oi (1994) also reported: "The debts of a village or township are the responsibility of the collective. Interviews reveal that in a number of localities when a collective enterprise fails and defaults in its loans, the debt is paid off by the other enterprises regardless of the specifics of the contracting system."

4. According to Oi (1994), "Those who run the enterprise are dependent on the local government officials who appoint them. There is competitive bidding to win contracts, but local officials ultimately decide who will be given the contract."

5. Viewing the boundaries of the firm at the community level also helps clarify some of the confusion in the literature which typically interprets the boundaries of the firm for TVEs at the enterprise level. First, the disagreement over whether TVEs have clearly specified property rights (e.g., Weitzman and Xu 1994 vs. Naughton 1994) becomes less pronounced and will be probed from a new perspective. Rather the relevant question is the efficiency of the existing allocation of control rights (see Grossman and Hart 1986 and Hart and Moore 1990). Second, different views on the hardness of budget constraints of TVEs (e.g., Whiting 1995 vs. McKinnon 1994) can also be reconciled. Cross-subsidization among TVEs within a community can co-exist with the hard budget constraints of the community to which these TVEs belong.

6. Most TVEs are legal persons, while divisions in a corporation are not. In this respect, the structure of TVEs is more like a holding company.

7. Because the rights of community residents are restricted, community residents are more appropriately referred to as beneficiaries, rather than owners, of TVEs (Chang and Wang 1994).

8. Two special mechanisms of TVEs may have helped in part to contain some of the agency costs. First, TVEs' after-tax profits must be used mainly for the purpose of reinvestment and local public expenditure. Because the heads of townships and villages are appointed and dismissed by the county and township governments respectively, these restrictions can be enforced to some extent as the residents can voice their concerns to higher governments, although they cannot vote. Second, a township, especially a village, is a small community, and most township and village government officials and TVE managers are residents of the same community where TVE investments are located. Because community government officials and TVE managers interact with residents frequently (they usually have extensive family ties in the community), their activities can be better monitored by residents, which helps reputation mechanisms work.

9. North (1990) and North and Weingast (1989) discuss the issue in the historical perspective. The lack of credible commitment by the state under central planning, which induces the so called "ratchet effect," was a major topic in the literature of comparative systems (see Kornai 1980). Litwack (1991) links the lack of credible commitment to the lack of rule of law.

10. Under decentralization, regional governments at provincial, prefecture and county levels also have control over state bank branches and SOEs in their regions, thus these governments can also order a state bank branch to provide funds to a state enterprise in their regions.

11. "Resolution on Several Questions about Speeding Up Agricultural Development," December 1978, as quoted by Byrd and Lin (1990).

12. State Council document, August 30, 1989, as quoted by Whiting (footnote 100, p. 109, 1995).

13. As quoted by Whiting (p. 111, 1995).

14. Table 2, Table 28, and Table 6 in Zhang and Ronnas (1993). The data on loan size are for loans at the enterprise level. At the community level, the difference is even more striking, because on average each township has 8.2 township enterprises and each village has 1.4 village enterprises.

15. The threshold wealth $\underline{w}$ can be derived from the following "incentive compatibility" condition (assuming the entrepreneur has all the bargaining power): The entrepreneur has no incentives to divert funds if and only if.

$(1+a) - (1+r)(1-w) \geq \pi[(1+a) - (1+r)(1-w)] + (1-\pi)0 + b,$

which gives $w \geq \underline{w} = [-(a-r) + b/(1-\pi)]/(1+r).$

16. The qualitative results will remain even if we assume that the community government can divert the funds without monitoring managers.

17. The community government has incentives to monitor if.

$(1+a) - (1+r)(1-W) - c \geq \pi[(1+a) - (1+r)(1-W)];$

and the community government has no incentives to divert funds if

$(1+a) - (1+r)(1-W) - c \geq \pi[(1+a) - (1+r)(1-W)] + b.$

Both are satisfied if.

$W \geq \underline{W} = \max \{c/(1-\pi), b/(1-\pi)\}/(1+r) - (a-r)/(1+r) \geq \underline{w}.$

18. Although we have followed the logic of analysis by Dewatripont and Maskin (1995), our model setup and results differ from theirs: in their model, a soft budget constraint is associated with centralization of credit, and a hard budget constraint is associated with decentralization of credit. In our model, we take the state-controlled banking system as the given institutional environment, and show how a soft budget constraint arises in SOEs and a hard budget constraint in TVEs because of different control rights allocation over enterprises and banks.

19. The underlying "second-best" principle is quite general in studying institutions and political economy. For example, Spiller and Sampson (1994) argue that the apparently inefficient pricing schemes and regulatory structure in Jamaican telecommunications can be viewed as a second-best alternative that reflects a pragmatic response to the imperfect Jamaican government institutions in the areas of public utilities.

References

A Statistical Survey of China, Beijing: China Statistical Publishing House, various years.

Almanac of China's Finance and Banking, Beijing: China Finance Publishing House. 1993."

Byrd, William, "Entrepreneurship, Capital, and Ownership," chapter 9 in William Byrd and Qingsong Lin (eds.), *China's Rural Industry: Structure, Development, and Reform*, Oxford University Press, 1990.

Byrd, William and Allen Gelb, "Why Industrialize? The Incentives for Rural Community Governments," chapter 17 in William Byrd and Qingsong Lin (eds.), *China's Rural Industry: Structure, Development, and Reform*, Oxford University Press, 1990.

Byrd, William and Qingsong Lin, "China's Rural Industry: An Introduction," chapter 1 in William Byrd and Qingsong Lin (eds.), *China's Rural Industry: Structure, Development, and Reform*, Oxford University Press, 1990.

Chandler, Alfred Jr., *Strategy and Structure*, New York: Doubleday & Company, Inc., 1966.

Chang, Chun and Yijiang Wang, "The Nature of the Township Enterprise," *Journal of Comparative Economics*, 19: 434–452, 1994.

China Statistical Yearbook, Beijing: China Statistical Publishing House, various years.

Dewatripont, Mathias, and Eric Maskin, "Credit and Efficiency in Centralized and Decentralized Economies, *Review of Economic Studies*, October, 1995.

Grossman, Sanford and Oliver Hart, "The Costs and Benefits of Ownership: A Theory of Vertical and Lateral Integration," *Journal of Political Economy*, 94, 1986.

Hart, Oliver, and John Moore, "Property Rights and the Nature of the Firm," *Journal of Political Economy*, 98(6), pp. 1119–1158, 1990.

Holmstrom, Bengt, "Financing of Investment in Eastern Europe: A Theoretical Perspective," mimeo, MIT, 1995.

Jin, Hehui, and Yingyi Qian, "Ownership and Institutions: Evidence from Rural China," mimeo, Stanford University, 1997.

Kornai, Janos, *Economics of Shortage*, Amsterdam: North Holland, 1980.

Li, David D., "Ambiguous Property Rights in Transition Economies," *Journal of Comparative Economics*, 1996.

Litwack, John, "Legality and Market Reform in Soviet-Type Economies," *Journal of Economic Perspectives*, 5(4):77–90, Fall, 1991.

Ma, Rong, et al. *Zhongguo Xiangzhen Qiye de Fazhan Lishi he Yunxing Jizhi (Development History and Operating Mechanisms of China's Township Enterprises)*, Peking University Press, 1994.

McKinnon, Ronald, "Gradual versus Rapid Liberalization in Socialist Economies: Financial Policies in China and Russia Compared," No. 10 in the ICEG Sector Studies Series, a publication of the International Center for Economic Growth, 1994.

Ministry of Agriculture, China, *Xiangzhen Qiye Tongji Zilao 1978–85 (Township Enterprises Statistical Manual 1978–85)*, Beijing: Department of Rural Enterprises of Ministry of Agriculture, 1986.

Ministry of Agriculture, China, *Zhonghua Renmin Gongheguo Xiangcun Jiti Suoyouzhi Qiye Tiaoli Tiaowen Shiyi (Explanations of the Regulation on Township and Village Collective Enterprises of the People's Republic of China)*, Beijing: China Legal Press, 1990.

Ministry of Agriculture, China, *Xiangzhen Qiye Tongji Ziliao, 1992 (Statistical Materials of Township Enterprises, 1992)*, Beijing: China Legal Press, 1992a.

Ministry of Agriculture, China, *Zhongguo Xiangzheng Qiye Tongji Zhaiyao 1992 (A Statistical Survey of China's Township Enterprises 1992)*, Beijing: Department of Rural Enterprises of Ministry of Agriculture, 1992b.

Naughton, Barry, "Chinese Institutional Innovation and Privatization from Below," *American Economic Review*, vol. 84, no. 2, pp. 266–270, May, 1994.

Nee, Victor, "Organizational Dynamics of Market Transition: Hybrid Forms, Property Rights and Mixed Economy in China," *Administrative Science Quarterly*, 37, 1992.

North, Douglass C., *Institutions, Institutional Changes, and Economic Performance*, Cambridge University Press, 1990.

Oi, Jean, "Fiscal Reform and the Economic Foundations of Local State Corporatism in China," *World Politics*, vol. 45, no. 1, October, 1992.

Oi, Jean, *Rural China Take off: Incentives for Reform*, mimeo, Harvard University, 1994.

Qian, Yingyi, and Chenggang Xu, "Why China's Economic Reforms Differ: The M-Form Hierarchy and Entry/Expansion of the Non-State Sector," *Economics of Transition*, 1(2):135–170, June, 1993.

Qian, Yingyi, and Barry R. Weingast, "China's Transition to Markets: Market-Preserving Federalism, Chinese Style," *Journal of Policy Reform*, 1: 149–185, 1996.

Spiller, Pablo T., and Cezley I. Sampson, "Regulation, Institutions, and Commitment: The Jamaican Telecommunications Sector," Policy Research Working Paper 1362, The World Bank, October 1994.

Stiglitz, Joseph E. and Andrew Weiss, "Credit Rationing in Markets with Imperfect Information," *American Economic Review*, 71, 393–410, June, 1981.

Weitzman, Martin and Chenggang Xu, "Chinese Township Village Enterprises as Vaguely Defined Cooperatives," *Journal of Comparative Economics*, 18: 121–145, 1994.

Whiting, Susan, *The Micro-Foundations of Institutional Change in Reform China: Property Rights and Revenue Extraction in the Rural Industrial Sector*, Ph.D. dissertation, University of Michigan, 1995.

Williamson, Oliver, *Markets and Hierarchies*, New York: Free Press, 1975.

Wong, Christine, "The Maoist 'Model' Reconsidered: Local Self-Reliance and its Financing of Rural Industrialization," in William Joseph, Christine Wong and David Zweig (eds.), *New Perspectives on the Cultural Revolution*, Harvard University Press, 1991.

Wong, Christine, "Fiscal Reform and Local Industrialization," *Modern China*, 18(2):197–227, April, 1992.

Xiangzhen Qiye Tongji Ziliao, 1992 (*Statistical Materials of Township Enterprises*, 1992), Beijing, Department of Rural Enterprises, Ministry of Agriculture.

Zhang, Gang and Per Ronnas, "The Capital Structure of Township Enterprises," mimeo, Stockholm, 1993.

Zhonghua Renmin Gongheguo Xiangcun Jiti Suoyouzhi Qiye Tiaoli Tiaowen Shiyi (*Explanations of the Regulation on Township and Village Collective Enterprises of the People's Republic of China*), edited by the Ministry of Agriculture, Beijing: China Legal Press, 1990.

5 Insecure Property Rights and Government Ownership of Firms

1. Introduction

For the past two decades, China's transition to a market economy occurred in an environment without the rule of law to constrain the state. In particular, there was no commitment based on law and institutions designed to prevent the national and local governments from encroaching on private enterprises or to prevent the national government from encroaching on local governments. Hence, property rights (both cash flow and control over assets) were fundamentally unprotected against state predation. Without secure property rights, private enterprises played only a minor role during the period, and by 1993 the private sector accounted for only about 15 percent of national industrial output.

Despite this problem, China's economic performance has been remarkable. The main driving force of the economy has been the so-called "non-state" firms that have a form of government ownership. The share of this type of firm in the national industrial output increased from 22 percent to 42 percent between 1978 and 1993, while the share of state-owned enterprises (SOEs) declined from 78 percent to 43 percent [*China Statistics Yearbook* 1994, and Section 5 below]. One striking example of this type of non-state firm are local government-controlled enterprises in rural areas known as Township-Village Enterprises (TVEs), whose share in the national industrial output increased from 9 percent in 1978 to 27 percent in 1993.

In this paper, we study ownership of firms in an environment in which the state is unable to make a credible commitment not to expropriate their revenue. We argue that, although local government ownership compromises managerial incentives in comparison to private

With Jiahua Che; originally published in *Quarterly Journal of Economics*, May 1998, 113(2), pp. 467–496.

ownership, it may also limit national government predation, increase local public goods provision, and reduce costly revenue hiding. Because the local government carries out government activities, the interests of the national government are more aligned with those of the local government than with those of a private owner, and thus the local government may better serve the objectives of the national government. Hence, the national government may have less incentive to prey on local government-owned firms than on private firms when government activities provide important revenue-enhancing services.

We use a simple model to formalize the above idea. In our model the economy has two types of activities: business activities that generate revenue, and government activities that use existing revenues to provide local public goods to enhance future revenues. There are three types of players: the manager who operates business projects; the local government that provides local public goods and has the discretionary power to extract revenue from managers; and the national government that has the discretionary power to extract revenue from both managers and local governments. As a result of state predation, no revenue-based contracts are enforceable.

We examine and compare three types of ownership of firms: "private ownership," "local government ownership," and "state ownership" (i.e., national government ownership). In private ownership the manager controls the firm; under state ownership, the national government controls the firm. These two types of ownership are standard in the literature. Our focus here, however, is local government ownership, where the local government, which provides local public goods, controls the firm.[1]

In our model, ownership provides the owner with the control rights over a firm's books and accounts, thereby allowing him to hide and receive unobservable parts of the revenue. In this way, ownership credibly provides owners with incentives. But such revenue hiding is also costly. For example, it may restrict technology choice. The tendency toward revenue hiding is pervasive in transition and developing economies that do not have rule of law. In China for example, private enterprises on average have paid much less in taxes than their true value added would call for, and local governments have maintained sizable (hidden) "off-budget revenue accounts" outside their official budgetary accounts [Yang 1996]. By incorporating the possibility of revenue hiding, we extend the existing ownership theory of firms to an environment with an unconstrained state.

We show that, although private ownership provides the owner-manager with incentives through revenue hiding, it involves excessive revenue hiding and fails to provide incentives for local governments. State ownership has the advantage of reducing revenue hiding to a minimum and it enables the national government to collect a larger share of revenue that is observable. However, it provides no incentives for either managers or local governments because they expect to be completely expropriated by their owner—the national government. In either case, the national government has no incentives to limit predation on observable revenue from managers and local governments.

Under local government ownership, the local government integrates government activities and business activities. It provides local public goods to enhance revenues from business projects *and* exercises control over a firm's books and accounts. This affects the behavior of the local government and the national government in two ways. First, in the absence of incentives provided by revenue-based contracts, ownership rights enable the local government to receive unobservable revenue that provides it with incentives to carry out government activities. This, in turn, reduces the national government's predaceous incentives because less predation today enables the local government to improve local public goods provision and increase revenues tomorrow. Second, being less concerned about the national government's predation, the local government chooses more efficient, less-revenue-hiding projects. Thus, local government-owned firms generate more observable revenue that the national government does not prey upon. The fundamental reason for securer property rights under local government ownership is that government activities better serve the interests of the national government in terms of future revenue. The downside of local government ownership is the lack of incentives for managers.

The following example illustrates the basic principle underlying our mechanism. Suppose that there are two projects: project A yields first period returns ($10, $100) and project B yields ($50, $80), where the first components are observable and the second are not. The local government activity needs an expenditure of either $4 or $12, which enhances the second period return by ($8, $8) and ($40, $40), respectively, if the local government makes an "effort," where, again, the first components are observable and the second components (net of effort) are not; the second period returns are all zero if the local government does not make an effort. For simplicity, we assume here that only observable revenue can be used for the local government's expenditures and the managerial effort does not matter (these restrictions will be relaxed in the formal model).

Under private ownership the local government has no incentive to make an effort since it cannot be compensated in a credible way. Then the manager would not choose project B since the national government would take away $50 and leave nothing to the local government, which would make the second period returns zero. Thus, the manager chooses project A, and the national government takes away the entire $10 and does not provide any revenue to the local government.

Under local government ownership, if the local government chooses project A, the national government gives back $4 to the local government and the local government exerts an effort to enhance the business project's return. As a result, in the second period, the national government gets $8 and the local government gets $8 (net of effort). Overall, the national government gets net $(10–4+8) = $14 and the local government gets net $(100+8) = $108. This is the incentive effect, that is, the local government has an incentive to make an effort, and the national government preys less on the local government. Moreover, if project B is chosen, the national government will give the local government $12 as a result of relaxing the liquidity constraint, which enhances the second period returns of the project—$40 to the national government and $40 (net of effort) to the local government. Because $(80+40) > $(100+8), the local government has an incentive to choose the more efficient project B. This is the less-revenue-hiding effect. In the end, the national government gets a two-period net revenue $(50–12+40) = $78 and the local government gets $(80+40) = $120.

Our model incorporates elements of the two main strands of the literature on the theory of the firm—the ownership models and multi-task models. First, our model contains some of the elements of the incomplete contract models of ownership (e.g., Grossman and Hart [1986] and Hart and Moore [1990]) and government ownership of firms (e.g., Schmidt [1996], Shleifer and Vishny [1994], and Hart, Shleifer, and Vishny [1997]). However, our model has a different institutional setting where an unconstrained state exists, which makes contract incompleteness (or more precisely, the absence of contracts) endogenous. Second, our model relates to the multi-task models of Holmstrom and Milgrom [1991, 1994]. Our model features several tasks in government and business activities. The allocation of these tasks, in connection with ownership, becomes crucial for determining incentives, revenue-hiding, and the extent of state predation.

The idea of local government ownership protecting firms in adverse political circumstances is also contained in some recent studies on China's TVEs (e.g., Chang and Wang [1994] and Li [1996]). However, these papers assume, rather than explain, that the local government is useful. Therefore, it is not clear why the local government is able to offer protection, and it is also not possible to assess what are the limits to the local government's role. In this paper we endogenize the capability of local governments to secure property rights by analyzing how their activities can better serve the interests of the national government.

Our focus on institutional responses to insecure property rights is similar to that in Greif, Milgrom, and Weingast [1994]. In a repeated game framework they argue that merchant guilds in the late medieval period served as an institutional mechanism to protect merchants' property rights against abuses by the city governments of trading centers, which was achieved by coordinating punitive actions among merchants against intrusive city governments. In a similar spirit, our paper regards local government ownership as an organizational response to the problem of state predation. In contrast to their institutional setting, managers in our context cannot escape the sphere of the state's power, and they are not allowed to form organizations to punish either national or local governments. However, local government ownership of business firms provides interesting mechanisms for limiting state predation.[2]

The rest of the paper is organized as follows: Section 2 introduces a simple model. Section 3 analyzes the model. Section 4 generalizes the model to a setting with multiple localities. Section 5 applies our theory to interpret China's experience. Section 6 concludes.

2.   A Simple Model

Consider a simple model with one business project in one locality. The technology of the economy consists of two activities and two periods. The first activity is "business activity"—one task of which concerns an "operation decision" about a business project. We call the individual who operates the business project a "manager" (denoted by M). The manager's (unobservable) "effort," a, enhances the first period return, $R_1 = R(a) > 0$ for all $a \geq 0$, which is increasing and concave in a, at a cost, $D(a)$, which is increasing and convex in a. The second period expected return, $R_2 > 0$, is independent of a for simplicity.

Both R_1 and R_2 have an "observable" part and an "unobservable" part. The division of R_2 is fixed, $(1-\lambda)R_2$ is observable, and λR_2 is not. The division of R_1 between the observable part and the unobservable part is determined by project type, q ($0 \leq q \leq 1$): For any given q, $(1-q)R_1$ is observable and $\alpha(q)R_1$ is not. And another task of the business activity concerns "control decision" of choosing q. We intend for this control decision to correspond to the control over the books and accounts of a firm, which ultimately determines revenue hiding. For example, we may think of high q projects as more cash-intensive projects. Incorporating the possibility of revenue hiding is essential for studying ownership issues in an environment with an unconstrained state. However, revenue hiding is costly, and the net hidden revenue, $\alpha(q)$, is such that $\alpha(q)$ is concave, $\alpha(0) = 0$, $\alpha'(q) < 1$ for all q. We also require that $\alpha'(1) < 0$, the condition that captures the situation where hiding every penny (i.e., $q = 1$) is extremely costly and thus the maximum revenue hiding is $\bar{q} < 1$, where $\alpha'(\bar{q}) = 0$.[3]

Ownership of a business project is defined as (i) the right of undertaking the task of control over the project type, and (ii) the right of receiving an unobservable part of the revenue.[4] This definition of ownership combines the notion of control and income. Here, income is naturally linked to control because if the owner of the project chooses a technology to hide some parts of the revenue, then he is the one who knows how to recover it. The decision to choose the type of project is irreversible: once the project is chosen and revenue is hidden, it is too late for someone else to reverse the decision. Furthermore, we assume that where to hide revenue can only be decided once at the beginning of period 1. This rules out the possibility of an ownership shift between periods.

The second activity is "government activity" that involves the task of providing local public goods. Local public goods have the potential to increase the second period return, R_2. Provision of local public goods requires an individual to operate, whom we call the "local government" (denoted by G). The effectiveness of local public goods provision in enhancing business projects depends on two factors: the local government's (unobservable) effort, g, and total expenditure, A, spent on the government activity. We write $R_2 = gh(A)$, where h is an increasing and concave function of A. For simplicity, we only allow for two effort levels: $g = 0$ or $\bar{g} > 0$ with the associated costs $C(0) = 0$, and $C(\bar{g}) = C > 0$. In reality, local government activities have a wide range, from maintaining social order (e.g., preventing riots) to providing basic living conditions (e.g., sanitary facilities), and from building local infrastructure (e.g., roads) to coordinating development in the locality.

Following the standard Grossman–Hart–Moore framework, we assume that one person can only do one task: either operate a business project or provide a local public good. Regardless of ownership assignment, M always operates a business project, G always provides local public goods, and M and G are not the same person.[5]

The national government in the economy is denoted by S. To capture the idea that both the national and local governments are not constrained by the rule of law, we assume that the local government can tax away any observable revenue from the manager, and the national government can tax away any observable revenue from either the manager or the local government. However, we impose a "limited liability" constraint, that is, the maximum amount the national or local government can tax away is limited to the observable amount of revenue.[6] Notice that, given our assumption of a lack of credibility of any revenue-based contracts (including loan contracts), the national government cannot spend more in the second period than it collects in the first period.

We consider three types of ownership: private ownership when M has control over project type q and receives unobservable revenue; local government ownership when G has those rights; and state ownership when S has those rights. The sequence of the play is as follows. At the beginning of period 1, the owner of the business project selects type q project and M makes an effort decision, a. Then the first period return is realized, $(1-q)R_1$ is observable and $\alpha(q)R_1$ is not. At the end of period 1, the national government preys on observable revenues from managers and local governments and decides how much revenue E (out of $(1-q)R_1$) is given to G for government activity. Simultaneously, the owner receives unobservable revenue and decides how much unobservable revenue e (out of $\alpha(q)R_1$) to spend for the government activity. This determines the total expenditure $A = e + E$. In the second period the local government decides on effort g for the government activity and then the second period return is realized, $(1-\lambda)R_2$ is observable and λR_2 is not. The national government takes away the observable part. The time line is represented by Figure 5.1.

Let I_k and J_k be consumption by k ($k = M, G, S$) in period 1 and 2, respectively, and δ be the common discount factor. The utility functions of the three players are specified as follows:

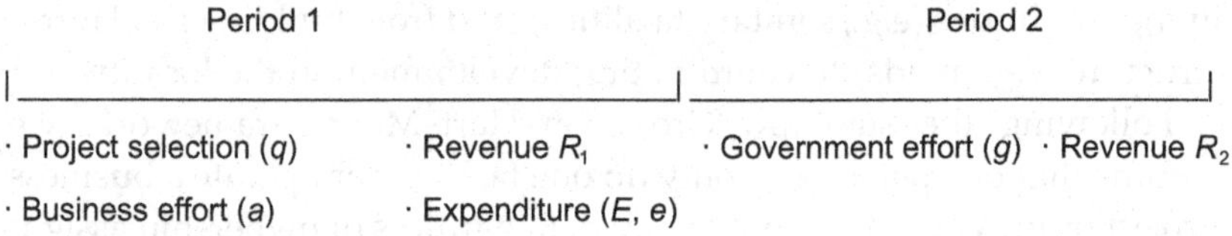

Period 1   Period 2

|_____|_____|

· Project selection (q)   · Revenue R_1 · Government effort (g)   · Revenue R_2

· Business effort (a)   · Expenditure (E, e)

Figure 5.1
Timeline

$$U_M = [I_M - D(a)] + \delta J_M;$$

$$U_G = I_G + \delta[J_G - C(g)];$$

$$U_S = I_S + \delta J_S.$$

Note that there is no intrinsic difference between G and M in terms of preferences, and that the national government is only concerned with its own revenue/consumption.

We first describe the benchmark "first-best" allocation. Because revenue hiding is costly, $q^{FB} = 0$. The first-best allocation maximizes total social surplus $U_M + U_G + U_S$ by choosing non-negative a, g, E, I_M, I_G, I_S, J_M, J_G, and J_S (no storing is possible):

$$\max [I_M + I_G + I_S - D(a)] + \delta[J_M + J_G + J_S - C(g)]$$

subject to: $I_M + I_G + I_S + E \le R(a)$,

$$J_M + J_G + J_S \le gh(E),$$

$I_k \ge 0, J_k \ge 0$ ($k = M, G, S$), $E \ge 0$, $g = 0$ or $\bar{g}$.

In the interesting case (i.e., $g = \bar{g}$), the above maximization problem is equivalent to:

$$\max R(a) - E - D(a) + \delta[\bar{g}h(E) - C]$$

subject to: $0 \le E \le R(a)$.

Then, there exists $\gamma \ge 0$, such that in the first-best allocation (a^{FB}, E^{FB}):

$$(1+\gamma)R'(a^{FB}) = D'(a^{FB});$$

$$\delta\bar{g}h'(E^{FB}) - 1 = \gamma;$$

$$\gamma(E^{FB} - R(a^{FB})) = 0.$$

If revenue-based contracts were enforceable, the first-best allocation could be achieved under private ownership provided that $\bar{g}h(E^{FB})$ is sufficiently large. To see this, let M have control over q. Let the contract awarded to the manager be such that the manager receives w_m in the second period if the first period observable revenue equals $R(a^{FB})$ and zero otherwise. Let a contract awarded to the local government be such that it receives w_g if the second period observable return is $(1-\lambda)\bar{g}h(E^{FB})$ and zero otherwise. Finally, let the national government receive all the residuals.

In this situation, the manager will choose $q = q^{FB} = 0$ and $a = a^{FB}$ if and only if

$$\delta w_m - D(a^{FB}) \geq \max_{q,a}[\alpha(q)R(a) - D(a)],$$

where the left hand side is the maximum amount of rents the manager can earn. The local government will choose $g = \bar{g}$ if and only if

$$w_g \geq C.$$

In order to make this set of incentive compatible contracts feasible, the second period observable revenue has to be large enough, that is,

$$(1-\lambda)\bar{g}h(E^{FB}) \geq w_g + w_m,$$

or equivalently,

$$(1-\lambda)\bar{g}\,h(E^{FB}) \geq C + (1/\delta)\{\max_{q,a}[\alpha(q)R(a) - D(a)] + D(a^{FB})\}.$$

This is possible if $\bar{g}h(E^{FB})$ is sufficiently large.

3.   Local Government Ownership as an Organizational Response to State Predation

From now on we assume that revenue-based contracts are not enforceable as a result of state predation. We first present private ownership and state ownership as two benchmark cases before focusing on local government ownership.

Private Ownership

We denote $(q_M, a_M, e_M, E_M, g_M)$ as an equilibrium under private ownership. Under private ownership the manager has control over q and receives an unobservable part of revenue $\alpha(q)R(a)$ in the first period and $\lambda gh(e+E)$ in the second period. In the second period, because the local government is deprived of ownership, it cannot be motivated in the absence of revenue-based contracts, thus $g_M = 0$. Because the local government's effort is essential to the second period revenue, expecting $g_M = 0$, the manager spends nothing on local public goods ($e_M = 0$) and the national government leaves nothing for the local government ($E_M = 0$). At the end of the first period, the national government expropriates all observable revenue from the private firm. Anticipating this, at the beginning of the first period, M chooses q and a to maximize $\{\alpha(q)R(a)-D(a)\}$, which gives $\alpha'(q) = 0$ and $\alpha(q)R'(a) = D'(a)$. Therefore, we obtain

Proposition 1. Under private ownership:

(i) the local government has no incentive for government activities ($g_M = 0$);
(ii) both the manager and the national government leave the local government no revenue for government activities ($e_M = E_M = 0$);
(iii) the manager has moderate incentives to make an effort ($0 < a_M < a^{FB}$); and
(iv) the manager hides revenue to the maximum degree ($q_M = \bar{q}$).

Under the threat of state predation, if q were low, the manager would have no incentives to supply a. The manager chooses high q to hide revenue: although it is productive in terms of providing incentives for exerting effort a, it is costly because resources are wasted on revenue hiding. At the same time, the national government cannot motivate the local government to exert effort g for government activities. This double inefficiency characterizes the situation of private ownership under state predation: excessive revenue hiding and under-supply of effective government services.

State Ownership
We denote (q_S, a_S, E_S, g_S) as an equilibrium under state ownership. Now S has control over the choice of q and receives the unobservable part of the revenue. As the national government receives both the observable and unobservable revenues, it has an incentive to reduce the inefficiency from revenue hiding to a minimum. However, under state ownership both the manager and local government are deprived of ownership, and thus, in the absence of revenue-based contracts, the national government is unable to motivate either the manager or the local government in a credible way. Therefore, neither of them has an

incentive to perform. Anticipating this outcome, the national government will not leave any revenue to the local government. We have

Proposition 2. Under state ownership:

(i) the local government has no incentive to make an effort for government activities ($g_S = 0$);
(ii) the national government leaves the local government no revenue for government activities ($E_S = 0$);
(iii) the manager has no incentive to make an effort ($a_S = 0$); and
(iv) the national government does not hide any revenue ($q_S = 0$).

Comparing Proposition 2 with Proposition 1, we find that parts (i) and (ii) are the same, that is, both private ownership and state ownership fail to provide incentives to the local government, and consequently, the national government has no incentive to prey less on the local government (under both private and state ownership, any observable revenue a local government collects will be taken away by the national government). The main difference between private ownership and state ownership lies in parts (iii) and (iv) of Propositions 1 and 2: private ownership provides the manager with the incentive to make an effort and state ownership gives the national government all the revenue. Therefore, from the national government's perspective, the trade-off between private ownership and state ownership is that between a smaller share of a bigger pie and a bigger share of a smaller pie. The national government prefers private ownership to state ownership when managerial incentives are relatively more important (i.e., $R(a_M)/R(0)$ is large), or revenue hiding by private owners is less severe (i.e., $\bar{q}$ is small), due to, say, a better tax collection system. Otherwise, the national government prefers state ownership to private ownership.

Local Government Ownership
We denote (q_G, a_G, e_G, E_G, g_G) as an equilibrium under local government ownership. Now, the local government chooses q and receives an unobservable part of the revenue. In the second period after q, a, E, and e are chosen, the local government chooses $g = \bar{g}$ if and only if

$$\lambda \bar{g} h(e+E) > C.$$

At the end of period 1, after q and a are chosen and R_1 is realized, the national and local governments choose simultaneously the amounts of expenditure for the government activity from their own budgets. For any given e, the national government chooses E and I_S to

max $I_S + \delta(1-\lambda)\bar{g}h(e+E)$

(P1) subject to: $E + I_S \leq (1-q)R(a)$,

$E \geq 0$ and $I_S \geq 0$.

For any given E, the local government chooses e and I_G to

max $I_G + \delta\lambda\bar{g}h\,(e+E)$

(P2) subject to: $e + I_G \leq \alpha(q)R(a)$,

$e \geq 0$ and $I_G \geq 0$.

Proposition 3. Under local government ownership, the manager has no incentive to make an effort ($a_G = 0$). However, when $C > 0$ is sufficiently small, for any given $q \leq \bar{q}$ chosen in period 1:

(i) the local government has incentive for government activities
($g_G = \bar{g}$); and
(ii) the total amount of expenditure for government activities $e_G + E_G > 0$, and furthermore, the national government leaves the local government with $E_G > 0$ for government activities when $0 < \lambda < 1/2$.

Proof: See Appendix.■

Proposition 3 demonstrates the incentive effect local government ownership has on both the local and national governments. Ownership allows the local government to receive unobservable revenues, and thus to receive benefits from government activities in a credible way, so that it provides the local government with an incentive to perform government activities. Moreover, when the future benefit to the national government is sufficiently large (i.e., $1-\lambda > 1/2$), the interests between the national and local governments are aligned. Since the national government sees that the local government can serve its interests, it therefore has incentive to leave revenue to the local government, that is, to prey less on local government-owned firms.

We next investigate the effect of ownership on the behavior of revenue hiding/project choice. Let $E^* = \text{argmax}\,\{\delta(1-\lambda)\bar{g}h(E)-E\}$ be the amount of the observable revenue that the national government would like to spend on local public goods provision in a situation without liquidity constraint and without any expenditure provided by the local government. Similarly, let $e^* = \text{argmax } \{\delta\lambda\bar{g}h(e)-e\}$ be the amount of the unobservable revenue that the local government would like to spend on local public goods provision in a situation without liquidity constraint and without any expenditure provided by the national government. We obtain

Proposition 4. Let $0 < \lambda < 1/2$. Under local government ownership, when $C > 0$ is sufficiently small:

(i) the local government hides less revenue than does an owner of a private firm (i.e., $q_G < q_M = \bar{q}$), provided that the national government's budget is binding in the sense that $(1-\bar{q})R(0) < E^*$; and
(ii) the local government does not hide revenue at all (i.e., $q_G = 0$), provided that the local government's budget is binding in the sense that $R(0) < e^*$.

Proof: See Appendix.■

Proposition 4 illustrates the second effect of local government ownership that concerns project choice and the extent of revenue hiding. Because under local government ownership the local government has the incentive to carry out government activity, an increase in local government expenditure will lead to a higher return to the national government in the second period. Therefore, if the national government is liquidity constrained (i.e., $(1-\bar{q})R(0) < E^*$), it will have incentive to leave more revenue with the local government when more observable revenue becomes available in the first period. The national government's incentive simply reflects the fact that when the local government carries out government activity in addition to business activity, the local government serves the interests of the national government better than does a private owner. Anticipating that the national government will leave more revenue, the local government will hide (strictly) less revenue compared with what a private owner will, who will hide the maximum. This is because the marginal cost of less revenue hiding is zero at the maximal level of revenue hiding (i.e., $\alpha'(\bar{q}) = 0$), whereas the marginal benefit from less revenue hiding is positive for the local government under local government ownership (but zero for a private owner under private ownership).

While the less-revenue-hiding result depends on the national government's liquidity constraint, the no-revenue-hiding result requires a stronger condition, that is, the local government's liquidity constraint (i.e., $R(0) < e^*$).[7] Under condition $R(0) < e^*$, the local government has incentive to spend all of its budget on local public goods, which is also the objective of the national government, and thus, the interests of the local and national governments become congruent. Therefore, the local government completely internalizes the cost of revenue hiding and hides no revenue at all.

We should note that if revenue-based contracts were enforceable, the cost of revenue hiding would be internalized through explicit contracting among the manager, the local government, and the national government. Only when such contracts are not enforceable (as under state predation), does integration of the two activities under local government ownership become a useful alternative for the purpose of reducing the cost of revenue hiding.[8]

Our model highlights the essential reason why local government-owned firms suffer less from state predation than do private firms. That is, the local government undertakes government activity that will bring future benefits to the national government in addition to those benefits brought by the business activity. As a result, when the local government integrates both the government and business activities, it becomes more useful to the national government than a private owner who performs only the business activity.[9]

However, for expository simplicity, we have assumed that only the government activity uses the first-period revenue to enhance the second-period revenue, while the business activity does not. In a slightly more general setup, both the government and business activities may enhance future revenue of the business project by using first-period revenue. Nonetheless, under local government ownership the local government carries out both activities; whereas under private ownership the manager carries out only the business activity. Therefore, the government activity enhances the second period return in addition to the business activity. Consequently, the local government is still more useful to the national government than is a private owner in this more general setup, and the essence of our analysis remains.

In order to focus on the mechanism, we have characterized government activity only in terms of its effect on enhancing future revenue of the business project, but we have not explicitly modeled the government activity as providing public goods. However, it is straightforward to introduce a public goods provision that enhances multiple (instead of one) business projects within one locality. It is easy to see that the essence of our analysis of local government ownership still remains. In this scenario a private agent who owns one business project may not have sufficient incentive to carry out the government activity because he is able to capture only a small portion of the total benefits of local public goods provision. However, under local government ownership, the local government, which owns many business projects, has a stronger incentive to make an effort to provide local public goods.[10]

The fact that our model has only one local government suggests that it may be applied more broadly to a government agency that is not local in the sense that it controls a piece of territory or that people can move between locations.[11] Therefore, our analysis can be applied to a situation where one government agency has the authority to confiscate revenues from all other agents in the economy, and another government agency can undertake a government activity to benefit the first government agency. When the second government agency owns business projects, it has incentive to carry out the government activity, and thus brings more benefits to the first government agency than a private agent would bring under private ownership. Consequently, ownership of the business projects by the second government agency, as compared with ownership by a private agent, may suffer less from the first government agency's predation.

We have so far focused on how the rights to observable revenue can (or cannot) be secured under alternative types of ownership. In our framework the national government not only preys on observable revenue, but also may have the ultimate right to determine whether to allow the existence of a particular type of ownership. Therefore, only if the national government prefers one ownership type to another, does that type of ownership and the associated allocation of control rights become "secure." Clearly, the advantage of local government ownership is having a higher second-period return. This implies that the national government prefers local government ownership if the national government is more patient or the local government's effort is more important. Other things being equal, the national government may prefer private ownership if managerial effort becomes crucial. Finally, the national government will prefer state ownership if private ownership entails too much revenue hiding and if the local government under local government ownership is very difficult to motivate. Therefore, we obtain

Proposition 5. Assume that $0 < \lambda < 1/2$. Then, other things being equal,

(i) the national government more likely prefers local government ownership if the national government is more patient (i.e., δ is larger) or the local government's effort is more important (i.e., $\bar{g}$ is larger);
(ii) the national government more likely prefers private ownership if the manager's effort is more important (i.e., $R(a_M)/R(0)$ is larger); and
(iii) the national government more likely prefers state ownership if revenue hiding is more serious (i.e., $\bar{q}$ is larger) and the local government is harder to motivate (i.e., λ is smaller).

4. Revenue Redistribution across Localities

In order to highlight the mechanism by which local government ownership may entail securer property rights as compared with private ownership, the previous sections assume only one locality in the economy. In this section we generalize our model to include N localities, and there is still one business project in each. This generalization gives rise to the possibility of revenue redistribution by the national government across localities. One consequence is that, although the national government may still face an aggregate liquidity constraint, this constraint can be potentially relaxed vis-à-vis an individual locality due to the possibility of revenue redistribution.

Such an extension has no effect on our results on private and state ownership. Under private ownership in all localities the manager in each locality hides revenue to the maximum; the national government preys on private firms and leaves no revenue to local governments; and the local governments have no incentives to provide local public goods. Under state ownership in all localities, the national government does not hide revenue, but it also has no incentive to give revenue to local governments, and neither managers nor local governments have incentives because of the fear of expropriation by the national government.

We now show that such an extension does not change our qualitative results on local government ownership either. Under local government ownership in all localities, at the end of the first period, after q_i's are chosen, the national government has $(N-\Sigma_i q_i)R(0)$ at its disposal. Given any choice $(e_1, ..., e_N)$ by the local governments and anticipating $(g_1, ..., g_N)$, the national government chooses I_S and $(E_1, ..., E_N)$ to

$$\max I_S + \delta(1-\lambda)\Sigma_i g_i h(e_i + E_i)$$

(P3) subject to: $\Sigma_i E_i + I_S \leq (N - \Sigma_i q_i)R(0)$,

$E_i \geq 0$ ($i=1,...,N$) and $I_S \geq 0$.

Given any $(E_1, ..., E_N)$, and given e_j, $j \neq i$, local government i, anticipating g_i, chooses e_i and I_i to

max $I_i + \delta \lambda g_i h(e_i + E_i)$

(P4) subject to: $e_i + I_i \leq \alpha(q_i)R(0)$,

$e_i \geq 0$ and $I_i \geq 0$.

First, the extension to multiple localities will not change our results about the incentive effect of local government ownership because those results do not rely on the assumption of the liquidity constraint of the national government. Therefore, we obtain that, under local government ownership, higher local government effort and less national government predation will continue to prevail, as the following proposition demonstrates

Proposition 6. Under local government ownership in all N localities, managers have no incentive to make efforts ($a_G = 0$). However, when C is sufficiently small, for any given $q \leq \bar{q}$, at a symmetric equilibrium in the second period:

(i) the local government has incentive for government activities ($g_G = \bar{g}$); and
(ii) the total amount of expenditure for government activities $e_G + E_G > 0$, and furthermore, the national government leaves the local government with $E_G > 0$ for government activities when $0 < \lambda < 1/2$.

Proof: See Appendix.■

Second, when the national government freely redistributes all the observable revenues across localities for local government expenditures, its liquidity constraint can potentially be relaxed vis-à-vis an individual locality, even though it continues to face an aggregate liquidity constraint. However, our less-revenue-hiding results continue to hold as long as the national government's aggregate budget constraint is binding, as shown below.

Consider the situation in which local government j unilaterally deviates to hide marginally less revenue than other localities (i.e., $q_j < q$, $q_i = q$ for all $i \neq j$). Then an extra amount of observable revenue $(q - q_j)R(0)$

is made available to the national government. Suppose that the local government's budget constraint is not binding at q (i.e., $e < \alpha(q)R_1(0)$). Then, despite the reduction of unobservable revenue due to less revenue hiding, local public goods expenditure in locality j remains the same as in other localities, as well as the marginal return to the national government for additional local expenditure. Therefore, the national government will optimally equalize local expenditure by allocating exactly $1/N$ of the extra observable revenue to all localities. Hence, the benefit of the deviation of less revenue hiding to local government j is strictly positive for any finite N. But at maximum revenue hiding $q = \bar{q}$, the marginal cost of less revenue hiding is zero ($\alpha'(\bar{q}) = 0$). Hence local government j has a net gain from hiding less revenue when all other localities hide to the maximum. Therefore, all localities hiding to the maximum cannot be an equilibrium.

What is more interesting is the situation where the local government's budget is binding (i.e., $e = \alpha(q)R_1(0)$). Then the benefit for less revenue hiding is always larger than the cost, given any level of revenue hiding in other localities. To see this, suppose that all other localities hide revenue at $q > 0$. When the local government's budget is binding, local government j, by hiding less revenue, reduces the unobservable revenue as well as the expenditure in local public goods in its own locality relative to other localities. This increases the marginal return to the national government's expenditure in this locality relative to that in other localities. Therefore, it is optimal for the national government to fully compensate this locality for the amount lost due to reduced hidden revenue, and to give an additional $1/N$ of the extra amount from the efficiency gain. Hence, local government j has a net gain from hiding less revenue than other localities hide for any $q > 0$. Therefore, any (symmetric) revenue hiding by all localities cannot be an equilibrium when the local government's budget is binding.

For the same reason, if the local government's budget is binding at $q = 0$, then revenue hiding by a local government when all other localities do not hide revenue will induce the national government to leave less revenue in that locality. Furthermore, because revenue hiding is costly, the total amount of both the national and local governments' expenditures in that locality will be reduced. Therefore, unilateral revenue hiding is not profitable and no revenue hiding is the only equilibrium when the local government's budget is binding, regardless of the number of localities.

Therefore, we obtain

Proposition 7. Let $0 < \lambda < 1/2$. For all finite N, when C is sufficiently small, at a symmetric equilibrium under local government ownership in all N localities:

(i) the local government hides less revenue than an owner of a private firm hides (i.e., $q_G < q_M = \bar{q}$), provided that the national government's aggregate budget is binding in the sense that $N(1-\bar{q})R(0) < NE^*$; and

(ii) no revenue hiding (i.e., $q_G = 0$) is a unique symmetric equilibrium, provided that the local government's budget is binding in the sense that $R(0) < e^*$.

Proof: See Appendix.∎

5. Interpreting China's Experience

In this section we use our theory to interpret some interesting features of China's reforms. For the past two decades China's transition has occurred in an environment where there was a lack of secure property rights based on the rule of law. The national government did not allow private enterprises to operate until 1981. Even when legislation or regulations allowed private enterprises to operate, security of private property rights was still not guaranteed. The national government attacked private enterprises on several occasions during general political crackdowns, including the "anti-spiritual pollution" campaign of 1983, the "anti-bourgeois liberalization" campaign of 1987, and most recently, after the Tiananmen incident of 1989. In August of 1989 the national government attacked "individual and private entrepreneurs who used illegal methods to seek huge profits and thereby create great social disparity and contribute to discontent among the public" and launched a series of investigations into the tax records of individuals and private firms.[12]

Despite the lack of secure property rights, China's economic landscape has changed significantly since reforms started in the late 1970s. Historically, state-owned enterprises (SOEs) were the predominant type of ownership in China.[13] In 1978, the share of SOEs in national industrial output was as much as 78 percent, but since then the significance of SOEs has declined steadily even without any privatization. By 1993, the share of SOEs in national industrial output had dropped to 43 percent, and the remaining 57 percent came from non-state enterprises. While the development of private enterprises had been constrained by the lack of secure property rights, the phenomenal expansion of local government-owned industrial firms was the driving force behind the remarkable performance of the non-state enterprises. In 1993, about three quarters of the non-state industrial output, or 42 percent of the national total (about equal in size to that of the SOEs), was produced by non-state enterprises that involve government ownership other than the national government.[14] Within this category the rural TVEs represent the largest subsector, and they alone accounted for about one-half of the industrial output within the non-state sector.[15]

Interestingly, property rights are securer in local government-owned enterprises than in private enterprises. The national government's regulations have been less hostile to TVEs than to private enterprises. Collective enterprises (i.e., local government-owned firms) including TVEs have always been allowed to operate legally. As early as the mid-1970s amid the wave of "agriculture mechanization," some rural areas began to launch commune-brigade enterprises (the predecessors of TVEs) [Byrd and Lin 1990]. The national government tolerated these enterprises at the beginning and supported them later.

At the same time, these local government-owned firms, compared with private firms, often provided more revenue to local governments, invested more in local public goods, and also provided more revenue and other services to the national government. Indeed, the national government stipulated that the TVE after-tax profits should be essentially used for two purposes: reinvestment and provision of local public goods.[16] Nationwide in 1985, about 46 percent of the after-tax profits of TVEs were reinvested, and 49 percent were used for local public expenditure [A Statistical Survey of China 1992, p. 67]. In 1992, 59 percent of the after-tax profits of TVEs were reinvested and 40 percent were used for local public expenditure [A Statistical Survey of China 1993, p. 67].

Casual observations indicate a similar story. The interesting contrast between two cities—Wuxi of Jiangsu province and Wenzhou of Zhejiang province—is well-known. These two cities represent two extremes of ownership structure in rural industries. In Wuxi, TVEs have been dominant and private enterprises almost do not exist, while Wenzhou has been dominated by private enterprises. Correspondingly, in Wuxi the income from TVEs has been the chief revenue source for the township and village governments. During 1971–1978, as much as 148 million yuan (or 148 yuan per capita) in profits from these firms went into agricultural machinery, bridges and power stations, field terracing, and other agricultural investments [Song and Du 1990]. In contrast, township and village governments in Wenzhou were "impotent in performing their administrative functions." "Basic facilities and public works in Wenzhou were rather backward, considering the rate of capital accumulation." "Cultural, public health, and other public undertakings were lagging behind other areas" [Song and Du 1990].

The same picture is reflected in some recent econometric studies as well. Using panel data from 28 provinces in China between 1986 and 1993, Jin and Qian [1998] investigated the relationship between the share of TVEs relative to private enterprises in rural nonfarm enterprises and the revenue shares of the national and township/ village governments.[17] They found that the share of TVEs increased the revenue shares of both the national and township/village governments, after controlling for the level of per capita income and other geographic and political variables. This indicates that both the national and township/village governments benefit from local government ownership.

These salient features of China's reforms can be interpreted along the lines of our analysis. According to it, local government-owned enterprises have securer property rights than private enterprises have because the national government expects them to better serve its interests. As indicated by the aforementioned evidence, the national government indeed benefits from these enterprises: they provide more revenues to the national government, and they also spend more on local pubic goods, which, in addition to increasing future revenues, also serve the interests of the national government directly (for example, through increased agricultural production or social stability). Seen in this light, the relative success of local government-owned firms in leading the remarkable performance of the Chinese economy in the past two decades can be better understood.

6. Conclusions

In this paper we have presented an analysis of the ownership of firms under insecure property rights. We argue that local government ownership can be perceived as an organizational response to state predation. When the local government controls two activities—government and business—together, the interests of the national and local governments become better aligned than those between the national government and a private owner. In the absence of revenue-based contracts, giving ownership rights to the local government provides an incentive because the local government can hide some revenue. Correspondingly, the national government finds it in its own interest to prey less on local government-owned firms than on private firms. As a result, the local government under local government ownership may hide less revenue as compared with what a private owner may hide. This analysis helps in understanding the relative success of local government-owned enterprises in China in the absence of a rule of law.

Two main insights have come out of our study. First, a certain type of government ownership has emerged as an organizational response to imperfect state institutions, which may work better than either conventional private or state ownership. Though not the first-best choice, this type of ownership can reduce the adverse effects of state predation in the absence of institutions to constrain the state. The positive role of the government identified here is not a cure for "market failure"; rather, local government ownership in our paper is perceived to overcome "state failure."

Second, when revenue-based contracts are problematic, integrating local government and business activities can be in the interests of both the national and local governments and can also be efficiency enhancing. While such an integration has no apparent advantage when complete contracts are feasible, under state predation integration helps internalize the externalities between alternative activities. In such circumstances, the allocation of tasks interacts with that of ownership to generate interesting new features concerning the relationship between the government and firms.

In future research we will investigate an extension of the model to include an additional dimension of the decisions on local public goods provision. Such decisions can be allocated to either the national or the local government so that one can study the issue of centralized and decentralized provision of local public goods. Because fiscal decentralization is an important and distinct feature of Chinese reform, such an extension may shed light on the comparison of China to other countries and on the comparison between pre-reform and post-reform China as well.

Appendix: Proofs of Propositions

Proof of Proposition 3. (i) Obvious.

(ii) In the second period, the local government chooses $g = \bar{g}$ if and only if

$$\delta\lambda\bar{g}h(e + E) > C.$$

We note that $e + E \geq \min \{e^*, \alpha(\bar{q})R(0)), E^*, (1-\bar{q})R(0)\} > 0$. Then there exists C, for all $C < C$ and q, $g = \bar{g}$.

(iii) $e_G + E_G > 0$ by (i). Assume $0 < \lambda < 1/2$. Given any e_G, the first order conditions of the optimization problem (P1) yield:

(1) $\delta(1-\lambda) h'(e_G + E_G) \leq \xi$ ($<$ if and only if $E_G = 0$),
(2) $1 \leq \xi$ ($<$ if and only if $I_S = 0$).

Given any E_G, the first order conditions of the optimization problem (P2) yield:

(3) $\delta\lambda\bar{g}h'(e_G + E_G) \leq \eta$ ($<$ if and only if $e_G = 0$)
(4) $1 \leq \eta$ ($<$ if and only if $I_G = 0$).

If $e_G = 0$, we must have $E_G > 0$ since $e_G + E_G > 0$. Suppose $e_G > 0$ but $E_G = 0$. From (1) and (2), we have:

$$\delta(1-\lambda)\bar{g}h'(e_G + E_G) < \xi = 1.$$

From (3) and (4), we have:

$$\delta\lambda\bar{g}h'(e_G + E_G) = \eta \geq 1.$$

This leads to a contradiction as $\lambda < 1/2$. Therefore, $E_G > 0$.

Q.E.D.

Proof of Proposition 4. (i) Let $(1-\bar{q})R(0) < E^*$. We first show that $I_S = 0$ for $\bar{q}$ (and in its small neighborhood as well). Suppose that $I_S > 0$ at $\bar{q}$. By Proposition 3, $E_G > 0$. Then (1) and (2) imply that

$$\delta(1-\lambda)\bar{g}h'(e_G + E_G) = \xi = 1.$$

This implies, by $\lambda < 1/2$, that

$$\delta\lambda\bar{g}h'(e_G + E_G) < 1.$$

By (3) and (4), $e_G = 0$. Hence, $E_G = E^*$, which violates $(1-\bar{q})R(0) < E^*$. Therefore, $I_S = 0$ and $E_G = (1-\bar{q})R(0)$.

Let

$$V(q) = \alpha(q)R(0)-e(q) + \delta\lambda\bar{g}h(e(q) + (1-q)R(0)),$$

where $e(q)$ is the maximizer subject to constraints $0 \le e \le \alpha(q)R(0)$.

By the generalized envelope theorem,

$$dV(q)/dq = \alpha'(q)R(0)-\delta\lambda\bar{g}h'(e(q) + (1-q)R(0))R(0) + t_2\alpha'(q)R(0),$$

where t_2 is the Lagrangean multiplier associated with the constraint $e \le \alpha(q)R(0)$. Since $\alpha'(\bar{q}) = 0$, $dV(q)/dq < 0$ at $\bar{q}$, that is, it is profitable to reduce q below $\bar{q}$.

(ii) Because $\lambda < 1/2$, $e^* < E^*$. Therefore, $(1-q)R(0) \le R(0) < e^* < E^*$ for all $q \le \bar{q}$. Then the argument in (i) shows that $I_S = 0$ and $E_G = (1-q)R(0)$ for all $q \le \bar{q}$.

Furthermore, because $e_G + E_G \le R(0) < e^*$, then for all q,

$$\delta\lambda\bar{g}h'(e_G + E_G) > \delta\lambda\bar{g}h'(e^*) = 1.$$

Therefore, $I_G = 0$ and $e_G = \alpha(q)R(0)$ for all q.

In the first period, the local government chooses q to

$$\max \delta\lambda\bar{g}h([\alpha(q)+1-q]R(0)),$$

and the optimal solution is $q = 0$.

Q.E.D.

Proof of Proposition 6. Follow exactly the proof of Proposition 3. The first order conditions of (1)–(4) are replaced by the following:

Given any $(e_1, \ldots, e_N)$, the first order conditions of the optimization problem (P3) yield:

(5) $\delta(1-\lambda)\bar{g}h'(e_i+E_i) \le \xi$ ($<$ if and only if $E_i = 0$),
(6) $1 \le \xi$ ($<$ if and only if $I_S = 0$).

Given $(E_1, \ldots, E_N)$, the first order conditions of the optimization problem (P4) yield

(7) $\delta\lambda\bar{g}h'(e_i + E_i) \le \eta_i$ ($<$ if and only if $e_i = 0$)
(8) $1 \le \eta_i$ ($<$ if and only if $I_i = 0$).

Q.E.D.

Proof of Proposition 7. (i) Let $N(1-\overline{q})R(0) < NE^*$. We first show that $I_S = 0$ if $q_i = \overline{q}$ for all i. Suppose that $I_S > 0$. By Proposition 6, $E_i > 0$. Then (5) and (6) imply that

$$\delta(1-\lambda)\overline{g}h'(e_i+E_i) = \xi = 1.$$

This implies, by $\lambda < 1/2$, that

$$\delta\lambda\overline{g}h'(e_i+E_i) < 1.$$

By (7) and (8), $e_i = 0$. Hence $E_i = E^*$, which violates $(1-\overline{q})R(0) < E^*$. We conclude that $I_S = 0$.

Consider a possible small unilateral deviation by local government j from $\overline{q}$ to $q_j = \overline{q}-\varepsilon$ ($\varepsilon > 0$ small). Because $I_S = 0$, the national government will choose $(E_1, ..., E_N)$ so that

$$e_{-j} + E_{-j} = e_j + E_j,\text{ and}$$

$$(N-1)E_{-j} + E_j = (N-1)(1-\overline{q})R(0) + (1-q_j)R(0),$$

where $-j$ denotes $i \neq j$. We solve for

$$(9)\ \ E_j(q_j) = \{(N-1)(1-\overline{q})+(1-q_j)\}R(0)/N-(e_j-e_{-j})(N-1)/N.$$

Let

$$V(q_j) = \alpha(q_j)R(0)-e_j(q_j) + \delta\lambda\overline{g}h(e_j(q_j) + E_j(q_j)),$$

where $e_j(q_j)$ is the maximizer subject to constraints $0 \leq e_j \leq \alpha(q_j)R(0)$.

By the generalized envelope theorem,

$$dV(q_j)/dq_j = \alpha'(q_j)R(0)-\delta\lambda\overline{g}h'(e_j(q_j) + E_j(q_j))R(0)/N + t_2\alpha'(q_j)R(0),$$

where t_2 is the Lagrangean multiplier associated with the constraint $e_j \leq \alpha(q_j)R(0)$. Since $\alpha'(\overline{q}) = 0$, $dV(q_j)/dq_j < 0$ at $\overline{q}$, that is, it is profitable for local government j to reduce q below $\overline{q}$.

(ii) Because $\lambda < 1/2$, $e^* < E^*$. Therefore, $(1-q)R(0) \leq R(0) < e^* < E^*$ for all $q \leq \overline{q}$. Then $I_S = 0$ if $q_i = q$ for all i. Furthermore, because $e_G + E_G \leq R(0) < e^*$, then for all q,

$$\delta\lambda\overline{g}h'(e_G + E_G) > \delta\lambda\overline{g}h'(e^*) = 1.$$

Therefore, $I_G = 0$ and $e_G = \alpha(q)R(0)$ for all $q \leq \overline{q}$.

To show that $q_i = 0$, $e_i = 0$, $E_i = R(0)$, for all i, is an equilibrium, consider a deviation by local government j to $q_j = \varepsilon > 0$. As $\delta\lambda\overline{g}h'(R(0)) >$

1, we must have $e_j = \alpha(q_j)R(0)$. Therefore, replacing $\bar{q}$ by $q = 0$ and substituting $e_{-j} = 0$ and $e_j = \alpha(q_j)R(0)$ into (9), we obtain

$$E_j(q_j) = \{(N-1)+(1-q_j)\}R(0)/N-\alpha(q_j)R(0)(N-1)/N.$$

Let

$$V(q_j) = \delta\lambda\bar{g}h(\alpha(q_j)R(0) + E_j(q_j)).$$

Then

$$dV(q_j)/dq_j = \delta\lambda\bar{g}h'(\alpha(q_j)R(0) + E_j(q_j))(\alpha'(q_j)-1)/N < 0.$$

Therefore, local government j has no incentive to deviate.

To show uniqueness, suppose $q_i = q > 0$, $e_i = \alpha(q)R(0)$, and $E_i = (1-q)R(0)$ for all i is an equilibrium. Consider a small unilateral deviation by local government j from q to $q_j = q + \varepsilon$. As $\delta\lambda\bar{g}h'(R(0)) > 1$, we must have $e_j = \alpha(q_j)R(0)$. Replacing $\bar{q}$ by q and substituting $e_{-j} = \alpha(q)R(0)$ and $e_j = \alpha(q_j)R(0)$ into (9), we obtain

$$E_j(q_j) = \{(N-1)(1-q)+(1-q_j)\}R(0)/N-(\alpha(q_j)-\alpha(q))R(0)(N-1)/N.$$

Thus,

$$dE_j/dq_j = -\{\alpha'(q_j)+(1-\alpha'(q_j))/N\}R(0) < 0.$$

Therefore,

$$dV(q_j)/dq_j = \delta\lambda\bar{g}h'(\alpha(q_j)R(0) + E_j(q_j))(dE_j/dq_j) < 0,$$

that is, local government j has incentives to reduce q. A contradiction.

Q.E.D.

Notes

* We are grateful to Masahiko Aoki, Abhijit Banerjee, Avner Greif, Oliver Hart, Dilip Mookherjee, Andrei Shleifer, Yijiang Wang, and three referees for helpful comments and discussions.

1. The distinction between "state ownership" and "local government ownership" reflects diverse ownership forms inside the government hierarchy in countries like China, where there are not only national government-owned "national public firms," but also local government-owned (or other types of lower level government agency-owned) "local public firms."

2. We choose not to appeal to the reputation argument for securing property rights. It is well known that multiple equilibrium outcomes are possible in the reputation model. In fact, in China the state has historically exploited private property rights. From this per-

spective, one can view our paper as analyzing a situation in which the reputation mechanism has failed to generate a good equilibrium outcome.

3. Suppose there is an increasing convex cost function $c(q)$ for transferring observable revenue to unobservable revenue, where $c(0) = 0$, $0 < c'(0) < 1$, and $c'(1) > 1$. Thus the net unobservable revenue will be $\alpha(q) = q - c(q)$ and there exists $\bar{q} < 1$, such that $\alpha'(\bar{q}) = 0$.

4. Receiving an unobservable revenue can be called "cream off," as in Hart [1988].

5. We do not study the issue of whether the national government itself carries out local government activities. Using the principal-agent framework, we implicitly assume that the national government cannot do everything due to its limited time or knowledge, and thus local governments and managers are needed and incentive problems arise.

6. We use the term "limited liability" here, not as a legal constraint, but to mean that the national government is unable to take away unobservable revenue from managers or local governments (and the same is true for the local government vis-à-vis managers). One way to rationalize this assumption is to consider a situation where the unobservable revenue generated is $R^o + R^u$ with probability $1-\varepsilon$ and R^o with probability ε ($0 < \varepsilon < 1$). Suppose that the utility of a manager or local government becomes infinitely negative if wealth falls below zero, and further suppose that the national government cannot inflict infinitely negative utility upon the manager and the local government in any state of the world (perhaps because it fears their desperation). Then the national government may not be able to extract anything beyond R^o and the manager or the local government receives at least $(1-\varepsilon)R^u$ in expected terms. Therefore, it is as if R^o is "observable" and $(1-\varepsilon)R^u$ is "unobservable" and the maximum amount the national government can tax is limited to the "observable" part of the revenue. When ε is small, our results should continue to go through.

7. Notice that under the assumption $\lambda < 1/2$, $\lambda < 1-\lambda$. Hence, by the definition of e^* and E^*, $e^* < E^*$.

8. We have assumed that ownership cannot shift between periods. Let us consider what would happen if an ownership shift were allowed. It is generally not optimal to have private ownership in the first period and local government ownership in the second period, because the manager in the first period has no incentive to hide less revenue. However, state ownership in the first period and local government ownership in the second period will weakly dominate local government ownership in both periods. Such a peculiar outcome is due to our simplifying assumption that local government services have no effect in the first period. To avoid this outcome, we can suppose that there is a second project which starts in period 2 and finishes in period 3, with a period 2 return of $R_1(a, gh(A))$ and a period 3 return of $g'h(A')$. Then state ownership of this second project in its first period and local government ownership in its second period generally will not weakly dominate local government ownership of this project in both periods, because state ownership reduces the local government's returns in period 2, and thus generally reduces the local government's incentive to exert effort g in period 2.

9. There may be other reasons that a local government can better serve the interests of the national government than a private agent can. For instance, certain institutional factors could lead to a situation where a local government's preference differs from that of a private agent but is similar to that of the national government. One particular example would be that the local government represents the preference of a "median voter" in the locality, and thus it could be more credible (i.e., have more incentive) to

provide local public goods than a private business owner could. We thank Abhijit Banerjee for suggesting this possibility.

10. Therefore, the difference between a local government and a private agent here becomes the degree of integration of business projects.

Although we can interpret our model more broadly, we do not consider our model applicable to ownership of firms by the government agencies providing national public goods. This is because an agent who provides a national public good is unlikely to internalize a large portion of the benefits generated from the public good in the absence of revenue based contracts unless he integrates a huge number of firms in the economy. This would be, although not modeled here, prohibitively costly. This is perhaps an important reason why we observe that firms owned by the local government, which is responsible for local public goods provision, have grown rapidly in economies like China's without a rule of law, but firms owned by the government agencies responsible for national public goods provisions have not.

11. The analysis is similar if there are, for example, a tax collection ministry in charge of extracting tax revenues and an electricity ministry in charge of delivering power instead of a national government and a local government. When the electricity ministry, by delivering power, provides revenue-enhancing activities to business projects, it may make sense for the electricity ministry to own the business projects rather than allowing managers to own them under the predation of the tax collection ministry.

12. State Council document, August 30, 1989, as quoted by Whiting [1995, footnote 100, p. 109].

13. SOEs are (national government-owned) national public firms and most of them were present during the planning era. Although the supervision authority of many SOEs is delegated to provincial, city, and county governments, many control rights over SOE assets are held by the national government because all SOEs are subject to nationwide unified accounting standards, tax regulations, investment and wage control, employee welfare obligations, etc. In contrast, the national government does not hold similar control rights over the assets of non-state enterprises [Qian 1996].

14. Before 1993, firms in China were classified into four general categories: SOEs, collective enterprises, small private enterprises (employing fewer than eight people), and "others." The others category included two types of ownership: mixed ownership with the government holding the majority of shares (such as new entrepreneurial firms affiliated with government agencies, joint ventures between foreign firms and the government, stock companies, and holding companies) and private ownership (such as large private enterprises, foreign firms, and mixed ownership with the government holding the minority of shares). We have made a rough estimate of the 50:50 division of the others category between government ownership and private ownership, and combined the collective enterprises with government-owned firms in the others category to obtain the figures for local government-owned firms [*China Statistical Yearbook* 1994, p. 373 and p. 375].

15. Previous research has documented that within TVEs local (township or village) governments are in control to make "strategic decisions" in areas such as finance and investment, although managers of individual TVEs run their daily operations [Chang and Wang 1994; Li 1996; and Che and Qian 1998]. On the other hand, the national government does not have ownership and control rights over TVEs. Therefore, TVEs are indeed local government-owned firms.

16. "The part retained by the enterprise should be no less than 60 percent of the total, … [and] should be mainly used for the increase of the funds for production development in technological transformation and expansion of reproduction, and also for the appropriate increase of welfare funds and bonus funds." "The part remitted to the owner of the enterprise should be used mainly for the support of construction of agricultural infrastructures, agriculture technology services, rural public welfare, renewal and transformation of enterprises, or development of new enterprises" [Article 32, Chapter 5, Ministry of Agriculture 1990, p. 137].

17. Notice that there are no SOEs in rural areas, only TVEs and private enterprises.

References

A Statistical Survey of China, Beijing: China Statistical Publishing House, 1992 and 1993.

Byrd, William, and Qingsong Lin, "China's Rural Industry: An Introduction," chapter 1 in William Byrd and Lin Qingsong (eds.), *China's Rural Industry: Structure, Development, and Reform*, Oxford: Oxford University Press, 1990.

Chang, Chun, and Yijiang Wang, "The Nature of the Township Enterprises," *Journal of Comparative Economics*, 19:434–452, 1994.

Che, Jiahua, and Yingyi Qian, "Institutional Environment, Community Government, and Corporate Governance: Understanding China's Township-Village Enterprises," *Journal of Law, Economics, and Organization*, 14(1):1–23, 1998.

China Statistical Yearbook, Beijing: China Statistical Publishing House, 1994.

Greif, Avner, Paul Milgrom, and Barry R. Weingast, "Coordination, Commitment, and Enforcement: The Case of the Merchant Guild," *Journal of Political Economy*, 102(4):745–776, 1994.

Grossman, Sanford, and Oliver Hart, "The Costs and Benefits of Ownership: A Theory of Vertical and Lateral Integration," *Journal of Political Economy*, 94:691–719, 1986.

Hart, Oliver, "Incomplete Contracts and the Theory of the Firm," *Journal of Law, Economics, and Organization*, 4(1):119–39, 1988.

Hart, Oliver, and John Moore, "Property Rights and the Nature of the Firm," *Journal of Political Economy*, 98:1119–1158, 1990.

Hart, Oliver, Andrei Shleifer, and Robert W. Vishny, "The Proper Scope of Government: Theory and an Application to Prisons," *Quarterly Journal of Economics*, CXII(4):1127–1162, November, 1997.

Holmstrom, Bengt, and Paul Milgrom, "Multi-task Principal-Agent Analysis: Incentive Contracts, Asset Ownership and Job Design," *Journal of Law, Economics, and Organization*, 7:24–52, 1991.

Holmstrom, Bengt, and Paul Milgrom, "The Firm as an Incentive System," *American Economic Review*, 84:972–991, 1994.

Jin, Hehui, and Yingyi Qian, "Public vs. Private Ownership of Firms: Evidence from Rural China," *Quarterly Journal of Economics*, forthcoming, 1998.

Li, David D. "Ambiguous Property Rights in Transition Economies," *Journal of Comparative Economics*, 23:1–19, 1996.

Ministry of Agriculture, China, *Zhonghua Renmin Gongheguo Xiangcun Jiti Suoyouzhi Qiye Tiaoli Tiaowen Shiyi* (*Explanations of the Regulation on Township and Village Collective Enterprises of the People's Republic of China*), Beijing: China Legal Press, 1990.

Qian, Yingyi, "Enterprise Reform in China: Agency Problems and Political Control," *Economics of Transition*, 4(2):427–447, October, 1996.

Schmidt, Klaus, "The Costs and Benefits of Privatization: An Incomplete Contracts Approach," *Journal of Law, Economics, and Organization*, 12(1):1–24, 1996.

Shleifer, Andrei, and Robert W. Vishny, "Politicians and Firms," *Quarterly Journal of Economics*, CIX:995–1025, November 1994.

Song, Lina, and Du He, "The Role of Township Governments in Rural Industrialization," in William Byrd and Lin Qingsong (eds.), *China's Rural Industry: Structure, Development, and Reform*, Oxford: Oxford University Press, 1990.

Whiting, Susan, *The Micro-Foundations of Institutional Change in Reform China: Property Rights and Revenue Extraction in the Rural Industrial Sector*, Ph.D. thesis, Department of Political Science, University of Michigan, 1995.

Yang, Zhigang, "China's Off-Budget Revenue Accounts," mimeo, Institute of Public Finance and Trade, Chinese Academy of Social Sciences, 1996.

6 Public vs. Private Ownership of Firms: Evidence from Rural China

1. Introduction

In studying economies in transition from plan to market, no single issue has received more attention from economists and policy makers than the one of property rights and ownership of firms. In Eastern Europe and the former Soviet Union, one observes mass privatization of old state-owned enterprises (SOEs) and the emergence of new private (including newly privatized) enterprises. In China, old SOEs also declined even without privatization, and new private enterprises flourish. However, there is a puzzle concerning China's successful Township-Village Enterprises (TVEs).

TVEs are neither private enterprises nor SOEs. While SOEs are (central government-owned) national public firms, TVEs are rural (community government-owned) local public firms controlled by community (township or village) governments. Between 1979 and 1993, the TVE share of the national industrial output expanded from 9 percent to 27 percent, while the share of rural private enterprises increased from 0 to 9 percent (*China Statistical Yearbook* 1994). Combining TVEs with private enterprises in 1993, rural industries as a whole produced 36 percent of the national industrial output, and rural industries and services employed 123 million people, accounting for about one half of the national non-farm employment. Rural industries, and in particular TVEs, have made major contributions in sustaining China's 10 percent annual growth during its transition to markets.

Why are there many community publically owned TVEs? The conventional theory on the ownership of firms has largely focused on private and national-public enterprises. Recently, several new theories have been proposed to explain TVEs. A large body of this literature has

With Hehui Jin; originally published in *Quarterly Journal of Economics*, August 1998, 113(3), pp. 773–808.

viewed TVEs as local (i.e., community) government ownership taking advantage of the existing institutional environment to achieve certain government goals.

Several possible objectives of community government are studied. In the context of rural China, the three most relevant goals of a community government are considered to be the community government's revenue (e.g., Byrd and Gelb [1990], Oi [1992, 1994], Che and Qian [1998b]), non-farm employment (e.g., Rozelle and Boisvert [1994]), and per capita income, all of which provide its financial and political support. Theories suggest that community government ownership of TVEs can be a more effective instrument than private ownership in achieving the government's objectives when contracts are incomplete (e.g., Shleifer and Vishny [1994] and Che and Qian [1998b]).

Theories also relate the ownership of firms to the specific institutional environment during the process of transition and development. Three institutional factors are emphasized which might give more political and economic advantages to TVEs rather than to private enterprises, given the goals of the community government: the central government's influence, the community government's power, and underdevelopment of the market. These factors can operate through several channels. Theories suggest that TVEs are favored in credit rationing by the central government or in the imperfect capital market (e.g., Wong [1988, 1991], Byrd [1990], Che and Qian [1998a]), and TVEs may use their political connections with the central government-owned SOEs to smooth transactions when the product market is underdeveloped (e.g., Nee [1992], Otsuka [1996]). Another possibility is that TVEs are vehicles for the community government to cash in the value of land under its control in the absence of asset markets (Naughton [1994, 1996]). Other theories propose that TVEs are better protected politically by the community government's power in the absence of secure property rights under the rule of law (e.g., Chang and Wang [1994], Li [1996], Che and Qian [1998b]), and TVEs benefit from the community government which was empowered by the initial collective assets and experiences before the reform (e.g., Chang and Wang [1994], Putterman [1994], Luo [1990]).

All of these theories seem plausible, but none of them has been investigated empirically.[1] In this paper, we use a set of provincial data to carry out an empirical analysis on TVEs vs. private ownership of firms. Inspired by the above theories but limited by the data available, we will focus on two empirical issues. First, how do the three factors concerning the institutional environment of firms explain the observed provincial variation of ownership distribution between TVEs and private enterprises? And second, how effectively does community government ownership of TVEs, as opposed to private ownership, help the community government to achieve the three objectives? We find that TVEs, relative to private enterprises, are favored in a province where the central government's influence is greater through a larger state supply of credit and more state industrial enterprises. TVEs are also favored where the community government's power is stronger through having more collective assets under its control at the beginning of the reform and stronger local political strength. On the other hand, private enterprises, relative to TVEs, are more likely to develop in an environment of less anti-market ideology and better market development through more product market expansion and urbanization. We also find some evidence on the effectiveness of TVE ownership in pursuing the community government's goals: The TVE share in the rural non-farm sector increases the community government's share of revenue and, somewhat surprisingly, the state's (all governments above the township level) share of revenue as well, but more so for the former. The TVE share also raises rural non-farm employment and rural real per capita income, but it does not increase income for the given levels of non-farm employment and/or local public goods provision.

These results help in understanding the nature of TVEs and private enterprises and provide several insights which may have implications beyond China. First, the distribution of firms between local public and private ownership reflects the institutional features in the process of transition from plan to markets and economic development, which can be summarized by three factors: the central government's influence, the local community government's power, and market development. Second, ownership of TVEs may serve as an effective instrument for both the community and central governments to raise more revenue and for the community government to retain a larger share. This provides some evidence on the incentives of all levels of government, especially the community government, to develop TVEs. Indeed, development of TVEs helps the government avoid revenue crises which are often observed in other transition and developing economies. Third, although TVEs generate a higher level of rural non-farm employment and a higher revenue share for the community government than private enterprises, they do not increase per capita income for the given levels of non-farm employment and/or local public goods provision. Because of the relatively high capital-labor ratio in TVEs, this finding may indicate that TVEs are not as efficient as private enterprises.

The rest of the paper is organized as follows. Section 2 provides a brief description of TVEs and their roles in China's economic reform. Section 3 summarizes theories on ownership of TVEs and their major testable implications. Section 4 discusses estimation methods. Section 5 describes the construction of regression variables. Section 6 presents results on the provincial variation of the relative share of TVEs vs. private enterprises in rural industry. Section 7 reports results of the effect of TVE ownership on the community government's objectives. Section 8 concludes.

2. TVEs and China's Economic Reforms

The Chinese economy is divided into "urban" and "rural" areas, which is an administrative rather than economic concept inherited from the planning era. Firms in the urban area consist of state-owned, collectively-owned, privately-owned, and "other" (including foreign) firms. State-owned enterprises are national public firms owned by the central government and supervised by the four upper levels of government: central, provincial, prefecture, and county (a municipality can have a rank of the latter three). Firms in the rural area are called rural enterprises, which consist of two ownership types: community public firms (TVEs) and private firms. In China, the state sector refers to SOEs in urban areas and the non-state sector refers to the rest.

Between 1978 and 1993, the share of the state sector in the national industrial output declined from 78 percent to 43 percent, while the share of rural enterprises increased from 9 percent to 36 percent (the rest came from other urban enterprises such as collectives or private and foreign firms) [*China Statistical Yearbook* 1994]. These relative share changes have occurred without any privatization of old SOEs. In 1993, total rural enterprise employment reached 123 million, accounting for about one-half of the national non-farm employment. Clearly, rural enterprises have played an essential role in China's economic reform.[2]

Within the rural enterprise sector, both TVEs and private enterprises flourish, but until recently, TVEs have played a more important role in rural industrialization than private enterprises. At the end of 1992, China had about 50 thousand townships and 800 thousand villages. On average, each township (with a population of about 18 thousand) had 8.2 township-run enterprises, and each village (with a population of about 1,000) had 1.4 village-run enterprises [*China Statistical Yearbook* 1993]. In 1993, there were about 1.5 million TVEs with 52 million employees, and the shares of TVE output and employment in rural industry were 72 percent and 58 percent respectively, with the remaining shares coming from private enterprises [*China Township Enterprises Statistical Yearbook* 1994]. The TVE subsector is indeed significant by both absolute and relative measures.[3]

TVEs are local community public firms owned and controlled by the township or village government (Chang and Wang [1994]; and Che and Qian [1998a]). TVEs are not private enterprises. As compared with private enterprises, TVEs receive substantial assistance from the community government (see section 3 below) and also suffer from problems typically found in public firms, such as weaker managerial incentives and greater political intervention from the community government [Zhang 1996].

On the other hand, the local community government-owned TVEs differ significantly from the central government-owned SOEs. Although both the theoretical and empirical parts of our paper are about TVEs and private enterprises and are not about the comparison between TVEs and SOEs, it is worthwhile to summarize the important differences between TVEs and SOEs as useful background.

Some empirical works have found that TVEs are much more efficient than SOEs in terms of productivity growth (e.g., Jefferson and Rawski [1994]). At the enterprise level, TVEs differ from SOEs in the following three aspects. First, TVEs have not been under state allocation plans for either input or output. In the early periods, the central government tolerated TVEs for the purpose of agricultural mechanization; indeed, many TVEs started as agricultural machine repairing shops. Later, TVEs expanded their scope of operation to pursue local industrialization. Second, TVE workers are not state employees who receive job security and welfare from the state. Unlike SOE employees, TVE workers can be laid off.[4] Third, although TVEs have softer budget constraints than private enterprises, they have much harder budget constraints than SOEs. TVEs receive proportionally far fewer loans than SOEs and were hit badly during the retrenchment period.[5]

A more thorough understanding of the difference between TVEs and SOEs requires a deeper knowledge about township and village governments.[6] Under China's highly decentralized fiscal system, fiscal "self-sufficiency" has been a basic principle for the rural community governments [Wong 1997]. These community governments retain and use a large proportion of the revenues they generate on the one hand, and they receive no or very few fiscal budgetary transfers from higher level governments on the other.[7] At the same time, the authority of township and village governments in some important aspects is more constrained as compared to the central government and even to higher level local governments such as provincial governments. For example, although township and village governments may have connections with SOEs and exert some influence on the state financial institutions, they do not control them. Moreover, township and village governments are unable to erect trade barriers since their jurisdictions are geographically too small. Therefore, as compared to the central and higher level local governments, township and village governments have more constrained authority and have relatively hard budget constraints from the fiscal and financial channels. These are possibly fundamental reasons for TVEs to perform better than SOEs, although both are government-owned (Qian and Weingast [1996]; and Che and Qian [1998a]).

3. Theories of TVEs

Due to their unconventional features and relative success, China's TVEs have recently stimulated quite a lot of research. The traditional theory on public ownership postulates that benevolent governments as owners of firms maximize social welfare to cure market failures in the presence of monopoly power or externalities. In contrast, theories on TVEs are positive in nature. Most theories intend to explain TVEs as local (i.e., community) government firms taking advantage of the existing institutional environment to achieve certain government goals.[8]

Because the community government plays a central role in TVEs, theories about them start with the goals of the community government in developing TVEs. In the late 1970s, rural China was characterized by a large amount of surplus labor, a low level of income, and a poor local government revenue base. Economic reform has since proceeded in the direction of fiscal decentralization, under which township and village governments were able to retain a large portion of their revenues while obtaining few revenue transfers from the higher level. Consequently, the most relevant objectives of a community government are considered to be an increase of the government's revenue, creation of non-farm employment, and an increase of rural income. Conceivably, the first provides financial support and the latter two provide political support for the community government.[9]

All of the aforementioned objectives of the community government can be achieved by rural industrialization. However, it is not obvious whether community government-owned firms (TVEs) or private firms are more effective in achieving the government's goals. An important consideration is the incompleteness of contracts, which entails the relevance of allocation of ownership of firms in general and government ownership of firms in particular (Shleifer and Vishny [1994], and Hart, Shleifer, and Vishny [1997], Che and Qian [1998b]). Theories on TVEs relate the ownership of firms to the specific institutional environment in which the firms are operating. During the process of transition and development, both government and market institutions are problematic. Three factors concerning the institutional environment of firms which might give more political and economic advantages to TVEs rather than to private enterprises are: the central government's influence, the community government's power, and under-development of the market.

In what follows, we first discuss several channels through which the three institutional factors may play important roles in the development of rural industrial firms. They are financing of investments, transaction costs, urbanization, security of property rights, and collective heritage. We then discuss the three objectives of the community government for developing TVEs.

Ownership and the Institutional Environment

The first theory proposes that TVEs have distinct advantages in financing investment compared to private enterprises because of the central government's influence and/or under-development of the capital market. The start-up capital for private enterprises comes mainly from owners with little coming from bank loans. Given the limited amount of personal financial resources, private enterprises have difficulty growing. In contrast, TVEs are able to access a larger pool of capital, in particular, bank loans, with the help of the community government [Wong 1988, 1991].

TVEs may have an advantage over private enterprises in financing investment because the community government can make use of its political connections with the central government-owned state banks to channel loans to TVEs. The state banks are also more willing to lend to TVEs because ideological discrimination against private enterprises makes lending to the latter politically riskier. TVEs may also have possible advantages in financing investment due to the under-development of market financial institutions and the imperfect capital market (Byrd [1990]; Che and Qian [1998a]). For example, the community government is able to share risks by cross-subsidization among its many diversified enterprises, thus reducing the default risks borne by banks. The community government can also reduce agency costs in borrowing because of its larger endowment in physical and financial assets. From both perspectives, this theory implies that the relative share of TVEs is positively correlated with the supply of credit from state financial institutions to all rural enterprises, but negatively correlated with the extent of financial market development.

Second, the "transaction costs" theory similarly relates TVEs to the partial liberalization of the economy with the co-existence of the central government's influence and under-development of the market. Nee [1992] contends that China's economy is characterized by declining but still functioning central government planning institutions on the one hand, and emerging but weak market institutions with poorly specified and enforced property rights on the other. TVEs, with help from the community government, have a lower transaction cost in dealing with the existing SOEs, which enable them to access the SOEs' technology and materials. Quite often, TVEs and SOEs establish a long term relationship through subcontracting [Otsuka 1996]. On the other hand, private enterprises have lower transaction costs in dealing with other enterprises in competitive markets, because, for example, private entrepreneurs have higher marketing ability. This theory suggests a positive relationship between the share of TVEs and the importance of links with the state industrial sector, and a negative relationship between the TVE share and product market development.

Third, Naughton [1994, 1996] views developing TVEs as vehicles for the community government to convert community assets (i.e., land) to cash flow under the situation in which the development of asset markets lags behind that of product markets. He implicitly assumes an imperfection of the land rental market so that the only way of transforming land value into income streams is to directly operate businesses on it. He argues that because land close to urban areas is more valuable, communities closer to them have more incentives to transform assets into income streams by developing TVEs. However, one may also argue that a higher degree of urbanization can be associated with better market development, and thus reduce the disadvantages of small private enterprises in doing business through more accessible outlets for output, increased support for specialized inputs, labor market pooling, and technological spillovers. Naughton's testable hypothesis is the positive correlation between the share of TVEs in a community and its "urban proximity," which is a measure of the proximity of the community to urban centers weighted by urban population.

The fourth theory concerns the security of property rights of firms and associates the advantages of TVEs over private enterprises with the local community government's power for political protection. China's reform has proceeded in an environment which lacks a rule of law. As part of the political institutions, the community government can provide better political security to their own enterprises (Chang and Wang [1994]). The community government's protection of TVEs becomes more effective than that of private enterprises because ownership gives the community government better information about the operation of firms (Li [1996]).

Che and Qian [1998b] endogenize the community government's role in securing TVE property rights under a predatory state. Under TVE ownership, the community government integrates government activities (i.e., community public goods provision) and business activities, and it can better serve the interests of the central government. Consequently, the central government is less predatory toward community government-owned firms (TVEs) than private firms, and property rights under TVEs become more secure. In such a case, both the central government and the community government can benefit from TVE ownership.[10] This theory implies that the share of TVEs vs. private enterprises is positively correlated with the local political strength of the community government against pressure from the central government, but negatively correlated with the change of nationwide ideology in favor of the market economy.

The fifth theory relates TVEs to the history of China's economic planning and development. Because of 20 years spent implementing the commune system, the community government in rural China had already accumulated an unusual amount of physical and human capital by the late 1970s. One might argue that this particular historical experience empowered the community government, and thus gave TVEs organizational advantages over private enterprises (Chang and Wang [1994] and Putterman [1994]). However, one might also argue that this legacy provided more incentives for the community government to suppress private enterprises instead, in order to, for example, reduce competition in the skilled labor market [Luo 1990]. In either case, the "history matters" theory implies that the relative share of TVEs in the late 1980s and early 1990s should positively correlate with the strength of the rural collective sector at the beginning of reform, which is the community government's initial power base.

Ownership and the Community Government's Objectives

First, several studies have emphasized the revenue goals of the community government in developing TVEs. Both Byrd and Gelb [1990] and Oi [1992, 1994] stress the effect of fiscal decentralization that has made community governments independent fiscal entities. Community governments are able to retain and use a large proportion of the revenues they generate, and they are also subject to hard fiscal budget constraints due to limited fiscal revenue transfers from the higher level government. These authors then argue that, under this circumstance, community governments turn to TVEs for a revenue source.

However, these authors did not explain why the revenue objectives of the community government can be better achieved by developing TVEs. Conceivably, in a developed market economy, government ownership of firms may not help increase government revenue, and even worse, the inefficiency associated with public ownership is likely to decrease both profits and government revenue as compared with private ownership. One plausible explanation for the positive linkage between TVE ownership and community government revenue is based on incomplete contracts (Che and Qian [1998b]). Due to inadequate accounting and taxation institutions, the community government finds it hard to tax private firms. However, the community government can better extract revenue from TVEs because ownership gives it control over, and information about, operation of the firms. In the model of Che and Qian [1998b], because the community government also carries out revenue-enhancing local government activities by providing local public goods, both the community government and the central government can benefit from TVEs in terms of their own revenues. This theory implies that we may not only expect a positive correlation between the TVE shares and the revenue share of the community government, but also a positive correlation between the TVE shares and the revenue share of the central government.

Second, creation of non-farm employment in a community ranks very high on the list of community leader's concerns [Rozelle and

Boisvert 1994], and is often a motive claimed by the community government itself for developing TVEs. Reduction of rural underemployment is especially important in China because of some restrictions on and/or costs of labor migration from the rural to urban areas. Although an increase of non-farm employment is generally efficiency-enhancing in rural China, there may also be the possibility of inefficient excess employment. Whether developing TVEs is more effective than developing private enterprises to increase non-farm employment depends on the net effect of several factors. On the one hand, because TVEs are able to mobilize more capital than private enterprises, they may bring in more capital investment, which leads to more non-farm employment. In addition, the ownership rights give the community government the power to force TVEs to employ workers at the high level it desires. On the other hand, private enterprises typically have much lower capital-labor ratios [Zhang and Ronnas 1996], and thus they may provide more employment opportunities for a given level of capital investment.

The third often-claimed objective of the community government in developing TVEs is raising per capita income within the community. Because of the restrictions on and/or costs of labor migration, one way TVEs could contribute to raising per capita income is through increased local employment opportunities. Another way TVEs could contribute to raising per capita income is through an increased local public goods provision due to the improvement of the community government's revenue, because local public goods are usually under-supplied in the rural areas. On the other hand, inefficiency associated with the community government's political intervention may reduce per capita income. Therefore, developing TVEs could also be less effective than developing private enterprises to increase rural income.

4.   Estimation Method

The above theories inspired us to address the following two empirical questions. First, suppose that the community government's objectives are the same across provinces. Then, how do the three factors concerning the institutional environment of firms explain the observed provincial variation of ownership distribution between TVEs and private enterprises? Second, how effectively do TVEs, as opposed to private enterprises, help the community government achieve the objectives of increasing government revenue, non-farm employment, and per capita income?

We use provincial data from 1986 to 1993.[11] There are 28 provinces, excluding Tibet and Hainan. We incorporate Hainan into Guangdong in our data because Hainan separated from Guangdong and obtained a provincial status only in 1988. An advantage of such comprehensive data, as compared with survey data from a few provinces, is that it covers an entire country which has great variation across provinces.

We use the following econometric model to examine the provincial variation of ownership distribution. Let p_{it} be the probability of observing a worker (or unit of output) being employed (or produced) by TVEs, rather than private enterprises, in province i in year t, and X_{it} represent various aspects of the factors concerning the institutional environment of firms. We assume that p_{it} is a logit function of X_{it}:

$$p_{it} = \exp(\alpha_i + \gamma_t + X_{it}'\beta + u_{it})/[1 + \exp(\alpha_i + \gamma_t + X_{it}'\beta + u_{it})],$$

where α_i's represent provincial fixed effects, γ_t's yearly fixed effects, and u_{it}'s are error terms. This formulation has the property that the "odds ratio" has a log-linear functional form

$$\ln[p_{it}/(1-p_{it})] = \alpha_i + \gamma_t + X_{it}'\beta + u_{it}. \tag{1}$$

Equation (1) is a reduced form, where the endogenous variable p_{it} is regressed on exogenous variables X_{it}. Clearly, u_{it}'s of the same province in different years are highly correlated. Furthermore, there may also be a provincial specific error component and the variances of u_{it}'s may vary across provinces. To address these problems, we compute Huber–White robust standard errors allowing for group errors by provinces using the procedure suggested by Deaton [1995]. We report ordinary least squares estimation results with t-ratios based on Huber–White robust standard errors.

As will be described below, several of our variables (for example, initial collective assets) are not time varying, and thus they would be absorbed into provincial fixed effects α_i's in the estimations including all provincial dummies. Therefore, instead of using all provincial dummies, we use 6 region dummies in our regressions to capture some pre-existing regional differences. We group the 28 provinces into 6 regions according to geographic location: North, South, Southwest, Northwest, Coastal, and huge cities (for details see next section). We also report estimation results from regressions without these region dummies.[12]

To investigate the effectiveness of TVE ownership in achieving the alternative government's objectives, we estimate the structural equations with causality going from the share of TVEs to government revenues, non-farm employment, and per capita income. The general form of the equations we use is given by:

$$y_{it} = \alpha_i + \gamma_t + p_{it}\theta + Y_{it}'\delta + Z_{it}'\gamma + v_{it}. \tag{2}$$

where y_{it} represents the dependent variables we are interested in, i.e., the community government's and the state's shares of revenue, rural non-farm employment, or per capita income; p_{it} is the share of TVEs relative to private enterprises; Y_{it} are endogenous variables including a subset of y_{it}'s; Z_{it} are exogenous variables, for example, per capita cultivated land and urbanization; and v_{it} is an error term. We again use 6 region dummies to capture some pre-existing regional differences.

The error term v_{it} in equation (2) may not only be correlated with Y_{it}, but also with p_{it}, the TVE shares. This arises from the possibility that, while the ownership distribution may indeed have an effect on the government's revenues, employment and income, there may be another structural equation, say $p_{it} = g(y_{it}, X_{it}, Z_{it})$, where the causality runs from the latter to the TVE shares. For example, community governments with a higher share of revenues may have a larger capability to finance their enterprises, which in turn leads to a higher share of TVE ownership. Thus, both Y_{it} and p_{it} should be treated as endogenous variables in equation (2). To correct for the endogeneity problem, we use an instrumental variable method to estimate equation (2). The set of instrumental variables includes X_{it} from equation (1) and Z_{it} from equation (2), as well as all region and year dummies. In addition, we also report the results from the ordinary-least-squared estimations. For both ordinary-least-squared and instrumental variable estimations, we report t-ratios based on Huber–White robust standard errors allowing for provincial group effects.

In our specification, some variables in X_{it} which have direct effects on TVE shares are not present in equations (2). This differentiates them from the equations with reverse causality running from the government revenue to the TVE shares and thus makes them identifiable. In fact, these equations are overidentified. It is arguable that some of the instrumental variables should also be included as independent variables. To address this issue, we perform an overidentification test [Newey 1985]. An insignificant χ^2 statistic will justify the exclusion of these instruments from the equations, and will also indicate that any proper subset of the instruments should produce the same estimation of coefficients. Because our panel data have grouped errors, we adjust the test statistics as suggested recently by Hoxby and Paserman [1997].

5. Construction of Variables

To examine provincial variation of ownership, we use the relative share of TVEs vs. private enterprises in rural industrial employment and output respectively for p_{it}.[13] We focus on industry (and thus exclude services) to avoid the further problem of the heterogeneity of technologies between industry and services. The X_{it} includes the following variables representing various aspects of the three factors concerning the institutional environment of firms.

We have two variables representing the central government's influence. The first is the state supply of credit. The credit here refers to "rural enterprise loans" from the Agricultural Bank of China (ABC) and Rural Credit Cooperatives (RCCs), which are the two major credit sources for both TVEs and private enterprises. This variable is then normalized to represent the amount of loans per employee in real terms obtained by all rural enterprises from state financial institutions.

The second variable is the size of state industry measured by the per capita state industrial real output in a province. It serves as an index of the potential linkage of a rural enterprise with SOEs in the province. Because TVEs developed much later than SOEs, this variable is exogenous to TVEs.[14]

For the local government's power, we also have two variables. The first is collective heritage, which is measured by the per capita collective fixed assets in 1980. It indicates the initial base of the rural collective sector and is a proxy for the accumulated physical and human capital under the control of the community government at the beginning of reform. Because of few private assets at the time, it was also an approximate value of per capita wealth. However, since this wealth was under direct control of the community governments, it captures elements of collective heritage.

The second variable concerns local (i.e., community) political strength. The political strength and organizational capability of local community leaders are hard to measure. We use the following measurement as a proxy for community political strength: the percentage of rural households in a province NOT adopting the *Dabaogan* form of the Household Responsibility System in agriculture at the end of 1983. The *Dabaogan* form is based on fixed renting, and community governments are not involved at all in any production decision-making and revenue sharing arrangements with households.

The *Dabaogan* form initially started spontaneously in the late 1970s in a few provinces, and it was soon welcomed enthusiastically by households across the country. The central government endorsed the *Dabaogan* form as early as 1980. For three consecutive years starting in 1982, the Party Central Committee issued three No. 1 Party Circulars to put pressure on community governments across the country to adopt this form, and by the end of 1984, nearly 100 percent of households had done so. Communities which had not adopted it by the end of 1983 demonstrated the community governments' political strength to resist pressure from both above and below. We interpret this resistance as coming from community governments rather than higher levels of local governments because the adoption of this form was not uniform at the county and provincial levels.

We have three variables to measure market development. The first is private financial assets at the end of the previous year to indicate financial market development.[15] Because the data for total private financial assets is not available, the total rural household savings deposits are used instead,[16] which is a reasonably good proxy if the amount of household savings deposits is roughly proportional to the amount of total household financial assets. We normalize private household savings deposits in a province by its rural gross output. This measure is parallel to the usual measure for "financial deepening," which is the ratio of total financial assets in the economy to total GDP. Therefore, our index of private financial assets is not an index of the level of private wealth, but the level of the development of rural financial markets.

The second variable is product market development. We use the total transaction volume in rural free markets in a province divided by its total rural gross output to measure the development of the product market. The transaction volume in the rural free market indicates overall private trading activities in the markets of farm products and consumer goods, as well as producer goods. A higher index means a better opportunity for enterprises to obtain a supply of materials from, and to sell their outputs to, the market. Because the local industrial enterprises only account for a very small proportion of the total trans-actions in these markets, this index can be thought of as exogenous.

Finally, urbanization is also potentially associated with the extent of market development. We use the index of urbanization measured by the share of urban population in the total population. We use the 1990 census data because it is the most appropriate for our purposes.[17] A related, but different, index for urbanization is the urban proximity index constructed by Naughton [1996], which is a weighted average of the inverse of distance from the center of a province to selected major cities, using the city population as weight. The two indices give very similar results so we will only use urban population in our reports.

In addition, we use year dummies for each year between 1987 and 1993 to capture any changes over one particular year as compared with the previous year. Because macroeconomic policy changes over years have been somewhat controlled by the variables such as the state credit supply, we interpret time dummies as representing the nationwide shift of official ideology regarding plans and markets due to changes in the Party line. From 1986 to 1993, the overall trend of the Party line was moving in a more liberal direction with the major exception of 1989 due to the Tiananmen Square incident. The years of 1992 and 1993 were particularly so when Deng Xiaoping made his famous trip to the south-ern China to promote market-oriented reform and the Chinese Com-munity Party subsequently endorsed "socialist market economy" as its official Party ideology.

We use 6 region dummies to capture pre-existing regional differ-ences among 28 provinces. We divide China into North and South (according to climate and pattern of agricultural activities) and East and West (the West is mountainous and the East is relatively flat) to obtain four regions: North and South in the East, and Southwest and Northwest in the West. We then separately list 6 coastal provinces as one region because they were one step ahead in reforms and opening up to foreign trade and investment. Finally, we single out the three huge cities of Beijing, Tianjin, and Shanghai because they are small in geographical size and do not have large rural areas like all the other provinces.

In examining the community government's objectives, consider first the government's revenue. The net income of the rural economy is generated from three sources. The first two sources are the income generated by farm households and private enterprises respectively.

Part of this income is paid to the state (all governments above the township and village level) as taxes, part goes to community governments under the names of "collective reserves" and "administrative fees," and the remaining part is retained by households. The third source is the income generated by TVEs. Part of this income is submitted to the state as taxes and fees, but a major part goes to households as wages and bonuses, and the remainder (including retained profits) is controlled by community governments. From the destination perspective, the net income of the rural economy is distributed among three entities: the state (all governments above the township and village level), the community (township and village) government, and households. The state's revenue includes all state taxes and fees remitted to the government above the township. The community government revenue is the income received by township and village governments, including retained profits from TVEs. The remaining income belongs to households.[18]

In addition to the community government's and the state's shares of revenue, our dependent variables also include rural non-farm employment and the rural income level. We use share of the rural non-agricultural labor force in the total rural labor force to measure the level of rural non-farm employment. We measure the income level by the rural real per capita income at the 1980 price.

We use the share of TVEs in rural enterprise employment in both industry and services as our independent variable to measure the importance of TVE ownership relative to private ownership. This is because our dependent variables concerning income and employment also include the sources from both industry and services.

The summary statistics of the above variables are reported in Table 6.1. Our data set has a much smaller sample variation over time than across provinces. This is not surprising because most variables are characterizations of the institutional environment which shift slowly over time at the provincial aggregate level and our data covers only 8 years. Three variables, local political strength, the share of urban population, and initial collective assets, are not time varying. Among the rest, the variances over time of the share of TVE industrial employment and output account for about 2 percent and 8 percent of total variances respectively, and those of the revenue shares of the community government and the state represent about 8 percent and 12 percent of the total variances respectively. Only the variances over time of the state supply of credit and private assets are significant,

Table 6.1
Summary Statistics of Variables

	Mean	Minimum	Maximum	Standard deviation
Employment share of TVEs in rural industry	0.585	0.226	0.970	0.169
Output share of TVEs in rural industry	0.681	0.342	0.990	0.140
State supply of credit	1.006	0.243	6.238	0.816
Size of state industry	0.101	0.024	0.584	0.109
Log of initial collective assets	4.926	3.523	6.231	0.547
Local political strength	0.094	0.002	0.606	0.128
Private financial assets	0.139	0.014	0.318	0.055
Product market development	0.084	0.008	0.241	0.044
Share of urban population	0.311	0.147	0.732	0.162
State share in rural net income	0.073	0.025	0.283	0.048
Community government share in rural net income	0.082	0.011	0.255	0.056
Share of non-farm employment in total rural labor force	0.233	0.068	0.771	0.148
Rural per capita real income	0.317	0.167	0.829	0.128
Share of TVEs in rural enterprise employment	0.494	0.198	0.970	0.180
Per capita community government revenue	0.072	0.003	0.885	0.118
Per capita cultivated land	1.441	0.476	4.824	1.074

Note: Precise variable definitions and sources are presented in the chapter appendix

accounting for about 42 percent and 34 percent of the total variances respectively.

6. Estimation Results: Provincial Variation of Ownership

Table 6.2 reports the regression results for the provincial variation of ownership distribution between TVEs and private enterprises. We initially included in our regressions the variables of adult education (measured by the percentage of the rural labor force having at least primary schooling) and the per capita cultivated land. They are not significant and we later dropped them. Table 6.2 also reports the regression results by excluding region dummies, which show slight changes only.[19]

First, the coefficients for the supply of credits from state financial institutions are positive and significant, while the coefficients for

Table 6.2
Ownership and the Institutional Environment—The Logit Model

	Share of TVEs in rural industrial employment			Share of TVEs in rural industrial output		
Intercept	-2.076	-1.596	-2.195	-0.444	0.370	-0.577
	[2.547]	[2.217]	[2.069]	[0.455]	[0.592]	[0.476]
State supply of credits	0.274	0.480		0.363	0.538	
	[5.200]	[4.687]		[3.650]	[4.365]	
Size of state industry	0.746	1.322	1.487	1.866	2.957	2.846
	[1.324]	[2.170]	[2.902]	[2.529]	[3.972]	[4.523]
Log of initial collective assets	0.698	0.563	0.690	0.522	0.292	0.506
	[3.838]	[3.318]	[2.929]	[2.444]	[1.625]	[1.928]
Local political strength	1.532	2.062	1.356	2.319	2.902	2.079
	[3.739]	[4.049]	[3.732]	[4.679]	[4.329]	[4.065]
Private financial assets	-0.009	-2.785		-0.102	-2.506	
	[0.006]	[2.375]		[0.057]	[1.507]	
Product market development	-7.476	-5.452	-6.586	-7.503	-5.155	-6.375
	[5.782]	[2.998]	[4.536]	[4.441]	[2.439]	[3.247]
Share of urban population	-1.977	-1.636	-1.574	-3.440	-3.137	-2.913
	[2.627]	[1.605]	[1.938]	[2.855]	[2.220]	[2.285]
Region dummy for huge cities	0.568		0.788	0.509		0.806
	[2.057]		[2.525]	[1.070]		[1.483]
Region dummy for coastal	0.391		0.572	0.283		0.520
	[3.177]		[3.737]	[1.426]		[2.259]
Region dummy for Southwest	0.253		0.251	0.312		0.307
	[1.751]		[1.411]	[1.457]		[1.332]
Region dummy for Northwest	-0.243		-0.208	-0.201		-0.164
	[1.730]		[2.456]	[1.024]		[1.049]
Region dummy for North	-0.349		-0.308	-0.482		-0.433
	[2.181]		[1.875]	[2.530]		[2.130]
Year dummy for 1987	-0.041	-0.015	-0.022	-0.082	-0.062	-0.058
	[1.221]	[0.523]	[0.838]	[1.735]	[1.325]	[1.564]
Year dummy for 1988	-0.083	-0.083	-0.077	-0.060	-0.065	-0.052
	[4.434]	[4.635]	[4.266]	[2.915]	[3.258]	[2.433]
Year dummy for 1989	-0.006	0.002	0.006	-0.012	-0.006	0.003
	[0.282]	[0.104]	[0.316]	[0.390]	[0.196]	[0.113]
Year dummy for 1990	-0.105	-0.102	-0.048	-0.201	-0.193	-0.127
	[3.282]	[2.544]	[1.917]	[3.748]	[3.516]	[2.429]
Year dummy for 1991	-0.047	0.009	-0.009	0.021	0.067	0.069
	[0.930]	[0.224]	[0.485]	[0.261]	[0.923]	[1.417]
Year dummy for 1992	-0.121	-0.177	-0.050	-0.164	-0.216	-0.071
	[3.986]	[4.898]	[2.570]	[3.938]	[5.063]	[2.677]
Year dummy for 1993	-0.123	-0.236	-0.055	-0.125	-0.222	-0.034
	[2.700]	[4.153]	[1.600]	[1.762]	[2.881]	[0.682]
R^2	0.929	0.875	0.911	0.847	0.782	0.815

Notes: (1) The functional form of the dependent variable is given by equation (1) in Section 4. (2) Sample size is 224. (3) The t-statistics are in parentheses, which are based on Huber-White robust standard errors allowing for group errors by provinces.

private financial assets are not significant. This gives some support to
the financial theory of TVE ownership. A large supply of state non-
agricultural loans can increase the relative share of TVEs because, with
the help of the community government, these loans are more likely to
go to TVEs to support their development. However, the more important private financial assets in the rural economy, which indicate more
developed informal financial markets, seem to affect both TVEs and
private enterprises equally.

Second, the coefficients of product market development are all negative and significant, which suggests that product market development
favors private enterprises. On the other hand, the effect of the size of
state industry on TVEs is positive and significant. Therefore, a larger
state industrial sector seems to favor TVEs, for example, through subcontracting. These results seem to be consistent with the transaction
cost theory of TVEs.

Third, we were able to reproduce Naughton's [1996] result of a positive correlation between the share of TVEs in a province and its "urban
proximity" (or our urbanization index) in univariate regressions for our
extended sample period. Casual observation often gives the impression
that TVEs are predominant in provinces with a high degree of urbanization or proximity to major cities, which is indeed captured by the
univariate regressions.

However, the positive correlation no longer holds when other variables are being controlled. By adding the size of state industry, the
coefficient of urbanization becomes insignificant in the output equation, suggesting that urbanization picked up some effects from the size
of state industry in univariate regressions. By further adding any one
of the four variables—initial collective assets, local political strength,
state supply of credit, or product market development—the coefficient
of urbanization becomes negative in the output equation and insignificant in the employment equation. With all explanatory variables
included, we find that the coefficient of urbanization (and that of
Naughton's urban proximity index as well, which is not reported
here) becomes negative and significant. This provides some evidence
showing that urbanization favors private enterprises through better
market development. For example, private enterprises can take advantage of being located near urban areas for a more accessible outlet for
output, increased support for specialized inputs, labor market pooling,
and technological spillovers.

Fourth, the local political strength seems to play an important role in favoring TVEs, as indicated by its positive and significant coefficients. A greater capability of community leaders to resist pressures from higher levels of government provides more effective political protection for TVEs relative to private enterprises, and therefore favors their development. As will be shown in the next section, a higher share of TVEs gives the community government more revenue; therefore, the community government has the incentive to provide more protection to TVEs than to private enterprises. The evidence seems to support the theory of the security of property rights.

Examining the year dummies we find a general trend of decline of TVEs relative to private enterprises in this time period. The evidence also indicates that political retrenchment in 1989 stopped this decline temporarily, but it did not reverse this trend. On the other hand, there is some evidence of an acceleration of private enterprises relative to TVEs after 1992. It seems that a nationwide ideological shift toward conservatism does not effectively reduce the share of private enterprises in the rural economy immediately, but an ideological shift in a liberal direction leads to significant prosperity for private enterprises. Perhaps the mere removal of existing restrictions on private enterprises induces an instant response, but adding new restrictions has little immediate effect as it takes time to establish effective enforcement.

Finally, the initial collective assets have a positive and significant effect on the TVE's shares in later years. According to one interpretation, those provinces with a larger base of accumulated physical and human capital controlled by the community government prior to the reform tend to give organizational advantages to TVEs relative to private enterprises. According to the alternative interpretation, a larger collective base provides community governments with higher incentives to suppress private enterprises. Both interpretations are consistent with the view that the community government's initial power base is crucial in the development of TVEs. They seem to accord well with the "history matters" theory of TVEs and demonstrate the "path dependent" nature of institutional changes in agreement with North [1991].[20]

In the above regressions, there may be a potential endogeneity problem concerning the variables of "state supply of credit" and "private financial assets."[21] The state supply of credit may rise when TVEs demand more credit,[22] and similarly, private assets would be higher with more private firms.[23] We dealt with this problem in two ways. First, we ran regressions by excluding these two variables and the results are reported in Table 6.2. The results show that our estimations of other coefficients are not sensitive to the inclusion of these two variables. Second, we also looked at the "average TVE share" over our sample period as a function of *ex ante* provincial characteristics from the period before our sample. We first used only initial collective assets (1980), local political strength (1983), and the 1982 share of urban population as *ex ante* characteristics, and later added the 1986 data of state supply of credit, private financial assets, product market development and the size of state industry as additional *ex ante* characteristics. We report the results, which are quite similar to our previous findings, in Table 6.3. This again shows that our results are not driven by the potential endogeneity problem.

In summary, our results seem to suggest that the variation in the share of TVEs vs. private enterprises among provinces can be explained by three factors: the central government's influence, the community government's power, and the extent of market development. TVEs, relative to private enterprises, are favored in provinces where the state supply of credit is large and the potential linkages with the state industry are large. TVEs are also favored where the community government's political strength is strong and the initial collective assets under its control are large. On the other hand, private enterprises, relative to TVEs, are more likely to develop if there are more developed product markets, more urbanization, and a less hostile ideological environment toward markets.

What can be said about the magnitudes of the estimates? By looking at the effect of a 1 percent increase in the independent variables at the mean on the change of the TVE share, we find that the most significant variables in the employment equation are initial collective assets (0.17 percent), urbanization (0.15 percent), and product market development (0.15 percent). In the output equation, the most significant variables are urbanization (0.23 percent), product market development (0.14 percent), and initial collective assets (0.11 percent). In other words, the most significant variables concern the local government's power and market development.

We also looked at how much actual inter-provincial differences can be explained by the alternative independent variables in order to make some assessment of their economic importance. Take the pair of Shanghai (with the highest share of TVEs) and Guizhou (with the lowest share of TVEs) as an example. All the variables together (excluding

Table 6.3
Ownership and the Institutional Environment—the Logit Model Average TVE Shares and *Ex Ante* Provincial Characteristics

	Share of TVEs in rural industrial employment		Share of TVEs in rural industrial output	
Intercept	-3.913	-2.498	-2.367	-1.046
	[4.192]	[3.288]	[2.362]	[1.094]
State supply of credits		0.499		0.448
		[3.457]		[1.744]
Size of state industry	1.692	0.151	2.787	1.126
	[2.737]	[0.399]	[3.867]	[1.264]
Log of initial collective assets	0.833	0.771	0.663	0.632
	[3.677]	[4.793]	[2.778]	[2.928]
Local political strength	1.324	1.246	1.924	1.957
	[6.653]	[4.073]	[4.492]	[2.816]
Private financial assets		-1.261		-1.594
		[0.566]		[0.510]
Product market development		-7.782		-7.696
		[6.328]		[4.713]
Share of urban population	-1.590	-2.025	-3.320	-4.158
	[1.815]	[4.928]	[2.576]	[4.263]
Region dummy for huge cities	1.239	1.064	1.486	1.342
	[3.075]	[3.739]	[2.286]	[2.755]
Region dummy for coastal	0.786	0.412	0.723	0.387
	[2.835]	[3.171]	[2.339]	[2.027]
Region dummy for Southwest	0.324	0.034	0.416	0.450
	[1.266]	[1.987]	[1.773]	[1.730]
Region dummy for Northwest	0.123	-0.110	0.185	-0.027
	[0.512]	[0.679]	[0.788]	[0.116]
Region dummy for North	0.022	-0.242	-0.077	-0.326
	[0.078]	[1.555]	[0.275]	[1.791]
R^2	0.892	0.959	0.838	0.907

Notes: (1) The functional form of the dependent variable is given by equation (1) in Section 4. (2) Shares of TVEs are averages over 1986–1993; share of urban population is the 1982 data; state supply of credit, private financial assets, produce market development, and size of state industry are the 1986 data; and local political strength is 1983 data and initial collective assets are 1980 data as in the rest of the paper. (3) sample size is 28. (4) The t-statistics are in parentheses, which are based on White heteroskedasticity consistent standard errors.

region and year dummies) explain about 86 percent of the difference in the TVE share in employment and 89 percent in output. The two most important variables are the initial collective assets and product market development for employment (together they explain 69 percent of the difference), and the initial collective assets and the size of state industry for output (together they explain 65 percent of the difference). We also take a less extreme pair, Jiangsu (a coastal province) and Sichuan (an inland province), both having state industrial sectors of a moderate size. In this case, all the variables together (excluding region and year dummies) explain 73 percent of the difference in the TVE share in employment and 58 percent in output. The two most important variables are the initial collective assets and the product market development for both employment and output; together they explain 62 percent of the difference for employment and 44 percent of the difference for output. Again, the local government's power and market development seem to be the most important factors.

7.   Estimation Results: Ownership and the Community Government's Objectives

Table 6.4 reports the results from ordinary-least-squared and instrumental variable estimations for the effect of TVE ownership on the government's revenue. The table also reports chi-squared statistics for the over-identification test, adjusted for group errors. The null hypothesis that all the instruments are legitimate and can be excluded from the revenue share equations cannot be rejected at the 10 percent level. The following discussions are based on the instrumental variable estimations.

The state's share of revenue is positively related to real per capita income, which seems to be consistent with similar trends in other countries. For a given level of real per capita income, the TVE share in rural enterprise employment has positive effects on both the community government's and the state's shares of revenue, and more so for the community government. This seems to suggest that ownership of TVEs is an effective instrument for both the community government and the state to raise more revenue, and for the community government to obtain a larger share.

These results provide some evidence on the fiscal incentives of the community government in developing TVEs, which tends to confirm numerous previous findings from anecdotes and case studies

Table 6.4

Ownership and the Community Government's Objectives: The Government's Revenue

	OLS		IV	
	State share	Community government share	State share	Community government share
Intercept	-0.066	0.001	-0.098	-0.074
	[3.879]	[0.042]	[7.356]	[3.255]
Share of TVEs in rural enterprise	0.108	0.112	0.114	0.242
employment	[3.690]	[4.292]	[3.896]	[4.316]
Net per capita rural income	0.181	-0.055	0.285	-0.006
	[3.741]	[0.957]	[7.742]	[0.108]
Local political strength	-0.073	0.026	-0.095	0.018
	[2.819]	[0.966]	[5.468]	[0.811]
Region dummy for huge cities	0.048	0.126	0.019	0.056
	[3.197]	[4.426]	[1.679]	[2.549]
Region dummy for Coastal	0.003	0.039	-0.010	0.008
	[0.267]	[2.497]	[1.795]	[0.639]
Region dummy for Southwest	0.008	-0.010	0.013	-0.002
	[1.002]	[1.278]	[1.496]	[0.144]
Region dummy for Northwest	0.003	0.002	0.008	0.004
	[0.458]	[0.212]	[1.193]	[0.423]
Region dummy for North	0.014	0.032	0.015	0.039
	[2.376]	[4.615]	[2.779]	[3.897]
χ^2 [dof]			4.532 [5]	2.354 [5]
Standard errors	0.015	0.021	0.016	0.024

Notes: (1) A full set of year dummies is included in each specification. (2) Endogenous variables are the share of TVEs in rural enterprise employment and net per capita rural income. Instruments are local political strength, region dummies, year dummies, state supply of credit, size of state industry, private financial assets, product market development, share of urban population, log of initial collective assets, and per capita cultivated land. (3) Sample size is 224. (4) The t-statistics are in parentheses, which are based on Huber-White robust standard errors allowing for group errors by provinces. (5) The χ^2 statistics are for the overidentification test for the legitimacy of the instruments, adjusted for provincial group errors.

(e.g., Byrd and Gelb [1990] and Oi [1992, 1994]). However, somewhat surprisingly, our results indicate that the state also benefits from TVEs in terms of its own revenue.[24] This result provides some evidence on the fiscal incentives of the central government for having more TVEs developed. Together, these findings give some support to the theory of the revenue goals of both the community government and the central government in developing TVEs (Che and Qian [1998b]).

The revenue effect of TVEs may have some implications for transition and developing economies. All transition economies have been experiencing government revenue shortfalls due to the collapse of the planning-based mechanism of revenue extraction. At the same time, all levels of government often find it difficult to tax new private firms due to the lack of market-based taxation institutions [McKinnon 1991]. On the other hand, the governments in developing economies, for political reasons, often bias the revenue allocation toward urban areas which hinders rural development [Bates 1987]. The above results provide some empirical evidence that TVEs helped reduce the severity of these two problems.

Interestingly, local political strength has a negative effect on the state's share of revenue and positive effects on the revenue shares of the community government and households, given the TVE's share in rural enterprise employment.[25] These results may suggest a conflict of interest between the community government and the central government (but not between the community government and households). For the given level of a TVE share, the political strength of community leaders plays an important role in increasing the combined community income at the expense of state taxes. This result shows that our variable of local political strength captures the ability of local resistance to pressure from above rather than below.

But stronger local political power also has an indirect positive effect on the state's revenue through the increased TVE's share, as is shown in section 6. Therefore the total effect of local political strength on the state's share of revenue is not necessarily negative. We have run alternative regressions in which the state's share and the community government's share of revenue are regressed on all exogenous variables X_{it} in equation (1), and found that the total effect of local political strength on the state's and community government's shares of revenue is respectively positive and significant. This suggests that both the central government and the community government benefit from local political strength. This looks paradoxical, but it is consistent with the predictions of models considering commitment problems (e.g., Aghion and Tirole [1997], Che and Qian [1998b]). In such a situation, one party may gain by giving away some information or power to another party. Thus, we can view the local political power of community governments as a device to secure their revenues against the central government's arbitrary extraction and, at the same time, also make the central government better off through, say, improved incentives of the community government.

Table 6.5 reports the results of the effect of TVE ownership on rural non-farm employment and per capita income from both ordinary-least squared and instrumental variable estimations. The table also reports chi-squared statistics for the over-identification test, adjusted for group errors. The null hypothesis that all the instruments are legitimate and can be excluded from the employment and income equations cannot be rejected at the 10 percent level. The following discussions are based on instrumental variable estimations.

The TVE's share in rural enterprise employment has a positive effect on the share of rural non-farm employment in the total rural labor force even with the control of per capita community government revenue (a proxy for local public goods provision). This provides some evidence that TVEs are able to create more non-farm employment opportunities than private enterprises. Thus, although private enterprises generally have a lower capital-labor ratio than TVEs, perhaps a lack of access to capital may be sufficiently severe to hinder their ability to increase non-farm employment. Although our result seems to support the theory that TVEs help increase non-farm employment, it does not necessarily mean that TVEs are more efficient in creating non-farm employment than private enterprises, given that capital is scarce and labor abundant in rural China.

We also find that the TVE's share in rural enterprise employment has a positive and significant effect on per capita income when not conditioned on the non-farm employment of the rural labor force and local public goods provision. But for a given share of non-farm employment in the rural labor force and the level of local public goods provision, that effect becomes negative. These results seem to indicate that the effect of TVEs on increasing per capita income works only through expansions of non-farm employment and local public goods provision. Furthermore, taking into account the fact that TVEs have a higher capital-labor ratio than private enterprises, these results seem to indicate that TVEs are not as efficient as private enterprises.

In summary, we find some evidence on the effectiveness of TVE ownership in pursuing the community government's goals: TVEs seem to increase the revenue shares of the community government and the state, as well as to increase rural non-farm employment and income, but they do not increase income given the levels of non-farm employment and local public goods provision.[26]

Table 6.5
Ownership and the Community Government's Objectives: Non-Farm Employment and Per Capita Income

	OLS				IV			
	Share of non-farm employment in rural labor force		Net per capita rural income		Share of non-farm employment in rural labor force		Net per capita rural income	
Intercept	-0.005 [0.148]	-0.034 [0.856]	0.2197 [4.508]	0.156 [3.465]	-0.009 [0.188]	-0.096 [1.946]	0.371 [3.773]	0.131 [3.646]
Share of TVEs in rural enterprise employment	0.348 [5.003]	0.402 [5.286]	-0.047 [0.517]	0.202 [2.448]	0.356 [3.444]	0.532 [6.685]	-0.531 [2.311]	0.255 [4.265]
Share of non-farm employment in rural labor force			0.507 [2.238]				0.892 [1.690]	
Per capita community government revenue	3.182 [4.410]		2.700 [2.406]		3.792 [3.414]		6.697 [2.026]	
Per capita cultivated land	-0.036 [3.331]	-0.037 [3.282]	0.015 [1.029]	-0.005 [0.360]	-0.036 [3.418]	-0.037 [3.578]	0.031 [1.149]	-0.005 [0.415]
Share of urban population	0.081 [0.785]	0.091 [0.825]	0.144 [1.958]	0.198 [1.349]	0.080 [0.805]	0.095 [0.925]	0.088 [0.494]	0.200 [1.441]
Region dummy for huge cities	0.124 [2.123]	0.203 [2.964]	-0.022 [0.233]	0.148 [1.462]	0.100 [1.926]	0.144 [2.210]	-0.081 [0.817]	0.125 [1.693]
Region dummy for Coastal	0.055 [2.247]	0.061 [2.384]	0.027 [0.807]	0.063 [2.183]	0.049 [1.983]	0.036 [1.321]	0.045 [0.867]	0.053 [2.377]

Table 6.5 (continued)

	OLS				IV			
	Share of non-farm employment in rural labor force		Net per capita rural income		Share of non-farm employment in rural labor force		Net per capita rural income	
Region dummy for Southwest	-0.031 [1.381]	-0.032 [1.244]	-0.014 [0.862]	-0.031 [2.859]	-0.030 [1.491]	-0.025 [0.768]	-0.143 [0.306]	-0.028 [2.122]
Region dummy for Northwest	0.035 [1.618]	0.036 [1.568]	-0.055 [2.751]	-0.035 [1.890]	0.035 [1.668]	0.040 [1.489]	-0.078 [1.962]	-0.034 [1.878]
Region dummy for North	0.081 [3.249]	0.089 [3.416]	-0.054 [2.145]	-0.003 [0.131]	0.080 [3.459]	0.095 [3.457]	-0.112 [1.997]	0.001 [0.006]
χ^2 [dof]					7.454 [4]	5.439 [5]	0.363 [3]	7.461 [5]
Standard errors	0.037	0.041	0.043	0.052	0.037	0.042	0.058	0.053

Notes: (1) A full set of year dummies is included in each specification. (2) Endogenous variables are the share of TVEs in rural enterprise employment, share of non-farm employment in rural labor force, net per capita rural income, and per capita community government revenue. Instruments are per capita cultivated land, region dummies, year dummies, local political strength, state supply of credit, size of state industry, private financial assets, product market development, share of urban population, and log of initial collective assets. (3) Sample size is 224. (4) The t-statistics are in parentheses, which are based on Huber-White robust standard errors allowing for provincial group errors. (5) The χ^2 statistics are for the overidentification test for the legitimacy of the instruments, adjusted for provincial group errors.

8.   Concluding Remarks

We found evidence that the variation in the share of TVEs among provinces can be explained by the central government's influence, the community government's power, and market development. We also found evidence on the effectiveness of TVE ownership in pursuing the community government's goals of the government's revenue, non-farm employment, and rural per capita income.

While our focus in the paper is the variation among provinces in China, it is useful to emphasize the common institutional elements throughout China under the reform. As already mentioned in Section 2, common to all provinces, township and village governments are all independent fiscal entities under fiscal decentralization—they are subject to hard fiscal budget constraints and they are able to retain a large proportion of the revenue they generate. In addition, township and village governments have the authority as well as the responsibility to participate in enterprise development. These considerations help explain why we do not observe many TVE-types of firms in other transition and developing economies. In those economies, the fiscal systems are typically very centralized so that local governments are not independent fiscal entities, and relatedly, local governments are often prohibited from becoming directly involved in enterprise development.

Since 1994, TVEs themselves have been evolving and some of them have been transformed into a new corporate form known as a "joint-stock cooperative," which is a mix of employee/manager ownership and cooperatives. These changes deserve further research.

Appendix: Definitions and Data Sources of Variables

Employment share of TVEs in rural industry: TVE employment divided by total employment in rural enterprises (TVEs plus private enterprises) in industry. 1986 figures are taken from [TESM 1986] and others from [CTESY 1988–1994].

Output share of TVEs in rural industry: TVE output divided by total output in rural enterprises (TVEs plus private enterprises) in industry. 1986 figures are taken from [TESM 1986] and others from [CTESY 1988–1994].

State supply of credit: total volume of "rural enterprise loans" from the ABC and RCCs at the end of the previous year [CRFSY 1989–1993] divided by TVE's output price index, and then normalized by the total rural enterprise (TVE plus private enterprises) employment (1,000 yuan/employee) [CTESY 1988–1994]. The TVE's output price index is constructed based on the gross output value of TVEs in current and constant prices [CTESY 1986–1994].

Size of state industry: gross industrial real output of state enterprises [CSY 1987–1994] divided by population [CPY 1991–1994] (10,000 yuan/ person).

Initial collective assets: collective fixed assets in 1980 [TESM 1986] divided by rural population [CAY 1981] (yuan/person).

Local political strength: share of rural households NOT adopting the *Dabaogan* form of the Household Responsibility System in agriculture at the end of 1983 [CRSY 1985].

Private financial assets: total rural household savings deposits at the end of the previous year [CRFSY 1989–1993] divided by total rural gross social products [CRSY 1987–1994].

Product market development: total transaction volume in rural free markets [CICAS 1990, CDTSY 1991–1994] divided by total rural gross social products [CRSY 1987–1994].

Share of urban population: urban population in the 1990 census divided by total population [CPY 1991]. The 1982 data used in Table 6.3 are urban population in the 1982 census divided by total population [CPY 1983].

State share in rural net income: state (governments above the township level) taxes and fees collected in rural areas [CAY 1987–1994] divided by rural net income [CAY 1987–1994].

Community government share in rural net income: township and village government revenue from all sources and retained profits in TVEs, divided by rural net income [CAY 1987–1994].

Share of non-farm employment in total rural labor force: total rural labor force minus rural agricultural labor force divided by total rural labor force [CRSY 1987–1994].

Rural per capita real income: rural net per capita income [CAY 1987–1994] deflated by rural consumer price index (1980 = 1, constructed based on annual rural consumer price indices from [CSY 1981–1994]) (1,000 yuan/person).

Share of TVEs in rural enterprise employment: TVE employment divided by total rural enterprise (TVE plus private enterprise) employment in industry and services [TESM 1986, CTESY 1987–1994].

Per capita community government revenue: township and village government revenue from all sources and retained profits in TVEs, divided by rural population and deflated by rural overall price index [CAY 1987–1994] (1,000 yuan/person).

Per capita cultivated land: total cultivated land divided by rural population [CRSY 1987–1994] (mu/person).

Region dummies: Huge Cities (Beijing, Tianjin, and Shanghai); Coastal Region (Liaoning, Shangdong, Jiangsu, Zhejiang, Fujian, and Guangdong); South Region (Hunan, Hubei, Jiangxi, and Guangxi); Southwest Region (Sichuan, Guizhou, and Yunnan); Northwest Region (Shaaxi, Gansu, Ningxia, Qinghuai, and Xinjiang); and North Region (Heilongjiang, Jilin, Inner Mongolia, Shanxi, Anhui, Hebei, and Henan).

Notes

* We are grateful to Takeshi Amemiya, Masahiko Aoki, Avner Greif, D. Gale Johnson, Anjini Kochar, Michael Kremer, Lawrence Lau, David D. Li, Guo Li, John McMillan, Jonathan Morduch, Barry Naughton, Douglass North, Albert Park, Dwight Perkins, Louis Putterman, Jan Svejnar, Frank Wolak, two referees, especially Lawrence Katz and Andrei Shleifer, and seminar participants at University of Southern California, Harvard University, Stanford University, the Universities of California at Berkeley and San Diego, University of Michigan, University of Pittsburgh, and the World Bank for helpful comments and discussions.

1. The only empirical work on the issue that we are aware of is that of Naughton [1996], who, in univariate regressions, finds a positive correlation between the share of TVEs in a province and its "urban proximity." We show later that his result will not hold in multivariate regressions.

2. This is in accordance with the general East Asian model of rural-based development [Hayami 1996].

3. However, TVEs and rural industrialization in China were not planned and actively supported by the central government at the initial stage. This historical fact is reflected

in the following quote from Deng Xiaoping on June 12, 1987: "The greatest achievement that was totally out of our expectation is that rural enterprises [both TVEs and private enterprises] have developed" [*Economic Daily*, June 13, 1993].

4. In fact, in response to a central government austerity program, total TVE employment fell from 48.9 million in 1988 to 47.2 million in 1989, and further to 45.9 million in 1990. In contrast, employment in the state-sector increased during the same period [*China Statistical Yearbook* 1992].

5. During the late 1980s and early 1990s, the total size of SOE industrial output was about twice that of TVEs. However, for each year between 1986 and 1992, loans to all rural enterprises accounted for only about 8 percent of all non-agricultural loans, while loans to SOEs accounted for about 86 percent. During the retrenchment period in the late 1980s, the share of new loans to rural enterprises in total non-agricultural areas declined from 10.2 percent in 1988 to 6.8 percent in 1989, and the share of new loans to SOEs increased from 82.9 percent in 1988 to 90.5 percent in 1989 [*Almanac of China's Finance and Banking* 1993].

6. Before 1994, the leaders of village (township) governments were appointed by township (county) governments. Evidence suggests that community economic performance, especially TVE performance, is an important criteria used for appointments [Whiting 1995]. After 1994, the leaders of village governments have been directly elected by village residents and those of township government are still appointed by county governments.

7. Byrd and Gelb [1990] report a high correlation between county (one level above township) revenues and expenditures within a province in the 1980s, which leads to what they called "ineffective redistribution" across counties and townships in the rural area. Wong [1997] also reports that in the 1990s the rural sector is still very much neglected by the fiscal system. Counties face hard fiscal budget constraints, and, on average, they have inadequate revenues to finance their expenditure responsibilities.

8. In an alternative approach, Weitzman and Xu [1994] point to the Chinese culture for the success of TVEs which they view as vaguely defined cooperatives. We leave this theory out because we are unable to measure variations of the Chinese culture across provinces inside China.

9. Consider other possible objectives of government. Maximization of the budget is not quite relevant given the fixed and limited fiscal transfers from higher level government; maximization of votes is irrelevant because the leaders of townships and villages were not elected before 1994; lobbying for central government projects is not very realistic because the central government usually does not have projects located in rural areas; and promotion to counties does not look very attractive compared to running a profitable enterprise, given the low salary for civil servants and limited power of those offices (on the last point, see Byrd and Gelb [1990]).

10. This would imply that it is possible that local political strength can also benefit the central government.

11. Data of many variables before 1986 is not available. Data after 1994 is not available at the time of this writing. Even if it exists, it may present some problems because since 1994 a new category of ownership emerged known as "joint stock cooperatives," in addition to TVEs and private enterprises, but no unified national rule has yet been established to distinguish this form from TVEs and private firms.

12. In addition, we have also run all corresponding regressions for single years and for the averages over 1986–1993. The results are similar and are reported in the earlier version of the paper.

13. The appendix describes the precise construction of regression variables and their sources.

14. An alternative index would be the total transaction volume between SOEs and the rural industry within a province, but no such data is available. Even if such data were available, it might not be able to capture all aspects of the linkages between SOEs and rural enterprises because such linkages have many dimensions through subcontracting, technology transfers, skill training, trade credit, etc.

15. Outside the state financial institutions, the rural financial market has developed rapidly since the mid-1980s. A study estimates that the capital flows through the informal financial markets were larger than those through the formal state financial institutions after 1990 [Liu 1993].

16. Although rural household savings deposits are the main liability components of the ABC and RCCs, loans to rural enterprises constitute only a small part of their assets as agricultural loans are the major part. Hence, the household savings deposits and state credit to rural enterprises are two different variables.

17. Two other more readily available sets of data are from the *China Statistical Yearbook*, one a non-agricultural population and the other a population of designated cities and towns. But neither of them is appropriate: the former is downward biased, and the latter is upward biased.

18. A more refined approach would distinguish further between farm and non-farm incomes accrued to the three entities. Unfortunately, no such data is available.

19. We also estimated the linear probability model and the results (available upon request) are similar.

20. The "history matters" theory is supported by additional evidence. Simply examining the data over the 8 year period reveals that TVEs grew faster than private enterprises in the provinces where they were initially strong, but more slowly in the provinces where they were initially weak.

21. It is also possible that local political strength is enhanced by TVEs. But our variable of "local political strength" poses less of a problem because it is from 1983 and the dependent variables are after 1986.

22. This might be the case if the state banks had preferred to lend to TVEs and, if there are few TVEs, diverted the loans for other purposes rather than lending to private enterprises. However, because most other loans in rural areas are agricultural loans, which are known to be less attractive to banks than loans to rural industry (including private enterprises), this consideration is less likely to be important.

23. Private assets would also be lower with more TVEs if TVEs had raised a large part of their capital directly from households because household bank deposits would be correspondingly reduced. In the period we consider here, however, this kind of direct financing is not significant [Zhang and Ronnas 1996].

24. In comparison, Oi [1994] reports from her field work that the county government sometimes complained that their revenue was squeezed by TVEs.

25. The results on the household revenue share equation can be derived from the state's and community government's revenue equation because the three revenue shares add up to one.

26. In the estimations including provincial fixed effects, the effect of TVE ownership on the state's share of revenue remains positive and significant while that of the community government's share of revenue becomes insignificant; and the effect of TVE ownership on non-farm employment remains positive and significant while that on income is insignificant. These results (available on request) are consistent with the above findings.

References

Aghion, Philippe, and Jean Tirole, "Formal and Real Authority in Organizations," *Journal of Political Economy*, 105(1):1–29, February, 1997.

Bates, Robert, *Essays on the Political Economy of Rural Africa*, Berkeley: University of California Press, 1987.

Byrd, William, "Entrepreneurship, Capital, and Ownership," chapter 9 in William Byrd and Qingsong Lin (eds.), *China's Rural Industry: Structure, Development, and Reform*, Oxford: Oxford University Press, 1990.

Byrd, William and Allen Gelb, "Why Industrialize? The Incentives for Rural Community Governments," chapter 17 in William Byrd and Qingsong Lin (eds.), *China's Rural Industry: Structure, Development, and Reform*, Oxford: Oxford University Press, 1990.

CAY, *China Agricultural Yearbook*, 1981–1994 annual issues, Beijing: China Agricultural Press.

CDTSY, *China Domestic Trade Statistical Yearbook*, 1991–1994 annual issues, Beijing: China Statistical Press.

Chang, Chun and Yijiang Wang, "The Nature of the Township Enterprise," *Journal of Comparative Economics*, 19:434–452, 1994.

Che, Jiahua and Yingyi Qian, "Institutional Environment, Community Government, and Corporate Governance: Understanding China's Township-Village Enterprises," *Journal of Law, Economics, and Organization*, forthcoming, April, 1998a.

Che, Jiahua and Yingyi Qian, "Insecure Property Rights and Government Ownership of Firms," *Quarterly Journal of Economics*, forthcoming, May, 1998b.

CICAS, *China Industrial and Commerce Administration Statistics 40 Years*, Beijing: China Statistical Press, 1990.

CPY, *China Population Yearbook 1991*, Beijing: China Population Press, 1991.

CRFSY, *China Rural Finance Statistical Yearbook 1989–1994* annul issues, Beijing: China Statistical Press.

CRSY, *China Rural Statistical Yearbook 1984–1994* annual issues, Beijing: China Statistical Press.

CSY, *China Statistical Yearbook 1981–1994* annual issues, Beijing: China Statistical Press.

CTESY, *China Township Enterprises Statistical Yearbook 1987–1994* annul issues, Beijing: China Agricultural Press.

Deaton, Angus, "Data and Econometric Tools for Development Studies," in J. Behrman and T. N. Srinivasan (eds.), *Handbook of Development Economics, Volume III,* Elsevier Science B.V., 1995.

Hart, Oliver, Andrei Shleifer, and Robert W. Vishny, "The Proper Scope of Government: Theory and an Application to Prisons," *Quarterly Journal of Economics,* CXII(4):1127–1162, November, 1997.

Hayami, Yujiro, "Toward an Alternative Paradigm of Economic Development: An Introduction," in Y. Hayami (ed.), *Rural-Based Development of Commerce and Industry: Selected Experience from East Asia,* the World Bank, 1996.

Hoxby, Caroline, and Daniele Paserman, "Overidentification Tests with Grouped Data," mimeo, Harvard University, 1997.

Jefferson, Gary and Thomas Rawski, "Enterprise Reform in China's Industry," *Journal of Economic Perspectives,* 8(2), 47–70, Spring, 1994.

Li, David D., "Ambiguous Property Rights in Transition Economies," *Journal of Comparative Economics,* 23:1–19, 1996.

Liu, Jianjin, "A Study of Borrowing and Lending Behavior of Rural Households in China," *China Rural Economy (Zhongguo Nongcun Jingji),* No. 12, 1993.

Luo, Xiaopeng, "Ownership and Status Stratification," chapter 7 in William Byrd and Qingsong Lin (eds.), *China's Rural Industry: Structure, Development, and Reform,* Oxford: Oxford University Press, 1990.

McKinnon, Ronald, "Financial Control in the Transition to A Market Economy from Classical Socialism," in C. Clague (ed.) *The Emergence of Market Economies in Eastern Europe,* Oxford: Basil Blackwell, 1991.

Naughton, Barry, "Chinese Institutional Innovation and Privatization from Below," *American Economic Review,* 84(2):266–270, May, 1994.

Naughton, Barry, "Why are [some of] China's Rural Industries Publically Owned?" mimeo, University of California at San Diego, 1996.

Nee, Victor, "Organizational Dynamics of Market Transition: Hybrid Forms, Property Rights and Mixed Economy in China," *Administrative Science Quarterly,* 37:1–27, 1992.

Newey, Whitney, "Generalized Method of Moments Specification Testing," *Journal of Econometrics,* 29(3):229–256, September, 1985.

North, Douglass, "Institutions," *Journal of Economic Perspectives,* 5(1):97–112, Winter, 1991.

Oi, Jean, "Fiscal Reform and the Economic Foundations of Local State Corporatism in China," *World Politics,* 45(1):99–126, October, 1992.

Oi, Jean, *Rural China Take off: Incentives for Reform,* book manuscript, Harvard University, 1994.

Otsuka, Keijiro, "Rural Industrialization in East Asia," mimeo, Tokyo Metropolitan University, 1996.

Putterman, Louis, "On the Past and Future of China's Township and Village Owned Enterprises," mimeo, Brown University, 1994.

Qian, Yingyi, and Barry R. Weingast, "Institutions, State Activism, and Economic Development: A Comparison of State-Owned vs. Township-Village Enterprises in China," Chapter 9 in M. Aoki, H. Kim, and M. Okuno-Fujiwara (eds.) *The Role of Government in East Asian Economic Development: Comparative Institutional Analysis*, Oxford University Press, 1996.

Rozelle, Scott and R. N. Boisvert, "Quantifying Chinese Village Leaders' Multiple Objectives," *Journal of Comparative Economics*, 18:25–45, February, 1994.

Shleifer, Andrei, and Robert W. Vishny, "Politicians and Firms," *Quarterly Journal of Economics*, CIX:995–1025, November, 1994.

TESM, *Township Enterprises Statistical Material 1978–1985*, Beijing: Ministry of Agriculture, 1986.

TESM, *Township Enterprises Statistical Material 1986*, Beijing: Ministry of Agriculture, 1987.

Weitzman, Martin and Chenggang Xu, "Chinese Township Village Enterprises as Vaguely Defined Cooperatives," *Journal of Comparative Economics*, 18:121–145, 1994.

Whiting, Susan, *The Micro-Foundations of Institutional Change in Reform China: Property Rights and Revenue Extraction in the Rural Industrial Sector*, Ph.D. dissertation, Department of Political Science, University of Michigan, 1995.

Wong, Christine, "Interpreting Rural Industrial Growth in the Post-Mao Period," *Modern China*, 14(1):3–30, 1988.

Wong, Christine, "The Maoist 'Model' Reconsidered: Local Self-Reliance and its Financing of Rural Industrialization," in William Joseph, Christine Wong, and David Zweig (eds.), *New Perspectives on the Cultural Revolution*, Cambridge: Harvard University Press, 1991.

Wong, Christine, *Financing Local Governments in the People's Republic of China*, Oxford University Press, 1997.

Zhang, Gang, "Government Intervention versus Marketization," in Per Ronnas (ed.), *Rural Industries in Post-Reform China: An Inquiry into Their Characteristics*, International Labor Organization and South Asia Multi-Disciplinary Advisory Team, New Delhi, 1996.

Zhang, Gang, and Per Ronnas, "The Capital Structure of Township Enterprises," in Per Ronnas (ed.), *Rural Industries in Post-Reform China: An Inquiry into Their Characteristics*, International Labor Organization and South Asia Multi-Disciplinary Advisory Team, New Delhi, 1996.

III GOVERNMENT AND REFORM: FEDERALISM, CHINESE STYLE

7 Federalism, Chinese Style: The Political Basis for Economic Success in China

1. Introduction

The remarkable success of China's economic reforms—fostering economic growth averaging 9 percent per year over the past fifteen years—seems to defy conventional wisdom. Consider the following:

- Economic reform appears to have been successfully pursued without any political reform.
- The central government seems to retain considerable political discretion, including the ability to reverse suddenly the reform process or to impose onerous exactions on successful enterprises.
- Finally, there have been few attempts to provide the central feature of private markets, a system of secure private property rights. Nor has an attempt been made to develop a commercial law (for example, property and contract law) or an independent court system for adjudication.

Each of these factors bodes ill for economic reform. Without political reform, economic returns remain at the mercy of political predation. Political discretion, in turn, implies that there are no impediments to the government reversing the reforms. In this context, leadership turnover would allow the new government not only to reverse the reforms, but also to confiscate considerable wealth and to punish those who were successful under the reforms. Alternatively, problems may occur during unexpectedly hard times. With severe budget problems and a population clamoring for "solutions, now," the immediate need for revenue produces powerful pressure for a partial or wholesale reversal of the reforms. This type of discretion typically kills the prospects of any reform program.[1] Because economic agents know in advance that

With Gabriella Montinola and Barry R. Weingast; originally published in *World Politics*, October 1995, 48(1), pp. 50–81.

political discretion affords no protection for their economic success, they are unlikely to put their effort and wealth into undertakings that put them at risk, and hence the reforms will fail. These problems are seemingly further exacerbated in China by the lack of a system of private-property rights—a clear, necessary condition for a successful market system. All these factors point toward poor performance for Chinese economic reform.

The actual performance of the Chinese reforms provides a striking contrast to these expectations. Over the past fifteen years, China's performance potentially parallels that of the other high-growth East Asian economies. The juxtaposition of the conventional wisdom with experience demands an explanation.

The purpose of this paper is to provide such an explanation. We argue that the problem with the conventional wisdom is several fold. First, it provides too narrow a definition of political reform. Second, although it asks the right question about political discretion, the inappropriate definition of political reform leads it to the wrong conclusion. Third, though much is wrong with the system of property rights in China, looking for a system of such rights as exists in the West has confused many analysts. Rights are not as secure in China as they could be, and the absence of a law of property and contracts along with a judicial system to enforce it remains a significant lacuna in the reform process. Yet, property rights are not completely insecure and without political foundation. Indeed, political reform in China has placed considerable limits on the discretion of the central government. These limits, in turn, provide the beginnings of a strong and credible political foundation for many market-oriented enterprises throughout the successful regions of China.

To understand the basis for these claims, we begin with the notion of political reform. In the common parlance, political reform focuses on democratization and hence the separation of the Chinese Communist Party (CCP) from the state.[2] On this important component of reform, China has made little progress. Nearly all the formal aspects of democracy are absent, notably, individual rights of free speech and political participation, a viable system of competition for political office and a set of constitutional limits on the state. As democracy is one of the most central aspects of political freedom, China's record speaks for itself.

Yet, democratization does not encompass all aspects of political reform. So what has changed? We emphasize three principal factors. First, not only has political decentralization enhanced the powers of local government, but it has also altered central-local government relations in several critical ways that are difficult, though not impossible, to reverse.[3] Second, a major shift in ideology underpins the reforms, with the CCP moving from a dogmatic emphasis on the Maoist version of Marxism-Leninism to a pragmatic, market-oriented approach. Although the rhetoric of socialism has been retained (for example, the recent emphasis on the "socialist market economy"), the staunch anti-market, anti-private initiative, anti-private gain focus has been removed. Third, China has for the first time under the communists opened its economy.

In our view, these changes have resulted in a new political system that we characterize as *federalism, Chinese style*. This system, in turn, provides considerable political protection for China's reforms, including limits on the central government. Viewed from the perspective of the individual, this system differs considerably from federalisms in the developed West.[4] Viewed from the perspective of the political relationships among the different levels of government, China's political de-centralization shares much in common with Western federalisms. The modern Chinese system includes a division of authority between the central and local governments. The latter have primary control over economic matters within their jurisdictions. Critically, there is an important degree of political durability built into the system.

As we argue, the Chinese system provides a partial basis for a special kind of federalism called *market-preserving federalism*.[5] Central to the success of market-preserving federalism is the element of political durability built into the arrangements, meaning that the decentralization of power is not merely at the discretion of the central political authorities. And here, conventional wisdom's focus on the relationship between the national government and the individual results in erroneous judgments, for this focus ignores the relationship between the central authorities and the provincial and lower governments. The latter relationships have not only changed dramatically, but have done so in ways that are difficult to undo. They thus provide a degree of commitment.

Nonetheless, the new economy is not without its limitations. An understanding of how China's current system differs from a more complete system of market-preserving federalism provides some guide to both its current problems and solutions to them. First, China lacks an adequate mechanism for policing the internal common market. This absence explains in part why many local governments have focused on trade barriers and aggressive anti-market policies within their jurisdiction. Second, political decentralization has yet to be institution-alized to ensure its long-term stability. A third problem is the absence of private property rights and a commercial law, as many have noted. These limitations should not be seen as economically debilitating; rather they should be seen as problems that need to be addressed in the near future.

This paper proceeds as follows. The next section discusses the theory of federalism and is divided into two parts. The first examines the necessary political foundations of market-preserving federalism while the second examines the economic consequences of federalism. Sections 3 and 4 turn to federalism, Chinese style, paralleling the two parts of section 2. Section 3 discusses whether and how the conditions of market-preserving federalism hold in China. Section 4 reveals the remarkable parallel between the predicted effects of market-preserving federalism and China's decentralization. This approach also helps order the seemingly chaotic variety of behavior in the different prov-inces and localities. Much of this variation, especially the trends in behavior, policy, and economic outcomes, is as predicted by the theory of federalism. Several imperfections of the system are also noted. Our conclusions follow in Section 5.

2.   The Theory of Market-Preserving Federalism

Political Foundations of Market-Preserving Federalism
A fundamental dilemma faces a government attempting to build and protect markets: it must not only be strong enough to enforce the legal rights and rules necessary to maintain the economy, but it must also be strong enough to commit itself credibly to honoring such rules.[6] In the absence of credible limits on governmental behavior, nothing prevents the government from taking away wealth from the citizens for its own purposes. This behavior may take many forms: an outright con-fiscation of wealth, onerous taxation, or inflationary financing by print-ing money. The absence of a credible commitment, in turn, adversely affects the "positive incentives" of economic agents. Because rational actors understand that this political environment reduces their eco-nomic benefits *ex post*, they will withhold their efforts, investments, and information *ex ante*, thus jeopardizing economic growth.

Another form of the lack of commitment can be seen in a govern-ment that is unable to impose a "hard budget constraint" on itself and other economic agents.[7] In this case, the government continues to bail out or subsidize troubled institutions and agents.[8] Lack of commitment fails to provide "negative incentives" to economic institutions and agents, who rationally distort their efforts, typically leading to wasteful investment and low productivity. Put simply, the soft-budget constraint eliminates the need for sensible planning since mistakes are not costly to the decision makers.[9]

Reputation is often held as an important mechanism to achieve credible commitment, but it alone is hardly sufficient. Political institutions are also necessary because, in the appropriate form, they provide for a balance of power that can make commitment credible.[10]

One set of political institutions that play this role are those surrounding federalism. Understanding the implications of federalism requires a clear notion of how it is sustained, that is, of its political foundations. Most studies simply take federalism as an exogenously specified system, focusing on its effects. For the purposes of studying the consequences of federalism in the developed West (for example, in Switzerland or the United States), this often involves no great loss. For the purposes of implementing and perfecting a new system of federalism, however, an appreciation of its political foundations proves essential.

The fundamental feature of federalism is decentralization; however, not all systems of decentralization are federal. To understand federalism, we must identify its principal characteristics. As a special type of federalism, *market-preserving federalism* encompasses a set of conditions that governs the allocation of authorities and responsibilities among different levels of government:

(F1) A *hierarchy* of governments with a *delineated scope of authority* (for example, between the national and subnational governments) exists so that each government is autonomous in its own sphere of authority.

(F2) The subnational governments have primary *authority over the economy* within their jurisdictions.

(F3) The national government has the authority to police the *common market* and to ensure the mobility of goods and factors across subgovernment jurisdictions.

(F4) Revenue sharing among governments is limited and borrowing by governments is constrained so that all governments face *hard budget constraints*.

(F5) The allocation of authority and responsibility has an *institutionalized degree of durability* so that it cannot be altered by the national government either unilaterally or under the pressures from subnational governments.

These conditions represent an ideal type of institutional arrangement of a market-preserving federalism. The purpose of these institutions is in part to limit the degree to which a political system can encroach on markets.[11]

Condition 1 contains the defining characteristic of federalism. But formalized decentralization alone does not generate federalism's market-preserving qualities. These require the addition of conditions 2–5.

From the perspective of preserving market incentives, the authority of the national government over markets is limited to policing the common market across regions (condition 3) and providing national public goods, which should not be left to the subnational level governments (for example, monetary policy).

The institutional arrangements of federalism recognize a critical difference between the national government and the subnational governments: there is only one of the former but many of the latter. The natural limits on the discretionary authority of the subnational level governments are induced by competition among jurisdictions. But this competition is beneficial only if there are no trade barriers and the entire nation becomes a common market (condition 3). Without condition 3, each subnational government would become something of a *de facto* "national government" in its jurisdiction, and its discretionary authority over the economy again would limit its ability to make a credible commitment. Condition 2 thus enhances the effects of condition 3. If decentralization remained at the discretion of the national government, the latter could intervene in the economy first by using its discretion (in the absence of condition 2) to compromise the system of federalism and then to intervene.

The constraint of condition 4 has two parts, one for fiscal revenue transfers between levels of governments, and one for borrowing through the financial system. The hard budget constraint in the fiscal channel limits revenue sharing and equalization among governments, especially through soft grants. The hard budget constraint in the financial channel restricts open-ended access to capital markets, especially borrowing from the central bank. Condition 4 applies to both the national government and the subnational governments. A hard budget constraint for the latter is necessary because it directly ties local revenue to local economic prosperity. A local government's financial problems remain its own, providing important incentives for local officials to oversee and ensure their government's fiscal health. If, in contrast, local governments were readily bailed out of their financial problems, they would have considerably fewer incentives to worry about the consequences of their choices. The constraint on the national government is necessary in part because a soft budget constraint would allow it to use monetary discretion to get around the limits on its authority.

Condition 5 provides for credible commitment to the federal system and thus for limits on the national government's discretionary authority. Not only must there be decentralization, but that decentralization must not be under the discretionary control of the national government. Condition 5 addresses the enforcement problem and is critically important. It is also likely, however, that an individual country, due to its own unique history and complicated social conditions, may require a different arrangement.

Market-preserving federalism's balance of power between the national and subnational governments is superior to either a complete centralization with a unitary government or a complete decentralization with each region an independent state. Under complete centralization or decentralization, the national government's authority is not limited through internal institutional arrangements; hence a potential danger exists for the discretionary authority to encroach on markets.

Before turning to the economic implications of market-preserving federalism, we pause to discuss the relationship between the conditions underlying market-preserving federalism and various systems of federalism throughout the world. Our approach shows that whether a nation calls itself federal—"de jure federalism"—is irrelevant.[12] What matters is whether the various conditions hold. Many de jure federalisms are nothing like market-preserving federalisms, for example, in Argentina, Brazil, and India. In these cases, conditions 2 and 5, and often condition 4, fail. The failure of conditions 2 and 5 implies that the political discretion and authority retained by the central government in these systems greatly compromises their market-preserving qualities. As discussed later in this section, these conditions are a necessary component of federalism's market-preserving qualities.

The contrast between market-preserving federalism and the decentralization of the former Soviet Union is also instructive. The Soviet system was characterized by administrative decentralization without authority. Lower governments were largely administrative units of the central government with little autonomous political power, let alone power over their local economies. The center also carefully controlled factor mobility. Hence all but condition 1 failed in that system.[13]

In sum, though many forms of political decentralization exist, only a narrow subset is characterized by market-preserving federalism.

The Economic Effects of Market-Preserving Federalism

The most important implication of market-preserving federalism is the induced competition among jurisdictions,[14] which produces a number of salutary effects. First, no government has a monopoly of regulatory authority over the entire economy. Any subnational government that seeks to use its authority for purposes of monopolization or other political ends is at a considerable disadvantage because it cannot impose its will on the entire economy. When a particular jurisdiction imposes an onerous restriction on its firms, the latter face a competitive disadvantage relative to competing firms from other jurisdictions that are not bound by the restriction. Producers outside the particular jurisdiction are not bound by these rules and, hence, their costs will be lower and they will outsell those firms bound by the restriction.

Second, competition among jurisdictions extends to factors of production, such as capital and labor. Jurisdictions are thus induced to provide a hospitable environment for factors, typically through the provision of local, public goods such as establishing a basis for secure rights of factor owners, the provision of infrastructure, utilities, access to markets, and so on. Those jurisdictions that fail to provide these goods find that factors move to other jurisdictions. Local economic activity and tax revenue decline as a consequence.

Third, the hard budget constraint implies that local governments can go bankrupt. This provides them with incentives for proper fiscal management.[15] Local enterprises, local politicians, and citizens in particular areas hardly want their government to spend more money than is prudent. Bankruptcy would greatly hinder the ability of local governments to finance needed public goods, such as those needed to attract foreign capital and lower business costs.

Finally, market-preserving federalism provides the political foundations for markets.[16] By placing the authority over markets in the hands of lower governments, it fosters local economic prosperity. By keeping the central government out of this activity, it prevents massive intervention of political goals that distort markets for other purposes. Once established, markets are difficult to alter since national political forces are deflected from this issue and, at the local level, it is hard for a group with any particular goal to capture the lion's share of the local governments. In turn, the implication is that some governments are always likely to retain their pro-market focus. Market-preserving federalism, therefore, diminishes the prevalence of rent-seeking and patronage systems. The latter can only survive in areas with political protection from market forces, a phenomenon that market-preserving federalism is designed to eliminate.

Predictions Following the Inception of Market-Preserving Federalism. Following the imposition of a system of federalism we should observe a diversity of policy choices and experiments. People in different political jurisdictions are likely to have markedly different interests, expectations, and capabilities. We should, therefore, observe that they choose a range of policies to promote their goals.

As the results of these experiments and policies become known, individuals and policymakers will update their expectations about the effects of various policies. Thus, decentralization under market-preserving federalism results in an important degree of feedback, which would not be present under a unitary system that imposes a single national experiment over all regions.

Competition among jurisdictions provides incentives to replace poorly chosen strategies with variants of strategies that appear to succeed elsewhere. To the extent that some jurisdictions are better at promoting markets, generating wealth, and caring for the needs of their citizens, their policies are likely to be imitated by others that have been less successful. Still, we do not expect the appearance of uniformity among jurisdictions for several reasons. First, individuals and firms will sort themselves into jurisdictions; to the extent, for example, that they require different types of public goods. Second, resources and access to markets imply that a variety of economic and political differences will survive.[17] Finally, individuals are likely to vary in their tastes for public goods, as well as in their ability to pay for them.

Predictions When Market-Preserving Federalism Remains Incomplete. The set of predictions just noted will vary in systematic ways if particular components of market-preserving federalism are missing. We discuss the implications of two limitations on market-preserving federalism. The first concerns the absence of a common market, allowing individual jurisdictions to erect trade barriers. The principal difference is that the common market is highly unlikely to be sustained without explicit protection from the central authorities.[18] This implies that some areas, particularly those not likely to perform well under competition with jurisdictions, are likely to erect trade barriers to firms and products from other areas. A federalism of this sort (which is only incompletely market-preserving) will produce seemingly contradictory results. Some areas will promote markets while others will closely control their economy, especially from influence outside the jurisdiction.

We also expect this juxtaposition to be more pronounced in jurisdictions just after a system of federalism is imposed than in a more mature system, especially in an economy like China's with only limited experience with markets. Limited exposure to markets naturally generates suspicion of them and of their potential dependence on outsiders. The feedback provided by multiple jurisdictions that conduct independent experiments is important for the next stage. As the market grows in those areas that commit themselves to it, the tendency of other jurisdictions toward protectionism will diminish. The experience with markets will reveal new information about how they allow local governments to provide for the needs of citizens. Even in the presence of strong trade barriers, fiscal pressures will push insulated areas to substitute market mechanisms for those activities that have been demonstrated elsewhere to be superior providers of particular goods and services. Nonetheless, some regions may never foster markets.

The second explicit limit on market-preserving federalism concerns the absence of centralized control over the monetary system. To the extent that the authority over credit, for example, is not centralized, but remains, at least in part, at the discretion of lower governments, several problems are likely to emerge. The most obvious is inflation as each government over grazes the "commons," causing too much growth in the money supply. The second problem is a consequence of the first. Decentralized access to credit under these circumstances also softens the hard budget constraint as governments that increase their exposure can always borrow more in the short run. This induces moral hazard— for example, too much borrowing to finance too many investments, many of which would not be financed were it not for access to credit in this manner.

3. Federalism, Chinese Style

The decentralization in China differs from Western federalism in several important respects. First, the latter virtually always root federalism in an explicit system for protecting individual rights. Second, Western federalism typically has strong, explicit constitutional foundations. Third, it is almost always associated with political freedom, representation, and democratization. None of these factors are present in China. Notice, however, that as defined above, market-preserving federalism in no way depends on these factors. Instead, it depends on the political relationships among levels of government with no reference to an explicit or constitutional basis or its promotion of individual rights and political freedom.

In this section, we present evidence from China on each of the five conditions, both positive and negative, underlying market-preserving federalism. As we show, with some important qualifications, the conditions are satisfied.

The differences between Western and Chinese federalism noted above constitute the first aspect of federalism, Chinese style. The second aspect concerns the specific nature of the institutional changes of decentralization underpinning the reforms, the increased reliance on markets, and openness to the outside world. Perhaps the most significant steps toward reform taken by the Chinese central government were its decentralization of authority from the central to local governments and, to a lesser degree, the state-owned enterprises. The idea of decentralization in China is not new—it experienced two previous waves of "administrative decentralization," the Great Leap Forward in 1958 and the Cultural Revolution in 1970. Decentralization in the 1980s differed, however, in that it is combined with financial incentives, reliance on market mechanisms, increased control for lower governments over their economies, and a new openness to international markets. These features generate far reaching consequences for political institutions and economic performance.[19]

Decentralization of Authority

Even before the current economic reform began in 1979, a large number of state-owned industrial enterprises in both light and heavy industries were controlled by local governments rather than the central government. In 1978, the share of industrial output of state-owned enterprises controlled by the central government was less than one-half of the national total.[20] In the early 1980s, as a result of the reforms, many state-owned enterprises controlled by the central government were delegated to local governments. By 1985, state-owned industrial enterprises controlled by the central government accounted for only 20 percent of the total industrial output from such enterprises at or above township level. At the same time, provincial and city governments controlled 45 percent, county governments 9 percent, and the rest came from township enterprises.[21]

Unlike previous decentralizations which were carried out within the framework of central planning, provincial and local governments under the market-oriented reforms enjoyed a wide range of authority within the market environment. More and more foreign capital, for example, flowed into firms and projects that were not controlled by the central government. The total foreign investment in China increased from $4.5 billion in 1985 to $19.2 billion in 1992 (among the largest investors were Hong Kong, Taiwan, U.S., and Japan). At the same time, the share of foreign investment administered by provinces (rather than ministries of the central government) increased from 35 percent in 1985 to 68 percent in 1992.[22]

Many reform policies were also delegated to provinces and local governments. For example, China did not liberalize prices in one stroke. The dual-price system was a common practice in China in the 1980s, with one planned price and another market price. A little known fact is that, for many goods, moving from a dual-price system to a single-price system was not carried out solely by the central government, but also by local governments. Decisions about prices were largely delegated to lower-level governments. (Exceptions to this generalization are some nationally important goods, like energy and transportation services.) Many governments have extended their authority to pursue reform to liberalize the prices. With grain prices, which had been under the control of the central government, Guangdong took the lead in liberalization in 1992, and many other provinces have since followed suit.

Decentralization of authority is particularly associated with the establishment of special economic zones, coastal open cities, and development zones. In 1979 China established four special economic zones: Shenzhen; Zhuhai; Shantou, adjacent to Hong Kong in Guangdong Province; and Xiamen, in Fujian Province across the Taiwan strait.[23] Subsequently, Guangdong and Fujian gained substantial autonomy in developing their regions when the central government granted them authority to pursue reform "one step ahead." Not only did these areas enjoy lower tax rates, but they gained more authority over economic development. For example, they have the authority to approve foreign investment projects up to $30 million, while other regions' authority remains much lower.

In 1984 the central government declared fourteen coastal cities as "coastal open cities," conveying to them new authority that paralleled power granted earlier only to special economic zones. In the early 1990s treatment of special economic zones was extended to various inland regions. For example, some inland cities along the Yangtze River and cities bordering Russia obtained similar authority as the coastal cities. Furthermore, many inland cities, which did not qualify for these special treatments as a whole, established numerous "development zones" inside their regions to enjoy part of the tax benefits and autonomy.

Fiscal Incentives: The Fiscal Contracting System
Starting in 1980, China implemented a fiscal revenue-sharing system between any two adjacent levels of governments.[24] Although schemes vary across both regions and time, the basic idea is that a lower-level regional government contracts with the upper-level regional government on the total amount (or share) of tax and profit revenue (negative values imply a reverse flow of subsidies) to be remitted for the next several years; the lower-level government keeps the rest. This system was maintained until the end of 1993, and a new fiscal system was introduced in the beginning of 1994.

Consider fiscal contracting schemes between the central and provincial governments (lower-level fiscal contracting is similar). In the first step, revenue income in each province is divided between "central fixed revenue," all of which is remitted to the center, and "local revenue," which is subject to sharing. In the second step, a particular formula of sharing is determined. There were six basic types of sharing schemes for the thirty provinces and five cities during 1988–1993.[25]

(1) **Fixed sharing**: a fixed proportion is remitted to the center (three provinces/cities);

(2) **Incremental sharing**: a certain proportion is retained up to a quota, and then a higher proportion is retained in excess of the quota (three provinces/cities);

(3) **Sharing up to a limit with growth adjustment**: the localities retain a specified proportion that is within a specific percentage of revenue from the previous year, and then retain all above that quota (ten provinces/cities);

(4) **Fixed quota delivery**: a specified, nominal amount is remitted to the center (three provinces/cities);

(5) **Fixed quota with growth adjustment**: the fixed amount remitted to the center is increased at a contracted rate (two provinces/cities);

(6) **Fixed subsidies** (fourteen provinces/cities).

The importance of these new fiscal arrangements is that they induce a strong positive relationship between local revenue and local economic prosperity for all provinces and cities, thus providing local officials with an incentive to foster that prosperity. Schemes (4) to (6), which cover nineteen out of thirty-five provinces or cities, at the margin allow local governments to retain 100 percent of local revenues. Scheme (3), which covers another ten provinces and cities, has the same effect when the increased revenue limits for sharing are not a binding constraint. Even in scheme (2), the marginal remittance rate is regressive.

The fiscal contracting in budgetary revenue described above is only one aspect of fiscal decentralization; the other is the expansion of the so-called "extra-budgetary" funds (certain categories of revenues collected by the local governments and ministries, including some retained profits of state-owned enterprises). In the early 1990s, the extra-budgetary revenue reached about the same level as budgetary revenue. Unlike the budgetary revenue, which is subject to sharing with the higher governments, the extra-budgetary revenue is wholly retained by the local government. Moreover, the local government has complete authority over the determination of taxes or fees that fall into the categories of "extra budget." The decentralized nature of extra-budgetary revenues also increases local government security from predation by the central government, as such revenues are easier to hide from the higher governments. These funds are especially valuable to local governments as their use is more flexible than budgetary revenues.

By way of summary, these changes provide for substantial independence of the governments in China, from the provincial to the township, which ensures that governments in each region assume primary responsibility for economic development in that region. Hence, these governments possess both significant fiscal autonomy from the central government and considerable independent authority over their economies.

Notice the striking contrast between this system and that of the former communist system, including the former Soviet Union and Eastern Europe. In the latter, the central authorities retained the discretionary authority to the profits "earned" by producers, typically using this authority both to take resources from those firms with positive earnings and to bail out those with negative earnings. This discretionary redistribution was described in the Soviet Union by the Russian word *uravnilovka*, which translates as "equalization" or "leveling off."[26]

The Common Market Condition
In contrast to the decentralizations accompanying the Great Leap Forward and the Cultural Revolution, decentralization in the current reform is associated with increasing marketization. The development of good and factor mobility across regions is considerable, but remains imperfect. On the one hand, there are clear signs of increased factor mobility over time, as evidenced by the huge "floating migrant" population and the foreign-capital inflow. On the other hand, decentralization has increased the incentives as well as the range of political means for local governments to erect trade barriers, resulting in the so-called "dukedom economies" phenomenon which has worried the central government and economists. This form of protectionism has occurred most often in the markets of high profit-margin manufacturing goods (such as automobile, tobacco products, and alcohol) and raw materials in short supply (such as cotton, silkworm cocoons, tobacco, and aluminum).

The imperfect common market implies that some areas have used their political freedom to maintain considerable trade barriers.[27] We offer two examples. First, consider automobile assembly. The total production of automobiles in China was around 1.2 million in 1992, despite the fact that it had more than 126 assembly factories, with an average production of 10,000 units.[28] Almost all provinces have their own automobile factory. Such an inefficient scale can be maintained only in the presence of substantial government protection: tariffs at the national level and various trade barriers at the regional level.[29]

Second, in 1985 Jiangxi Province liberalized hog procurement.[30] As a result of the large demand from rich neighboring provinces, such as Guangdong and Fujian, hog prices increased rapidly. To maintain the welfare of its urban constituents, the local governments of Jiangxi attempted to keep the urban retail pork price of local government-owned food companies at a low level. The local governments thus spent a large amount of their budgets on subsidizing hog sales in local cities. As it was more profitable for rural households to sell hogs to neighboring rich provinces where hog prices were much higher, hogs were exported out of the region. At the end of 1985, the Jiangxi provincial government reacted to this situation (in which the "Jiangxinese raise hogs and Cantonese consume pork") by establishing tax offices on the provincial border. Their purpose was to develop a so-called "hog development fund" derived from hog sales out of the region. Since this fund actually could be captured by any level of authorities that charged it, many county and even township governments in Jiangxi set up tax offices. In response, hog production decreased dramatically.[31]

As these examples suggest, the imperfect policing of the common market allows local governments to insulate themselves from competition by erecting trade barriers. These barriers also allow the emergence of corruption. In insulated regions beyond the reach of the central government, local officials can take advantage of their power for personal gain. In the presence of open competition, this type of corruption is harder to sustain because of market pressure.

The Hard Budget Constraint Condition

At all levels of government, fiscal budget constraints are relatively hard due to the declining tax revenues and the limited intergovernmental budgetary transfers under the fiscal revenue sharing schemes. The one exception is the state banking system, which has become the most significant source of the soft budget constraint for governments at or above the county level.

China's state banking system features a central bank supervising four major specialized state banks. The banking institutions in China evolved from the planning era in which the central bank and each of the four specialized banks established a branch in every province, municipality and county. Under regional decentralization, the regional governments at provincial, municipality, and county levels also gained great influence over credit decisions through the regional branches of the central bank and specialized banks. The local bank branches were under the "dual subordination" principle (*shuangchong lingdao*): they were subordinated to the banking hierarchy as well as to the local government. As reform proceeded, the latter carried more weight. *Ex ante*, the local governments were directly involved in the credit-plan formulation and might impose loans on specialized banks. *Ex post*, the local governments had the authority to decide whether the enterprise should pay back the loan.

The absence of a unified monetary system has allowed local governments access to credit in a way that has expanded the money supply. When all local governments behave in this manner, the result is inflation. Yet not one of them has an incentive to stop; each province claims that overheating is caused by the other provinces, not by itself. This has the structure of the "tragedy of the commons" and is the main reason that the monetary system is a national public good: it must be controlled by a single authority, and best by a national one.[32]

The Case for Township and Village Governments

Central, prefecture, municipal, and county governments all have full authority in the Chinese governmental hierarchy to regulate the market through administrative methods. But township and village governments have very limited authority. Historically, their responsibility was confined to agriculture and rural governance and they had no control over state-owned enterprises (SOEs) and no access to the state banking system. These institutional constraints have made the township and village governments somewhat different from the higher level governments: township and village governments operate under a hard budget constraint and without trade barriers. Both conditions were somewhat relaxed, however, for higher level governments in China. In this sense, the Chinese federalism seems to better approximate a market-preserving one at the township and village levels than at higher levels.

One result of China's reform is the spectacular growth of the market in the flourishing sector of township-village enterprises (TVEs), which are owned by township and village communities and controlled by township and village governments.[33] By the end of 1993, TVEs produced 30 percent of the total industrial output in China. This remarkable success of TVEs can be understood from the incentives facing these firms. First, the structure of these firms affords residual claim rights (in essence, the rights to profits) to township and village governments. Second, two forms of limits are imposed upon the township and village governments and their firms. The first limit is that these governments do not have the authority to enact protectionist policies. They cannot use political means to protect their firms, for example, by erecting trade barriers to keep out competition. The second limit is a hard budget constraint. Not only may they go bankrupt, but the local governments, in contrast to the central government that can print money, cannot endlessly bail them out. In 1989, for example, about three million TVEs went bankrupt or were taken over by other TVEs. In the same year almost all loss-making state-owned enterprises were bailed out by the state.[34] Furthermore, total credit going to the TVE sector was no more than 8 percent of the total outstanding loans, despite the fact that this sector produced more than 25 percent of total industrial output at the time.[35] Although both TVEs and SOEs are "owned" by governments, their incentives and hence their behavior are far different.[36]

Durability and Irreversibility of Federalism, Chinese Style
Decentralization began with the delegation of considerable economic authority to local governments. These governments assumed primary authority over economic matters within their jurisdiction. We have also suggested that the reforms have provided considerable limits on the discretion of the central government. They are also often associated with the emergence of strong regional economic powers, such as Guangdong Province. These limits seem to endow the reforms with a degree of durability, making reversal more costly, if not impossible. Three events after the Tiananmen Square uprising in 1989 demonstrate these conclusions.

(1) After Tiananmen Square, 1989–1991. The single best indication of the linkage between durability of reform and decentralization concerns the events following Tiananmen Square, especially between 1989 and 1991 under the austerity program. During that period, the conservatives gained the most political, ideological, and military power for a possible reversal. Li Peng tried to recentralize investment and financial powers but failed. The governor of Guangdong refused to cooperate, and many other governors followed.[37] This, however, is only part of the story.

This incident suggests the striking new power of local governments to shape decisions by the central government. On several previous occasions when the economy faced difficulties (for example, in 1962 and 1981), Chen Yun, an advocate for central planning, succeeded in compelling the provincial governments to "help the central government overcome the difficulties," that is, to turn over more revenue to the central budget. The contrast between this situation and Li Peng's failed attempt illustrates our point: the limits on the discretion of the central government provides for the durability of reforms.

Five considerations support this claim. First, by this time, the price of recentralization had increased. In order to recentralize, the central government would have to undertake substantial new obligations by providing social safety-net expenditures. A major retrenchment would increase the regime's financial obligations while the economy would shrink as firms, successful under markets, withered. This raises immediate financial problems: How would these obligations be financed? Fiscal problems of this magnitude raise the specter of the former Soviet Union's failure, surely a possibility to be avoided. Further, a major retrenchment would risk considerable social problems.

Second, some regions have already accumulated sufficient wealth in ways that do not allow the central government to easily confiscate the revenue because the regional governments followed a strategy of "storing wealth in people and in enterprises." The regional governments also have greater vested interest in continuing the reform.[38]

Third, incentive structures within the government and the Party have altered considerably. In advanced regions, many officials no longer care to be promoted to posts in the higher level government.[39] This is because officials enjoy a higher level of autonomy, which also translates into higher financial benefits, at a lower level of government. This provides a striking contrast to the earlier period in which most officials wanted to climb the Party ladder. Thus, in Guangdong Province today, township officials do not want to be promoted to the county level, municipal officials do not want to be promoted to the provincial level, and provincial officials do not want to be promoted to the central government.

This difference reflects an important change in political incentives. Local political officials are now far less beholden to the central authorities. In the past, central authorities retained a variety of incentives to control the behavior of lower officials: fiscal control of local government operations allowed them to manipulate local decision making, and individuals were promoted for appropriate behavior and punished for behavior deemed inappropriate. Each of these incentives has been weakened under the current arrangements. Although the central government retains control over the army and over the appointment and dismissal of high-level personnel, the power of these tools is weaker than when they were combined with the more micro-level incentives employed during previous eras.

Fourth, the fall of socialism in Eastern Europe and the former Soviet Union has had an important impact on China. China's immediate reaction to the collapse of these communist regimes was recentralization, but the Chinese government soon realized that its legitimacy could only be sustained by economic growth. A reversal of the reforms that cut off access to international markets would result in significant shrinking of domestic production and unemployment, thus dramatically increasing the demands on the central government. An outright reversal of the reforms would greatly expand the central government's fiscal commitments while dramatically contracting the economy, putting the regime at risk. Complementing this financial incentive is the economic stake due to openness to the international market, in particular, pressure from the booming East Asian neighbors. Further, the sheer growth of the market economy makes the imposition of a new round of central control of the economy difficult, if only because the central government no longer retains the capacity to monitor the vast new economy.

A final aspect of the reforms, as often claimed, is that a majority of Chinese people seem to have gained economically under the reforms, including farmers, workers, and even most bureaucrats. A widespread feeling that reforms have left people better off places a large constraint on any attempt to reverse reforms.

(2) Deng's southern tour, 1992. The above evidence suggests that the reforms were not reversed after the Tiananmen Square incident in part because of the increased political power of local governments. Amid the political deadlock within the central government at the end of 1991, Deng Xiaoping made his now famous southern tour to the province of Guangdong. Among his stops were several special economic zones. Using the regional support for continued reforms, Deng's visit tipped the political balance of the central government. This resulted in the central government's official declaration in October 1992 to build a "socialist market economy."[40] Ending the deadlock revealed two inter-related elements about the security of the reforms. First, it indicated that the immediate threat to the reforms after Tiananmen had failed. Second, the failure of the retrenchment revealed that the reforms were protected by a degree of durability.

(3) Rationalization and institutionalization, 1993–1994. Further evidence for the durability of the reforms and decentralization is provided by the recent controversies over recentralization.

In the transition from a planned to a market economy, certain types of overshooting in decentralization have not been avoided. Several problems have thus emerged from the lack of central authority, raising calls for a recentralization. The crucial question is this: Will the central government use the occasion for centralization and reversal to the old system, or will it have to justify its action as an integrated part of more reforms, that is, a process of rationalization of market institutions? We provide two examples below indicating the latter path.

In the first half of 1993 the economy seemed to become "over-heated," reflecting problems of macroeconomic imbalance similar to those experienced in 1988. This caused instability in the foreign exchange market. At first, the government attempted to control the exchange rate through administrative methods by imposing a ceiling, but this failed. The market exchange rate was later stabilized in July 1993 when the central bank sold dollars rather than imposing ceilings. This intervention was followed soon by the implementation of foreign-exchange reform on January 1, 1994, which unified the previous official and market rates and essentially achieved trade-account convertibility.

Second, amid the continuing decline of central government revenue as a proportion of GDP from 31 percent in 1978 to 15 percent in 1992 (within-budget consolidated revenue), the call for an increase of government revenue comes together with a proposal for enacting a more formal system of fiscal federalism, which was implemented in January 1994. The new fiscal system, which resembles that of the United States, established a two-tier tax-administration system (national and local) that separates taxes into national, local, and shared taxes. It also simplifies tax rates and makes them more uniform. Furthermore, rule-based transfer formulas are being studied for possible implementation in the future. The reason for such a shift toward a formal fiscal federalism is that it appears impossible (prohibitively costly) to collect more revenue through methods of centralization, and fiscal federalism is the only alternative that will satisfy both central and local governments. Importantly, it holds the promise of resolving the problems of an overly weak government without removing the beneficial effects of the decentralization. A direct recentralization, in contrast, would threaten to remove this essential political component underlying the success of the economic reforms.

Summary. A range of factors contributes to the durability of the reforms, limiting the discretion of the central government to attempt a reversal. First, as a result of the reforms, new, rival power centers have emerged in China. Local governments, particularly those in areas with the largest growth, now have substantial independent sources of revenue, authority, and political support. Second, although local officials are still appointed and dismissed by the central government, their authority is implied and enhanced by their access to and control of local information and resources (for example, in the case of "extra-budgetary revenue"). Third, the gradual decline of the personal authority of national leaders and the rise of local governments have weakened the reach of the Chinese Communist Party into the lower levels of government; many lower government officials now bestow their loyalty on localities, not the central government. Fourth, as the private market economy has expanded, the ability of the central government to monitor and control local economic behavior has weakened enormously. Finally, as noted above, any attempt by the center at economic retrenchment would strain its financial capacity, raising the specter of the fall of the Soviet Union.

These changes endow the economic reforms with a degree of political durability. Each serves to raise the costs of a recentralization of political authority and an economic retrenchment, although this effect was often unintended. The short-lived attempt at recentralization following Tiananmen Square is consistent with this logic, as are the recent institutional and tax changes reflecting an attempt to correct for overshooting in decentralization. Our argument does not imply that a retrenchment is impossible, but that it would be costly and might fail, thus making it less likely.

4. The Effects of Federalism, Chinese Style

The economic approach to market-preserving federalism outlined in section 2 yields predictions about economic performance following the onset of federalism. We now turn to investigate some of the varied economic responses to federalism, Chinese style, over the past fifteen years.

Economic policy-making by provincial and local governments reveals a wide range of behavior over the past fifteen years.[41] Many areas initially chose to remain unchanged. Others sought to reinforce the status quo. Still others, of course, chose the path of reform. Moreover, this pattern of policy choice has not remained stationary but has changed over time, in part reflecting the emerging evidence about the consequences of the different policies. Competition among jurisdictions is evident in many forms.

Competition among Jurisdictions: Experimentation, Learning, and Imitation

Following the predictions of the economic approach to federalism, jurisdictions in China initially chose different policies. As the results became known, some of those with inferior policies adopted the superior ones. First, failed experiments were discarded while successful ones were expanded and imitated. Second, there has emerged a large range of seemingly puzzling results that appears inconsistent with marketization. Many governments pursue strikingly interventionist policies, for example, by erecting trade barriers and preventing competition from firms from neighboring provinces. Moreover, there are widespread reports of overcompetition. How do we make sense of all this? The following series of cases reveal patterns consistent with the theory developed above.

(1) Heilongjiang's "Project 383."   Bordering Russia, Heilongjiang is China's most Northeastern province, and a conservative one.[42] In an effort to demonstrate their dedication to the old system, Heilongjiang's officials announced "Project 383" in 1989. This policy was designed to achieve a significant reduction in the rate of price increases (from 17 percent in the previous year to 13 percent) for the 383 goods in the official basket used to calculate the inflation index. The policy proved very costly and was criticized by the government—for example, members of the financial bureaucracy—and the public. The contrast with Guangdong was apparent to all. Guangdong had freed prices on the same set of goods and, due to reforms, prices had fallen. Guangdong's policies had thus achieved the same results but without significant financial participation by the government. Reports from economists suggest that Project 383 has been abandoned.

This episode represents an important instance of the learning that takes place during the experimental process. Given its goals and expectations, Heilongjiang initiated Project 383. It decided that the project was a failure, not because the province changed its goals, but because market methods had proved more effective.

(2) Two prefectures. The process of choosing different strategies followed by the comparison of results and the adoption of the superior strategy occurred in two similar prefectures just across the provincial border, Shaoguan in Guangdong and Binzhou in Hunan.[43] When reform was first adopted in Guangdong in 1980, many commodity prices in Guangdong rose above those in Binzhou since the reform was not carried out in Hunan. As a result, resources from Binzhou flowed to Guangdong. The Binzhou government set up tax offices on the border in an attempt to stop this outflow. These attempts did not bring prosperity to Binzhou. Years later when the people in Binzhou compared themselves with their neighbor, Shaoguan, they found that, although both had similar initial economic conditions, Shaoguan had significantly benefited from economic reform in Guangdong. People in Binzhou urged the government to undertake reform.

In 1988 the central government allowed Binzhou to adopt some reform measures. This enabled Binzhou to enjoy the benefits of opening markets to Guangdong. The prefecture government withdrew all its tax offices along the border with Guangdong. Soon the adjacent areas between Binzhou and Guangdong prospered and interregional trade reached a record level. Importantly, the Binzhou government obtained far more tax revenue from these businesses than from those border tax offices.[44]

(3) Coordinating labor flows. China's floating labor population, estimated variously between 60 and 100 million workers, is so large that it can overwhelm the ability of local governments to provide basic services, such as water, food, sewage, transportation, security, and housing.[45,46] In part, due to the congestion caused by these migrants, several provinces have begun to manage and coordinate these flows.[47] For example, in early 1992, Guangdong, Hunan, Guangxi, and Sichuan established an interregional labor coordination center to help coordinate labor movements among these four provinces. Under the new regulations, migrant workers in Guangdong must obtain approval from labor management organizations of their home province. Guangdong, in turn, agrees to provide labor demand information to the other three provinces.

A comparison of labor flow into Guangdong and Shanghai reveals the effect of these organizations. For both areas, the labor inflow of 1993 was the largest in history. Yet the two regions responded very differently. In Guangdong, transportation was much more reliable than in previous years. The crime rate dropped sharply compared with the same period (spring) of the previous year. Many firms provided their own transportation for workers hired from other regions. Likewise some local governments of other provinces also provide transportation for workers from their regions. In contrast, large numbers of migrants flowed into Shanghai trying to find work in the recently established Pudong Developmental Zone. The development zone only needed approximately 500,000 to 600,000 workers. But the labor arriving in Shanghai on the two days of January 31 and February 1 more than doubled this figure. Many people were detained in the train station or on the streets. On January 31, the Shanghai municipal government sent an emergency request to neighboring provinces asking them to stop labor flowing to Shanghai. In the meantime, Shanghai started to deport those migrants who could not find jobs.

The difference between these two regions occurred in part because Guangdong had experienced the large amount of labor inflow much earlier than Shanghai. Therefore, Guangdong and its neighboring provinces have learned much more about the markets and what they can do about it. The market capacity appears to have reached a sufficient scale in Guangdong so that organized labor markets will pay off.

Competition among Jurisdictions: Factor Mobility
Beyond experimentation and imitation discussed above, there is a more explicit type of competition for resources, particularly labor and foreign capital. Here, too, localities with more efficient economies outcompete less efficient ones.

(1) Organized labor export and capital import in Sichuan Province.
Evidence of labor mobility is striking. Although many restrictions
remain on migration, the floating labor pool is enormous by any standard.[48] Labor moves from areas of surplus to areas of need. An interesting story concerns labor export from Sichuan province.[49] Total labor
exported from this province has reached 3 million per year. Remittances from migrants have totaled as much as 3–5 billion yuan annually, accounting for 10 percent of net farmer income in the province.
Provincial authorities have attached great importance to labor export.
The vice governor of Sichuan province pointed out that labor export
has become an important means of developing backward local economies. It requires less capital and yields quick and high returns. Individuals leave with nothing and return with what is, by local standards,
a fortune. Their annual incomes are largely higher than 1000 yuan, and
some have assets over 1 million. They bring back capital to invest in
the local economies, promoting the local economy and township-
village enterprises.

To foster the process of labor export and capital import, the Sichuan
provincial government established a labor development office headed
by the vice governor. Different levels of local government authorities
established organizations that are responsible for managing labor
exports and the provision of training to improve skills. Some counties
established county-township-village hierarchical labor service systems,
providing auditing, monitoring services, and coordination with tax
bureau and financial institutions.

(2) Competition for foreign capital. There is also considerable competition among regions—provinces, townships, cities, special economic
zones, and developmental zones—for foreign capital. Two of the main
ingredients in this competition are, first, the laws, regulations, and
taxes that promote economic development, including secure property
rights and private returns (known as the "software"); and second,
infrastructure (such as transportation and port facilities) and access to
markets (known as the "hardware"). There are now over one thousand
zones designed to attract foreign capital. There is considerable evidence
that foreign capital flows toward those areas where a high return is
likely.

As noted in Section 3, not only has foreign investment increased, but
the share of regional control also has increased dramatically. Closely
related is another recent trend that might be termed "development

zone" fever.[50] Under the efforts of several levels of local authorities, development zones mushroomed in the 1990s. According to the national bureau of land regulation, in 1991 there were only 117 development zones for the entire country. For 1992, it estimated the number to be 2,700.[51] In some cases, the cause for this development zone fever is that local governments try to attract foreign investment or business (so-called "building a nest to attract the phoenix"). In other cases, it is related to the emerging real estate business which is extremely profitable in China. This fever, however, does not automatically turn on the flow of foreign investment. In many instances, there are not complementary, well-established facilities and other conditions that suit large amounts of capital investment. This puts pressure on the local governments to further improve infrastructure and complementary facilities.

Dynamics of Competition among Jurisdictions: Trends and Momentum

As discussed above, successful aspects of reform and marketization are being imitated in many areas in China. The divergence in success and prosperity of seemingly similar towns, cities, and regions encourages those who struggle to copy those who thrive. Competition for factors implies that the various levels of government must provide secure promises to maintain reform and encourage investment.

Shaanxi's learning from and imitation of Guandong's system of opening trade illustrates the trend in imitation of the successful areas.[52] The governor of Shaanxi Province observed that the reason that Guangdong province achieved fast economic growth was that its markets were open and interregional trade was not blockaded. Shaanxi, in contrast, maintained considerable trade barriers, including large numbers of tax offices across its different counties and prefectures. In 1991, the provincial government released its control over 125 commodity prices and withdrew 12,289 tax offices. The commodity trade soon flourished. In the second half of 1991, the business tax of commerce increased by 20.1 percent over the same period of 1990.

The central government attached great importance to Shaanxi's experience. The state council made copies of Shaanxi government's documents about its reform policy and sent them to other provincial governments. Many provinces, such as Gansu, Yunnan, Sichuan, Henan, Jilin, Ningxia, and Jiangsu, responded earnestly. Before long, Jiangsu established a "market guidance and coordination council"; Guizhou organized a "coordination team for market circulation reform." Many provinces have now incorporated the development of a market system into their socioeconomic development plans.

As part of this effort, authorities from various regions are actively studying the political and economic arrangements within the most successful regions. For example, in 1991, Jiangsu province sent a group of seventy-three government officials to the southern part of Shaanxi province, which is a very poor area.[53] This was the first cross-province exchange of government officials. After one year, they helped many counties, organizations, and firms in that area establish cooperative connections with those in Jiangsu province. Due to their efforts, the southern part of Shaanxi has attracted more than two hundred projects, including more than ten million yuan and a range of different types of personnel from other regions. These officials also helped to train over twenty-two hundred local personnel; they provided information to local firms; and they helped promote the firms' sales on international markets. The official exchange enabled the rich province of Jiangsu to develop markets and resources in Shaanxi province.

Summary
This section indicates that a range of behavior under the reforms is consistent with the predictions of market-preserving federalism. Experimentation, learning, and adaptation all follow from the inception of local political freedom over the economy. Local governments compete with one another for factors and in the international market for exports.

The illustrations provided in this section do not prove our hypothesis, for they are not a representative sample of behavior. They nonetheless provide a sufficient basis to establish the plausibility of our contentions.

5. Conclusions

An economic system faces a fundamental dilemma: not only does it depend on the political system for specifying and enforcing property rights and contracts, but it also depends on the political system to protect the market from political encroachment. The developed economies of the West learned to mitigate this problem long ago, and, for many purposes, economists can ignore them. But the same cannot be said for developing countries, particularly those with long histories of unconstrained government.

The central hypothesis of this paper is that the form of decentraliza-tion inherent in the reforms in China—what we have called "federal-ism, Chinese style"—provides an important set of limits on the behavior of all levels of government. By design, decentralization directly limits the central government's control over the economy. It also induces competition among local governments, serving both to constrain their behavior and to provide them with a range of positive incentives to foster local economic prosperity.

The constraints of federalism, Chinese style, are especially important for China for a second reason. The other forms of credible limits on government typical of the developed West, notably, popular elections and a separation of power, appear not to be politically feasible for China at this time. Consequently, federalism may be one of the few ways in which a large, non-democratic state can provide credible limits on its behavior.

The discussion in sections 3 and 4 reveals that a substantial range of economic behavior exhibited in China is consistent with our central hypothesis. These case studies illustrate the range of experimentation, learning, and imitation that has occurred in many areas of China. The observation of the results of particular experiments provides informa-tion to all provinces, not just the one conducting the experiment. These observations have changed expectations nationwide. Yes, many indi-viduals have gotten rich, as some had warned, but so too have many province, township, and village governments. This unexpected but striking fiscal power has played a significant role in the comparisons across jurisdictions, as several of the above cases illustrate. The remark-able ability of the reforms to generate resources for many local govern-ments has had substantial consequences. Not only did this allow them to provide for the welfare of its residents, often far better than nearby areas that had fought marketization, but it helped change the minds of many who were initially skeptical of reform.

The results of experiments have thus proved critical to the recent history of China, underscoring the importance of the federalism with its institutionally created *absence* of a single government with monop-oly control over the economy. When there is only one government and it claims that the market would fail to provide for citizens and social needs, who can credibly claim otherwise, especially in the pres-ence of the obvious initial costs of marketization? In contrast, if many regions can choose policies for themselves, all can compare the results, including those which do not wish to initiate reform policies.

The successive comparisons over the past fifteen years, in combination with other factors, such as the conservatives' failure in 1989–92, underpin the new push toward markets over much of China.

Our explanation overlaps with and departs from Shirk's important work. Like Shirk, we emphasize decentralization and the incentives of local governments in the success of economic reform.[54] In comparison to our argument, Shirk places greater weight on the political organization of local governments and their control over the economy, arguing that local political officials should be viewed as creating systems of patronage and loyalty. We believe that there is considerable truth in Shirk's assertion. Because the approval of officials is necessary for enterprises, and because their protection is part of the maintenance of enterprise property rights and contracts, local governments play a more central role in the economy than local governments in Western Europe or the United States.

Nonetheless, Shirk's argument about particularism and patronage requires qualification. As stated, it applies in broad form to the patronage systems common in Latin America and Africa. Yet those economies have performed, respectively, poorly and abysmally. Missing from Shirk's approach is an explanation of the limits on the degree of economic extraction of local governments in China, without which there would be no spectacular economic success.

Our approach suggests an answer: the system of federalism and the inherent jurisdictional competition places striking limits on this system of patronage and political spoils. So too does competition on the international market. Were particularism and patronage in a particular locality to place onerous restrictions or burdens on these firms, they simply could not succeed in international competition. China's striking economic success suggests that local government particularism differs significantly from that in Latin America and Africa. These issues deserve further research.

Before concluding, we would like to discuss briefly some of the limits of our analysis. First, the evidence provided in sections 3 and 4 is intended to demonstrate the plausibility of our approach; it does not represent a systematic empirical test. The latter would require further analysis and more systematic data from an appropriately constructed sample of provinces, but no such data is available at this time. Second, although our approach does not rely on arguments about Chinese culture, we do not imply that Chinese culture is irrelevant. Undoubtedly culture is central to the ability of individuals and groups who have taken advantage of new opportunities under reform. Our argument emphasizes that Chinese economic success reflects, in part, institutional changes. A more complete approach would show how to integrate our institutional analysis with the relevant aspects of Chinese culture.

China's transition toward a market system is at a critical moment. The success of the past fifteen years of reform is a tremendous asset, not only in terms of economic benefits achieved, but also in terms of political institutions restructured. On the other hand, the institutional foundation underpinning a secure market system in China is far from rationalized and secure. We have discussed problems that arise from too weak a central government: internal trade barriers and soft budget constraints of various levels of government are just two phenomena that reflect such a problem. It is fortunate for China's economic success that both are less a problem for the township and village levels of government in China. There are, however, problems from a central government that is too strong, and this is the danger of recentralization per se. Without further institutional constraints, a financially independent central government would pose potential dangers to the reform's progress over the past fifteen years, especially if run by leaders far less favorable to the reforms than Deng Xiaoping.

Notes

* The authors gratefully acknowledge the helpful conversations of Masahiko Aoki, Nina Halpern, Anne Krueger, John Litwack, Ronald McKinnon, Paul Milgrom, Douglass North, Jean Oi, Gérard Roland and Susan Shirk; and the research assistance of Jiahua Che. This paper was prepared under a cooperative agreement between the Institute for Policy Reform (IPR) and the Agency for International Development (AID), Cooperative Agreement No. PDC-0095-A-00–1126–00. Qian's research was also supported by Research Incentive Fund from the Office of Technology Licensing (OTL) at Stanford University. Views expressed in this paper are those of the authors and not necessarily those of IPR, AID, or Stanford.

1. See McKinnon, Ronald I., "Financial Control in the Transition from Classical Socialism to a Market Economy," *Journal of Economic Perspectives* (1991) 5: 107–22; North Douglass C. *Structure and Change in Economic History*. New York: Cambridge University Press.1981; and North, Douglass C. *Institutions, Institutional Change, and Economic Performance*. New York: Cambridge University Press. 1990; Root, Hilton. [Madagascar MS.]1993; Weingast, Barry R. "The Economic Role of Political Institutions: Market-Preserving Federalism and Economic Growth." *Journal of Law, Economics, and Organization (Spring, 1995)*.

2. Hartford, Katherine, "Socialist Agriculture is Dead; Long Live Socialist Agriculture! Organizational Transformation in China, pp. 31-61 in Perry, E. & C. Wong, eds. *The Political Economy of Reform in Post-Mao China*. Cambridge, MA: The Council on East Asian Studies/Harvard University. 1985; Saich, T. "Much Ado About Nothing: Party Reform

in the 1980s" in Gordon White, ed. *The Chinese State in the Era of Economic Reform*. London: Macmillan Professional and Academic Ltd. 1991.

3. Shirk, Susan L. *The Political Logic of Economic Reform in China*. Berkeley: University of California Press, 1993.

4. Federalism in the West is nearly always associated with political freedom and the protection of individual rights. See Weingast, "The Economic Role of Political Institutions" for details of these federalisms, including a discussion of how federalism provided the important political foundations for the impressive growth of England in the 18th Century, and the United States in the nineteenth century.

5. Weingast "The Economic Role of Political Institutions"; See also McKinnon, "Market-Preserving Fiscal Federalism" (Working paper, Department of Economics, Stanford University, 1994).

6. North, *Institutions.*; Weingast, "The Economic Role of Political Institutions."

7. Kornai, Janos, *Economics of Shortage*, North-Holland, 1980.

8. Although the most pervasive forms of the soft budget constraint are observed in the centrally planned economy where the government controls nearly everything, the problem is general in all modern economies. Indeed, the exploding savings and loan problem in the United States resulted from a version of this problem. So, too, is the rampant inflation typical of many Latin American regimes.

9. McKinnon, "Market-Preserving Fiscal Federalism."

10. Weingast, "The Economic Role of Political Institutions."

11. McKinnon, "Market-Preserving Fiscal Federalism"; Weingast, "The Economic Role of Political Institutions."

12. See Williamson, Oliver. "The Institutions and Governance of Economic Development and Reform," Unpublished WP, UC Berkeley, 1994.

13. In contrast, eighteenth century England was characterized by market-preserving federalism, although the English did not call their system federal. See Weingast, "The Economic Role of Political Institutions."

14. This section summarizes an extensive literature in economics, including the classic work of Tiebout and Oates. For a review of this literature see Rubinfeld, Daniel. "Economics of the Local Public Sector," *Handbook of Public Economics*, vol. II, A. J. Auerbach and M. Feldstein, eds. New York: Elsevier. 1987.

15. McKinnon, "Market-Preserving Fiscal Federalism."

16. Weingast, "The Economic Role of Political Institutions."

17. See, e.g., Krugman, Paul. *Geography and Trade*. Cambridge, MA: M.I.T. Press. 1991.

18. For example, the common market in early nineteenth century United States could not have been sustained without the ever-vigilant policing of the Supreme Court. Policing the market against encroachments by state governments proved a major use of its constitutional powers. These cases reveal the remarkable diversity and cleverness of the states in their efforts to erect such barriers. See Weingast, Barry R. "The Political Foundations of the Antebellum American Economy," Working Paper, Hoover Institution, Stanford University, 1993); Similarly, such barriers are a major reason underlying the movement for economic and political union in Europe. See Garrett, G. "The International

Cooperation and Institutional Choice: The European Community's Internal Market." *International Organization* (1992) 46:535–62.

19. Qian and Xu provide a detailed analysis of how and why this happened in China. Based on this analysis, they also provide an institutional explanation of differences between economic reforms in China and in Eastern Europe and the Soviet Union. See Yingyi Qian and Chenggang Xu, "Why China's Economic Reforms Differ: The M-form Hierarchy and Entry/Expansion of the Non-State Sector," *The Economics of Transition*, 1(2), pp. 135–170, June, 1993.

20. Wong, Christine, "Between Plan and Market: The Role of the Local Sector in Post-Mao China," *Journal of Comparative Economics*, 1987.

21. Qian and Xu, "Why China's Economic Reforms Differ."

22. See *China Statistical Yearbook* (various issues).

23. Hainan was added as the largest special economic zone when it was organized as a separate province in 1988.

24. See, e.g., Oi, Jean, "Fiscal Reform and the Economic Foundations of Local State Corporatism in China," *World Politics* (October 1992) 45:99–126; Oksenberg, Michael and James Tong, "The Evolution of Central-Provincial Fiscal Relations in China, 1971-1984: The Formal System," *The China Quarterly* (1991):1–32; and Wong, Christine, "Fiscal Reform and Local Industrialization," *Modern China*, vol. 18 no. 2, April, 1992.

25. The five cities are below the provincial level but have independent budget agreements with the center. The following is based on: Bahl, Roy and Christine Wallich, "Intergovernmental Fiscal Relations in China," Working Papers, Country Economics Department, World Bank, WPS 863, 1992; Wong, Christine, "Central-Local Relations in An Era of Fiscal Decline: The Paradox of Fiscal Decentralization in Post-Mao China," *The China Quarterly* (1991) 128:691–715; Wong, "Fiscal Reform and Local Industrialization."

26. For discussion of the Russian case, see Litwack, John, "Discretionary Behavior and Soviet Economic Reform," *Soviet Studies*, 1990; and Litwack, John, "Legality and Market Reform in Soviet-Type Economies," *Journal of Economic Perspectives* (1991) 5(4), pp. 77–89.

27. See Wong, "Central-Local Relations." In a recent comprehensive study of China's internal market, the World Bank concluded that "despite considerable progress in the substitution of allocation by the price mechanism, markets for both goods and factors of production (capital, labor and foreign exchange) are still regionally fragmented." "Links with the overseas exterior appear to have been easier to develop than links with other provinces, both in terms of the mobility of goods and some factors, particularly capital investment. There has been some tendency for individual provinces to behave as separate countries, rather than as parts of a single large country." World Bank, "China: Internal Market Development and Regulation," Country Operation Division, China and Mongolia Department, November 24, 1993.

28. *People's Daily*, overseas edition, October 11, 1993, p. 2.

29. For example, it is reported that one provincial government instructed its automobile registration department to refuse to issue license plates to unauthorized automobiles produced outside the province.

30. *Source:* C. Wang, "Hog Production Problems in Jiangxi Province," *Economic Study*, May, 1988.

31. Though the details differ, this pattern was repeated in 1986 and 1987.

32. This conclusion is standard in the fiscal federalism literature. See e.g., Oates, Wallace. *Fiscal Federalism.* New York: Harcourt, Brace, Jovanovich. 1972.

33. A burgeoning literature studies this topic. See, e.g., Byrd, William and Qingsong Lin, eds., *China's Rural Industry: Structure, Development and Reform.* Oxford University Press, 1990; Nee, Victor and Su Sijin, "Institutional Change and Economic Growth in China: The View from the Villages," *Journal of Asian Studies,* 1990.49; Oi, "Fiscal Reform"; Qian and Xu, "Why China's Economic Reforms Differ"; Weitzman, Martin and Chenggang Xu, "Chinese Township-Village Enterprises as Vaguely Defined Cooperatives," *Journal of Comparative Economics,* forthcoming 1994; Chang, Chun and Yijiang Wang, "The Nature of the Township Enterprise," forthcoming, *Journal of Comparative Economics,* 1994; Walder, Andrew, "The Varieties of Public Enterprises in China: An Institutional Analysis," mimeo, Harvard University 1994; Che, Jiahua and Yingyi Qian, "Boundaries of the firm and Governance: Understanding China's Township-Village Enterprises," mimeo, Stanford University, 1994.

34. *People's Daily,* March 23, 1990, overseas edition.

35. *Almanac of China's Finance and Banking.* Beijing: China's Financial Publication House, 1992.

36. This topic is further explored in Yingyi Qian and Barry R. Weingast, "Institutions, State Activism, and the Role of Government in Economic Development" in Masahiko Aoki, Masahiro Okuno-Fujiwara, and Hyung-Ki Kim, eds., *The Role of Government in East Asian Economies: Comparative Institutional Analysis* (New York: Oxford University Press, forthcoming).

37. Shirk, *Economic Reform in China.*

38. Paralleling these problems is the substantially diminished reach of the central planning system. Put simply, the central government no longer has the administrative apparatus to monitor and plan the economy as necessary under the older system.

39. Shirk, *Economic Reform in China.*

40. It should be noted that reforms in many southern regions went ahead despite actions from the central government during the period of 1989 and 1991.

41. Additional evidence is provided by Steve Lewis, "Marketization and Government Credibility in Shanghai: Federalist and Corporatist Perspectives" (Manuscript, Washington University, 1994).

42. *Source:* "Heilongjiang Province implements Project 383 to control prices," *Price Theory and Practice,* July, 1990.

43. *Economic Daily,* 1991.11.25.

44. Stories of this type can be replicated manyfold. As an additional example, we note the comparison of Nanyang and Xiangfan, two cities in Henan and Hubei provinces, respectively. The latter made much faster progress, and when this was reported in the *Economic Daily* in 1984, the former designed a new set of developmental programs to learn from and imitate the advanced regions. Five years later, the city was ranked as one of the best among middle and small size cities within the nation (*Economic Daily,* December 6, 1991).

45. Sources: *Economic Daily*, 1991.5.15. and 1992.7.4; and *Outlook*, 1993.2.22.

46. See, for example, Solinger, Dorothy. "The Floating Population as a Form of Civil Society," Paper for 43rd Annual Meeting of the Association for Asian Studies, New Orleans, April 11–14, 1991.

47. Undoubtedly there are other factors underlying these policies, for example, keeping the benefits of local services (such as education) for local residents. Moreover, under other circumstances, these mechanisms could be used to cartelize labor markets, or for other political purposes.

48. Solinger, "The Floating Population."

49. *Financial Times* (China) 1993.3.9; *People's Daily*, 1993.1.2.

50. Sources: *People's Daily*, 1993.1.30; *South Weekend*, 1993.3.5; *Guangming Daily*, 1993.6.29.

51. Among the new development zones, only ninety-five are approved by the various departments of central government. Most development zones were established by different local authorities, from provincial governments down to township governments.

52. *Source: Financial Times* (China), 1992.4.1.

53. *Source: Economic Information Daily*, 1992.5.3.

54. Shirk's more extensive discussions allow her to treat a much wider range of topics central to the reforms success, for example, the importance of gradualism, the initial role of agrarian reform, and the political mechanisms underpinning reform within the central government. See Shirk, *Economic Reform in China*, and Susan Shirk, *How China Opened Its Door*. Washington, DC: Brookings, 1994.

8 Federalism as a Commitment to Preserving Market Incentives

Traditional economic theories of federalism emphasize two well-known sources of benefits from decentralization. First, Hayek (1945) suggested that, because local governments and consumers have better information than the national government about local conditions and preferences, they will make better decisions. Second, Tiebout (1956) argued that competition among jurisdictions allows citizens to sort themselves and match their preferences with a particular menu of local public goods. In this spirit, Musgrave (1959; see also Oates 1972) showed how the appropriate assignment of jurisdictions over public goods and taxes can increase welfare.

Although these theories study central features of federalism, they do not completely characterize the function and benefits of federalism. First generation economic theories ignore the problem of why government officials have an incentive to behave in the manner prescribed by the theory. They take for granted that political officials provide public goods and preserve markets.

Notice the parallels between the first generation approach to federalism and the neoclassical theory of the firm. Both treat the organizations they study—firms and governments—as black boxes run by people who act benevolently—for shareholders or citizens. Both theories provide only a modest explanation for why managers or government officials would behave in the prescribed manner.

The question we address is, how do governments commit to providing efficient public goods and preserving market incentives? The answer lies in the governance structure of the state (Williamson 1997). Preserving markets requires that the state be effective yet limited. Several mechanisms are known to further this objective, such as the rule of law, horizontal separation of powers (e.g., into the executive,

With Barry R. Weingast; originally published in *Journal of Economic Perspectives*, Fall 1997, 11(4), pp. 83–92.

judiciary and legislative branches), and democracy, but all are imperfect. In this paper, we suggest that federalism—the appropriate decentralization from the central to local governments—provides another solution.

Influenced by advances in the new theory of the firm,[1] we offer a new, second generation economic theory of federalism. The theory of the firm studies a wide range of incentive problems that plague firms, assuming that no natural reason compels managers to favor shareholders. The theory shows how firm institutions and governance structures can be structured so that, interacting with the market, they align incentives of managers with the interests of shareholders. As with the theory of the firm, we assume there is no natural reason for political officials to further the interests of citizens. Like firm managers, if given the opportunity, political officials will appropriate the lion's share of the rents from political decisionmaking. Again in parallel with the theory of the firm, we argue that the appropriate political institutions align incentives of political officials and citizen welfare.

In what follows, we study the problem of how governments preserve markets. Efficient markets require two related aspects of credible commitment by the state. The state must maintain "positive" market incentives that reward economic success. When the government is tempted to take away too much income and wealth generated by future success, individuals have no incentives to take risks and make effort today. In the terms of North (1990), this is the "state predation" problem. The state must also commit to "negative" market incentives that punish economic failure; if the government is tempted to bail out failed projects or continue costly, inefficient public programs, individuals have no incentives to avoid mistakes and waste. In the terms of Kornai (1986), this is the "soft budget constraint" problem.

Thriving markets thus require that governments solve this problem through credible commitment (North 1990; Weingast 1995). Historically, as North (1981, 1990) suggests, most states have failed to achieve sufficient credible commitment to markets. This does not mean that political officials are malevolent, however. In the developed world, problems typically arise for a different reason. Political officials may be sufficiently honest and possess good intentions. Nonetheless, in the name of good intentions, they often produce bad economic policies. Political officials face pressure to provide benefits to a range of groups and constituencies; they may levy too high tax on economic success in the name of poor people; they may mandate the provision of private benefits through regulation; and they may be tempted to borrow too much from future generations. Political officials also face pressure to intervene to save jobs by rescuing ailing firms and bailing out bad projects. In combination, these activities compromise the positive and negative incentives necessary for markets.[2]

We approach this question using the insights and analytical tools from the new theory of the firm. Two lines of ideas are relevant for studying federalism. First, the allocation of information and authority directly affects the degree of commitment. In particular, efficiency can arise in a dynamic setting if the principal gives up some information and authority. Second, competition can be used as a disciplinary device in the presence of managerial incentive problems, forcing managers to reflect the interests of shareholders.

We have only tentative beginnings on these problems.[3] Paralleling arguments in the theory of the firm, we suggest how the features of federalism—decentralization of information and authority and inter-jurisdictional competition—can provide credible commitment to secure economic rights and preserve markets. Specifically, providing the central government less information and power in particular areas increases the credibility of commitment. This combines with the induced competition among local jurisdictions to provide local political officials with the incentives to pursue citizen interests. In addition, we also identify some factors relevant for sustaining federalism. This approach goes well beyond the traditional studies of federalism and decentralization in the spirit of Hayek and Tiebout.

Our approach rests on the important work of several economists. Buchanan has long drawn attention to problems with the assumption of benevolent government (Buchanan and Tullock 1962; Buchanan and Brennan 1980), though we disagree with his modeling strategy of assuming a malevolent government. A range of models (e.g., Epple and Zelenitz 1981; Courant and Rubinfeld 1981; Inman and Rubinfeld 1979) show how inter-jurisdiction competition limits but may not eliminate inefficiency, given particular features of local public goods provision, such as immobile land. More recently, Inman and Rubinfeld (1997) have articulated a complex positive theory about how the politics of public expenditure programs and budgeting introduces a range of inefficiencies.

The Incentive Effects of Decentralized Information and Authority

Through the appropriate decentralization of information and state power, federalism can establish positive incentives to limit the state predation problem and negative incentives to reduce the soft budget constraint problem. In a dynamic setting, for example, the principal can sometimes increase efficiency by giving up some information and authority. Increasing *ex post* transaction costs may be essential for credible commitments and thus for *ex ante* efficiency.

The notion of increased efficiency through less information and limited authority differs from Hayek's idea. It has also been a consistent theme in the recent theory of the firm and regulation. Consider several examples. First, lack of commitment not to use *ex post* information creates the phenomena of "ratcheting up" planned quotas and inefficient regulation, leading to pervasive incentive problems (Laffont and Tirole 1989). Second, in the theory of firm ownership, one cost of vertical integration is the lack of credible reward by the integrated firm to the manager when the former controls cost information (Riordon 1990). For the same reason, inefficiencies arise with public ownership because of the government's superior information about the firm (Schmidt 1996). Third, in an organization, reducing information channels linking lower decision makers to the top decision makers can be beneficial because it reduces wasteful influence activities (Milgrom and Roberts 1990, 1992). Fourth, under certain circumstances, limiting the authority of the principal credibly provides a subordinate with the incentives to take "initiatives." These limits grant the subordinate more "real authority" through controlling more information despite her lack of "formal authority" (Aghion and Tirole 1997). Finally, diffused information and authority is also the key argument in the endogenous theory of hard vs. soft budget constraint (Dewatripont and Maskin 1995).

Studies of federalism typically illustrate their principles using the state governments of the United States or the national and supranational governments of Europe. In addition to drawing on those cases, we believe that modern China provides a striking example of the economic benefits of federalism. China has emphasized economic reform through devolution of authority from the central to local governments, in contrast to the more centralized reform in Eastern Europe and the former Soviet Union. Along several critical dimensions, China's central government has explicitly limited its information as a way of credibly committing the center not to repeat the pernicious behavior of the Mao era. For example, the central government allows local governments to maintain various "extra-budget" and "off-budget" accounts. Limited knowledge about these budgets commits the central government not to tax them, which in turn encourages local governments to generate prosperity and revenue. The central government also issues large quantities of cash, facilitating cash transactions which are far less prone to state predation. Also, the state permits private savings accounts with state banks under false names, and thus credibly commits not to confiscate bank deposits for a particular person. Of course, the central government can still confiscate a portion of all deposits by taxation or inflation, but the political costs would be high. Although not completely binding its own hands, the central government's devolution of information and authority makes it harder to use those hands.

The allocation of authority also has profound implications for the hardness of budget constraints at different levels of government. McKinnon (1997) observes that American state governments are not only constrained in their taxing, but also more constrained in their borrowing than the federal government. Because the American federal government is backed up by the central bank (money issuing authority), therefore it can issue bonds at a privileged rate. No other financial institution or government can do this, implying that the federal government has a softer budget constraint. In comparison, the American states and local governments do not have direct access to the central bank. Nor, in contrast to Canada for example, do states have indirect access to the central bank through soft federal transfers to states. Furthermore, state borrowing is largely confined to issuing bonds for capital improvement, not general consumption. These limits have important incentive effects. They prevent states from endlessly bailing out ailing enterprises and from expenditure levels beyond their fiscal means. These limits therefore help preserve negative market incentives and provide local governments with the incentive to husband their economies.

This contrasts with the emerging federal system in the European Community. Because each European nation retains its own central bank, these "middle-level" governments have softer borrowing constraints. They may therefore bail out loss-making firms to a degree that American states cannot afford. The case of Canada is in between the United States and Europe. Canadian provinces do not have direct access to the central bank. Nonetheless, through the large transfers of federal revenue, provinces have indirect access to the central bank.[1]

The effect of decentralized allocation of information and authority in achieving credible commitment also helps explain why some local government owned enterprises perform better than state-owned enterprises (SOEs). Because the central government is concentrated with ownership and control of both industrial enterprises and banks, it is unable to credibly commit to high-powered incentives for enterprise managers. Without binding itself to any fixed rules, the state is always tempted to reduce rewards to enterprises and managers when it observes outstanding performances. Moreover, the state's knowledge of which state owned enterprises are ailing combines with its access to the central bank to imply an absence of commitment to a hard budget constraint. For this reason, governments of all stripes—including Western European or the former socialist—tend to bail out ailing national enterprises.

China's recent economic success provides an important contrast. Over the past fifteen years, local township and village enterprises (TVEs) have provided the engine of Chinese economic growth. These local government-owned enterprises have remarkably different governance structures from SOEs and thus face better positive and negative incentives (Che and Qian 1997; Qian and Weingast 1996b). By fully controlling the assets of TVEs, the local governments have access to information that not available to the central government, and thus they are able to resist state revenue predation in a credible way (for example, through revenue hiding). Moreover, because the local governments are empowered with the responsibility of local public goods provision, the state finds in its own interest to prey less on TVEs than on private firms because it expects some revenues to be used for local public goods provision. Most importantly, local governments' power is limited because they do not control state banks and cannot create money. This governance structure, where banks have credits but local governments have control and information over firms, serves as a commitment device to hard budget constraint in the way analyzed by Dewartripont and Maskin (1995).

The Incentive Effects of Jurisdictional Competition

Competition among jurisdictions forces governments to represent citizen interests and to preserve markets. In Tiebout, jurisdictional competition among local governments increases efficiency through sorting and matching. Our approach suggests that, in addition, jurisdictional competition serves as a disciplinary device to punish inappropriate market intervention by lower government officials.

Again, our argument here parallels those commonly made in the recent model about corporate control and the theory of the firm, which stress how markets encourage good behavior by corporate managers (Holmstrom and Tirole 1989). For example, managerial labor market provides a degree of discipline because a manager who performs poorly is, among other things, more likely to receive low future wages. Competition in the product market also gives managers an incentive to pursue the shareholder interests of the firm. Finally, a number of economists have argued that the threat of a firm takeover in the capital market is the ultimate weapon against managerial misconduct.

Just as market competition pressures firm managers to reflect the interests of shareholders, competition among local governments helps limit government's predatory behavior. Mobile resources quickly leave jurisdictions with inappropriate behavior. Competition for mobile sources of revenue prevents local political leaders from imposing debilitating taxes or regulation (Buchanan 1995; Weingast 1995). In the best case, only those economic restrictions that residents are willing to pay for will survive. Examples of this effect abound in the literature. Romano's (1985) famous studies of corporate chartering in the United States explain how New Jersey emerged as the primary locus of chartering for major corporations late in the 19th century, but when that state moved to extract rents from these firms, a large number moved to Delaware, which has since remained the home of most large corporations.

Similar arguments also suggest how federalism's jurisdictional competition leads to the endogenous emergence of harder budget constraints for lower governments (Qian and Roland 1996). Politicians in every type of political system tend to bail out inefficient firms or spend on wasteful public consumption. In a federal system, however, the mobility of resources across regions raises the opportunity costs to local governments of bailing out inefficient firms or wasteful public expenditures. Ceteris paribus, jurisdictions that consistently make inefficient expenditures will not be able to attract mobile resources to jurisdictions. Therefore, competition endogenously hardens lower governments' budget constraints and changes the incentives of local politicians. In recent years, local governments' budget constraints in China have become harder, in part because local governments compete in spending their resources to attract foreign investments. They thus have higher incentives to stop subsidizing failing state firms.

A main concern about federalism is that, in the absence of centrally-mandated policies of redistribution, it may increase inequality across regions (for example, Rose-Ackerman and Rodden 1997). The recent American South provides a complex illustration. The destructive Civil War caused the South to fall from the richest American region to the poorest, and so it remained for many decades. Since 1950, however, the faster growth of the American South is at least partly the result of competition among southern state governments in offering flexible labor markets and less generous welfare provisions than the Northern states. This attracted investment on vast scale, along with help from factors such as the interstate highway system and the commercialization of air conditioning (McKinnon 1995, 1997). Jurisdictional competition can therefore reduce regional inequality without centrally-mandated redistribution.[5] Moreover, as McKinnon suggests, the lack of federal redistribution may even be a necessary condition. In contrast to the American federal system, which has no strong tradition of revenue sharing or equalization grants from the federal government, regional equalization grants in Europe and Canada seem to have impeded this natural process of "equalization through competition." As McKinnon (1995, 1997) argues that, in the Mezzogiorno region of Italy and the poor maritime provinces of Canada, large intergovernmental transfers inhibit their labor markets from adjusting in the American mode.[6]

Sustainability of Federalism

To this point we have focused on how federalism helps a state credibly commit to preserving markets. For federalism to have this effect, however, it must be sustainable. To survive, federal systems require institutions that make them self-enforcing: political officials must have an incentive to abide by the rules of federalism. This issue is clearly outside the scope of first generation theories of federalism, but it is an important focus of the second generation theories. Recent formal models address this question by using repeated games (Bednar 1997, de Figueiredo and Weingast 1997; Weingast 1995, 1997). Page constraints limit our discussion to indicating but a few factors relevant for sustaining federalism.

Three decades ago, Riker (1964) suggested that federal systems were inherently unstable (see also Bednar 1997). DeFigueiredo and Weingast (1997) capture the problem in the two fundamental dilemmas of federalism: First, what prevents the central government from destroying federalism by overwhelming the lower governments? Second, what prevents the constituent units from undermining federalism by free-riding and otherwise failing to cooperate? Federal instability arises because the two fundamental dilemmas imply a tradeoff: institutions and powers designed to mitigate the first dilemma exacerbate the second, and vice versa.

Students of federal stability identify a number of considerations. We here note two.[7] First, the central government must be given sufficient resources to police shirking by lower governments; second, the lower governments must police central government abuse of its authority by retaliating in concert against abuses (de Figueiredo and Weingast 1997).

We provide two brief illustrations of the second principle. First, Weingast (1998) stresses the importance of institutions to create a self-enforcing balance between state and national authority in the antebellum United States.[8] The "balance rule" constituted a critical institution for this purpose, giving both the north and the south an equal number of states. Both sections worried that the other would capture the national government, forcing bad policies on the other. Balance granted both sections a veto over national policymaking. In combination with the separation of powers system, balance helped keep most issues off the national agenda. The result was a strong system of market-preserving federalism, with the powers of the national government limited to providing national public goods, such as a stable monetary system, national defense, and policing the common market.

Recent events in China also reveal the importance of local government resistant against encroachment by the central government. Because federal institutions devolve authority, resources, and information away from the central government, they provide local governments with some incentives and tools to protect their newfound authority. Nonetheless, if lower governments fail to act in concert, the central government can encroach on the federal system. In China, for example, the central government tried to reverse local political authority underpinning market-oriented reform in the aftermath of Tiananmen Square in 1989. Led by the Governor of Guangdong, the governors of many provinces resisted so that the central government eventually backed down (Montinola, Qian, and Weingast 1995; Shirk 1993).

Conclusions

This paper attempts to sketch a new theory of federalism that complements traditional ones. We appeal to the theory of the firm to find a range of problems in federal systems ignored by traditional theories. Incentive problems, for example, occur throughout government hierarchies as in firms, even when public officials are motivated to serve others instead of being corrupt or malevolent. We argue that political institutions serve a similar role for government officials as firm institutions do for firm managers. Appropriately designed institutions help align the interests of public officials with citizens. Importantly, we also show that federalism helps government officials maintain the positive and negative incentives necessary for thriving markets.

Notes

1. See, e.g., Coase (1937), Grossman and Hart (1986), Holmstrom and Tirole (1989), Milgrom and Roberts (1992), and Williamson (1985).

2. These problems are exacerbated in the developing world, where government officials often face few incentives against syphoning off resources for personal gain.

3. Our work draws on the following: Frye and Shleifer (1997), North and Weingast (1989), McKinnon (1995, 1997), Montinola, Qian, Weingast (1995), Qian and Roland (1996), Qian and Weingast (1996a), Shleifer (1996), Weingast (1995), and Wildasin (1996, 1997).

4. Wildasin (1997) also studies central government grants to local governments for local public goods. He argues that a kind of externality arises in which large jurisdictions are more likely to face soft budget constraints than small jurisdictions. The reason is the "too big to fail" phenomenon that follows because the failure to bail out larger jurisdictions has far more severe consequences for the economy. Wildasin concludes that decentralization with smaller lower level governments leads to harder budget constraints.

5. Although jurisdictional competition allowed the south to catch up, federalism also allowed the pernicious Jim Crow system discriminating against African Americans.

6. Wildasin (1996) discusses the redistribution effect of factor mobility.

7. Other works address this question: Ordeshook and Svetsova (1997) and Riker (1964) emphasize the importance of political parties in limiting the encroachment of politicians. Bednar, Eskridge, and Ferejohn (1997) emphasize the national courts. Weingast (1997) discusses how a constitution can create a focal solution to certain coordination problems created by federalism.

8. Weingast (1997) also discusses the importance of a focal solution to coordinate citizen and lower government retaliation for federal abuse of authority. From the beginning of the republic, Americans were deeply suspicious of the national government, preferring political power to be vested in state and local governments. Reflecting this suspicion, the two parties that dominated national elections during the first half of the 19th century—the Jeffersonians and, later, the Jacksonians—built their majority support in the nation on various notions of states' rights. Parties advocating a substantially greater political role for the national government could not compete in national elections.

References

Aghion, Philippe and Jean Tirole, "Formal and Real Authority in Organization," *Journal of Political Economy*, 105:1, 1–29, February 1997.

Bednar, Jenna. "Federalisms: Unstable by Design?" Paper delivered at the Conference on the Law and Economics of Federalism, University of Minnesota Law School, May 2 and 3, 1997.

Bednar, Eskridge, and Ferejohn, "A Political Theory of Federalism," WP, Hoover Institution, Stanford University, 1997.

Brennan, Geoffrey, and James M. Buchanan, *The Power to Tax: Analytical Foundations of a Fiscal Constitution*. New York: Cambridge University Press, 1980.

Buchanan, James, "Federalism as an Ideal Political Order and an Objective for Constitutional Reform," *Publius*, 25,2: 19–27, Spring, 1995.

Buchanan, James M., and Gordon Tullock. 1962. *The Calculus of Consent*. Ann Arbor: University of Michigan Press.

Che, Jiahua, and Yingyi Qian, "Institutional Environment, Community Government, and Corporate Governance: Understanding China's Township-Village Enterprises," *Journal of Law, Economics, and Organization*, forthcoming, 1997.

Coase, Ronald, "The Nature of the Firm," *Economica* 4, 1937: 386–405. Reprinted in Coase, R., *The Firm, the Market and the Law*, Chicago, University of Chicago Press, 1988.

Courant and Daniel Rubinfeld, "On the Welfare Effects of limited Taxation," *Journal of Public Economics*, 289–316, 1981.

de Figueiredo, Rui J., and Barry R. Weingast, "Self-Enforcing Federalism: Solving the Two Fundamental Dilemmas," mimeo, Stanford University, April, 1997.

Dewatripont, Mathias and Maskin, Eric, "Credit and Efficiency in Centralized and Decentralized Economies," *Review of Economic Studies*, October, 1995.

Epple, Dennis, and Alan Zelenitz., "The Implications of Competition among Jurisdictions: Does Tiebout Need Politics?" *Journal of Political Economy*, 1981.

Frye, Timothy, and Andrei Shleifer, "The Invisible Hand and the Grabbing Hand," *American Economic Review*, 87:354–58, May, 1997.

Grossman, Sanford, and Oliver Hart, "The Costs and Benefits of Ownership: A Theory of Vertical and Lateral Integration," *Journal of Political Economy*, 94, 1986.

Hayek, Friedrich A., "The Use of Knowledge in Society," *American Economic Review*, 35: 519–30, 1945.

Holmstrom, Bengt and Jean Tirole, "The Theory of the Firm," in R. Schmalensee and R. Willig (eds.) *Handbook of Industrial Organization*, vol. 1, Amsterdam: North-Holland, 1989.

Inman, Robert P., and Daniel L. Rubinfeld, "The Judicial Pursuit of Local Fiscal Equity," *Harvard Law Review*, 92: 1663–1750, 1979.

Inman, Robert P., and Daniel L. Rubinfeld, "Rethinking Federalism," *Journal of Economic Perspectives*, 11(4): 43–64, Fall, 1997.

Kornai, Janos, "The Soft Budget Constraint," *KYKLOS*, 39(1), 3–30, 1986.

Laffont, Jean-Jacques, and Jean Tirole, "The Dynamics of Incentive Contracts," *Econometrica*, 1989.

Musgrave, Richard, *Theory of Public Finance: A Study in Public Economy*, New York: McGraw, 1959.

McKinnon, Ronald, "Intergovernmental Competition in Europe with and without a Common Currency," *Journal of Economic Policy Modeling*, 463–78, October, 1995.

McKinnon, Ronald, "Market-preserving Federalism in the American Monetary Union," in *Macroeconomic Dimensions of Public Finance: Essays in Honour of Vito Tanzi*, M. Blejer and T. Ter-Minassian (eds.), London: Routledge, 73–93, 1997.

Milgrom, Paul, and John Roberts, "Bargaining Costs, Influence Costs, and the Organization of Economic Activity," in *Perspectives on Positive Political Economy* (J. Alt and K. Shepsle, eds.) Cambridge, Cambridge University Press, 1990.

Milgrom, Paul, and John Roberts, *Economics, Organization, and Management*, Prentice Hall, 1992.

Montinola, Gabriella, Yingyi Qian, and Barry R. Weingast, "Federalism, Chinese Style: The Political Basis for Economic Success in China," *World Politics*, October, 1995.

North, Douglass, *Structure and Change in Economic History*, New York: Norton, 1981.

North, Douglass, *Institutions, Institutional Changes and Economic Performance*, Cambridge University Press, 1990.

North, Douglass C. and Barry Weingast, "Constitutions and Credible Commitments: The Evolution of the Institutions of Public Choice in 17th Century England," *Journal of Economic History*, 1989.

Oates, Wallace, *Fiscal Federalism*, New York: Harcourt Brace Jovanovich, 1972.

Ordershook, Peter, and Olga Svetsova, "Federalism and Constitutional Design," *Journal of Democracy*, 8(1): 27–42, 1997.

Qian, Yingyi, and Gerard Roland, "Federalism and the Soft Budget Constraint," CEPR Discussion Paper, No. 481, Stanford University, 1996.

Qian, Yingyi, and Barry Weingast, "China's Transition to Markets: Market-Preserving Federalism, Chinese Style," *Journal of Policy Reform*, 1:149–185, 1996a.

Qian, Yingyi, and Barry Weingast, "Institutions, State Activism, and Economic Development: A Comparison of State-Owned vs. Township-Village Enterprises in China," chapter 9 in M. Aoki, H. Kim and M. Okuno-Fujiwara (eds.) *The Role of Government in East Asian Economic Development: Comparative Institutional Analysis*, Oxford University Press, pp. 254–275, 1996b.

Riker, William, H., *Federalism: Origin, Operation, and Significance*, Boston, Little Brown, 1964.

Riordan, Michael, "What is Vertical Integration?" in M. Aoki, B. Gustafsson and O. Williamson (eds.) *The Firm As a Nexus of Treaties*, Sage Publications, 1990.

Romano, Roberta. 1985. "Law as a Product: Some Pieces of the Incorporation Puzzle," *Journal of Law, Economics, and Organization*. 1.

Rose-Ackerman, Susan, and Jonathan Rodden, "Does Federalism Preserve Markets?" mimeo, Yale University, 1997.

Schmit, Klaus, "The Costs and Benefits of Privatization," *Journal of Law, Economics and Organization*, 1996.

Schleifer, Andrei, "Government in Transition," mimeo, Harvard University, 1996.

Shirk, Susan, *The Political Logic of Economic Reform in China*. Berkeley: University of California Press, 1993.

Tiebout, Charles, "A Pure Theory of Local Expenditures," *Journal of Political Economy*, 64:416–24, 1956.

Weingast, Barry R, "Constitutions as Governance Structures: The Political Foundations of Secure Markets," *Journal of Institutional and Theoretical Economics*, 149, 1993.

Weingast, Barry R, "The Economic Role of Political Institutions: Market-Preserving Federalism and Economic Growth," *Journal of Law, Economics and Organization*, 11: 1–31, 1995.

Weingast, Barry R. "Political Foundations of Democracy and the Rule of Law," *American Political Science Review* (1997) 91: 245–63.

Weingast, Barry R. American Democratic Stability and the Civil War: Institutions, Commitment, and Political Behavior," in Robert Bates, et. al., eds. *Analytic Narratives*. Princeton: Princeton University Press (forthcoming, 1998).

Wildasin, David E., "Factor Mobility and Redistributive Policy: Local and International Perspectives," mimeo, Vanderbilt University, December, 1996.

Wildasin, David E., "Externalities and Bailouts: Hard and Soft Budget Constraints in Intergovernmental Fiscal Relations," mimeo, Vanderbilt University, 1997.

Williamson, Oliver, *The Economic Institutions of Capitalism: Firms, Markets, Relational Contracting*, New York: The Free Press, 1985.

Williamson, Oliver, "The Institutions and Governance of Economic Development and Reform," chapter 13 in his *The Mechanism of Governance*, New York: Oxford University Press, 1996.

9 Regional Decentralization and Fiscal Incentives: Federalism, Chinese Style

1. Introduction

Reforming the government is a crucial component of both the transition from a planned to a market economy and economic development. Creating thriving markets in these economies typically requires transforming a highly centralized and interventionist government into one that supports the market and fosters decentralized economic activities. Democracy, separation of powers, and the rule of law are among the important institutions that allow citizens to hold the government accountable for its economic actions and to secure markets from arbitrary state intrusion. By devolving power from the central to local levels, federalism is another institution that helps implement a limited yet effective government conducive to market development.

Economic theories of federalism have traditionally emphasized allocative benefits of decentralization in the provision of public goods and services, such as education and health care. There are two related ideas. First, Hayek (1945) discussed the use of knowledge in society, emphasizing that local governments have better access to local information, which allows them to provide public goods and services that better match local preferences than the national government. Second, Tiebout (1956) introduced the inter-jurisdictional competition dimension and argued that such a competition provides a sorting mechanism to better match public goods and services with consumers' preferences. Drawing on these ideas, Musgrave (1959) and Oates et al. (1972) built a theory of fiscal federalism, stressing among other things the appropriate assignment of taxes and expenditures to the various levels of government to improve welfare.

With Hehui Jin and Barry R. Weingast; originally published in *Journal of Public Economics*, September 2005, 89(9–10), pp. 1719–1742.

Our main concern in this paper is the relationship between fiscal incentives facing local governments and local government promotion of market development in the local economy. Recent experiences of transition and developing economies have shown that a central barrier to economic development in these countries is from the governments, especially local governments, as their policies are often hostile to local business development. Local government policies, such as business regulation and levies, may have either favorable or adverse effects on the entry and expansion of local business enterprises. This leads to two types of government role that have been identified in the literature (Shleifer and Vishny 1998): The government either plays the role of the "grabbing hand" by restricting and preying on productive enterprises and protecting unproductive ones, or it plays the role of the "helping hand" by supporting productive enterprises and disciplining unproductive enterprises.

Our study of federalism centers around the question of how the central–local governmental relationship affects the local government's behavior toward business enterprises and market development. A crucial issue is what kind of federalism better aligns local government incentives with promoting markets and productive enterprises.[1] Interjurisdictional competition can serve as an important incentive device, as emphasized by Tiebout and Brennan and Buchanan (1980): competition rewards local governments friendly to markets as factors of production move to their regions, while it punishes heavily interventionist local governments as they lose valuable factors of production. But this mechanism is not perfect, competition may result in the phenomenon known as "race to the bottom."

Another mechanism, the focus of this paper, concerns the fiscal incentives of local government. This mechanism works when pro-business local government policy promotes local business development, which rewards local governments by increasing the local tax revenue base. A critical aspect of this incentive, however concerns whether the local government is able to keep a significant portion of the increased tax revenue that results from their policy decisions. If so, they have strong fiscal incentives to support market development. On the other hand, if a local government's fiscal reward is unrelated to, or even worse, negatively related to its policy effort, it has no fiscal incentives to support local business.

Studies on China's transition to markets have long noticed the general local government support for local business development, especially in the non-state sector (e.g., Montinola et al. 1995). What are the reasons for the local governments in China to play the "helping hand" for local business development? Using a provincial panel data set, we conduct an empirical study on the Chinese style of federalism with a focus on provincial government's fiscal incentives.

We report three empirical findings. Our first two findings both concern the change in fiscal incentives facing provincial governments after the reform. First, in assessing the "fiscal contracting system" operating between the central and provincial governments from 1980 to 1993, we find that the discrepancy between *ex ante* contracts and *ex post* implementation declined over time and was relatively small on average. These small differences imply that the fiscal contracts between center and province were credible. We also find that cases of extra subsidies were much more common than cases of extra revenue remittance. This suggests that, as far as the central-provincial relations in China, the "soft budget constraint" problem (Kornai 1988) was a greater problem than the "predation" problem.

Second, we find a strong correlation between the current provincial budgetary revenue and its expenditure for the period of 1982–1991 when the "fiscal contracting system" was implemented, about four times as large in the magnitude as the before reform period of 1970–1979, and such a strong correlation remained in the post-1994 period when the "fiscal contracting system" was replaced by the "separating tax system." The finding provides the evidence that provincial governments in China faced much stronger *ex post* fiscal incentives after the reform.

Our third finding concerns the effects of fiscal incentives on provincial economic development and reform. We use the *ex ante* marginal revenue retention rate of provincial governments, as specified in the fiscal contracts between the central and provincial governments in the period between 1982 and 1992, as the measure of fiscal incentives faced by provincial government.[2] We find that stronger fiscal incentives are associated with faster development of non-state enterprises in terms of the employment growth rates in rural enterprises and in all non-state enterprises, even controlling for the conventional measurement of fiscal decentralization. Similarly, stronger fiscal incentives are also associated with greater reform in state-owned enterprises, as measured by the increased shares of contract workers in the total state employment and bonuses in total employee wages.

With these results in mind, we compare federalism, Chinese style, with federalism, Russian style. Studies of Russia's transition stress the problematic role of the government in reform. Shleifer (1997) and Frye

and Shleifer (1997), for example, provide evidence that local governments in Russia have been playing the role of "grabbing hands" that
retard private business development. Zhuravskaya (2000) finds that the
existing revenue sharing schemes between the Russian regional and
local governments provide the latter with no fiscal incentives to increase
their tax base: increases in local government revenues were almost
entirely exacted by the regional government. The lack of fiscal incentives in part explains why local governments in Russia prey on private
businesses.

Our perspective suggests that the distorted incentives faced by local
governments in part explain the different disappointing performances
of the Chinese and Russian reforms. Interestingly, Russia has done
more than China in terms of privatization of state-owned enterprises
and liberalization of markets (Shleifer 1997; Frye and Shleifer 1997;
de Figueiredo and Weingast 2001; Lavrov et al. 2000; OECD 2000). But
apparently it has failed to provide local governments with appropriate
fiscal incentives to pursue local prosperity. Liberalization and privatization without altering government fiscal incentives are insufficient to
produce meaningful economic reform.

We emphasize the critical importance of government fiscal incentives for successful reform. In addition to fiscal incentives, political
incentives facing local governments also matter in comparing the
Chinese and Russian federalism (Blanchard and Shleifer 2000). A complementary approach studying the political incentives facing local governments in China has recently begun. For example, Maskin et al.
(2000) documented an empirical correlation between the provincial
economic performance and the provincial representation in the Party
Central Committee. Li and Zhou (2004) found evidence that the central
government uses personnel control over promotion and dismissal of
provincial top leaders to induce provincial economic growth.

The remainder of the paper is organized as follows. Section 2
describes the changing fiscal system in China during the reform. Section
3 develops our theoretical perspective. Section 4 describes the data and
the construction of variables. Section 5 assesses the credibility of the
"fiscal contracting system" for the period of 1982–92. Section 6 examines the *ex post* link between provincial revenue collection and its
expenditure before and after reform. Section 7 estimates the effects of
fiscal incentives on provincial development and reform. Our conclusions follow.

2. Fiscal Relations Between the Central and Provincial Governments in China

China's fiscal system has five hierarchical levels of government: (1) central; (2) provincial; (3) prefecture; (4) county; and (5) township.[3] In this paper, we will focus on the central–provincial fiscal relations. The central-provincial fiscal relations have evolved over time in three distinct phases: the pre-reform phase prior to 1979, the transitional phase of 1980–1993, and the post-1994 phase.

Prior to the reform of 1979, the fiscal relations between the central and provincial governments are best described as the one of "unified revenue collection and unified spending" (*tongshou tongzhi*). Basically, the provincial governments collected most of revenue generated from within the province, on average over 80 percent, which included taxes and (mostly) profits from state-owned enterprises. Then the central government made a plan of spending for each province. This system earned a nickname "eating from one big pot" (*chi daguofan*), which captured its essence.

Starting 1980, the central–provincial fiscal relations altered in a dramatic way. Between 1980 and 1993, the institution governing the central and provincial fiscal relations is the so called "fiscal contracting system" (*caizheng chengbao zhi*), also known by its nickname "eating from separate kitchens" (*fenzao chifan*). Under the fiscal contracting system, provincial governments entered into relatively long-term fiscal contracts (typically five years) with the central government. Because of their experimental nature, the contractual arrangements varied across provinces and over time. The fiscal contracting system worked as follows (Wong 1997; Bahl 1999): First, "central fixed revenue" was defined to include customs duties, direct tax or profit remittance from the central government supervised state-owned enterprises (SOEs), and some other taxes. All other revenue falls under the heading "local revenue." On average, the local revenue accounted for about 66 percent of total government budgetary revenue over these years. Second, the local revenue was then divided between the central and provincial governments according to pre-determined sharing schemes. For example, between 1980 and 1987, Guangdong province agreed to remit a fixed amount per year, and between 1988 and 1993, it agreed to remit an amount that increased by a fixed 9 percent per year. Guizhou province agreed to receive subsidies that increased by a fixed 10 percent per year. On the other hand, Jiangsu province agreed to remit a fixed share of revenue to the central government. Over time, many provincial governments retained 100 percent of the total local revenue at the margin, which effectively made them residual claimants over the local revenue.

The actual (*ex post*) expenditure of local government did not necessarily match that from the sharing scheme for several reasons. After the division of local revenue according to the sharing scheme, some extra remittance and transfer payments took place between the central government and the provinces. For example, the central government sometimes "borrowed" funds from the provinces. On the other hand, the central government also made additional transfer payments (not specified in the sharing schemes) to provinces, which generally fell into two categories: earmarked subsidies (*zhuanxiang butie*), such as price subsidies for urban residents compensating them for food price increases, and matching grants (*peitao buokuan*), such as funds for highway building. Clearly, the larger this type of *ex post* redistribution, the less important the pre-determined revenue sharing schemes.

Starting 1994, the "fiscal contracting system" was replaced by "separating tax system." Under the new system, "local revenue" has been redefined as revenues from local taxes and the local portion of the shared taxes (Bahl 1999). The major local taxes are now the income taxes from all enterprises other than central government enterprises, business tax from the sales of services, and personal income tax. The most important shared tax is the value added tax (VAT), of which 25 percent belongs to the provincial government, uniform across provinces. The post-1994 phase has eliminated the variations of the revenue sharing rules from the 1980–1993 phase.

In addition to the budgetary revenue, another category of revenue exists called "extra-budgetary revenue," which consists of tax surcharges and user fees levied by central and local government's agencies, as well as some earnings from SOEs. The extra-budgetary revenue emerged in the 1950s but only became institutionalized after the reform. Unlike the budgetary local revenues, the extra-budgetary local revenues are not subject to sharing with the central government. In 1978, total extra-budgetary revenue was about 10 percent of the GDP while total budgetary revenue was about 31 percent. In 1993, the extra-budgetary revenue was up to 16 percent of the GDP and the budgetary revenue was down to 16 percent of the GDP (*Statistical Yearbook of China* 1995). While about three-quarters of the extra-budgetary funds are earnings retained by SOEs and by their supervisory government agencies at the central and local levels, about 30 percent of the extra-budgetary funds are used for government expenditures to supplement the budgetary funds (Fan 1996).

3. Fiscal Incentives and Economic Development: A Theoretical Perspective

How do fiscal incentives of local government contribute to the local economic development? As Hayek stressed, decentralization of authority has the benefits of more efficient use of dispersed local knowledge possessed by the local government. In contrast, centralization of government authority is costly because information transmission from local to central government is often distorted and incomplete. But decentralization of authority is meaningless if the central government takes away all revenue generated in the local economy as a result of local government's action. This suggests a link between fiscal incentives of local government and local development which is a function of local government's policy.

Consider the following very simple model for the purpose of illustration. Let $Y(e)$ be the value created by the local business development, which is a function of local government's "effort" e. This effort is related to local government's policies concerning local productive enterprises, such as the non-state enterprises. These policies could reduce excessive regulation and controls over business entry, speed up of approval of projects and permits, eliminate of onerous fees imposed on firms, or fight against unfavorable ideology toward the development of non-state firms. This effort is also related to reform efforts in non-productive state enterprises in order to reduce their losses. Because effort here is interpreted as policies rather than public goods provisions such as those in education and health care, its effect on the local economy is immediate. Higher local government effort means more favorable local business environment and thus higher value of the local economy $Y(e)$, which means a larger government revenue base.

We also assume that the revenue generated y is positively related to local economy Y. Then the relationship $y(Y(e))$ implies that total revenue generated $y(e)$ is an increasing function of e. Note that in our interpretation e is not revenue collection effort by the local government, rather, it is the local government's policy effort in supporting productive business in its locality. On the other hand, effort e has a cost to local government $C(e)$, which is also increasing in e. Such a cost could be the forgone bribes received by the local government officials, or more generally, the costs spent to facilitate local business development.

The first step in the fiscal contracting system is the designation of "central revenue" and "local revenue." For simplicity we assume that out of the total revenue generated y, vy is designated as "local revenue" and $(1-v)y$ as "central revenue." The second step specifies the marginal provincial revenue retention rate which we denote as z; the province may also pay the center a fixed remittance (or subsidy) R. The provincial government's revenue retention is then given by $zvy(e) - R$. In the third step, the central government makes transfers T to local government. Therefore, the final local government's expenditure is determined by $zvy(Y(e)) - R + T$.

We assume that local government maximizes local expenditure net of cost of effort by choosing effort level e:

$$\max \{zvy(e) - R - c(e) + T\}. \tag{1}$$

Under the usual assumptions of concavity of $y(e)$ and convexity of $c(e)$, the optimal effort level e^*, as well as the local economy $Y(e^*)$, is an increasing function of revenue retention rate z:

$$de^*/dz > 0,$$

and

$$dY(e^*)/dz > 0, \tag{2}$$

assuming that v is constant. That is, the larger the marginal fraction of revenues a local government is allowed to keep, the stronger the local government's incentives to increase its revenue base, which in turn means better government policy to pursue local economic prosperity. This implies that strong links between local expenditures and local revenue help align the interests of local governments to local development.

In the above model, the central government delegates the tasks of supporting local business development to local governments because the latter have better local knowledge. The central government cannot dictate local effort level e because local effort is not easily observable or measurable. For example, even if the central government could announce a nationwide policy to support productive enterprises, it is still up to the local government to enforce such a policy. During enforcement, local circumstances play important role. Therefore, the above model already incorporates the assumption about the importance of local information. Hence the central government is limited to using the revenue retention rate, z, to motivate local governments by aligning the interests of local government with local prosperity.

This implication of the above simple model differs in an important way from the conventional perspective on revenue sharing between the central and local governments. While arguing for the benefits of decentralization of expenditure, the conventional fiscal federalism view does not consider a strong linkage between local governments' own revenue and their expenditures desirable. This view instead focuses on allocative distortions under decentralized revenue collection. It therefore recommends a centralized revenue collection together with decentralized expenditure system, allowing sizeable transfers from the central to local governments to fill the local revenue-expenditure gap. The traditional view therefore implies no necessary relationship between local expenditure and local revenue generated. In contrast, the above model stresses the importance of local governments' incentives in pursuing prosperity in the local economy which serves as the local revenue base. For that purpose, it is natural to emphasize the potential benefit of linking local governments' revenue with their expenditure.

Our model is especially relevant for transition and developing economies for several reasons. For transition economies, the pervasive revenue redistribution practice under central planning had long distorted local governments' incentives, and correcting this distortion has been an urgent need. Developing countries generally have excessive regulation over business development, and local governments in these countries also have more discretions affecting the well-being of local business. Therefore, for these countries, aligning the fiscal incentives of local governments with local prosperity would have stronger effects on the local economy. In contrast, for developed countries, such a justification for local fiscal incentives may be weaker, because the formal legal environment is generally more hospitable to business.

Based on the above discussion, we conjecture that the higher the marginal proportion of revenue retained by the local governments, the faster development of the productive part of the local economy and more reform of the non-productive part of the local economy. Because onerous restrictions on enterprises reduce their revenue, lower governments facing stronger fiscal incentives are likely to impose fewer economic restrictions on and give more support for productive enterprises. However, local governments may fail to respond to fiscal incentives.

Alternatively, these incentives may result in protecting the local economy rather than expanding it. Therefore, empirical testing is required to determine the validity of the hypothesis.

4. Data and Variables

We use a panel data set of 29 provinces from 1970 to 1999, with a particular focus for the time period from 1982 to 1992.[4] We obtained our data from the official Chinese government publications at the national and subnational levels, including *China Statistical Yearbook* in various years published by the National Bureau of Statistics. Table 9.1 presents summary statistics of major variables for the period of 1982–1992.

Measurement of provincial and central government expenditures is standard. However, we make one adjustment to the fiscal expenditure data because the original data has an inconsistency: price subsidies

Table 9.1
Summary Statistics of Major Variables (1982–92)

	Mean	Minimum	Maximum	Standard Deviation
Ratio of local expenditure to central expenditure in a province	1.78	0.61	7.11	1.32
Provincial marginal revenue retention rate	0.84	0.11	1.00	0.23
Provincial marginal revenue retention rate (dummy)	0.57	0	1	0.50
Provincial budgetary revenue (100 million *yuan*)	53.56	1.30	222.64	42.01
Provincial budgetary expenditure (100 million *yuan*)	45.46	5.71	197.93	27.93
Provincial extra-budgetary revenue (100 million *yuan*)	44.21	0.46	160.47	33.89
Provincial extra-budgetary expenditure (100 million *yuan*)	42.20	0.49	161.40	32.96
Provincial growth of rural non-agricultural employment	0.06	-0.04	0.26	0.05
Provincial growth of non-state-non-agricultural employment	0.09	-0.11	0.56	0.11
Share of contract workers in total state employment in a province	0.09	0.00	0.33	0.06
Share of bonuses in total wage in state enterprises in a province	0.15	0.06	0.45	0.05

were netted out from revenue and expenditure before 1986 but added to both revenue and expenditure afterward. Most of the price subsidies are the central government's earmarked transfers to local governments (Wong 1997). To make the data consistent throughout the sample period, we exclude the price subsidies from the government expenditure data after 1986. Because explicit provincial data on their price subsidy expenditures are unavailable, we use the following method to estimate them. First, we apply the central and local shares of price subsidies nationwide (Hofman 1993) to calculate the total local expenditures of the price subsidies for each year. Because the price subsidies are exclusively for urban residents and they are provided more or less uniformly across provinces, we then use the provincial share of urban residency in the country to allocate price subsidies to each province.

We investigate the marginal fiscal incentives facing local governments from both *ex post* and *ex ante* perspectives. To examine the *ex post* marginal fiscal incentives, we look at realized provincial *budgetary revenue* and *budgetary expenditure* separately. As explained in section 2, provincial budgetary revenue is the revenue generated in the province, excluding those revenues designated as the central government's fixed revenue. Provincial budgetary expenditure is the actual provincial government spending, after contractual obligations are fulfilled and renegotiation takes place. We also consider provincial *extra-budgetary revenue* and *extra-budgetary expenditure*. Although no sharing arrangements cover extra-budgetary revenue, the central government might extract a portion of these funds.[5]

We measure *ex ante* marginal fiscal incentives, defined as the contractual marginal retention rate of local revenue collection by provincial governments, as those determined by the fiscal contracts between the central and provincial governments during the period of 1980–1993. In contrast to the ratio of local to central government expenditure, the fiscal incentive variable measures how local governments are rewarded (or punished) *at the margin* from an increase (or decrease) in local revenue collection. Therefore, it is the right variable that should be used to the study on the effects of fiscal incentives.[6]

The data on provincial marginal retention rates in the fiscal contracts are collected from several publications including Chen (1988), Oksenberg and Tong (1991), Bahl and Wallich (1992), and Bahl (1999), which are in turn obtained from the Ministry of Finance in China, the central government agency that formulates these contracts. In some cases the data shows more than one marginal retention rate in a contract for different revenue brackets. In those cases we use the rate for the highest revenue bracket because the data reveals that all the provinces in fact ended up with that bracket.

We exclude the data of 1993 because it is distortionary due to the anticipation of a major change in the fiscal system in 1994. For example, one provision of the 1994 reform, announced in the fourth quarter of 1993, compensated local governments based on their 1993 figures of local expenditure. This provision gave an incentive for local governments to inflate the local expenditure figures toward the year end. We also use the 1992 data with caution, because in that year four provinces were selected for the experiment of a new tax system to be implemented nationwide in 1994. Therefore, these provinces were not officially on the fiscal contracting system any more. Dropping off these four data points has little effect on our results.

The provincial marginal revenue retention rates involve one complication. Starting in 1986, several large cities became fiscally independent from their provinces, directly contracting with the central government (they are known as "separately plan listed cities"). We have tried to incorporate the information on these city contracts into the provincial contracts by constructing an average provincial marginal retention rate using city revenue and provincial revenue (excluding the relevant city) as weights.[7] Figure 9.1 plots the average of the provincial marginal revenue retention rates and the share of provinces with 100 percent marginal retention rates.

The non-state sector in urban and, especially, rural areas is widely regarded as the engine of China's growth. We use two variables to measure the development reflecting the entry and expansion of non-state enterprises: *growth of rural enterprise employment*, which covers all non-agricultural activities in the rural areas, and *growth of non-state non-agricultural employment*, which includes both urban and rural non-state industry and services.

We study the reform within the state sector by examining two variables: the changes in the *share of contract workers in total state employment* and in the *share of bonuses in total state employee wages*. Prior to 1992, China did not privatize any state enterprise. Nonetheless state-owned enterprises underwent modest reforms. For example, many changed their employment practices by hiring workers on a contractual basis rather than giving them permanent positions. They also increasingly used bonuses as a form of payment in addition to fixed salary. Both

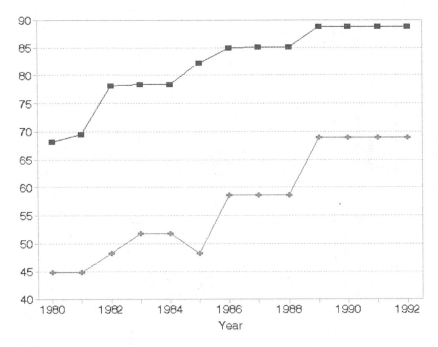

Figure 9.1
Provincial Marginal Revenue Retention Rates (1980–92). Note: The upper line is the average of marginal retention rates and the lower line is the share of the provinces with 100% marginal retention rates.

reforms were intended to improve workers' incentives. Groves et al. (1994) used similar variables as their major measurements of state-owned enterprise reform in China, and their data came from the enterprise level survey in four provinces.

5.   How Did Fiscal Incentives for Provincial Governments Change: Assessing the Credibility of the Fiscal Contracting System

We assess the credibility of the fiscal contracting system for the period of 1982–1992 by first comparing the actual provincial expenditure with the contractual revenue retention amount implied by the *ex ante* fiscal contracts (for example, the *ex ante* marginal retention rate times local revenue collection minus lump-sum remittance). This allows us to estimate the extent of *ex post* readjustment of revenue remittance and subsidies beyond the contracts. A small discrepancy between the *ex ante* contracts and *ex post* implementation implies that the fiscal contracts

Table 9.2
The Discrepancy between the *Ex Ante* Contracts and *Ex Post* Implementation

	(1) Budgetary revenue	(2) Unadjusted budgetary expenditure	(3) Price subsidies	(4) Budgetary expenditure	(5) Contractual budgetary revenue retention	(6) Weighted average of fiscal readjustment (%)	(7) Number of provinces
All provinces							
1982	863.5	572.4	0	572.4	521.7	10.9	28
1983	881.6	645.3	0	645.3	546.7	15.3	28
1984	968.5	800.1	0	800.1	602.8	24.7	28
1985	1185.0	1038.2	0	1038.2	852.0	18.3	28
1986	1324.5	1366.5	256.0	1110.5	992.4	9.4	28
1987	1466.4	1411.5	292.9	1118.7	1124.6	6.0	28
1988	1597.6	1650.2	315.0	1335.2	1267.3	6.9	28
1989	1926.5	1937.2	370.3	1566.8	1624.6	7.4	29
1990	1967.7	2105.5	380.8	1724.7	1657.4	6.6	29
1991	2258.1	2402.5	373.8	2028.8	1917.2	6.8	29
1992	2430.7	2564.6	321.6	2243.0	2085.1	7.3	29

Note: Hainan became a separate province in 1989 so the total number of provinces increased from 28 to 29.

are credible, whereas a big discrepancy would emerge if the central government systematically sought greater than the contracted amounts from high-performing provinces.

Fiscal readjustment (*ex post*) measures the difference between actual provincial expenditure and contractual revenue retention as implied by the fiscal contracts.[8] A negative value of fiscal readjustment means that the province spends less than the contractual provision entailed. We interpret the first case to be the one in which the province *ex post* remitted extra revenue to the central government, for example, if it were forced to "lend" revenue to the central government. These cases represent the central government's "predation." A positive value of fiscal readjustment indicates that the province *ex post* received extra subsidies from the central government, a signal of the "soft budget constraint" (Kornai 1988).[9] For any given year, we use the average of this variable across provinces weighted by provincial expenditure to measure the average deviation of implemented fiscal contracts from the promised ones.

Consider Table 9.2, which reports in column (6) the weighted average of the fiscal readjustment across provinces between 1982 and 1992, as measured by the absolute difference between actual expenditure and contractual revenue retention divided by expenditure. The data display a declining trend over time. After 1986, this variable fell below 8 percent.

This evidence suggests that the extent of *ex post* readjustments has become more limited over time. Further, after 1986, these adjustments have been relatively limited in scope. On average, actual provincial expenditures correspond reasonably well to their contractual revenue retention. Of course, we do not expect an exact correspondence due to *ex post* adjustments reflecting exogenous events that occur during the year, such as natural disasters. The evidence thus suggests that the fiscal contracts are credible.

Next we divide the provinces into two categories: extra remittance provinces, defined as those provinces whose actual expenditure fall short of contractual revenue retention, and extra subsidy recipient provinces, defined as those whose expenditure exceed contractual revenue retention. Examining the two groups separately, we find that there are generally fewer extra revenue remitting provinces (see column (7), Panel A of Table 9.3) than extra subsidized provinces (see column (7), Panel B of Table 9.3). This indicates that the *ex post* extra transfers from the center to provinces (i.e., the problem of soft budget

Table 9.3
Extra Remittances vs. Extra Subsidies

	(1) Budgetary revenue	(2) Unadjusted budgetary expenditure	(3) Price subsidies	(4) Budgetary expenditure	(5) Contractual budgetary revenue retention	(6) Weighted average of fiscal readjustment (%)	(7) Number of provinces
Panel A: Provinces paying extra remittance (budgetary expenditure < contractual revenue retention)							
1982	193.4	110.1	0	110.1	116.0	-5.3	6
1983	0	0	0	0	0	N/A	0
1984	0	0	0	0	0	N/A	0
1985	184.2	46.1	0	46.1	47.9	-4.0	1
1986	79.8	82.9	16.3	66.6	72.0	-6.6	1
1987	611.5	702.8	150.9	551.9	597.2	-6.5	14
1988	418.2	392.6	79.1	313.4	336.6	-5.9	6
1989	1368.3	1313.7	259.4	1054.3	1155.1	-7.7	19
1990	873.7	827.3	149.8	677.6	713.5	-4.3	10
1991	694.4	742.2	107.8	634.4	660.2	-3.5	7
1992	591.7	596.4	60.0	536.4	550.8	-2.4	4
Panel B: Provinces receiving extra subsidies (budgetary expenditure > contractual revenue retention)							
1982	670.2	462.3	0	462.3	405.8	12.2	22
1983	881.6	645.3	0	645.3	546.7	15.3	28
1984	968.5	800.1	0	800.1	602.8	24.7	28
1985	1000.7	992.1	0	992.1	804.1	19.0	27
1986	1244.7	1283.6	239.7	1043.9	920.4	9.6	27
1987	855.0	708.8	142.0	555.8	527.4	5.6	14
1988	1179.4	1257.6	235.8	1021.8	930.7	7.3	22
1989	558.3	623.5	111.0	512.5	469.5	6.9	10
1990	1093.9	1278.2	231.0	1047.1	944.0	8.1	19
1991	1563.8	1660.4	266.0	1394.4	1256.9	8.3	22
1992	1839.0	1968.3	261.7	1706.6	1534.3	8.8	25

Note: Hainan became a separate province in 1989 so the total number of provinces increased from 28 to 29.

constraints) is quantitatively more significant than extra transfers from the provinces to the center.[10]

Because of the potential for central government predation, the phenomenon of extra remitting provinces is of special interest. If the central government behaved in a predatory fashion—for example, if it consistently forced the more successful provinces to remit significant amount of additional revenue—the magnitude of this figure would be significant. The results in Panel A of Table 9.3 suggest that these additional remittances are small. After 1989, only one-third of the provinces remitted additional money, and the average amounted to a relatively small portion of their expenditure, under 4 percent.

Table 9.3 also reveals two aspects of a sudden increase in extra remittances from provinces to the central government in 1989. First, the average quantity of extra remittances increased to 7.7 percent of expenditures (see column (6), Panel A). Second, the number of provinces making the extra remittances jumped to 19 out of 28 (see column (7), Panel A). The table also shows a decrease in extra subsidies from the central to local governments as compared with other years, before and after (columns (6) and (7), Panel B).

The changes in 1989 are not surprising. In that year, conservatives in the government temporarily gained power after the Tiananmen Square incident, causing a temporary setback in reform. Importantly, Table 9.3 reveals two aspects of this setback. First, this change was relatively short lived: after 1989, the fiscal pattern returns to its previous trend. Second, the absolute amount was modest. Although many more provinces were subject to additional remittances in 1989, remittances averaged less than 8 percent of expenditures. Indeed, these data support the common anecdotal evidence in the literature that the setback in reform after Tiananmen Square was temporary. By the early 1990s, the number of provinces with extra remittances was small, as was the average magnitude of the extra remittance.

6. How Did Fiscal Incentives for Provincial Governments Change: Examining the *Ex Post* Link between Local Revenue and Expenditure

In this section, we provide evidence showing that reform has strengthened the fiscal incentives of provincial governments through a stronger link between (*ex post*) provincial marginal revenue collection and marginal expenditure. To that end, we look at the correlations between provincial *ex post* realized revenue and expenditure for both before and after reform. We run the following fixed effect model:

$$\text{(Local Expenditure)}_{it} = \alpha_i + \gamma_t + \beta \text{ (Local Revenue)}_{it} + \mu_{it}, \tag{3}$$

where (Local Expenditure)$_{it}$ is province i's local expenditure in year t, (Local Revenue)$_{it}$ is province i's local revenue in year t, the α_i's are provincial fixed effects, γ_t's are the year dummies, and μ_{it}'s are the disturbance terms. These tests are designed to examine the link between local expenditures and local revenues, after controlling for provincial inherent characteristics and nationwide changes over time.

Panel B of Table 9.4 reports the results for data from 1982 to 1991, in which row (1) shows a coefficient of 0.752 on provincial budgetary revenue in its budgetary expenditure equation. It means that, on average, a one *yuan* increase in provincial budgetary revenue results in about three-quarters *yuan* of provincial budgetary expenditure. Considering the fact that during this period the local budgetary revenue is on average about two-thirds of the total budgetary revenue, the results demonstrate that, in terms of budgetary revenue and expenditure, the fiscal system in China's reform has produced a strong link between local expenditure and local revenue generation. Further, row (2) shows an even larger coefficient—0.971—for the extra-budgetary expenditure equation, that is, the relationship for extra-budgetary revenue and expenditure becomes almost one-to-one.[11] This provides additional fiscal incentives for local governments.

To put the above results in perspective, we run the similar regression for the pre-reform period. Using data from 1970 to 1979, row (1) of Table 9.4 in Panel A reveals a very small coefficient on provincial budgetary revenue in the budgetary expenditure equation, 0.172. This result shows that, prior to economic reform, the central government extracted revenue from high revenue provinces while subsidizing low revenue provinces. Indeed, a coefficient of 0.172 indicates that, prior to the reforms, the central government, on average, extracted over 80 percent of any increase in local revenue.

One has to be careful in attempting to compare the above numbers from the pre-reform and post-reform periods because the definition of "local revenue" changed somewhat between the two periods. Indeed, after the 1980 reform, some revenues previously designated as "local revenue" were later designated as "central revenue," mainly because some previously local government supervised state-owned enterprises were taken over by the central government and their revenues

Table 9.4
The Correlations Between Local Revenue and Expenditure

		Panel A: 1970–79		Panel B: 1982–91		Panel C: 1995–99	
		β	R^2	β	R^2	β	R^2
	Fixed Effect						
(1)	Budgetary expenditure on budgetary revenue	0.172*** (6.172)	0.930	0.752*** (19.73)	0.968	0.998*** (18.95)	0.986
(2)	Extra-budgetary expenditure on extra-budgetary revenue			0.971*** (32.25)	0.991		
	First Difference						
(3)	Budgetary expenditure on budgetary revenue	0.086*** (3.840)	0.448	0.481*** (8.767)	0.707	0.942*** (11.44)	0.481
(4)	Extra-budgetary expenditure on extra-budgetary revenue			0.803*** (12.53)	0.674		

Notes: (1) Each regression includes a full set of year dummies. (2) Huber-White robust t-statistics are in parentheses. (3) Asterisks indicate variables whose coefficients are significant at the 10% (*), 5% (**), and 1% (***) levels.

subsequently became central revenue. One way to think of this is to consider the value v in equation (1). Reclassification of some local revenue into central revenue after the 1980 reform reduces v, assuming that it reduces the local revenue proportionally to a fraction of the original revenue.[12] To the extent that this occurred in practice it implies that, when we regress "local expenditure" on "local revenue," the estimated coefficient would be larger simply because v becomes smaller.

Examining our data reveals that such an effect is not quantitatively significant. The average share of local budgetary revenue in total government budgetary revenue is 84 percent for the period of 1970–1979 (with the maximum of 88 percent in a single year) as compared to 66 percent for the period of 1982–1991 (with the minimum of 59 percent in a single year). These figures imply that, on average, the 1982–1991 period local revenue share is about 0.79 times the share of the 1970–1979 period. Therefore, due purely to the effect of reclassification of local revenues after the reform and not attributed to any improvement in incentives, the estimated correlation coefficient β after the reform could have been boosted by about $1/0.79 = 1.27$ times (or by 1.48 times if the maximum and minimum values are used) on comparable basis. In other words, the comparable coefficient for the pre-reform period could be 0.218 instead of 0.172 (or 2.55 if the maximum and minimum values are used). Our estimated correlation during the reform, 0.752, is still 3.4 times that before the reform, instead of 4.4 times if reclassification of revenue is completely ignored . Therefore, the modest reclassification of revenues does not undermine our interpretation of the drastic improvement of local incentives after reform.

We also run the regression using the data from 1995 to 1999 to see how the fiscal incentives of local governments might have changed for the post 1994 period when the "fiscal contracting system" was replaced by the "separating tax system." Row (1) of Table 9.4 in Panel C shows a coefficient of 0.998 on provincial budgetary revenue in its budgetary expenditure equation. To make the results of the post-1994 period and the 1982–1991 period comparable, we need to consider the change in the definition of "local revenue." Starting in 1994, "local revenue" has been defined as revenues from local taxes and the local portion of the shared taxes (Bahl 1999). As a result of this change, the local revenue share of the total revenue shrank from 66 percent for 1982–1991 to 50 percent for 1995–1999, still a very high level. This implies that the average local revenue share for 1995–1999 is about 0.76 times the share for the 1982–1991 period. Because the marginal incentive of the local revenue for the 1995–1999 period is approximately 1, when we take into consideration the effect of the reduced scope of local revenue for this period, the estimated correlation coefficient β is still comparable to 0.752 as for the 1982–1991 period.

We also examine the first difference version of model (5.1) by regressing the change of local expenditure over one year on the change of local revenue over one year, still including the year dummies. Row (3) of Table 9.4 shows a coefficient of 0.481 on provincial budgetary revenue in its budgetary expenditure equation for the data of 1982–1991 in Panel B, a drop from 0.752—the fixed effect model estimation. This coefficient is 0.057 for the data of 1970–1979 in Panel A, an even bigger proportional drop from 0.172 as in the fixed effect model estimation. It is 0.942 for the data of 1995–1999 in Panel C, somewhat smaller than 0.998 as in the fixed effect model. However, the estimations from the first difference model may be biased toward zero since it may suffer from an error-in-variable or a misspecification problem.

We compare our findings on China with the related investigations of post-reform Russia. Zhuravskaya (2000) examined the fiscal incentives of local (i.e., city) governments in the region-local fiscal relationship in post-reform Russia, showing a striking pattern which she interpreted as predation. Using the data from 35 cities for the period 1992–1997 and regressing the change in the "shared revenue" between the regional and city governments on the change of the city's "own revenue," she finds that the coefficient is -0.90. She interprets this result as evidence that increases in a city's revenue are almost entirely offset by decreases in shared revenues from the region to the city. This implies that an increase in 1 ruble in city government's own revenue will result in only increase of 0.1 ruble in net revenue of the city government. Exaction of this magnitude destroys cities' incentives to increase their tax base.

Our above results suggest that, for the budgetary revenue and extra-budgetary revenue individually, the Chinese central government's post-reform treatment of provinces provides provincial governments with strong fiscal incentives.[13] Our data set from China does not allow us to perform the comparable investigations on province-city or prefecture-county fiscal relationships. However, studies on China's local fiscal reform document two aspects relevant for this discussion (Bahl and Wallich 1992; Wong 1997): first, throughout the 1980s, the fiscal contracting practice extended to all subnational levels of provinces, cities/prefectures, counties, and townships; and second, the subnational fiscal contracting usually mimicked the center-province fiscal contracting applied to their province. To the extent that the subnational level inter-governmental fiscal relationships resemble that between the center and provinces, local government incentives within the provincial setting should parallel those we find at the central-provincial level. Further research is needed to obtain subnational level results on China in order to make direct comparisons with the results on Russia.

7. How Provincial Governments Responded to Fiscal Incentives: Estimating the Effects on Development of Non-State Enterprises and Reform in State Enterprises

To investigate the effects of fiscal incentives on the local economy, we investigate the following model:

$$Y_{it} = \alpha_i + \gamma_t + \delta'Z_{it} + \sigma'W_{it\text{-}1} + u_{it}. \tag{4}$$

In equation (4), Y_{it} is a vector of variables measuring the development of the non-state sector and reform in the state sector in a province, and Z_{it} includes the variable of (*ex ante*) provincial marginal revenue retention rate which measures fiscal incentives as well as the variable of fiscal decentralization. The α_i's represent the provincial specific effects, which we assume are constant for each province, implying that our specification is a fixed effect model. The γ_t's are the year dummies, which are intended to capture the effects of nationwide macroeconomic fluctuation. As a common practice, we include $W_{it-1,}$ the lagged per capita GDP, for the purpose of controlling for the level of development. The u_{it}'s are the disturbance terms. Our fixed effect model implies that any correlations between Y and Z cannot be attributed to inherent provincial characteristics.

Table 9.5 presents our results on the effects of fiscal decentralization and fiscal incentives on the development of non-state enterprises. The dependent variable in Panel A of Table 9.5 is the growth of rural enterprise employment, a narrower measure of non-state sector development; the dependent variable in Panel B is the growth of non-state-non-agricultural employment in both urban and rural areas, a broader measure.

The two panels give similar results. Column 1 of Table 9.5 reveals that fiscal decentralization has positive effects on the development of non-state enterprises.[14] Column 2 shows that fiscal incentives also have positive and significant effects on the development of non-state enterprises.[15] Is this possible that the fiscal incentives variable simply picks up the effect from fiscal decentralization? Column 3 shows that this is not the case: the effect of fiscal incentives remains significant even after controlling for fiscal decentralization. This implies that fiscal decentralization alone is insufficient to explain the growth of the non-state sector, fiscal incentives have additional explanatory power. Quantitatively, if the marginal revenue retention rate in a province increases by 10 percentage points, then the growth rate of non-state enterprises in that province would increase by 1.01 percentage points, when it is measured for rural enterprises only, and 0.97 percentage points, when measured for both rural and urban non-state enterprises. Because the average growth rate of employment in rural enterprises is 6 percent and that of all non-state enterprises is 9 percent during this period, the estimated effects are economically quite significant.

One may worry about the reliability of our data on marginal revenue retention rates. To check the robustness of our estimations, we ran

Table 9.5

Fiscal Incentives and the Development of the Non-State Sector

Panel A. Dependent Variable: Growth of Rural Enterprise Employment

Independent Variable	(1)	(2)	(3)	(4)	(5)
Ratio of local expenditure to central expenditure in a province	0.051* (1.729)		0.038 (1.376)		0.047 (1.639)
Provincial marginal revenue retention rate		0.141** (2.145)	0.114* (1.837)		
Provincial marginal revenue retention rate (dummy)				0.056*** (2.677)	0.051** (2.493)
Per capita GDP$_{-1}$	0.004 (0.064)	0.043 (0.724)	0.023 (0.392)	0.040 (0.684)	0.020 (0.342)
Adjusted R^2	0.734	0.742	0.736	0.740	0.771

Panel B. Dependent Variable: Growth of Non-State-Non-Agricultural Employment

Independent Variable	(1)	(2)	(3)	(4)	(5)
Ratio of local expenditure to central expenditure in a province	0.050** (2.265)		0.039* (1.829)		0.048** (2.179)
Provincial marginal revenue retention rate		0.131*** (2.714)	0.104** (2.309)		
Provincial marginal revenue retention rate (dummy)				0.042** (2.449)	0.038** (2.298)
Per capita GDP$_{-1}$	-0.024 (0.486)	0.023 (0.464)	-0.006 (0.122)	0.017 (0.349)	-0.012 (0.235)
Adjusted R^2	0.757	0.763	0.761	0.759	0.791

Notes: (1) Each regression includes a full set of provincial dummies and year dummies. (2) Huber-White robust t-statistics are in parentheses. (3) Sample size is 319. (4) Asterisks indicate variables whose coefficients are significant at the 10% (*), 5% (**), and 1% (***) levels.

parallel regressions replacing the continuous marginal retention rate variable with a dummy variable. This is a kind of aggregation, intended to reduce the impacts of the possible error-in-variable problem in the measurement of the underlying variable. The dummy fiscal incentive variable takes value 1 if the marginal retention rate is 100 percent and 0 otherwise. The results of using the dummy fiscal incentive variable are reported in columns (4) and (5) of Table 9.5. In both regressions, the signs and significance of all our estimated coefficients of the dummy fiscal incentive variable remain the same. The evidence demonstrates that the error-in-variable problem, if it exists, is not serious enough to distort our qualitative results.

We carry out a similar investigation for the reform of state-owned enterprises. Panel A of Table 9.6 reports our results on the change of the share of contract workers in total state employment and Panel B on the change in the share of bonuses in total employee wages. In contrast to permanent workers, who are under the traditional socialist labor conditions of "iron rice bowls," contract workers do not have tenure and are more likely subject to market conditions. More contract workers relative to permanent workers mean that enterprises are better restructured to market orientation. Bonuses, as compared to fixed wages, represent a compensation form that is more closely linked to workers performance, a higher share of bonuses in total employee wages implies enterprise workers are better motivated.

We find that the degree of fiscal decentralization has no significant effects on both measures of reform (column 1). However, fiscal incentives have positive and significant effects in the specification for the change of the share of contract workers in total state employment (column 2, Panel A), such effects remain even after controlling for fiscal decentralization (column 3, Panel A). A 10 percentage point increase in the marginal revenue retention rate in a province is associated with a 0.50 percentage point increase in the share of contract workers. As for the change of the share of bonuses in total employee wages, incentives still have positive and significant effects (column 2, Panel B), except that the statistical significance is lost after controlling for fiscal decentralization (column 3, Panel B). Again, we replaced fiscal incentive variable with the corresponding dummy variable and reports the results in columns 4 and 5. Fiscal incentives still have positive and significant effects for the change of the share of contract workers in total state employment (column 4, Panel A), even after controlling for fiscal decentralization (column 5, Panel A), but not for the change of the share of bonuses in total employee wages (columns 4 and 5, Panel B).

We now turn to investigate the possibility of endogeneity problems. The marginal retention rates are treated as a predetermined variable in our model. The central government and the provinces renegotiate the fiscal contract rates every 3–5 years, and they remain rather stable within the intervals. The marginal retention rates either stay the same or are increased over time; none are adjusted downward, as Figure 9.1 demonstrates this feature in aggregate terms. This suggests some

Table 9.6
Fiscal Incentives and the Reform of the State Sector

Panel A. Dependent Variable: Change in the Share of Contract Workers in Total State Employment

Independent Variable	(1)	(2)	(3)	(4)	(5)
Ratio of local expenditure to central expenditure in a province	0.165 (0.257)		-0.366 (0.675)		0.048 (0.082)
Provincial marginal revenue retention rate		5.465* (1.714)	5.625* (1.914)		
Provincial marginal revenue retention rate (dummy)				1.549* (1.919)	1.545* (1.705)
Per capita GDP$_{-1}$	-0.540 (0.218)	0.165 (0.079)	0.343 (0.163)	0.078 (0.037)	0.563 (0.025)
Adjusted R^2	0.026	0.081	0.078	0.047	0.198

Panel B. Dependent Variable: Change in the Share of Bonuses in Total Employee Wages

Independent Variable	(1)	(2)	(3)	(4)	(5)
Ratio of local expenditure to central expenditure in a province	0.433 (0.772)		0.251 (0.665)		0.415 (0.796)
Provincial marginal revenue retention rate		1.877* (1.705)	1.700 (1.641)		
Provincial marginal revenue retention rate (dummy)				0.329 (0.473)	0.292 (0.319)
Per capita GDP$_{-1}$	-0.976 (0.667)	-0.580 (0.535)	-0.688 (0.629)	-0.733 (0.605)	-0.882 (0.687)
Adjusted R^2	0.445	0.450	0.449	0.443	0.518

Notes: (1) Each regression includes a full set of provincial dummies and year dummies. (2) Huber-White robust t-statistics are in parentheses. (3) Sample size is 319. (4) Asterisks indicate variables whose coefficients are significant at the 10% (*), 5% (**), and 1% (***) levels.

underlying momentum in the negotiation process. Indeed, the contractual arrangements started as an "experiment" and only expanded and strengthened over time. For one reason, both the central and provincial governments were not sure if they would work or how effectively they would work. For another reason, the experiment was also constrained by exogenous factors such as an ideology against high marginal retention rates (which was viewed as too capitalistic), and such a constraint was only relaxed over time.

One may worry that in the process of the experiment, the central government sets higher marginal retention rates for high growth and greater reform provinces. If this is the case, we cannot interpret the higher growth and greater reforms as a result of higher marginal retention rates. An unbiased estimation might be obtained by instrumenting the marginal retention rate variable. Lacking such an instrument, we go for the second-best solution: instead of looking for unbiased estimations, we check to see if our estimations are biased upward; in such a case, our interpretation of the results would be problematic. To this end, we regress marginal retention rates on the lagged growth rates of the non-state sector and on the lagged reform variables in the state sector respectively. Table 9.7 reports the results with the marginal retention rate as the dependent variable, while Table 9.8 with the dummy

Table 9.7
The Endogeneity Problem: Provincial Marginal Revenue Retention Rate

Panel A. Dependent Variable: Provincial Marginal Revenue Retention Rate

Independent Variable	(1)	(2)	(3)	(4)
Growth of rural enterprise employment$_{-2}$	-0.017* (1.654)	-0.018* (1.738)		
Growth of non-state-non-agricultural employment$_{-2}$			-0.007 (0.903)	-0.008 (1.087)
Per capita GDP$_{-2}$	-0.208** (2.384)		-0.215** (2.432)	
Adjusted R^2	0.847	0.835	0.846	0.834

Panel B. Dependent Variable: Provincial Marginal Revenue Retention Rate

Independent Variable	(1)	(2)	(3)	(4)
Change in the share of contract workers in state employment$_{-2}$	-0.086 (0.484)	-0.093 (0.503)		
Change in the share of bonuses in total employee wages$_{-2}$			-0.922** (2.169)	-1.043** (2.481)
Per capita GDP$_{-2}$	-0.140 (1.506)		-0.173** (2.021)	
Adjusted R^2	0.838	0.841	0.849	0.839

Notes: (1) Each regression includes a full set of provincial dummies and year dummies. (2) Huber-White robust t-statistics are in parentheses. (3) Sample size is 307 (Panel A) and 298 (Panel B). (4) Asterisks indicate variables whose coefficients are significant at the 10% (*), 5% (**), and 1% (***) levels.

fiscal incentive variable. In both tables, we found negative rather than positive coefficients; some of them are even statistically significant. That is to say, on average, high growth provinces are more likely to receive lower rather than higher marginal retention rates. Therefore, if our estimates are biased due to the endogeneity problem, it is more likely biased against our hypothesis: that is, we might have underestimated the claimed effect.

8. Conclusions

This paper studies the changing local government fiscal incentives and their impacts on market development. Many anecdotes suggest the

Table 9.8
The Endogeneity Problem: Provincial Marginal Revenue Retention Rate Dummy

Panel A. Dependent Variable: Provincial Marginal Revenue Retention Rate Dummy

Independent Variable	(1)	(2)	(3)	(4)
Growth of rural enterprise employment$_{-2}$	-0.020 (0.475)	-0.021 (0.478)		
Growth of non-state-non-agricultural employment$_{-2}$			-0.067 (0.876)	-0.065 (0.763)
Per capita GDP$_{-2}$	-0.512*** (2.821)		-0.499*** (2.807)	
Adjusted R^2	0.843	0.815	0.845	0.817

Panel B. Dependent Variable: Provincial Marginal Revenue Retention Rate Dummy

Independent Variable	(1)	(2)	(3)	(4)
Change in the share of contract workers in state employment$_{-2}$	-0.144** (2.405)	-0.075 (1.233)		
Change in the share of bonuses in total employee wages$_{-2}$			-0.007 (0.219)	-0.044 (1.235)
Per capita GDP$_{-2}$	-0.636*** (3.119)		-0.524*** (2.954)	
Adjusted R^2	0.845	0.815	0.842	0.815

Notes: (1) Each regression includes a full set of provincial dummies and year dummies. (2) Huber-White robust t-statistics are in parentheses. (3) Sample size is 307 (Panel A) and 298 (Panel B). (4) Asterisks indicate variables whose coefficients are significant at the 10% (*), 5% (**), and 1% (***) levels.

importance of fiscal incentives in the previous studies on China's reforms. The econometric results in this paper provide some systematic evidence on the economic significance of fiscal incentives. We find that the reforms considerably strengthened the fiscal incentives of provincial governments, and they are generally conducive to provincial economic development and reform. These results point to the important link between local government's fiscal incentives and local economic development.

Comparisons of local government's behavior toward local economic development between China and Russia are striking. Our study of federalism, Chinese style, and the other studies on federalism, Russian style (Zhuravskaya 2000; de Figueiredo and Weingast 2001), indicate that one crucial difference concerns the fiscal incentives provided for local governments to pursue market-supporting activities.

Our perspective yields an important insight about how federalism works in promoting economic development; namely, there exists a positive relationship between the strength of fiscal incentives faced by lower-level governments and local economic performance. Countries with strong fiscal incentives for local governments are expected to experience healthier local business development while those with low fiscal incentives are expected to experience the opposite. Instead of decentralization per se, we emphasize the importance of strong fiscal incentives. Whether this prediction holds empirically in other countries awaits further work.

Notes

* We would like to thank Alberto Alesina, Bill Evans, Roger Gordon, John McMillan, Peter Murrell, Barry Naughton, Gerard Roland, Seth Sanders, Robert Schwab, Andrei Shleifer, Shang-Jin Wei, David Wildasin, Alwyn Young, Heng-fu Zou, and the participants at the Fifth Nobel Symposium in Economics held in Stockholm in 1999 for helpful comments and discussions and the Center for Research on Economic Development and Policy Reform at Stanford for financial support.

1. The recent theory of "market-preserving federalism" studies the general question of how federalism can be structured to promote market development (e.g., McKinnon 1997; Qian and Roland 1998; Qian and Weingast 1996; Weingast 1995; Wildasin 1997; and Zhuravskaya 2000).

2. The conventional, more readily available data of the *ex post* ratios of revenue retention over collection measures only the average realized revenue retention and is thus less suitable for the study of the effects of fiscal incentives on other economic variables.

3. Below the township level, the village is an informal level of government. A municipality can be one of the levels of a province, prefecture, or county; most municipalities are at the prefecture level.

4. The data excludes Tibet. Hainan obtained a provincial status only in 1989, and we treat Hainan as a separate province throughout the sample period.

5. All provincial budgetary and extra-budgetary data are consolidated figures within a province.

6. Akai and Sakata (2002) used an *ex post* measure of fiscal "autonomy" (defined as the ratio of local expenditure over local revenue) in their study of the U.S. fiscal federalism. They found that this measure of fiscal autonomy contributes to economic growth at the state level in the U.S.

7. The incorporated information on "separately plan listed cities" includes Wuhan (1986–1992) in Hubei; Chongqing (1986–1992) in Sichuan; Shenyang (1988–1992) in Heilongjiang; Ningbo (1988–1992) in Zhejiang; and Qingdao (1991–1992) in Shandong. Information sources are the provincial and city statistical yearbooks.

8. Again, the data is adjusted for price subsidies after 1986: local portions of price subsidies are excluded from local expenditure. They were earmarked central government transfers and were determined solely by the number of urban residents anyway.

9. We make a few qualifications regarding the interpretation of the variable fiscal readjustment. First, we implicitly assume that each province has a balanced budget each year without carry-overs from the previous year or savings into the next year. This is basically true. Second, because our information about the fiscal contracts is limited to fixed subsidies/remittances and marginal retention rates, we have to omit other pre-defined transfers or transfers based on exogenous criteria such as natural disaster relief. However, such transfers are not significant. Third, because we look at net transfers (i.e., expenditure minus revenue retention), it is possible that two way transfers are high but net transfers are low. Despite these limitations, this variable provides useful information on the significance of *ex post* readjustment of fiscal revenue retention.

10. This may also due to the fact that we were unable to account for some earmarked subsidies.

11. Using the three year data of 1983, 1987, and 1990 individually, Knight and Li (1999) also found that the correlations between local extra-budgetary revenue and expenditure were generally higher than those between local budgetary revenue and expenditure, and the latter increased over time.

12. However, other possibilities of reclassification may not induce a bias as large as this. For example, if a reclassification decreases local revenue by a fixed amount (same for all provinces) but does not change v, then the estimated coefficients β for the two periods are comparable.

13. In a separate regression we also find that in China, increases in extra-budgetary revenue (roughly corresponds to "own revenue" in Russia) has little negative effect on the change of budgetary expenditure (roughly corresponds to "shared revenue" in Russia) as observed in Russia. The coefficient is actually positive, which in part reflects the fact that budgetary and extra-budgetary revenues have similar tax bases.

14. A previous study by Zhang and Zou (1998) reported a negative and significant effect of fiscal decentralization on provincial GDP growth during China's reform. We found that such negative effect would disappear and actually would turn into a positive effect if the set of annual time dummy variables is included in their regressions. This suggests that their findings perhaps resulted from the failure to filter out economy-wide cyclic effect.

15. Lin and Liu (2000) reported a positive effect of marginal retention rate on provincial GDP growth in the production-function-based growth regression. However, in their regressions they used the growth rate of investment instead of the growth rate of capital (or investment-output ratio) for capital input as standard in the literature, which makes their results hard to interpret. Furthermore, the t-value associated with the effect of marginal retention rate drops significantly, from 2.70 to 1.65, when the sample is restricted to the post reform period, suggesting the claimed effect might pick up the effects of other unmeasured reforms.

References

Akai, Nobuo, and Masayo Sakata. "Fiscal Decentralization Contributes to Economic Growth: Evidence from State-Level Cross-Section Data for the United States." Journal of Urban Economics, 52: 93–108, 2002.

Bahl, Roy. *Fiscal Policy in China: Taxation and Intergovernmental Fiscal Relations*. San Francisco: The 1990 Institute, 1999.

Bahl, Roy, and Christine Wallich. "Intergovernmental Fiscal Relations in China," Working Papers, Country Economics Department, The World Bank, WPS 863, 1992.

Blanchard, Olivier; and Andrei Shleifer. "Federalism with and without Political Centralization: China versus Russia." NBER Working Paper #7616, 2000.

Brennan, Geoffrey, and James M. Buchanan. *The Power to Tax: Analytical Foundations of a Fiscal Constitution*. New York: Cambridge University Press, 1980.

Chen, Rulong (ed.). *The Fiscal System in Contemporary China (Dangdai Zhongguo Caizheng)*, Beijing: China Social Science Press, 1988.

de Figueiredo, Rui J. P. Jr., and Barry R. Weingast. "Pathologies of Federalism, Russian Style: Political Institutions and Economic Transition." Paper prepared for delivery at the Conference, "Fiscal Federalism in the Russian Federation: Problems and Prospects for Reform," Higher School of Economics, Moscow, Russia, January 29–20, 2001.

Fan, Gang. "New Norms in Public Revenue and Expenditure," in Shuguang Zhang (ed.), *Case Studies in China's Institutional Change*, Shanghai People's Publishing House, 1996.

Frye, Timothy, and Andrei Shleifer, "The Invisible Hand and the Grabbing Hand." *American Economic Review*, May 1997, *87*, pp. 354–358.

Groves, Theodore, Yongmiao Hong, John McMillan, and Barry Naughton. "Autonomy and Incentives in Chinese State Enterprises." *Quarterly Journal of Economics*, 1994, *109*(1), pp. 183–209.

Hayek, Friedrich A. "The Use of Knowledge in Society." *American Economic Review*, 35, pp. 519–530, 1945.

Hofman, Bert. "An Analysis of Chinese Fiscal Data over the Reform Period." *China Economic Review*, 1993, 4(2), pp. 213–230.

Knight, John; and Shi Li. "Fiscal Decentralization: Incentives, Redistribution and Reform in China." *Oxford Development Studies*, 1999, 27(1), pp. 5–32.

Kornai, Janos. "The Soft Budget Constraints," *KYKLOS*, 1988, *30*(1), pp. 3–30.

Lavrov, Aleksei, John M. Litwack, and Douglas Sutherland. 2000. "Fiscal Federalist Relations in Russia: A Case for Subnational Autonomy." Working Paper, Organization of Economic Cooperation and Development (OECD), Paris, France.

Li, Hongbin, and Li-An Zhou. "Political Turnover and Economic Performance: The Incentive Role of Personnel Control in China." *Journal of Public Economics*, forthcoming, 2004.

Lin, Justin Yifu, and Zhiqiang Liu. "Fiscal Decentralization and Economic Growth in China." *Economic Development and Cultural Change*, October 2000, *49*(1), pp. 1–21.

Maskin, Eric, Yingyi Qian, and Chenggang Xu. "Incentives, Information, and Organizational Form." *Review of Economic Studies*, April 2000, *67*(2), pp. 359–378.

McKinnon, Ronald. "Market-Preserving Federalism in the American Monetary Union," in M. Blejer and T. Ter-Minassian (eds.), *Macroeconomic Dimensions of Public Finance: Essays in Honour of Vito Tanzi*. London: Routledge, 1997, pp. 73–93.

Montinola, Gabriella, Yingyi Qian, and Barry Weingast. "Federalism, Chinese Style: The Political Basis for Economic Success in China," *World Politics*, October 1995, *48*(1), pp. 50–81.

Musgrave, Richard, *Theory of Public Finance: A Study in Public Economy*, New York: McGraw, 1959.

National Statistical Bureau, *China Statistical Yearbook*, Beijing: China Statistical Publishing House, various years.

Oates, Wallace. *Fiscal Federalism*, New York: Harcourt Brace Jovanovich, 1972.

OECD. 2000. *OECD Economic Surveys: The Russian Federation*. Paris, France: Organization for Economic Co-operation and Development.

Oksenberg, Michel, and Tong, James. "The Evolution of Central-Provincial Fiscal Relations in China, 1971–1984: The Formal System." *China Quarterly*, March 1991.

Qian, Yingyi, and Gerard Roland. "Federalism and the Soft Budget Constraint," *American Economic Review*, December 1998, *88*(5), pp. 1143–1162.

Qian, Yingyi, and Barry R. Weingast. "China's Transition to Markets: Market-Preserving Federalism, Chinese Style," *Journal of Policy Reform*, 1996, *1*, pp. 149–185.

Shleifer, Andrei. "Government in Transition." *European Economic Review*, 1997, *41*, pp. 385–410.

Shleifer, Andrei, and Robert W. Vishny. *The Grabbing Hand: Government Pathologies and Their Cures*, Cambridge, MA: Harvard University Press, 1998.

Tiebout, Charles. "A Pure Theory of Local Expenditures." *Journal of Political Economy*, 1956, *64*, pp. 416–24.

Weingast, Barry R. "The Economic Role of Political Institutions: Market-Preserving Federalism and Economic Growth," *Journal of Law, Economics, and Organization*, April 1995, *11*, pp. 1–31.

Wildasin, David E. "Externalities and Bailouts: Hard and Soft Budget Constraints in Inter-Governmental Fiscal Relations," mimeo, Vanderbilt University, 1997.

Wong, Christine P. W. (eds.). *Financing Local Government in the People's Republic of China.* Hong Kong: Oxford University Press, 1997.

Zhang, Tao, and Heng-fu Zou. "Fiscal Decentralization, Public Spending, and Economic Growth in China." *Journal of Public Economics*, 1998, *67*, pp. 221–240.

Zhuravskaya, Ekaterina V. "Incentives to Provide Local Public Goods: Fiscal Federalism, Russian Style." *Journal of Public Economics*, June 2000, *76*(3), pp. 337–68.

IV INITIAL ORGANIZATIONAL CONDITIONS AND REFORM

10 Why China's Economic Reforms Differ: The M-Form Hierarchy and Entry/Expansion of the Non-State Sector

1. Introduction

Recently, there has been a revived interest among economists in China's economic reforms. Since 1979, economic reforms in China have generated significant growth across the board: the overall performance of the Chinese economy has been better than its own past record, better than most developing countries at similar development levels, and also better than Eastern Europe and the former Soviet Union, both before and after their radical transformations in 1989. It appears that China had no coherent reform programs, no commitment to private ownership, and no changes in the political system, and China's economy was still not fully liberalized. From both the theoretical and policy perspectives, China's different reform strategies and outstanding reform performances are particularly interesting and puzzling.

The economic reforms in China formally started in 1979 following the Third Plenum of the Eleventh Congress of the Chinese Communist Party in December 1978. The starting time was later than that of Yugoslavia (1950) and Hungary (1968), and was about the same as for Poland (1980) and earlier than the Soviet Union (1986). Between 1979 and 1991, China's GNP grew at an average annual rate of 8.6 percent, or at 7.2 percent on a per capita basis.[1] In 1992, the growth of GNP reached 12.8 percent.[2] Exports grew at a faster pace, so that China's export-GNP ratio increased from below 5 percent in 1978 to nearly 20 percent in 1991.[3] Also in this period, inflation was kept within a single-digit range except for three years (11.9 percent in 1985, 20.7 percent in 1988 and 16.3 percent in 1989); the household bank deposits to GNP ratio increased from 6 percent in 1978 to 46 percent in 1991; and the

With Chenggang Xu; originally published in *Economics of Transition*, June 1993, 1(2), pp. 135–170.

government budget deficit accounted for about 2–3 percent of GNP, about half of which was financed from bond issues (Table 10.1).

Even more convincing evidence of the success of the reform is the increase in consumption and consumer durable goods by an average Chinese consumer in physical terms. For example, between 1978 and 1991, an average Chinese consumer increased his/her consumption about three times for edible vegetable oil, pork, and eggs (Table 10.2). In rural areas, which account for about 75 percent of total population, the living space per person increased about 130 percent between 1978 and 1991 (Table 10.3). The average per household consumer durable goods, such as television sets, refrigerators and washing machines, also increased dramatically. For instance, in 1991, on average, every two rural households had one television set, and every urban household had more than one (Tables 10.4 and 10.5). There is no doubt that China is still a low-income developing country, but the evidence clearly reveals a substantial improvement in living standards due to economic reforms.

The Chinese economic performance is in contrast to that of Eastern Europe and the former Soviet Union. Even if the two-digit annual decline of GNP in 1990 and 1991 in these countries was largely transitory, the magnitude was still too large to be ignored. What is more important, but tends to be neglected, is the economic stagnation in Eastern Europe and the Soviet Union in the decade of the 1980s before the radical changes. According to official statistics, the average growth rate of GDP in Hungary was 1.8 percent between 1981 and 1985 and almost zero in 1988 and 1989. In Poland, the average GDP growth rate was less than 2 percent between 1981 and 1989.[4] The situation in the Soviet Union was no better.

Political considerations aside, two arguments often come into discussions on the differences between China and Eastern Europe. The first argument is about different levels of economic development: Eastern Europe and the Soviet Union were at a much higher development stage than China—China had a very low per capita income with a dominant agriculture sector while the Eastern European and Soviet economies were "over-industrialized."[5] The second argument is about different reform strategies: China has followed a gradual and piecemeal approach as opposed to the "big-bang" strategy in most of post-1989 Eastern Europe and the former Soviet Union, like the shock therapy for stabilization in Poland and Russia, and the rapid mass privatization in Czechoslovakia.[6]

We feel that both views are relevant but unsatisfactory, or at least are incomplete. China's level of industrialization was perhaps higher than most people would think. In 1978, China's gross industrial output value accounted for 62 percent of the total output value of society (35 percent in heavy industry and 27 percent in light industry), despite the fact that only 29 percent of the total labor force was employed in the non-agriculture sector. In terms of GNP, China's industry accounted for about half in 1978, as compared to 60 percent to 65 percent in Eastern Europe. Furthermore, in China, reforms have been more successful in the more industrialized regions with weak central government control (like provinces of Guangdong, Jiangsu, and Zhejiang). Reforms have been less successful in both the less industrialized regions (like the Northwest provinces) and the more industrialized regions with strong central government control (like Shanghai and provinces of Liaoning and Jilin); the latter share similar problems to those of the earlier Hungarian reform. This fact suggests that one cannot explain the success of the reforms by the low level of development alone.

The argument for gradualism also raises more questions than answers. First, the agricultural reform in China proceeded very fast in the early 1980s. The abolition of the commune system and the nationwide establishing of the household responsibility system (an ownership reform) was implemented almost in one stroke, and can thus be viewed as a "big bang." More importantly, Eastern Europe's radical transition should not be examined in isolation: it came after deep troubles or failures of many years of gradual reform. In fact, the Hungarian reform started in 1968 with some initial success, but then ran into difficulties in the 1980s. Ironically, in several respects China followed Eastern Europe's gradual reform measures. If China's gradualism is a success, why has it worked in China but not in Eastern Europe? On the other hand, why was China's success not a temporary one, and will China soon encounter problems similar to Hungary's?

In this paper, we propose a theory to explain the differences between China's reforms and those of Eastern Europe and the Soviet Union. We first make an observation and provide extended evidence showing that, unlike the case of Eastern Europe and the Soviet Union, sustained entry and expansion of the non-state sector in China during the reforms were forceful and fast enough to become an important engine of growth by the end of the 1980s.[7] We then theorize an institutional reason which is responsible for this phenomenal expansion and for the concurrent emergence of the market. We argue that the difference in the initial institutional conditions concerning the organizational structure of the planning hierarchy plays an important role in the different transition paths of China and Eastern Europe and the former Soviet Union. The organization structures of both Eastern Europe and the Soviet Union were of a unitary form based on the functional or specialization principles (the "U-form" economy), and, in contrast, the Chinese hierarchy has been of a multi-layer-multi-regional form mainly based on a territorial principle since 1958 (the "deep M-form" economy, or in short, the "M-form" economy). The M-form structure has been further decentralized along regional lines during reform with both increased authority and incentives for regional governments, which provided flexibility and opportunities for carrying out regional experiments, for the rise of non-state enterprises, and for the emergence of markets. Our institutional approach is able not only to incorporate and link together aspects of the arguments concerning the level of development and gradualism, but also to explain richer phenomena such as the successful use of experiments in China but not elsewhere.

Under the M-form organization in China, interdependence between regional economies is not as strong as that of the U-form organization in Eastern Europe and the Soviet Union, because each region is relatively "self-contained." Unlike in Eastern Europe and the Soviet Union, regional governments in China (be it province, county, township, or village) have had considerable responsibility for coordination within the region. In particular, a large number of state-owned enterprises, including many in heavy industries, were subordinated to the regional governments even before the economic reforms. Hence, each region was relatively self-sufficient, the scale of an enterprise was small, and industries were less concentrated. In this environment, regional experiments can be carried out in a less costly way because the disruptive effect to the rest of the economy is minimal. A successful experiment in one region also has greater relevancy to other regions since adjacent regions are similar.

When the M-form economy was further decentralized along regional lines in the reform and the constraints on local government were gradually removed, the bottom level regional governments (i.e., townships and villages in the rural areas, and districts and neighborhoods in the urban areas) gained substantial autonomy in developing their own regions. They establish enterprises outside the state sector and outside the plan. From their inception, these non-state enterprises (most of them are not private though) have been market-oriented. Furthermore, competition between regions for getting rich fast puts pressure on the local governments to concentrate on growth and their limited access to bank credits maintains discipline on their behavior. This explains how the rise of the non-state sector occurred by gradually weakening the existing hierarchical control without destroying the existing structure in one stroke.

Of course, administrative decentralization induces, at the initial stage, costs of regional conflict, market protection, wasteful duplication, inefficient small scales of production, and increased administrative intervention by local governments. We do not argue against these opinions, but we would like to focus on a neglected but important aspect of the benefits of a multi-layer-multi-regional form of organization, that is, the flexibility of the system for experiments and hence for institutional changes, and the opportunity provided to facilitate entry and expansion of the non-state sector outside the plan. The unexpected, and perhaps unintentional, growth of the non-state sector is critical for the success of China's economic reforms.

Based on Chandler's seminal work (1966), Williamson (1975) first used the terms "U-form" and "M-form" in his study of business firms in the U.S. The U-form referred to the unitary organizational form of the firm along functional lines in the second half of 1800s and early 1900s, while the M-form referred to the multi-divisional form of the firm organized by product, by technology, or by geography, which emerged in the 1920s. Compared with departments in the U-form firms, divisions in the multi-divisional firms are more self-contained and their responsibility for coordination and profit inside the division is high. The regional governments in our multi-layer-multi-regional structure economy share these features. However, our concept is not simply an application or an extension of the Chandler-Williamson concept from firms to economies. There are important differences between the two concepts. In a multi-divisional firm, decentralization occurs exactly at the level of the general office and the divisions, and each division is often organized by functions. In contrast, in our concept of the M-form economy, decentralization occurs at all levels of the hierarchy, that is, the M-form is *deep*. This is critically important: it is precisely because of the autonomy and incentives provided to the *bottom* levels of the regional governments in China, that the non-state sector was able to grow so fast.

The remaining part of the paper is organized as follows. Section 2 clarifies the definition of China's non-state sector and private sector.

Section 3 provides empirical evidence on the sustained entry and expansion of the non-state sector between 1979 and 1991. Section 4 first characterizes institutions of the U-form hierarchies of Eastern Europe and the Soviet Union and the M-form hierarchy of China before the reform, and then describes several Chinese reform policies that are responsible for further decentralization along regional lines. Section 5 gives a general and preliminary analysis of the costs and benefits of the M-form organization vis-à-vis the U-form and the implications for transition. Section 6 explains specifically how the phenomenal expansion of the non-state sector in China is made possible under its M-form hierarchical organization. The final concluding section discusses implications of the non-state sector for further reforms in China and lessons from the Chinese experience for other economies in transition.

2. What Is the Non-State Sector in China?

2.1. The Non-State Sector

Before defining the non-state sector,[8] we should first define the state sector. In China, according to the constitution, the state-owned enterprises are owned by the "whole people." In practice, every state-owned enterprise is affiliated with one of the following four levels of government: (1) central; (2) provincial (with a population size of dozens of millions); (3) prefecture (with a population size of several millions); and (4) county (with a population size of several hundreds of thousands). A municipality is treated as one of the levels of province, prefecture or county, with a majority being at the level of a prefecture. Typically, the responsible government delegates the supervision of "its" state-owned enterprises to the industrial ministries/bureaus. Therefore, even for the state-owned enterprises, they are not homogeneous in terms of control.

The non-state sector consists of all enterprises not in the state-sector, and it includes the private sector as a sub-sector. According to the location of its supervising government (if it has one), a non-state enterprise is designated as either an urban enterprise or a rural enterprise.[9] By 1991, there were three categories of non-state ownership in China's official statistics: "collective ownership," "individual ownership," and "other types of ownership." The table below provides a detailed picture with both official and alternative classifications:

OFFICIAL CLASSIFICATION	Collectives			Individual	Others
Urban	District Enterprises	Neighborhood Enterprises	Urban Cooperatives	Urban Individual	Private; Foreign joint ventures; Other joint ventures
Rural	Township Enterprises (TVEs)	Village Enterprises	Rural Cooperatives	Rural Individual	
ALTERNATIVE CLASSIFICATION	Community		Private		

(A) Collectives (*jiti*). Urban collectives include (i) enterprises that are affiliated with a district government under a municipality or a county ("large" collectives, *dajiti*); (ii) enterprises that are affiliated with a neighborhood under a district ("small" collectives, *xiaojiti*); and (iii) urban cooperatives (*chengzhen hezuo*). Many urban collectives are subsidiaries of state-owned enterprises which receive some transferred assets from the parent firms and hire their surplus employees or the employees' spouses and children. The advantages of subsidiaries being registered as collectives under the supervision of lower level government is less government control and more business flexibility.[10]

Rural collectives include (i) enterprises that are affiliated with a township (*xiang* or *zhen*) government; (ii) enterprises that are affiliated with a village (*cun*) government; and (iii) rural cooperatives (*nongcun hezuo*). The predecessors of township and village enterprises (TVEs) were commune and brigade enterprises (CBEs) emerging during the Great Leap Forward in 1958. The ownership form of township and village enterprises is truly a Chinese invention that has not been found elsewhere.

(B) Individual Business (*geti*). These are household/individual businesses hiring no more than 7 employees. Individual businesses have been allowed to operate since 1978.

(C) Other Types of Ownership (*qita leixing*). This category includes mainly (i) private enterprises hiring more than 7 employees (*siying*); (ii) foreign enterprises and joint ventures with foreigners (*sanzi qiye*); and (iii) other types of joint ventures (e.g., a joint venture between state and private enterprises) and joint-stock companies. These types of ownership did not emerge until the early 1980s.[11]

2.2. The Private Sector

Defining the non-state sector in China is easy, but defining the private sector is not. As seen above, a "private enterprise" is defined in China as a private business establishment hiring more than 7 employees. This narrow definition is on purpose, in order to circumvent ideological difficulties. For example, an individual/household hiring no more than 7 employees is classified as an "individual business," not as a "private enterprise," although it is certainly part of the private sector. So are sole foreign business establishments. As for joint ventures and joint-stock companies, strictly speaking, only those shares that are owned by foreigners and domestic private parties can be regarded as belonging to the private sector.[12] Some "cooperatives" are more like partnerships hiring many employees. This is especially true in Southern China, and in some areas they are called "joint stock cooperatives" (*gufen hezuo*). In addition, some township and village enterprises and urban district and neighborhood enterprises are *de facto* private enterprises with vaguely defined ownership under the name of collectives.[13]

Lacking further information and taking approximations, our definition of the private sector in China in this paper will include individual ownership, cooperative ownership, and other types of ownership under the official classification, and will exclude all of the township and village enterprises. We speculate that this should not give too much bias in either direction for data prior to 1992. The remaining part of the collectives, that is, enterprises affiliated with an urban district or neighborhood or with a rural township or village (TVEs), can be regarded as the community sector.

3.   Sustained Entry and Expansion of the Non-State Sector in China: Evidence

3.1. General Features

From 1978 to 1991, the share of the non-state sector in national non-agriculture employment increased from about 40 percent to 57 percent. However, this happened not because of privatization or conversion of state enterprises to non-state enterprises. It is mainly due to entry and expansion of new non-state enterprises. In fact, employment by the state sector increased from 75 million in 1978 to 107 million in 1991. Its share declined because employment in the non-state sector grew even faster: from 21 million to 44 million in the urban areas and from 28 million to 96 million in the rural area during the same period.

China's non-state sector is engaged in all kinds of activities: construction, transportation, commerce, service, and in particular, industry. This is perhaps a crucial difference between China's non-state sector and the private sector in Eastern Europe, particularly before 1989.[14] During the period from 1981 to 1990, the national average annual growth rate of gross industrial output was 12.6 percent, in which the state sector grew at 7.7 percent, collectives at 18.7 percent, individual business at 92.2 percent and other types of ownership at 42.7 percent. As a result, the share of the non-state industry in the national total has expanded gradually from 22 percent in 1978 to 47 percent in 1991, and accordingly, the share of the state sector in industrial output shrunk from 78 to 53 percent. To put this into a historical perspective, the share of the state sector in 1991 is already below the level in 1957, which was 54 percent (Table 10.6).[15]

The change of ownership composition of Chinese industry toward the non-state sector did not happen overnight. In fact, the process started before 1979. Although true private industry in China did not appear until the early 1980s, the collectives had grown from 11 percent out of the national total in 1969 to 22 percent in 1978, or about 1 percent increase in output share every year (Table 10.6). However, the dramatic shift of weight toward the non-state sector has been apparent since 1979: The non-state sector in industry has on average experienced an increase in industrial share 2 percentage points every year for 13 years.[16]

Accompanied by the high growth rate, the non-state sector is also more efficient than the state sector. The annual growth rate of total factor productivity of the non-state enterprises was much higher than that of the state enterprises.[17] If one ranks all China's provinces according to their shares of the non-state sector in industrial output, the top five, Zhejiang, Jiangsu, Guangdong, Shandong and Fujian, are precisely those provinces that have much higher growth than the national average.[18] An interesting counter example of the coastal region is Shanghai. Shanghai was one of the most important financial and industrial centers in the Far East before 1949 and was also the industrial base after 1949. Shanghai has a low share of the non-state sector in industry as compared to the national average: 22 percent in 1985 and 32 percent in 1990. For the period from 1984 to 1989, Shanghai's industry grew only 7.9 percent per annum, well below the national average. Shanghai's share of industrial output dropped from 10 percent in 1985 to only 6.8 percent in 1989, below that of Jiangsu, Shandong or Guangdong.

Three additional characteristics of the entry and expansion of the non-state sector in China should be especially emphasized. First, the substantial entry and expansion occurred not because of an intentional design of a reform program from the central government; on the contrary, it came largely from local initiatives. The central government's tolerance is mainly because it solves unemployment problems without much financial support from the state. Second, and related to the first, there has been a large variance in terms of organizational and developmental patterns of non-state-owned enterprises across regions. For example, while export and foreign investment have played important roles in some parts of Guangdong and Fujian, they are not so vital in many other high-growth provinces. On the other hand, township and village enterprises are a dominant force of the non-state sector in Jiangsu and Shandong, but individual, partnership, and private enterprises are much more important in Zhejiang.

Third, by 1991, collectives and joint-ventures were the dominant majority of the non-state sector, and privately-owned enterprises played a minor role on the national scale. The collectives and joint-ventures have a larger scale of operation, employ better technology, and absorb more human capital. This is because in China, there is still a lack of legal protection of private property rights, let alone commitment to private ownership. Private firms often face discrimination in obtaining credit, labor and material supplies (Nee 1992). Local government ownership like a township or a village enterprise can be viewed as an institutional response to such an environment, in which they have comparative advantages over both private and state ownership. They are "politically correct," protected by at least some level of government, and they also enjoy the flexibility of business operation that the state-owned enterprises are lacking.[19]

3.2. The Non-State Sector in the Rural Areas—Township, Village and Private Enterprises

Within the non-state sector, the largest and the most dynamic part is the segment of rural enterprises, also known as Township, Village, and Private Enterprises (TVPs). Between 1978 and 1991, the number of rural enterprises increased from 1.5 million to 19.1 million and employment increased from 28.3 million to 96.1 million. Between 1981 and 1990, the total output by rural enterprises grew at an annual rate of 29 percent, in which the industrial output grew at 28 percent, much higher than the national average of 13 percent. Exports by township and village enterprises (excluding private enterprises) increased at an average annual rate of 65.6 percent from 1986 to 1990 (Table 10.7).

About three-quarters of the total output of the rural enterprises came from industry in 1990, light industry accounting for 55 percent and heavy industry for 45 percent.[20] For example, in 1990, rural enterprises produced about one third of coal, 40 percent of canned food and one half of electric fans in China (Table 10.8). With the rapid growth of rural enterprises, their status in the national economy has changed from a subsidiary sector of agriculture to an important engine of growth. Between 1979 and 1990, as a percentage of the national total, employment increased from 23 percent to 39 percent, total output increased from 7 percent to 22 percent, and industrial output increased from 9 percent to 25 percent. Export from township and village enterprises (excluding private enterprises) accounted for 24 percent of the national total in 1990 (Table 10.9). By all measures, the Chinese rural enterprises had already expanded to more than half of the non-state sector and to about one-quarter to one-third of the national total by 1991.

The rapid growth of the rural enterprises has changed the industrial structure of the Chinese rural areas as well. In 1980, the share of agriculture in gross output value in rural areas was 69 percent and the share of non-agriculture was 31 percent, of which industry accounted for only 20 percent. Ten years later, in 1990, the share of agriculture output had dropped to 46 percent and the share of non-agriculture output increased to 54 percent, of which industry accounted for 40 percent.[21]

3.3. Emergence of the Private Sector

The private sector in China did not appear until the late 1970s and private industry only started in the early 1980s. There was a tremendous increase in the number of private industrial enterprises in the 1980s. In terms of share of industrial output, a significant decline in urban collectives (from 45 percent to 29 percent) was accompanied by a surge in individual rural business (from 4 percent to 11 percent) and other types of ownership (from 3 percent to 10 percent), as shown in Table 10.10. According to our definition, the private sector's share of industrial output inside the non-state sector increased from 13 percent in 1985 to 27 percent in 1990, doubling in five years. Using a more conservative estimate (only one half of the "others" counted as private), about 10 percent of the total national industrial output was produced by privately owned enterprises in 1990, up from 5 percent in 1985. The expansion of the private sector was remarkably faster in rural areas. Employment by the rural private sector was about 24 percent and total output about 14 percent of the rural total in 1984, the corresponding numbers increased to 49 percent and 33 percent, respectively, in 1988 (Table 10.11).

An important part of the private sector in China is "individual business." China restored individually or household operated business in 1978 and since then, this segment of the private sector has registered rapid growth in both urban and rural areas, largely in industrial and commercial enterprises. Between 1981 and 1988, the number of individually-run enterprises increased seven-fold, from 1.8 million to 14.5 million, and employment increased nine-fold, from 2.3 million to 23.0 million (Table 10.12).

4. The M-Form and U-Form Hierarchical Structures

The phenomenal entry and expansion of the non-state sector distinguishes China's reform from the Eastern European reforms. Among many reasons which may explain these phenomena are the institutional differences between the (deep) M-form organization in China and the U-form organization in Eastern Europe and the Soviet Union, and the subsequent Chinese reform policies of further decentralization along regional lines which had a major influence on both the transition path and performance.

4.1. The U-Form Hierarchy of Eastern Europe and the Soviet Union

In Eastern Europe and the Soviet Union the economies were organized in the U-form in which hierarchical information flow and control were organized into a unitary form by functional or specialization principle.[22] Most enterprises were grouped by industry and under the direct supervision of ministries, and regional governments were primarily subordinates of the center and their roles were limited to collecting information from below and implementing plans from above without much autonomy.[23]

In order to utilize fully economies of scale and to avoid conflicting operations, there was little overlapping of functions among ministries in a U-form hierarchical economy. Enterprises were highly specialized and their sizes were extremely large. This led to extraordinary industrial concentration. Because of the strong interdependence between enterprises across different regions, comprehensive planning and administrative coordination between ministries at the top level of the government were crucial for the normal operation of the U-form economy in the absence of the market. To show the complexity, for example, in the late 1970's there were 62 ministries under the Gosplan in the Soviet Union. There were about 48,000 plan "positions" for about 12 million products planned and coordinated by the Gosplan (Nove 1983).

There are several reasons why the Soviet economy was organized in the U-form. First, from the very beginning, the Soviets had an ideological obsession with economies of scale and gigantic factories.[24] The U-form organization takes full advantage of economies of scale and specialization. We often saw in the Soviet Union that one or a few gigantic firms produced one product for the whole economy. Particularly when the economy was at a lower stage of development and the objective was clear and the decision-making was relatively simple, the U-form organization was effective in mobilizing scarce resources to catch up quickly (Gerschenkron 1962). Second, when the Soviet Union began to establish a centralized economy in the 1920s, the U-form was the only way of organizing industrial activities within large corporations in the West, as the multi-divisional firms in capitalist economies had not yet emerged. The claims of Lenin and Kautsky about establishing a socialist economy as a gigantic factory also reflected the prevailing knowledge about economic organization at that time. Third, there were political reasons for the U-form organization, particularly under Stalin, to achieve better control by Moscow over the Soviet Republics and the Eastern European countries. Because each region of Eastern Europe and the Soviet Republic was made a branch of the grand hierarchy, all regions became strongly interdependent, and ultimately, were dependent on Moscow.

When the economy becomes more complex, defects in the U-form organization become serious. In order to change the organization structure, Nikita Khrushchev in 1957 abolished the ministries altogether and introduced 105 Regional Economic Councils (*Sovnarkhozy*), to which all the state enterprises were subordinated. However, this reform did not go very far and soon failed. Given the already very concentrated industrial structure, a change from a unitary form to a multi-regional form required both political changes and economic changes. The power of ministries would be weakened, large enterprises would be broken up or new duplicating enterprises would be established, and all of these were very costly. In 1965, blaming the growing "localism" of the *Sovnarkhozy* and the difficulties of coordinating a regionally operated planning apparatus, the regional coordination system was replaced by the former ministerial system (Gregory and Stuart 1981).

4.2. The M-Form Hierarchy of China

In China there are six administrative levels: central, provincial, prefecture, county, township (previously, commune), and village (previously, brigade). In urban areas, there are three levels: municipality, district, and neighborhood. In China's official language, regions at each level are called "blocks" (*kuaikuai*), as opposed to "branches" (*tiaotiao*), and bureaucratic supervision takes place along the lines of function and specialization.[25] Instead of mainly following functional or specialization principles like those in Eastern Europe and the Soviet Union, the Chinese economy is organized into a multi-layer-multi-regional form mainly according to territorial principle, in which each region at each layer can be regarded as an operating unit. Each unit is further divided along geographic lines and at the same time the unit controls its own enterprises along functional and specialization lines. Regions are relatively self-contained; that is, they are self-sufficient in terms of functions and supplies in production.

Directly under the control of the central government are 30 province-level regions (blocks) and a few dozen functional and industrial ministries (branches). Before the economic reform which began in 1979, industries in China were much less concentrated than those in Eastern Europe and the former Soviet Union and there was a large number of state-owned industrial enterprises not controlled by the central government. This is true for light industries, as well as for heavy industries. In 1978, the share of industrial output of state-owned enterprises controlled by the central government was less than one-half of the national total (Wong 1987). In the automobile industry, almost all enterprises in Eastern Europe and the Soviet Union were directly controlled by the central government and the number of the enterprises was rather small. In China, there were 58 enterprises making automobiles before the reform, and most of them were controlled by the local governments (Wang and Chen 1991). Consistent with this, the number of products directly under the central plan in China was much smaller, only 791 in 1979 (Zhu 1985), as compared to more than twelve million in the former Soviet Union in the late 1970s (Nove 1980). With a much reduced work load, the desired number of ministries in the center was much smaller than in the Soviet Union (less than 30 vs. more than 60).

The hierarchical structure of each region at each level is a copy of that of the central government. For example, a county has about ten to twenty townships. The county government controls the enterprises affiliated to the county government by functional line and specialization principal (e.g., finance, textiles, food processing, electronics, etc.), and it also oversees township governments within its territory. Similarly, a township controls its own enterprises in addition to the oversight of its villages.

The commune system in the rural area between 1958 and 1984 provides a good example showing some of the features of the bottom level of the M-form hierarchy. A commune (now township) government was a bottom-level government in China (only the level of village is below it). Far from having specialization and division of labor, a commune encompassed all kinds of activities of industry, agriculture, commerce, education, entertainment, and even military ("people's militia"). The counterpart of the commune in urban areas is the neighborhood committee, which similarly has many of its own collective enterprises.

It should be clear that the difference between China's M-form hierarchy and the Soviet Union and Eastern Europe U-form hierarchy is more than the relationship at the top level between the central government and the provincial government. On the one hand, the CMEA as a whole should not be regarded as a large M-form hierarchy in our sense, since within each CMEA country, the economy is organized exclusively according to functional lines. On the other hand, the internal structure of a province in China is different from that of an Eastern European country, even though the size may be similar. For example, Hungary with a U-form hierarchy has a different organizational structure from Guangdong province of China. As a province, Guangdong is a part of the large hierarchy of China. But Guangdong itself is also organized in an M-form, with multiple-regions consisting of prefectures, counties, townships and villages, and all of them are self-contained economic units.

There are several reasons why China's economic organization evolved into the M-form. First, historically, before the Chinese Communist Party fully took power of China in 1949, both the economy and the military forces in regions under Communist control were organized in an M-form. The organizational heritage and skills accumulated in history have a deep influence on the evolution of the organizational structure of the Chinese economy. Second, technologically, poor communication and transportation facilities in a large country make the M-form organization an easier choice for the Chinese. Third, politically, nationalism was less a problem in China than in the Soviet Union and Mao had many other means (for example, political movements) to hold the country together. Fourth, militarily, as Mao was worried about the Soviet and American air-raid invasion and the Third World War, industries were dispersed into inland areas and placed under the supervision of the regional governments. Finally, culturally, there is vast classical literature in China on the art of managing multi-regional organization because for more than two thousand years the Chinese empires were basically organized along regional lines.

China's M-form hierarchical structure has evolved since 1958. Because of ideological and political reasons, China's first five year plan (1953–57) was formulated with the help of the Soviet experts, which was a process of copying the Soviet model—the U-form organization—into the Chinese economy. Toward the end of the first five year plan, Mao was increasingly dissatisfied with the over-centralization and bureaucratization in the Soviet model. In his famous 1956 speech on the ten major relationships, Mao discussed the relationship between the central and the local governments and advocated the ideas of "mobilizing two initiatives of both central and local governments" (*diaodong zhongyang he difang liangge jijixing*) and "walking on two feet" (*liangtiaotui zoulu*), the latter referring to development of both central and local industries.[26] These ideas later became official government policies and were subsequently implemented.

Under Mao's initiative, China started to deviate from the Soviet model and moved toward the direction known as "administrative decentralization" within the hierarchy. Two major waves of administrative decentralization occurred in 1958 (the Great Leap Forward) and in 1970 (the Cultural Revolution): the central government's bureaucracy was trimmed; supervision authority of many state-owned enterprises was delegated from the ministries to provinces and cities or even counties; and local governments' initiatives for developing their regions were encouraged. The legacy of Mao had a great impact on the organizational structure of the Chinese economy. As far as the initial institutional conditions for economic reforms are concerned, China's multi-layer-multi-regional hierarchical structure prior to 1979 was already substantially different from that of the unitary hierarchical form inherited in Eastern Europe and the Soviet Union before their economic reforms.

4.3. Reform Policies of Further Decentralization Along Regional Lines in China

However, the role of local governments before the economic reform was still limited compared to that after the economic reform. Before 1979, as the fiscal system remained very centralized, the local government had little financial resources for regional development. Autonomy of the local governments was also limited given the constraint of central planning and the use of markets not being officially sanctioned. Furthermore, the Chinese economy was a closed one without informational and technological exchanges with the rest of the world.

The subsequent reforms since 1979 opened up the Chinese economy to the outside world. The scope of planning was gradually reduced and the use of the market was encouraged. More importantly, several reform policies were carried out that have meant authority, information, and incentives being decentralized to the regional governments. It is only after these complementary reform policies that initiatives of the regional governments were mobilized and the market emerged beyond the boundary of each region. The reform policies of decentralization were mainly reflected in the following aspects.

First, a fiscal revenue-sharing system between any two adjacent levels of governments was implemented starting from 1980.[27] Although schemes vary both across regions and in time, the basic idea is that a lower-level regional government enters into a contract with the upper-level regional government on the total amount (or share) of taxed-profits revenue (negative means subsidies) to be remitted for the next several years, and the lower-level government keeps the rest.

Consider, for example, the fiscal sharing schemes between the central and provincial (local) government. There are two categories of revenue incomes in any province: central revenues and local revenues. Division between the central and local revenues is by source (for example customs duties are central revenue and turnover taxes are local revenue) and by *affiliation of enterprises* (for example, profit taxes from centrally-controlled enterprises are central revenue and those from provincially-controlled enterprises are local revenue). Only local revenue is subject to revenue sharing, and there have been four major types of sharing schemes (Wong 1992): (A) to remit a lump sum (possibly with an annual increment) and retain the rest. (This applied to only two experimental southern provinces, Guangdong and Fujian, first); (B) to remit a portion which is fixed for four to five years. (This is for the majority of provinces); (C) to remit a portion which is set annually (this applied to the three cash cows of industrial cities—which have provincial ranks—of Beijing, Shanghai, and Tianjin); and (D) to receive a fixed amount of subsidies (this applied first to four poor provinces in the Northwest, and later to a total of nine provinces). Starting from 1988, most provinces shifted to schemes (A) and (D), which have the strongest incentive effects. For example, Shanghai entered into a contract with the central government to remit a fixed 10.5 billion yuan since 1988.

Second, the so-called "extra-budgetary" revenues (i.e., the second budget) of the local governments and ministries were expanded. 80 percent of these funds belongs to state-owned enterprises as retained profits over which the local governments and ministries have substantial control. Before the reform, the extra-budgetary revenue was relatively small, 9 percent of GNP in 1978 compared to the budgetary revenue of 35 percent of GNP. In 1991, the extra-budgetary revenue was up to 15 percent of GNP while the budgetary revenue was down to only 18 percent of GNP (Sicular 1992).

Third, the banking system in China was also decentralized with the separation of the central bank and the specialized banks in 1983. Although banks were still owned by the state, each regional branch of the specialized banks was required to link their total credit extension to deposits collected within the region (*cundai guagou*). In case deposits fell short in a specialized bank, it is the regional branch of the central bank (not the general office of that specialized bank) which is responsible for reallocating funds within the region or asking for refinancing loans from the central bank. This regionally based banking institution was also "deep," as the central bank in China has branches even at the county level. Although the banking system was somewhat re-centralized in terms of personnel appointments starting in the fourth quarter of 1988, the influence of the regional government (through regional branches of the central bank and specialized banks) on credit remained rather strong.

Fourth, more autonomy was granted and more responsibilities were assigned to the regional governments. These include the reduced planning scope of the central government, and the increased authority of local governments for determining prices, for setting up new firms, and for making investments with "self-raised funds," that is, funds drawn from the "extra-budget" or borrowed from banks.[28] At the same time, burdens of fiscal expenditure were also decentralized, and local government assumed greater responsibility for providing education, health, housing, local infrastructure, etc.

With these reforms, local governments have become almost residual claimants and have incentives to maximize local revenues.[29] Because the local governments' budgets are highly dependent on local enterprises, they have incentives to set up more enterprises using their newly gained authority. More firms mean more revenue, and more revenue means more resources for regional development. With such a decentralization, local governments do not receive a great deal of financial support from above and, consequently, their responsibilities to above are also small.

Decentralization along regional lines in the M-form hierarchy during the reform had a great impact on China's industrial structure. First, more state-owned enterprises were delegated to local governments. In 1985, the state-owned industrial enterprises controlled by the central government accounted for only 20 percent of the total industrial output from enterprises at or above township level, while the provincial and city government controlled 45 percent and county government 9 percent (Table 10.13). In 1987, the share of the eight largest steel firms controlled by local governments was 12.3 percent as compared to 47.1 percent for the eight largest steel firms controlled by the central government (Wang and Chen 1991). In contrast, almost all firms in the steel industry in Eastern Europe and the Soviet Union were directly controlled by the central governments. Second, Chinese industry has become even less concentrated. For instance, there are more than 100 color television assembly lines, and every province has at least one. The number of enterprises making automobiles increased from 58 before the reform to 116 in 1987 (Wang and Chen 1991).

Third, the average size of state enterprises in China is much smaller than that in Eastern Europe and the Soviet Union, and is quite close to that in the West. For example, in 1988, employment per enterprise in manufacturing was 806 in the Soviet Union and 460 in Hungary, as compared to 145 in China and 96 in Italy. In clothing, the corresponding figures were 6,600 in Czechoslovakia, 307 in Hungary, 80 in China, and 71 in Italy (Table 10.14). In spite of twenty years of reform, the average size of Hungarian enterprises remained substantially larger than that in the West.[30]

5.   The Costs and Benefits of the U-Form and M-Form Hierarchies and the Implications for Transition: A Preliminary Analysis

The costs and benefits of different forms of organization are determined by the essential features of the organizational structures.[31] The important organizational features of the unitary form of hierarchies of Eastern Europe and the Soviet Union (the U-Form) are: (i) organization mainly by functional or specialization principles; (ii) regional governments' roles are limited and supplementary; (iii) interdependence between regions is strong and coordination at the top is critical; and (iv) the size of enterprises is generally large and industries are very concentrated. In contrast, the organizational features of the multi-layer-multi-regional form of hierarchy in China are: (i) organization mainly by territorial principle in addition to functional or specialization principles; (ii) each region is relatively self-contained and interdependence between regions is relatively weak; (iii) coordination at all levels is important but at the top it is not particularly critical; (iv) the size of enterprises generally is small and industries are less concentrated; and (v) the above features extend many levels down to the very bottom.

This characterization helps to clarify the relationship and differences between our concepts of U-form and (deep) M-form economies and U-form and M-form firms in the literature. It looks as if that, because divisions in a multi-divisional firm are also organized by product, the organization of the Soviet economy is similar to a multi-divisional form rather than unitary form. That similarity, however, is superficial. From an organizational point of view, relationships between different ministries and the role of the center in Eastern Europe and the Soviet Union resemble the relationships between different functional departments in the U-form firms: interdependence between departments is strong, the coordinating role of the center is critical, etc. On the other hand, China's multi-regional form shares several essential properties of multi-division firms: each operating unit (division in a firm and region in an economy) is self-contained, much of the coordination is delegated to the operating unit, and performance evaluation of each unit is based on comparisons of performance between units. One of the differences between an M-form economy and an M-form firm is property (v) above, that is, the M-form economy in China is a multi-layer one, or it is deep.

Based on the above theoretical abstraction, we provide a general and preliminary analysis of the costs and benefits of the M-form and the U-form hierarchies and of their implications for transition to a market economy. The U-form and M-form organizations affect static and dynamic efficiencies as well as the evolutionary processes of the system.[32]

5.1 Economy of Scale, Specialization, and Industrial Concentration

The U-form economy was designed to explore scale economy through technological engineering and through specialization and division of labor.[33] The U-form organization is effective in mobilizing scarce resources and concentrating on a few high-priority objectives. Enterprises in the U-form economy consistently have the following three features: a large scale of operation, a narrow scope of products, and a high degree of vertical integration. This leads to two significant features of the U-form economy: a high degree of industrial concentration and a high level of regional specialization.

Compared to the U-form hierarchy, the M-form hierarchy is less efficient in utilizing scale economies. The automobile industry in China provides an extreme example: there are more than a hundred small-scale state-owned auto makers in China, each producing on average about ten thousand automobiles annually. It is typical that regional governments in China control both heavy and light industries, and therefore regions are less specialized in products and industries are less concentrated. This leads to criticism of China's "local industrialization" for inefficient scale and wasteful duplications, and for associated regional protectionism and segmented markets, in particular in the presence of distorted prices and taxes (Wong 1992).

On the beneficial side, duplication may reduce vulnerability and increase reliability of supplies under uncertainty. It may also induce competition and facilitate diffusion of technology into inland areas. Furthermore, less specialization may also be more beneficial: less specialization may reduce coordination costs (Becker and Murphy 1992), and less specialization may also make workers more efficient in learning and in operation, as shown by the Japanese experience (Aoki 1986).

5.2 Coordination

In the M-form economy of China, coordination is distributed at all levels of the hierarchy: regional governments have substantial responsibility for coordination in addition to the important (though not critical) coordinating role of the central government.[34] There are two reasons

which favor a more decentralized coordination vis-à-vis a more centralized one. First, to the extent that information is initially dispersed, local
governments have better information than the central government
simply because they are closer to the sites. Hence the local information
is better used by local governments than by the central government
for regional development. Second, decentralized coordination has
lower requirements for capability in communication and information
processing. The burden of communication and information processing
is reduced since fewer messages need to be transmitted and fewer
tasks need to be coordinated. Therefore, the M-form hierarchy has
advantages when there is a high degree of complexity in an economy
and the communication and information processing technologies are
backward.

However, decentralized coordination may also result in inefficiency
when a market is incomplete (Weitzman 1974, Bolton and Farrell 1990,
and Milgrom and Roberts 1992). In the case of China, interdependence
between economic activities in different regions is not strong, and a
more decentralized coordination is likely to be preferred to a more
centralized one as in the U-form, other things being equal.[35] In the
U-form organization, industries are highly concentrated, the regions
are highly specialized, and the operating units of ministries and enterprises alike are strongly interdependent. Hence, a rigorous coordination at the center is crucial for maintaining the normal operation of
the economy, and a decentralized coordination at the regional level
may not be efficient.

5.3 Responses to External Shocks

With little or no duplication and with strong interdependence between
different units in the U-form economy, once a shock hits one unit,
which may be the only one in the economy producing a particular type
of product, the trouble in that unit may spread to the whole economy.
This implies that the U-form economy is more fragile to external shocks.
In contrast, with many duplications and a weak interdependence
between units of the M-form hierarchy, the adverse effects of an external shock to one or several units on the whole organization will likely
spread in a slower and weaker way. That is, the effects of shocks in an
M-form hierarchy can be localized.

The effects of region-specific shocks and industry-specific shocks to
the U-form and M-form economies are also different. In the U-form
economy, regional shocks affect not only the local economy but also
affect the whole economy through strong regional interdependence.

The adverse effects of the collapse of the CMEA are a good example. In the M-form economy, a region-specific shock may not affect the economy as a whole because industries are spread out in many regions. The sustainability of the Chinese economy during the Cultural Revolution illustrates this point. During that period, some regional economies in China collapsed (due to factional conflicts), but the national economy did not: national income dropped in only two years (-7.2 percent in 1967 and -6.5 percent in 1968) and recovered quickly afterwards.

On the other hand, since different regions have similar industrial compositions, an industry-specific shock may affect all regions, but in a similar way. This may reduce the aggregate adverse effect for several reasons: each region is better capable of dealing with the shock locally since the magnitude of the shock is smaller, regions may adjust better to new environment by learning from each other since all regions face similar shocks, and the incentive may become less of a problem because the shock is transformed into a systematic one in the M-form organization rather than an idiosyncratic one as in the U-form organization (see below).

5.4 Incentives

In an U-form hierarchy, incentives of subordinates are designed to ensure implementation of commands from above since coordination at the center has the highest priority. Agents are subject to frequent and arbitrary control by their superiors, and thus they try to avoid any changes or risks (Ericson 1991). In an M-form organization, coordination at the center is not so critical, and thus providing semi-autonomy together with higher powered incentives to local governments may be optimal. Indeed, in China, local governments have not been subject to arbitrary control from above for tasks within their autonomy for more than twenty years. After further decentralization in the reform, local governments have more incentive to build up their regional empires and officials have less interest in promotion to a higher rank.

Because the regions are self-contained with delegated authority and because different regions engage in a similar composition of activities, aggregate indicators like growth in revenue or output reflect the true performance of the regional government rather than random noise. Therefore, tournament or yardstick competition between regions is a powerful tool for providing incentives by filtering out common or systematic uncertainties (Holmstrom 1982). In China regional governments often take great pride in being ranked in first place in a competition among neighboring regions. The public and the media also place great importance on such a ranking. This type of incentive would be less effective and more costly to provide to ministries in the U-form hierarchies because idiosyncratic uncertainty is more significant.

5.5 Commitment Through Decentralization

In any economy, incentives cannot be really created unless the government is able to make a credible commitment not to expropriate promised incomes and not subsidizing loss makers. Absence of such a commitment was a legacy of centralized economies that led to the "ratchet effect" ("excess" profits were constantly siphoned away, as shown by Berliner 1957) and "the soft budget constraint" (loss-makers were continually bailed out, as shown by Kornai 1980). This lack of credible commitment is a fundamental problem in centralized economies because the state is too powerful to tie its own hands. In contrast, credible commitment may be achieved under decentralization.

Dewatripont and Maskin (1991) argue that dispersed banks and decentralized information structures can harden the budget constraint. This is because when a bank is constrained by the funds available, additional financing must come from another bank. In such a case, inefficient *ex post* renegotiation (say, due to asymmetric information between the new and old banks) reduces the returns and thus the incentives of the new bank from refinancing.[36] This in part explains why the budget constraint is harder for township and village enterprises in China, since most of them borrow from small rural credit cooperatives.

During China's decentralization, many upper level government departments and bureaus were removed or merged, and the number of bureaucrats was cut down. According to Milgrom and Roberts (1990), this reduces information channels between the superior and the subordinates, which in turn reduces influence costs. Thus a better commitment may be achieved as less information reaches the top.

The central government in the former Soviet Union retained strong discretionary power during its reforms. In contrast, China's reform policy of decentralization of authority to local governments makes it difficult for the central government to use its discretion.[37] In his study of the history of economic development, Weingast (1993) emphasizes the role of decentralized political institutions in achieving credible commitment to thriving markets by the state. The crucial aspect of what he called "market-preserving federalism" is that the central government's authority to make economic policy must be limited and this authority must be placed in the hands of the local governments. This is viewed as the key to solving the "fundamental political dilemma of an economic system": a government strong enough to protect property rights is also strong enough to confiscate the wealth of its citizens. One of the key differences between China's and Russia's reforms, as seen by Weingast, is that China proceeded in this direction but Russia did not.

5.6 Experimental Approach, Learning, and Institutional Changes

In Eastern Europe and the Soviet Union, some experiments had been introduced in their reforms before 1989. However, the experiments were often unsuccessful; even when they were successful in the local area, they were rarely promoted nationwide. Economists tend to believe that regional experimentation is not the right approach to reform a planned economy. However, one major feature of the Chinese reform is its success in using local experiments and in adopting the "bottom-up" approach (Chen, Jefferson, and Singh 1992; McMillan and Naughton 1992). Then a question arises: why is China so special in using experimental approaches?

In a U-form organization, with a high degree of interdependence between operating units, allowing one or a few regions to do experiments may be very costly or perhaps not feasible. This is because experiments generate shocks and may disturb normal operations of the economy regardless of the success or failure of the experiments evaluated at the local level. This makes the scope of regional experiments more limited and chances of success smaller. Even when an experiment was a success in a particular industry or region, its relevancy to other industries and other regions is less significant because of heterogeneity across operating units. Given these features of the U-form hierarchy, economic reforms will more likely be carried out in an "top-down" fashion, in which decisions for change have to be more centralized to minimize transition costs. In this sense, the U-form organization makes the institution more rigid and more difficult to change through local experiments.

In the M-form organization, however, the regional interdependence is relatively weak, so even a failure in the experiment will not significantly disturb the whole economy. In this case, the regional experimental strategy of reform in an M-form organization is less costly and more feasible. Under the M-form structure, large scale regional experiments can be carried out, many regions have a chance to develop a large variety of "mutants," and the central government may be able to compare and select among various alternatives.[38] Furthermore, because adjacent regions are similar in terms of economic structure, a successful experiment in one region can be promoted relatively easily in other regions. Hence, under the M-form organization, reforms may proceed more efficiently with the "bottom-up" approach,[39] which provides a less costly way of learning to establish and to use market institutions in an unprecedented environment. This makes the M-form organization more flexible in the institutional evolutionary process.[40]

6. The M-Form Hierarchy and the Non-State Sector in China

6.1. Direct Effects of the M-Form Hierarchy on the Non-State Sector

The M-form organization is directly responsible for fast entry and expansion of the non-state sector under the condition that the existing hierarchy is not destroyed in one stroke. The most relevant aspects of the M-form organization are those associated with the two bottom levels of government, that is, township and village governments in the rural area, and district and neighborhood governments in the urban area. In what follows, local governments refer to the two bottom levels of government.

Incentives and Authority of Setting Up Non-State Enterprises The major responsibility of a local government in the M-form economy is regional development and welfare. Compared to their counterparts in the U-form economy, regional governments in China pay less attention to bargaining with the higher authorities because they have less to gain from bargaining within the hierarchy. The local government has to raise revenue on its own without much help from above, and so it has strong incentives to set up and to support local enterprises for revenue generating and employment purposes.[41] Some scholars even view a township or village as a "corporation," and the government of the township as the board of directors and the management team of the corporation (Oi 1992).

A field study found that a significant portion of the net profit of township and village enterprises was used for the administrative budget of township and village governments (Rural Policy Research Division of the Central Committee Secretariat 1986). In another sampling survey, researchers found that 77.5 percent of the village administrative budget came from the village enterprises and that most village government officials responded that one of the major motivations for setting up village enterprises was to expand their administrative budget (Li 1987).

A Harder Budget Constraint for Non-State Enterprises   One pervasive problem with state-owned enterprises is soft budget constraints (Kornai 1980). This problem is particularly serious for enterprises affiliated with central and provincial governments. However, at the bottom levels of the hierarchy, financial resources available to local branches of the state banks and rural credit cooperatives and to local governments are very limited, and non-state enterprises do not have easy access to subsidies and credits as do state-owned enterprises (but still better than private enterprises). This limited power of community governments disables them from bailing out loss-making community enterprises, thus enabling them to commit themselves to terminating troubled enterprises (Dewatripont and Maskin 1990). Hence, the budget constraints for non-state enterprises are much harder than the state-owned enterprises. With hard (or harder) budget constraints, community governments are more conscious about risks and profitability and, in the final analysis, the efficiency of their enterprises.

The number of township and village enterprises that went bankrupt during the 1989–1991 retrenchment could be used as evidence for the harder budget constraints in the non-state sector. In 1989, about three million township and village enterprises went bankrupt, or were taken over by other township and village enterprises nationwide, while in the same year almost all loss-making state-owned enterprises were bailed out by the state.[42] In 1990, the loss-making township and village enterprises accounted for 7.5 percent of all township and village enterprises and the figure dropped to 4.6 percent in 1991. In contrast, the loss-making state enterprises accounted for 31 percent of all the state enterprises in 1990.[43]

Horizontal Relationship Between Regions and Emergence of Markets
An important feature, which distinguishes the M-form hierarchy from the U-form hierarchy, is the horizontal, and potentially market-oriented, relationship between regions and between regional governments, despite the fact that the relationship between a local government and its superior or its subordinate is still vertical. Thus, horizontal relationships between regions have developed, first, to create a condition for

market-oriented transactions and trade among enterprises across regions and outside the scope of planning, and second, to generate competition between regions for getting rich first and fast; and third, to facilitate learning by one region through imitating another region for successful reform policies or development strategies. This is how the market mechanism in China emerged at such a fast pace within the existing hierarchical system.

In contrast, in the U-form hierarchy, transactions between two enterprises must advance through their common superior. The high degree of specialization requires rigorous administrative coordination and thus development of the horizontal relationship inside a U-form hierarchy may become damaging. It is then difficult for the market mechanism to emerge and evolve within the existing hierarchical system.[44]

Regional competition will not be efficient unless factors can move freely. During the reform period, constraints on capital and labor movement have been gradually relaxed, especially in the southern coastal areas. In fast growing areas like Guangdong and Jiangsu, many non-state enterprises hire more than half of their labor from inland provinces like Sichuan and Hunan.[45] Capital poured into these areas as well, as shown by the substantial increase in bank deposits in the last few years.[46]

Development of Entrepreneurship and Use of Local Knowledge
With their weak bargaining position in the hierarchy, low-ranking government bureaucrats' temptation to secure promotion within the hierarchy has been greatly reduced. Rather, many bureaucrats turned into entrepreneurs, either by quitting their jobs to join a business company or by running the government like a corporation. Instead of implementing commands from above, their major job is to use their autonomous power to make profits. Entrepreneurship has developed among many local government bureaucrats or Party cadres, a phenomenon which would be hard to believe in the U-form hierarchical economy or in the hierarchical government in the market economy.[47]

Government bureaucrats' knowledge and information about local economies and government policies, their connections with the local community, and their past experience in coordination are all valuable assets. In China, the existing organization is not destroyed in one stroke and government bureaucrats are transformed into entrepreneurs in the reform. Hence, the valuable organizational capital and human capital accumulated and embodied in the M-form hierarchy are better utilized in developing non-state enterprises (Qian and Stiglitz 1993). This is particularly important for China because of the scarcity of human resources.

The Roles of the Central and Higher Regional Governments Partly due to the unpopular political movements in the Cultural Revolution, the central government in China has committed itself to economic development as the "central task" since the beginning of economic reform. The government officially encouraged people to get rich, thereby allowing some people and some regions to become rich earlier or quicker than others. The reform policies of decentralization, which can be regarded as utilizing the features of an M-form organization, strongly encouraged local governments and entrepreneurs to experiment with various alternatives and hence opened up the way for a "bottom-up" reform.

In other respects, the roles of the central government in the Chinese reform are limited. The fast growth of the non-state sector is not in the plan of the government, but rather almost a spontaneous process under a relaxed political and economic environment. The central government acknowledged openly that the fast growth of the non-state sector was an unexpected surprise.[48] China's case demonstrates that with commitment to economic development and commitment to decentralization, whether this be conscious or not, reforms can go very far even with the limited role of the central government, given the M-form structure and incentives to lower-level government to expand non-state enterprises.

Compared to the central government's role in Eastern Europe and the former Soviet Union, China's central government is relatively passive in guiding the reforms. It has not provided any coherent plan for the reform. It gives a green light for local experimentation, and it approves and promotes successful reform measures discovered in the course of regional experiments.[49] At the same time, it also imposes limits on reforms or institutional changes; for instance, it continues to restrict the activities of state-owned enterprises and it is against mass privatization. The observed gradualism in China is, to a large extent, a reflection of these binding limits. However, the central government is pragmatic and it accommodates its policies to the new situation. The attitude of the central government toward township and village enterprises is a good example: it discriminated against township and village enterprises in the early 1980s, then turned to support them several years later after discovering their vitality.

Most provincial governments are authorized to experiment with different reform measures in their provinces within the limits set by the central government. This helps to explain why there are large variations in the reforms from province to province. In many cases, a higher level of regional government protected their lower level governments and the non-state enterprises at a time when the political atmosphere at the center turned against them.

6.2. Interactions Between the M-Form Organization and Other Reform Policies

Although we primarily emphasize the importance of the M-form hierarchy and decentralization policies for the entry and expansion of the non-state sector in China, we also regard many other reform measures, such as the open-door policy, the dual-price system and the success of agricultural reforms, as important. We argue, however, that the achievements of these measures are better understood within our analytical framework of the M-form organization.

The Open-Door Policy Thanks to the open-door policy, foreign technology and investments come to China, and non-state enterprises have a chance to access international markets and resources. For the enterprises which use input supply from abroad and sell their products in the international market, the existing planning system places little constraint on them and they are completely market-oriented. More generally, the open-door policy affects all non-state enterprises. Imports of ideas, concepts, technologies, and especially international market competition, helped to create a market environment that gradually eroded the old planning mechanism.

Linkages between the open-door policy and the features of the M-form organization, and its influence on the expansion of the non-state sector is significant. A crucial component of the open-door policy is the establishing of special economic zones, which are experimental regions not just for attracting foreign investments, but also for learning to establish and to use market institutions. In fact, all of those special zones are located outside the old industrial bases and in remote areas where the central government control is weak. This ensures the maximum autonomy of the special zones and isolation of potential adverse effects of experiments from the rest of the economy. A dominant majority of enterprises in the special economic zones are in the non-state sector. It is these special zones that pull up the neighboring non-state enterprises, as seen most strikingly in the Pearl River Delta of Guangdong.

The Dual-Price System   The dual-price system is by no means a brand new practice. It in fact originated before 1979. China has had two prices for grain (the official price and negotiated price) since the 1950s. During the administrative decentralization in 1958 and 1970, a large number of small non-state enterprises emerged under local governments' support. Because those enterprises were outside the scope of planning, the market price on top of the planned price had to be tolerated for these enterprises' survival. In the Cultural Revolution, the central planning system was crippled, and input allocations to many state-owned enterprises were not guaranteed by the plan. Thus, horizontal cooperation (*hengxiang xiezuo*) between regions and between enterprises, including semi-legal black markets and barter trading, started to develop within the state sector. The dual-price system of the 1980s is merely an official legalization and an increase of its scope of the existing practice.[50]

The dual-price system has been controversial among economists. Critics emphasize that it results in corruption, inefficient bargaining (that is, rent-seeking), and supply diversion from the state to the non-state sector, etc. (e.g., Wu and Zhao 1987; Murphy, Shleifer, and Vishny 1992). Advocates argue that facing a market price at the margin, the managers in the state sector will make the right decisions because the planned quotas become lump-sum tax subsidies in effect (e.g., Byrd 1987; McMillan and Naughton 1992). We focus on a different effect of the dual-price system. If for some reason the price cannot be liberalized in one stroke, introducing legalized markets for *all* goods (an important distinction between Chinese reforms and Eastern European reforms before 1989) has a critical benefit for facilitating entry and expansion of the non-state sector, although it is at the margin and is imperfect. This is because a necessary condition of fast growth of the non-state sector is the existence of markets for intermediate goods which include capital goods and materials. Although the state sector faces two prices for one product, the non-state sector faces only one price, the market price. In a more or less competitive environment with market price signals, the non-state enterprises are likely to be more efficient than the state sector, which is essential for fast expansion of the non-state sector.

The Success of Agriculture Reforms   The development of the non-state sector has benefited from agriculture reforms in at least three aspects: (i) capital accumulation, (ii) release of labor force, and (iii) creation of demands. However, surplus labor, financial savings, and potential of markets by themselves cannot be transformed into growth automatically. Institutions are required to facilitate trade, and entrepreneurs are needed to organize production and distribution. It is the M-form organization that provides the flexibility within the system for efficient utilization of these favorable conditions. For example, many entrepreneurs in the non-state sector were in fact Party cadres or former commune leaders, and their organizational experience and connections in the local government have been turned into assets for the non-state enterprises.

The success of the agricultural reform itself is helped by the M-form structure. The household responsibility system was based on experiments initiated by regional governments (villages, township, county, and province) before it was promoted nationwide by the central government. Strong motivation and initiatives by local governments, tolerance on the part of the central government, and rapid promotion of this system are all made possible by the M-form organization structure. In addition, with a more decentralized system, industrial supplies to agriculture like agricultural machinery and spare parts, chemical fertilizers, transportation services are more reliable and less vulnerable to external shocks. Individual households are also likely to deal with competitive suppliers, not a monopoly. These seem to be different from the situation in the former Soviet Union.

7.   Concluding Remarks

We have provided a comparative analysis of transition from institutional perspectives, and have addressed the issues of how initial institutional environments differ between China and Eastern Europe and the former Soviet Union, how reform and transition strategies in China depend on institutional conditions, and how the institutional changes of decentralization affect China's transition path and outcomes. In particular, the decentralized M-form organization has provided room for the fast entry and expansion of the non-state sector which made the economic transition relatively smooth compared to those in Eastern Europe and the former Soviet Union. In this final section, we briefly discuss the implications of the non-state sector for further reforms in China and lessons from the Chinese experience for other economies in transition.

7.1 Denationalization of the State Sector in China

The recent Eastern European experiences have shown that massive and fast privatization of the state sector is rather costly. Given the initial condition of the M-form organization, it may be easier and less costly for China to follow the evolutionary approach of developing the non-state sector rather than the revolutionary approach of massive and fast privatization. Eventually, the state sector will be forced to share a minor role in the national economy.[51]

This has important implications for the possibility of *denationalization*, instead of *privatization*, of state-owned enterprises in China in the future. Denationalization is a transformation process which includes: successful non-state enterprises taking over or merging with state enterprises, state enterprises being converted into joint ventures with either domestic or foreign non-state enterprises, state enterprises being reorganized into joint-stock companies, etc. In either case, the transformation may include the sale of small-sized state enterprises or the sale of parts of large- and medium-sized state enterprises.[52] In fact, recently, takeovers and mergers by non-state enterprises have already emerged in China and reorganization to joint stock companies has also become fashionable. With the crowding out effects of takeover, mergers, and transformation of ownership, the economy will eventually rely more on the non-state sector. This is perhaps an alternative way to privatization and a less painful path of transition for China.

To the extent that the majority of the non-state sector has community or local government ownership rather than private ownership at the present time, China can be better described as *"decentralized market socialism"* according to its ownership structure (Qian and Xu 1993). It is decentralized because non-state properties are not owned by the central government; it remains socialism because properties are owned by organized communities like townships or villages (von Mises 1981).[53] What is less clear at this point is whether this type of decentralized socialist ownership is a mere transitional phenomenon, or whether it is sustainable for a long time. In any event, decentralized market socialism is clearly a unique outcome of China's gradual transition process.

7.2 Lessons for Other Economies in Transition

We believe that the lessons which other transition economies can learn from China depend on correct understanding of China's reforms in the first place. Our analyses have demonstrated that the success of China's particular gradual reform strategies depends on its initial institutional conditions (as well as other issues of the micro- and macroeconomic environment which are not discussed here), that is, the transition is *path-dependent* evolutionary process. For this reason, China's experience cannot, and should not, simply be copied to other economies in transition. One of the important implications of our analysis is that the difference in the initial institutional conditions concerning the organizational structure of the planning hierarchy should be taken into account when making policy suggestions for other countries based on China's reform experience.

The central idea underlying our theory is that, in addition to ownership, the organizational structure of the economy matters. We have discovered several important linkages between the reform process and the organizational structure of centralized economies, which have policy implications, though tentative, for other economies in transition. First, decentralization and deconcentration of the state sector are desirable in their own right, and for facilitating entry and growth of private business (Aghion, Burgess, and Xu 1993). There are several reasons. (i) Although privatization, understood as a process of simply transferring ownership from the state to citizens, might be achieved relatively quickly, privatization as a mechanism to achieve an efficient organizational structure and competitiveness is bound to be a long historical process. Typically, the privatization process per se does not automatically change the industrial structure of the economy (the Czech Republic is an example). If the U-form structure is not changed, the fundamental problems related to the high degree of concentration may still remain after privatization. (ii) If for some reason privatization is delayed, then there is a need for explicit policies to maintain and restructure the existing state-owned enterprises. The policies of decentralization and deconcentration of state enterprises are beneficial in generating competition and improving performance (perhaps with the exception of the natural monopoly industries). And (iii) decentralization and deconcentration of the state sector will facilitate and speed up entry and growth of new private businesses, which is a vital part of privatization both in the long run and in the short run. The growth of the private sector in Eastern Europe and the former Soviet Union has so far remained limited to trade, services, and construction, while other sectors such as manufacturing industries have not yet been much affected. The monopoly and monopsony power of the concentrated state enterprises or newly-privatized firms is one of the major barriers to entry and growth. Decentralization and deconcentration will reduce these barriers. In addition, decentralization of financial institutions also helps private firms to access credit, which is again critical for the fast growth of the private sector.

Second, a competent and limited central government combined with many vigorous and competitive regional governments is the right balance of power for the state in transition. This amounts to reducing and restricting the discretionary power of the central government and strengthening the local governments' authority in regional reforms and development at the same time. The scope of the central government's authority should be restricted, and the central government should be competent in executing only those reform programs that regional governments cannot or are unwilling to do, for instance, reforms that are related to maintaining macroeconomic stability and preventing regional protectionism. The balance of power between the central and regional governments has several benefits: (i) decentralization helps to create competition among regions; (ii) with less discretionary power given to the central government, regional transition and development will be less affected by fluctuations in central government policies. This will reduce uncertainties resulting from the politically opportunistic behavior or from power struggles between different factions of the central government. And (iii) a better commitment can be achieved with the limited discretion of the central government, so the problems of the ratchet effect and the soft budget constraints can be mitigated.

Third, given the unprecedented and complicated nature of the transition from centralized to market economies, an experimental approach may be a less costly way of learning to establish and to use market institutions in transition. Economic theory does not provide sufficient guidance for the transition. Other countries' experience may be relevant, but must be adapted to each country's own situation. By the decentralized nature of market economy and by the very nature of the transition, a large amount of bottom-initiated institutional experimentation is needed to acquire knowledge in transition. Although the U-form structure is not suitable for large scale experiments, as we analyzed in this paper, it is still possible to establish some special areas for the purpose of experimentation. To avoid interfering with the normal operation of the economy, these regions should be located outside the old industrial bases and far away from central control, as was done in China. Alternatively, after decentralization and deconcentration of the state sector, the economy will be more suitable for local experiments.

Appendix

Table 10.1
China: Selected Macroeconomic Indicators 1978–1991

	Growth of GNP	National Retail Price Index	Urban Cost of Living Index	Household Bank Deposits/ GNP	Export/ GNP	Budget Deficit/ GNP
1978	11.7%	0.7%	0.7%	5.87%	4.67%	surplus
1979	7.6%	2.0%	1.9%	7.05%	5.31%	5.16%
1980	7.9%	6.0%	7.5%	8.94%	6.07%	2.85%
1981	4.4%	2.4%	2.5%	10.97%	7.70%	2.07%
1982	8.8%	1.9%	2.0%	13.01%	7.97%	2.18%
1983	10.4%	1.5%	2.0%	15.36%	7.55%	2.12%
1984	14.7%	2.8%	2.7%	17.45%	8.34%	1.75%
1985	12.8%	8.8%	11.9%	18.96%	9.45%	0.80%
1986	8.1%	6.0%	7.0%	23.08%	11.16%	2.15%
1987	10.9%	7.3%	8.8%	27.19%	13.01%	2.21%
1988	11.0%	18.5%	20.7%	27.12%	12.60%	2.49%
1989	4.0%	17.8%	16.3%	32.34%	12.29%	2.36%
1990	5.2%	2.1%	1.3%	39.77%	16.88%	2.91%
1991	7.7%	2.9%	5.1%	45.88%	19.30%	3.34%

Table 10.2
China: Annual Consumption Per Capita (kilogram)

	Grain	Edible Vegetable Oil	Pork	Poultry	Eggs	Seafood
1978	195.46	1.60	7.67	0.44	1.97	3.50
1991	234.50	5.89	17.44	1.98	7.10	6.79

Table 10.3
China: Living Space Per Person (square-meter)

	Urban	Rural
1978	3.6	8.1
1991	6.9	18.5

Table 10.4
China: Consumer Durable Per 100 Urban Households (sets)

	Color Television	Black/White Television	Washing Machine	Refrigerator
1981	0.59	57.06	6.34	0.22
1991	68.41	43.93	80.58	48.70

Table 10.5
China: Consumer Durable Per 100 Rural Households (sets)

	Color Television	Black/White Television	Washing Machine	Refrigerator	Tape Recorder
1985	0.80	10.94	1.90	0.06	4.33
1991	6.44	47.53	10.99	1.64	19.64

Table 10.6
China: Share of Gross Industrial Output Value by Ownership

		State-Owned	Non-State-Owned
Revolution	1949	26.25%	73.75%
	1957	53.77%	46.23%
Great Leap Forward	1958	89.17%	10.83%
Cultural Revolution	1966	90.18%	9.82%
	1969	88.71%	11.29%
	1970	87.61%	12.39%
	1971	85.91%	14.09%
	1972	84.88%	15.12%
	1973	84.02%	15.98%
	1974	82.41%	17.59%
	1975	81.09%	18.91%
	1976	78.33%	21.67%
	1977	77.03%	22.97%
	1978	77.63%	22.37%
Economic Reform	1979	78.47%	21.53%
	1980	75.97%	24.03%
	1981	74.76%	25.24%
	1982	74.44%	25.56%
	1983	73.36%	26.64%
	1984	69.06%	30.94%
	1985	64.86%	35.14%
	1986	62.27%	37.73%
	1987	59.73%	40.27%
	1988	56.80%	43.20%
	1989	56.06%	43.94%
	1990	54.60%	45.40%
	1991	52.84%	47.16%

Table 10.7
China: Average Annual Growth Rate of Rural Enterprises 1981–1990

	Number of Enterprises	Employment	Total Output	Industrial Output	Export
1981–90	29.2%	11.9%	29.1%	28.1%	
1986–90	8.6%	5.8%	25.4%	27.1%	65.6%

Table 10.8
China: Share of Selected Industrial Products Produced By Rural Enterprises 1990

Coal	Cement	Cotton Cloth	Paper	Electric Fan	Canned Food
33.1%	27.5%	21.4%	38.2%	46.5%	39.1%

Table 10.9
China: Share of Rural Enterprises in the National Economy 1979–1990

	Employment	Total Output	Industrial Output	Exports
1979	22.54%	7.18%	9.05%	
1985	35.27%	16.45%	18.81%	4.80%
1990	38.61%	22.27%	25.29%	23.7%

Table 10.10
China: Share of Industrial Output as Percent of the Non-State Sector 1985–1990

	Collectives			Individual	Others
Urban	District and Neighborhood		Cooperatives		
1985	45.17%		0%	0.98%	3.44%
1990	28.99%		0.50%	0.99%	9.65%
Rural	Township	Village	Cooperatives		
1985	22.28%	19.41%	4.44%	4.29%	
1990	22.48%	22.04%	4.45%	10.89%	

Table 10.11
China: Composition of Rural Enterprises 1984–1990

	Number of Enterprises		Employment		Total Output	
	Township and Villages	Cooperatives and Individuals	Township and Villages	Cooperatives and Individuals	Township and Villages	Cooperatives and Individuals
1984	30.72%	69.28%	76.46%	23.54%	85.63%	14.37%
1985	15.13%	84.87%	62.00%	38.00%	75.27%	24.73%
1986	11.40%	88.60%	57.21%	42.79%	71.34%	28.66%
1987	9.04%	90.96%	53.59%	46.41%	67.89%	32.11%
1988	8.42%	91.58%	51.27%	48.73%	67.47%	32.53%
1989	8.22%	91.78%	50.40%	49.60%	66.44%	33.56%
1990	7.86%	92.14%	49.57%	50.43%	65.28%	34.72%

Source: A Statistical Survey of Chinese Rural Enterprises, 1991.

Table 10.12
China: Expansion of Individual Business (million) 1981–1988

	Number of Enterprises			Employment		
		of which:			of which:	
	Total	Urban	Rural	Total	Urban	Rural
1981	1.83	0.87	0.96	2.28	1.06	1.22
1982	2.63	1.13	1.50	3.20	1.36	1.84
1983	5.91	1.71	4.20	7.47	2.09	5.38
1984	9.30	2.22	7.08	13.03	2.91	10.12
1985	11.71	2.80	8.91	17.66	3.85	13.81
1986	12.11	2.91	9.20	18.46	4.08	14.38
1987	13.72	3.38	10.34	21.58	4.92	16.66
1988	14.53			23.05		

Source: Beijing Review, February 27-March 5, 1989, and People's Daily, overseas edition, March 11, 1989.

Table 10.13
China: Distribution of State-Owned Industrial Enterprises by Administrative Levels (1985)

	Central Government	Provincial and City Governments	County Government
Number of Enterprises	3,825	31,254	35,263
Share in Total Industrial Output	19.57%	44.57%	8.98%

Source: 1985 Industrial Censor of China.

Table 10.14
Comparison of Size of Enterprises in China, Eastern Europe, the Soviet Union and the West, 1988 (Employment/Enterprise)

	Manufacturing	Food Products	Wearing Apparel
Czechoslovakia	2,930	1,609	6,600
The Soviet Union	806	290	402
Hungary	460	925	307
Yugoslavia	311	243	402
China	145	75	80
Italy	96	71	71
United Kingdom	35	67	25

Sources: (1) Industrial Statistics Yearbook 1988 Volume 1, United Nations, Geneva, 1989; (2) Business Monitor PA1002 Report on Census of Production, 1989, Central Statistical Office, UK; and (3) Statistical Yearbook of China, 1989 (pp. 255–291), State Statistic Bureau, Beijing.

Notes

* We would like to thank Philippe Aghion, Masahiko Aoki, Patrick Bolton, Avner Grief, Athar Hussain, Carla Krüger, Nicholas Lardy, John Litwack, Eric Maskin, John McMillan, Paul Milgrom, Dwight Perkins, Louis Putterman, Gerard Roland, Anna Seleny, Barry Weingast, Martin Weitzman, Jinglian Wu, and an anonymous referee for helpful discussions and comments. Qian's research is sponsored by the Center for Economic Policy Research (CEPR), the Hewlett Fund of the Institute of International Studies (IIS), and Center for East Asian Studies (CEAS) at Stanford University, and Xu's research is sponsored by the Center for Economic Performance (CEP) and the Suntory-Toyota International Center for Economics and Related Disciplines (STICERD) at London School of Economics.

1. Data sources in this paper are from *Statistical Yearbook of China* (various issues from 1985 to 1992), otherwise noted.

2. Statistical Communique of the State Statistical Bureau on the 1992 National Economic and Social Development, February 18, 1992.

3. The export-GNP ratios are calculated based on the official exchange rate and are biased upward. But the dramatic increase of export share in GNP during the reform is unmistakable.

4. The data source for Hungary and Poland is from Table 9.1 of Kornai (1992).

5. For example, Summers (1992) expressed this view when he highly praised China's reform performance. Sachs (1992) also expressed similar ideas during his interview with the Chinese *Journal of Comparative Economic and Social Systems*.

6. This view is reflected in Singh (1991), McMillan and Naughton (1992), and Chen, Jefferson, and Singh (1992).

7. We deliberately avoid the issue of the state sector. Evaluation of the reform in the state-sector has been controversial among China experts and Chinese economists.

8. We only focus on the non-agriculture sector in this paper.

9. An interesting and confusing fact is that many rural enterprises are located in urban areas. They are called "rural enterprises" simply because they are supervised by rural community governments (e.g., township or village governments) and the majority of their employees are not registered urban residents.

10. This is known as "one factory, two systems" (*yichang liangzhi*) in China, referring to the planned system for the state-owned part, and the market system for the collective part.

11. If a state-owned enterprise is converted to a joint-stock company or limited liability company ("corporatization"), or becomes a joint venture, it will be reclassified into the category of "others." As a result, it will not be regarded as "state-owned" any more, despite the fact that the state may still own the majority interest. This may cause interpretative problems regarding the non-state sector in the future as more and more conversions occur, starting in 1992.

12. About one-half of "others" can be counted as truly private.

13. For example, the famous computer company Stone Group is officially a "large collective" under Haidian district in the Beijing municipality, but actually run by a group

of private businessmen. In Wenzhou municipality of the Zhejiang province, any business establishment with more than three co-owners is classified as a "collective," and is often called a "township" or "village" enterprise.

14. See Kornai (1986) for the private sector development in Hungary before 1989.

15. In 1957 the first five year plan was finished. At that time, there were still many state-private jointly-owned enterprises (*gongsi heying*). One year later, during the Great Leap Forward in 1958, the share of the state sector jumped to 90 percent.

16. The Information Center of the State Planning Commission in China has already predicted that by the year 2000 only about one-quarter of industrial production will be produced by the state-sector in China. However, see footnote 11 for qualification to this statement.

17. From 1982 to 1987, the annual growth rate of the total factor productivity of the TVEs is 12.5 percent at the national level, and 15 percent in the coastal areas (Xu 1991). In contrast, from 1978 to 1985, the annual growth rate of the total factor productivity of the state-owned enterprises is 1.3 percent at the national level (Chen et al. 1988). Another piece of evidence comes from Xiao (1991). Using the provincial data from 1985 to 1987, Xiao shows a significant positive correlation between the total factor productivity of the provincial economies and the non-state sector share of the industrial output (with the exception of Shanghai).

18. These five provinces are all coastal provinces. Because of rapid growth, the share of industrial output of these five provinces in the national total rose from 30 percent in 1985 to 37 percent in 1990.

19. The fast entry and expansion of the non-state sector has considerable impact on the state sector through increased competition, which forces state-owned enterprises either to ask for more subsidies from the government or to change in order to survive. Given the shrinking government budget revenue, reforms of the state-owned sector become more urgent than ever.

20. *A Statistical Survey of Chinese Rural Enterprises, 1991.*

21. Byrd and Lin (1990) contains a detailed study of rural industry in four counties in China: Wuxi of Jiangsu, Nanhai of Guangdong, Shangrao of Jiangxi, and Jieshou of Anhui.

22. It is also known as the organization by "branches."

23. In the case of the Soviet Union, ministries of the central government controlled all enterprises in heavy industry while the regional governments controlled some light industrial enterprises.

24. Lenin had this famous remark in his book *The State and Revolution* (1917): "The whole of [socialist] society will become a single office and a single factory." This ideology can be attributed to Marx.

25. Strictly speaking, each functional or industrial bureau in a region is subject to "dual leadership" (*shuanchong lingdao*) of the regional government (by block) and of the upper-level functional or industrial department (by branch). But the former is more important than the latter.

26. "Our territory is so vast, our population is so large and the conditions are so complex that it is far better to have the initiatives come from both the central and the local authorities than from one source alone. We must not follow the example of the

Soviet Union in concentrating everything in the hands of the central authorities, shackling the local authorities and denying them the right to independent action." "The central authorities want to develop industry, and so do the local authorities." "The central authorities should take care to give scope to the initiative of provinces and municipalities, and the latter in their turn should do the same for the prefectures, counties, districts and townships; in neither case should the lower levels be put in a strait-jacket." (Mao 1977)

27. The nick-name for this fiscal decentralization is "eating in separate kitchens" (*fenzao chifan*).

28. Although in some cases getting project approved by the upper level government is still needed, which is known as "project registration" (*lixiang*).

29. To some extent, the local government holds "local government or regional property rights."

30. Many economists criticized these reform policies on the basis of their adverse macroeconomic consequences, for example, declining fiscal revenue, pro-cyclical effect of the fiscal sharing schemes (contract is not indexed to inflation), and loss of control over fiscal instruments and credit. All of these tend to undermine the macroeconomic stability of the economy (Lou 1991).

31. In order to make our points clearer, we need to make some abstractions which may make the descriptions diverge from reality. But the essential features of the situation are preserved in our abstraction.

32. Chandler (1966) and Williamson (1975, 1985) first analyzed the unitary form and multi-divisional form of large organizations in the U.S. The problems with the traditional Soviet-type planning system are also well-described (for example, Kornai 1992, and Ericson 1991). In addition, many experts on China have studied its problems from administrative decentralization, such as wasteful duplications, not exploiting scale economies, local protectionism, and market fragmentation (for example, Wong 1987, and Wu and Reynolds 1988).

33. In all centrally planned economies the curricula of universities were designed by the center to train the labor force for utilizing specialization and division of labor. The design of the fields of concentration has been narrowly focused and students were more specialized than their counterparts in market economies.

34. In a multi-divisional firm, day-to-day coordination is delegated to divisions, which enables the general office to concentrate on long-term and strategic decisions (Chandler 1966, and Williamson 1985).

35. The logic here is similar to Weitzman's thesis of price versus quantity (Weitzman 1974). The more decentralized mode of control (price in this case) is better when inputs complementarity is weak so that the marginal benefit curve is flatter.

36. Alternatively, Qian and Xu (1993) suggest that even if banks are large, as long as the projects are not being financed exclusively by one bank, then achieving agreement among many banks is more difficult at the time of renegotiation, which makes the budget constraint harder.

37. During the 1990 retrenchment, the central government tried to revoke fiscal revenue sharing schemes and to re-centralize investment decisions, but encountered

strong opposition from the governors of provinces led by the governor of Guangdong and gave up.

38. An important component of China's reform is the establishment of special economic zones with the explicit purpose of experimentation.

39. However, the bottom-up approach has its own limitations, for example, in the reforms of the tax system and the financial system.

40. Experimentation under the decentralized market system is important for the growth of the West, as economic historians Rosenberg and Birdzell (1986) explain: "This diffusion of authority was interwoven with the widespread use of experiment to answer questions of technology, marketing, and organization for which answers could be found in no other way; and with the emergence of great diversity in the West's modes of organizing economic activity."

41. The rapid growth of the commune-brigade enterprises in Jiangsu province in the mid-1970s had already shown the potential of the M-form structure in the development of non-state enterprises.

42. People's Daily, Overseas Edition, March 23, 1990.

43. *Zhongguo Xiangzhen Qiye*, No. 8, 1991.

44. Kornai (1992) is right that the horizontal market coordination is incompatible to the vertical bureaucratic system (of the U-form organization).

45. It is estimated that there are about 70 million "floating migrants" every year in recent years in China looking for temporary jobs (People's Daily, Overseas Edition, p. 8, March 10, 1993).

46. For example, specialized banks in Zhongshan municipality of Guangdong province borrowed about 2.1 billion yuan through inter-bank loans from other regions (Qian and Stiglitz 1993). In 1992, total bank deposits in Hainan province (now a special economic zone) was 20 billion yuan, an increase of 142.6 percent over the previous year; most of the increase consisted of deposits from other provinces (People's Daily, Overseas Edition, p. 2, March 3, 1993).

47. It is not uncommon to see a person has several titles on the name card: Party secretary, Chairman of the Board of Directors, and CEO of a township or village corporation.

48. Deng Xiaoping admitted in 1988 that the amazing growth of the township and village enterprises was completely unexpected and was the greatest achievement of the reform (*Zhongguo xiangzhen qiye*, 1989).

49. This strategy is known in China as the one of "groping for stones to cross the river" (*mozhe shitou guohe*).

50. Although there were similar phenomena in the Soviet Union (Berliner 1957), the influence there was far less important than that in China.

51. Lau (1992) studied the experience of Taiwan and South Korea where the reduction of the public enterprise sector has been achieved mainly through the growth of the private sector, rather than privatization of the state enterprises.

52. The denationalization process also likely incorporates spontaneous privatization.

53. Some economists further argue that even in the state-sector, many of the Chinese state-owned enterprises have become the *de facto* properties of local governments or regions (see Granick 1990).

References

Aghion, P., R. Burgess and C. Xu, "Organizational Restructuring During Transition," mimeo, Oxford University and London School of Economics, 1993.

Aoki, M., "Horizontal vs. Vertical Information Structure of the Firm," *American Economic Review*, December, 1986, pp. 971–83.

Becker, G., and K. Murphy, "The Division of Labor, Coordination Costs, and Knowledge," *Quarterly Journal of Economics*, November, 1992.

Berliner, J., *Factory and Manager in the USSR*, Cambridge, Mass: Harvard University Press, 1957.

Bolton, P., and J. Farrell, "Decentralization, Duplication and Delay," *Journal of Political Economy*, 98(4), August, 1990.

Byrd, W., "The Impact of the Two-Tier Plan/Market System in Chinese Industry," *Journal of Comparative Economics*, 11, 1987.

Byrd, W. and Q. Lin (eds.), *China's Rural Industry: Structure, Development and Reform*, Oxford University Press, 1990.

Chen, K, G. Jefferson, and I. Singh, "Lessons from China's Economic Reform," *Journal of Comparative Economics*, 16:201–225, 1992.

Chandler, A. Jr., *Strategy and Structure*, New York: Doubleday & Company, Inc., 1966.

Department of Rural Enterprises of Ministry of Agriculture, China, *zhongguo xiangzhen qiye tongji zhaiyao 1991* (*A Statistical Survey of Chinese Rural Enterprises 1991*), Beijing: Reform Press.

Dewatripont, M. and E. Maskin, "Credit and Efficiency in Centralized and Decentralized Economies," mimeo, Harvard University, 1990.

Ericson, R. E., "The Classical Soviet-Type Economy: Nature of the System and Implications for Reform," *Journal of Economic Perspective*, 5(4):11–27. 1991.

Gerschenkron, A., *Economic Backwardness in Historical Perspective*, Cambridge: Harvard University Press, 1962.

Granick, D., *Chinese State Enterprises: A Regional Property Rights Analysis*, Chicago: Chicago University Press, 1990.

Gregory, P. and R. Stuart, *Soviet Economic Structure and Performance*, New York: Harper & Row, 1981.

Holmstrom, B., "Moral Hazard in Teams," *Bell Journal of Economics*, 1982.

Kornai, J., *Economics of Shortage*, North-Holland, 1980.

Kornai, J., "The Hungarian Reform Process: Visions, Hopes, and Reality," *Journal of Economic Literature*, December 1986.

Kornai, J., *The Socialist System*, Princeton University Press and Oxford University Press, 1992.

Lau, L., "Growth versus Privatization -- An Alternative Strategy to Reduce the Public Enterprise Sector: The Experience of Taiwan and South Korea," mimeo, Stanford University, 1992.

Li, Y., "*cunban qiye de yunxing jizhi yu xiangzhen qiyie de fazhan -- 1986 nian nongcun guding guanchadian zhuanti fenxi*" (The Operation Mechanism of Village Enterprises and Growth of TVEs—An Analysis of the Results of the 1986 Rural Area Sampling Survey), mimeo, 1987.

Lou, J., "*Jiejue Zhongyang yu Difang Maodun de Guanjian shi Shixing Jingjixing Fenquan,*" (The Key to Solve the Conflict between the Central and Local Governments is Economic Decentralization), *Journal of Comparative Economic and Social Systems*, Beijing, 1, 1991.

Mao, T., "On the Ten Major Relationships," *The Selected Works of Mao Tsetung, Vol. 5*, Beijing: The Foreign Language Press, 1977.

McMillan, J. and B. Naughton, "How to Reform a Planned Economy: Lessons from China," *Oxford Review of Economic Policy*, 8, Spring, 1992.

Milgrom, P. and J. Roberts, "Bargaining Costs, Influence Costs, and the Organization of Economic Activity," in J. Alt and K. Shepsle (eds.), *Perspectives on Positive Political Economy*, Cambridge University Press, 1990.

Milgrom, P. and J. Roberts, *Economics, Organization, and Management*, Prentice Hall, 1992.

Murphy, K., A. Shleifer, and R. Vishny, "The Transition to a Market Economy: Pitfalls of Partial Reform," *Quarterly Journal of Economics*, August, 1992.

Nee, V., "Organizational Dynamics of Market Transition: Hybrid Forms, Property Rights and Mixed Economy in China," *Administrative Science Quarterly*, 37, pp1–27, 1992.

Nove, A., *The Soviet Economic System*, Boston: Allen & Unwin, 1980.

Oi, J., "Fiscal Reform and the Economic Foundations of Local State Corporatism in China," *World Politics*, vol. 45, no. 1, October, 1992.

Qian, Y. and C. Xu, "Commitment, Financial Constraints and Innovation: Market Socialism Reconsidered," in P. Bardhan and J. Roemer (eds.), *Market Socialism: The Current Debate*, Oxford University Press, forthcoming, 1993.

Qian, Y. and J. Stiglitz, "A Report on the China Trip for the World Bank Project "Public Policy and the Asian Economic Miracle,"" mimeo, Stanford University, 1993.

Rosenberg, N., and L. E. Birdzell, Jr., *How the West Grew Rich*, New York: Basic Books, 1986.

Rural Policy Research Division of the Central Committee Secretariat, "A Summary of Nationwide Rural Social - Economic Sampling Survey," *Zhongguo Nongye Nianjian (Chinese Agricultural Yearbook), 1986*, Beijing: China Agriculture Press. 1986.

Sachs, J., Interviews with *Journal of Comparative Economic and Social Systems*, Beijing, 3, 1992.

Sicular, T., "Public Finance and China's Economic Reforms," Harvard Institute of Economic Research Discussion Paper Number 1618, November, 1992.

Singh, I. J., "China and Central and Eastern Europe: Is There a Professional Schizophrenia on Socialist Reform," Research Paper Series, #17, Socialist Economies Reform Unit, The World Bank, July, 1991.

State Statistical Bureau, *Statistical Yearbook of China (Chinese edition)*, 1986, 1987, 1988, 1989, 1990, 1991, 1992. Beijing: China Statistical Press.

Summers, L. "The Rise of China," *International Economic Insights*, May/June 1992.

von Mises, L., *Socialism—An Economic and Sociological Analysis*, Indianapolis: Liberty Classic, 1981.

Wang, H. and X. Chen (eds.), *Chanye zuzhi ji youxiao jingzheng—zhongguo chanye zuzhi de chubu yanjiou (Industrial Organization and Effective Competition—A Preliminary Study of Chinese Industrial Organization)*," Beijing: China Economy Press, 1991.

Weingast, B., "The Economic Role of Political Institutions," mimeo, Stanford University, 1993.

Weitzman, M., "Price vs. Quantities," *Review of Economic Studies*, 1974, 41: 477–91.

Williamson, O. *Markets and Hierarchies*, New York: Free Press, 1975.

Williamson, O. *The Economic Institution of Capitalism*, 1985.

Wong, C., "Between Plan and Market: The Role of the Local Sector in Post-Mao China," *Journal of Comparative Economics*, 1987.

Wong, C., "Fiscal Reform and Local Industrialization," *Modern China*, vol. 18 No. 2, April, 1992.

Wu, J. and B. Reynolds, "Choosing a Strategy for China's Economic Reforms," *American Economic Review*, May, 1988.

Wu, J. and R. Zhao, "The Dual Pricing System in China's Industry," *Journal of Comparative Economics*, 11, 309–318, 1987.

Xiao, G., "State Enterprises in China: Dealing with Loss-Makers," *Transition*, the World Bank, vol. 2, no. 11, December 1991.

Xu, C., "Productivity and Behavior of Chinese Rural Industrial Enterprises," STICERD Discussion Paper, mimeo, London School of Economics, 1991.

Zhu, R. (ed.), *Dangdai Zhongguo de Jingji Guanli (The Economic Management of Contemporary China)*, Beijing: Chinese Social Science Press. 1985.

11 Incentives, Information, and Organizational Form

1. Introduction

A central theoretical question is how organization makes a difference to economic performance. Obviously, technology will have a great bearing on the way a firm or economy performs. But, by an *organization* we mean the hierarchy of managers built on *top* of technology, e.g., the way a corporation is subdivided into different divisions, and the way a planned economy (such as China or the former Soviet Union) is divided into different functional or regional governing bodies. In this paper we show how organizational form affects the quality of incentive schemes that can be given to managers.

Of course, in reality, the choice of productive technique and that of organizational structure may not be altogether independent decisions: to some extent, the former may dictate the latter and vice versa. But to focus on the effect of organization, we abstract from this interaction and assume that technology, modeled as a collection of plants, is *fixed*. In this way, we can explore the implications of alternative organizational forms erected on top of these plants.

Specifically, we show that different organizational forms give rise to different information about managers' performance. Therefore, we argue, they differ according to how effective incentives can be in encouraging good performance.

We focus on the comparison between two organizational forms: the M-form (multi-divisional form) and the U-form (unitary form). Both structures have figured prominently in corporate history (see Chandler 1962; Williamson 1975). A classic example of the U-form was the Ford Motor Company before the Second World War. In those days, Ford

With Eric Maskin and Chenggang Xu; originally published in *Review of Economic Studies*, April 2000, 67(2), pp. 359–378.

was organized into a number of functionally specialized departments: production, sales, purchasing, and so on. In other words, the various departments carried out complementary tasks; none was independent of the others. By contrast, General Motors under Alfred Sloan became the prototypical M-form; GM comprised (and still comprises) a collection of fairly self-contained divisions, e.g., Chevrolet, Pontiac, and Oldsmobile.

The terms 'M-form' and 'U-form' have been applied primarily to corporations. Recently, however, they have been brought into the study of comparative economic systems. In particular, Qian and Xu (1993) observed that an important difference between the economies of the former Soviet Union and China lies in their respective organizational structures. The Soviet economy was, in effect, a gigantic U-form; it consisted of approximately sixty specialized ministries, e.g., steel or mining.[1] Since 1958, however, the Chinese economy has more closely resembled an 'M-form;' it comprises a large number of reasonably self-sufficient regions (e.g., provinces, prefectures, etc.).

The potential benefits from the U-form—mainly exploitation of scale economies—have been discussed at length in the literature on the Soviet economy (e.g., Kornai 1992). What are the countervailing advantages of the M-form? We argue that one such benefit may be better incentives, deriving from the familiar principle of yardstick competition (see, for example, Lazear and Rosen 1981, Holmstrom 1982, Nalebuff and Stiglitz 1983, and Shleifer 1985). Indeed, relative performance evaluation appears to be widespread in China: provinces, cities, counties, townships, and villages are continually ranked by their performance in growth, output, foreign investment, etc.[2] Interestingly, there did not appear to be such competition between the specialized ministries of the Soviet Union. The question is, why not? After all, in theory, we could compare the steel minister's performance with that of the mining minister. Admittedly, this seems intuitively more difficult than comparing regions that produce more-or-less the same array of goods. But on what is this intuition founded?

One answer could be that the 'variation' between the performances of two regions producing similar outputs is likely to be lower (in the appropriate statistical sense) than that between the performances of two production ministries. If this is so, yardstick competition between two regions will be more effective in providing incentives than that between two ministries, and thus an M-form will dominate from the standpoint of providing managerial incentives. Of course, this comes down in the end to a matter of empirics. But here our analysis of data from 520 Chinese state-owned enterprises seems to support the hypothesis that it is "easier" to compare different regions than different industries. In any case, the more general lesson that we are trying to draw is that different organizational forms give rise to different *information* on which *incentives* can be based.

We proceed as follows. In section 2, we lay out the model. In section 3, we present our theoretical results. Proposition 2 shows that the M-form provides better incentives for middle-level managers provided that there is "less variation" in interregional performance than in inter-industry performance. The comparison is independent of utility functions of both the principal and agents. Proposition 1 establishes that it is *only* at the middle level that organizational form has any bearing on incentive issues: both top- and bottom-level managers' incentives turn out to be independent of whether the M-form or the U-form is employed.

Our empirical work is reported in section 4, where we argue that there is indeed higher "variation" in performance across industries than across regions. We also offer systematic evidence to show the use of yardstick competition in the Chinese economy. We make a few concluding remarks in section 5.

2. The Model

Consider an economy with two *regions*, A and B; two *industries*, 1 and 2; and four *plants*, one plant for each region-industry combination: 1A, 1B, 2A, and 2B, where plant ir produces industry i output (i=1,2) and is located in region r (r=A,B).[3] There are three kinds of *shocks*: shocks η hit all plants in the economy; shocks θ_i hit just plants in industry i, i=1,2; shocks δ_r hit region r, r=A,B. We assume that shocks are jointly normally distributed.

A shock has two effects: (i) to increase the variance of output of those plants it hits, and (ii) to *potentially* decrease the mean of their output. We emphasize the qualification "potentially" because it is the job of a *manager* "assigned" that shock to take steps (i.e., to exert effort) before the shock hits to prevent the mean from falling too far: the higher the effort, the smaller the fall (we suppose however, that a manager cannot affect the variance of the shock). Hence the economy-wide (top) manager is assigned η; an industry i manager (i=1,2) is assigned θ_i; and a region r manager (r=A,B) is assigned δ_r.

For example, imagine that η corresponds to a potential increase in the world price of oil. The top manager could attempt to limit the effect of a possible such increase by investing in the development of machinery running on liquefied coal. Similarly, suppose that δ_A corresponds to the consequences of a possible flood besetting region A. The region A manager might prepare for this eventuality by working out a contingent plan for reinforcing embankments along the river. Finally, assume that industry 1 is agriculture and that θ_i corresponds to the effects of a potential locust invasion. The agriculture manager could respond by stocking-up on suitable crop sprays.[4]

In this paper, we will focus on two particular but widely employed hierarchies of managers: the U-form and the M-form.

If the economy is set up as a U-form, then it is organized along industrial (ministerial) lines. Beneath the top manager, who is allocated shock η, there is a manager (minister) for each of the two industries (ministries). Then within each industry, there are managers for the two regional shocks (and for the two plants). Hence, a U-form is illustrated by 11.1.

If the economy is configured as an M-form, then it is organized along regional lines. In this case there is again a top manager, who is allocated shock η. Then, at the next level down, there is a manager (governor) in charge of each of the two regions. Next, within a region, there is a manager for each of the industrial shocks. The M-form is depicted in Figure 11.2.

Consider a manager who is allocated shock δ_r. Suppose that in the absence of his taking any corrective action, the shock induces an expected decrease of d in the output of each plant under him in the hierarchy. In the flood example above, d might correspond to the

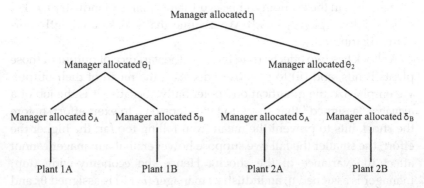

Figure 11.1
A U-form Organization

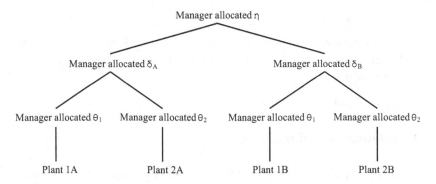

Figure 11.2
An M-form Organization

average fall in output if there were no enough embankment fortification.[5] Let e_r measure the extent to which the manager prepares for the flood (it corresponds to his *effort*): expected output is raised by e_r in all plants under him.

Now, because absolute levels play no role in our analysis, we can take the value of d, as well the means of all shocks, to be zero. Hence the output of a plant in industry i and region r, when the managers allocated the shocks θ_i, δ_r, and η hitting that plant exert efforts e_i, e_r, and e_η respectively, is

$$x_{ir} = e_i + e_r + e_\eta + \theta_i + \delta_r + \eta.$$

The cost of effort e is $C(e)$ where $C(0)=0$, and

$dC/de > 0$, and $d^2C/de^2 > 0$.

A manager's utility is given by

$U(t) - C(e)$,

where t is the manager's (monetary) payment and U is his von Neumann–Morgenstern utility function. Let $\underline{U}$ be the manager's reservation utility.

We will suppose that managers' efforts cannot be directly monitored. Hence, a manager's reward t will depend only on the observable outputs $\{x_{ir}\}$. The organizational problem is to choose a set M of managers and a set of reward schemes $t_j(\cdot)$ for each manager j so as to maximize the expected value of net output

$\Sigma_i \Sigma_r x_{ir} - \Sigma_{j \in M} t_j(\cdot)$,

subject to the constraints that each manager gets at least his reservation utility and that he chooses an effort level e^* that maximizes his own net expected utility:

$E[U(t(\cdot)) - C(e)]$.

3.   Information and Incentives

The central point of our paper is that different organizational forms give rise to different information on which incentives can be based. We are particularly interested in comparing managers' incentives in M-form and U-form organizations.

We will argue that if there is less "variation" (in the appropriate sense) in shocks across regions than across industries, the M-form dominates the U-form from the standpoint of incentives. To get a feel for the issues involved, let us consider an even simpler framework than that of our model. Suppose that there are two industries, 1 and 2, and that output in industry i is given by

$x_i = e_i + \varepsilon_i$,

where e_i is the effort of the manager in charge of shock ε_i, and $(\varepsilon_1, \varepsilon_2)$ are jointly normally distributed. Let us compare this with the case of two regions, A and B, where output in region r is given by

$x_r = e_r + \varepsilon_r$,

e_r is the effort of the manager in charge of shock ε_r, and $(\varepsilon_A, \varepsilon_B)$ are jointly normal.[6] All managers have preferences given by

$U(t) - C(e)$,

where t is a transfer that in the industrial case can depend on (x_1, x_2), and in the regional case on (x_A, x_B).

In which scenario can better incentives be provided? It turns out that a comparison of *conditional variances* is the key. If

$$\text{Var}(\varepsilon_A \mid \varepsilon_B) < \text{Var}(\varepsilon_1 \mid \varepsilon_2), \tag{1}$$

then manager A can be given better incentives than manager 1.[7] Moreover, if both

$$\min \{ \text{Var}(\varepsilon_A \mid \varepsilon_B), \text{Var}(\varepsilon_B \mid \varepsilon_A) \} < \min \{ \text{Var}(\varepsilon_1 \mid \varepsilon_2), \text{Var}(\varepsilon_2 \mid \varepsilon_1) \} \tag{2}$$

and

$$\max \{ \text{Var} (\varepsilon_A \mid \varepsilon_B), \text{Var} (\varepsilon_B \mid \varepsilon_A) \} < \max \{ \text{Var} (\varepsilon_1 \mid \varepsilon_2), \text{Var} (\varepsilon_2 \mid \varepsilon_1) \}, \qquad (3)$$

then both managers A and B can be given better incentives than manager 1 and 2.

The less noisy performance is as a function of effort, the easier it is to provide a manager with the incentive to supply effort. Condition (1) says that the residual noise that remains in manager A's performance after it is compared with that of manager B is smaller than the residual noise that remains in manager 1's performance after it is compared with that of manager 2.

To see that if (1) holds, manager A can be provided with better incentives than manager 1, fix an effort level e' for manager 2 and assume that managers choose effort levels noncooperatively. Suppose that $t_1(\cdot, \cdot)$ is an incentive scheme for manager 1 such that $t_1(x_1, x_2)$ is his transfer conditional on outputs (x_1, x_2). We will show that, if (1) holds, we can find a transfer scheme $t_A(\cdot, \cdot)$ as a function of (x_A, x_B) such that, if manager B exerts effort e', the scheme $t_A(\cdot, \cdot)$ is equivalent to $t_1(\cdot, \cdot)$. To see this, note that (1) is equivalent to

$$\sigma_A^2 - (\sigma_{AB})^2/\sigma_B^2 \leq \sigma_1^2 - (\sigma_{12})^2/\sigma_2^2,$$

where $\sigma_r^2 = \text{Var}(\varepsilon_r)$, $r=A,B$; $\sigma_{AB} = \text{Cov}(\varepsilon_A, \varepsilon_B)$; $\sigma_i^2 = \text{Var}(\varepsilon_i)$, $i=1,2$; and $\sigma_{12} = \text{Cov}(\varepsilon_1, \varepsilon_2)$.

Choose scalars

$$\alpha = \sigma_{AB}/\sigma_B^2 - \sigma_{12}/(\sigma_2^2\sigma_B^2)^{1/2},$$

$$\beta = (\sigma_2^2/\sigma_B^2)^{1/2}, \text{ and}$$

$$\gamma = (1-\beta)e'.$$

Also let z be a normally distributed random variable, independent of x_A and x_B, with mean $\alpha e'$ and variance $[\text{Var}(\varepsilon_1 \mid \varepsilon_2) - \text{Var}(\varepsilon_A \mid \varepsilon_B)]$. We claim that if managers 2 and B choose effort e', then for any choice of effort e by manager 1 and A, the two pairs of random variable (x_1, x_2) and $(x_A - \alpha x_B + z, \beta x_B + \gamma)$ have the same distributions. Hence, if we take

$$t_A(x_A, x_B) = t_1(x_A - \alpha x_B + z, \beta x_B + \gamma),$$

$t_A(\cdot, \cdot)$ will be equivalent to $t_1(\cdot, \cdot)$. But because all random variables are normal, it suffices to show that the two pairs have the same mean and the same covariance matrix for all e. In fact:

$E(x_A - \alpha x_B + z) = e - \alpha e' + \alpha e' = e = Ex_1;$

$E(\beta x_B + \gamma) = \beta e' + (1-\beta)e' = e' = Ex_2;$

$\text{Var}(\beta x_B + \gamma) = \beta^2 \text{Var}(x_B) = \sigma_2^2 = \text{Var}(x_2);$

$\text{Cov}(x_A - \alpha x_B + z, \beta x_B + \gamma) = \beta\sigma_{AB}^2 - \alpha\beta\sigma_B^2 = \sigma_{12}^2 = \text{Cov}(x_1, x_2);$

$\text{Var}(x_A - \alpha x_B + z) = \sigma_A^2 - 2\alpha\sigma_{AB} + \alpha^2\sigma_B^2 + [\text{Var}(\varepsilon_1 \mid \varepsilon_2) - \text{Var}(\varepsilon_A \mid \varepsilon_B)]$
$\quad = \sigma_A^2 - \sigma_{AB}^2/\sigma_B^2 + \sigma_{12}^2/\sigma_2^2 + \sigma_1^2 - \sigma_{12}^2/\sigma_2^2 - (\sigma_A^2 - \sigma_{AB}^2/\sigma_B^2) = \sigma_1^2$
$\quad = \text{Var}(x_1),$

as claimed.

We have been taking e' as fixed for managers 2 and B. But if (2) and (3) hold, a similar argument shows that manager B can be induced to choose the same effort level as manager 2.

So far we have been examining a setup that is simpler than the model that we are really interested in. Let us return, thereafter, to the model of section 2. As in the stripped-down framework, let us suppose that managers' effort cannot be directly monitored, so that their rewards can be based only on the vector of outputs

$(x_{1A}, x_{2A}, x_{1B}, x_{2B}).$

Let us also continue to assume that managers choose their effort levels noncooperatively.

We have argued that, at least in the stripped-down model, the M-form provides better incentives than the U-form for *middle-level* managers (those one level down from top management), provided that conditional variances for regions are smaller than those for industries. It may appear at first that the comparison should go exactly the other way, once we move down to bottom-level managers. After all, the bottom-level managers are industrial in the M-form and regional in the U-form. Moreover, were the comparison to flip, we would get no clear-cut answer about the M-form versus the U-form. However, it turns out that the incentives for bottom-level managers do not depend on whether an M-form or U-form is employed (nor do they for top-level managers). Thus it suffices to consider only the incentives of middle-level managers:

Proposition 1. Given any incentive scheme $t_\eta(x_{1A}, x_{2A}, x_{1B}, x_{2B})$ for the top manager (the one handling η) in the M-form, there exists an equivalent scheme $t_\eta'(x_{1A}, x_{2A}, x_{1B}, x_{2B})$ for the top manager in the U-form (in the sense that it induces the same effort level and gives the managers the same expected payoff), and vice versa. Similarly, given any incentive scheme $t_{ir}(\cdot)$ for the industry i manager under the region r manager in the M-form, there exists an equivalent scheme t_{ri}' for the region r manager under the industry i manager in the U-form, and vice versa.

Proof: Suppose that the industry 1 manager in region A (manager 1A) in the M-form faces incentive scheme $t_{1A}(x_{1A}, x_{2A}, x_{1B}, x_{2B})$. Moreover, suppose that, given their incentive schemes, the other bottom-level managers are induced to choose levels e_{2A}^*, e_{1B}^*, e_{2B}^* (where e_{ir}^* is the effort level of manager ir), the middle-level managers are induced to choose levels e_A^* and e_B^*, and the top manager level e_η^*. Now consider the U-form and suppose that the bottom-level managers other than A1 (the region A manager in industry 1) have incentive schemes that induce them to choose levels e_{A2}^{**}, e_{B1}^{**}, e_{B2}^{**}, the middle-level managers e_1^{**} and e_2^{**}, and the top-level manager e_η^{**}. Endow manager A1 with transfer function

$$t_{A1}'(x_{1A}, x_{2A}, x_{1B}, x_{2B}) = t_{1A}(x_{1A}+e_A^*+e_\eta^*-e_1^{**}-e_\eta^{**}, x_{2A}+e_A^*+e_\eta^*-e_2^{**}-e_\eta^{**}+e_{2A}^*- e_{A2}^{**}, x_{1B}+e_B^*+e_\eta^*-e_1^{**}-e_\eta^{**}+e_{1B}^*-e_{B1}^{**}, x_{2B}+e_B^*+e_\eta^*-e_2^{**}-e_\eta^{**}+e_{2B}^*-e_{B2}^{**}).$$

It is then straightforward to verify that, for any effort choice e by managers A1 or 1A, the random variables $t_{A1}'(\cdot,\cdot,\cdot,\cdot)$ and $t_{1A}(\cdot,\cdot,\cdot,\cdot)$ are the same. The argument for top managers is similar. Q.E.D.

Proposition 1 relies on a simple idea: the information available on which to base incentives is the same across organizational forms for both top- and bottom-level managers. However (as our stripped-down framework already suggests), the same is *not* true of middle-level managers. Indeed, a major theme of this paper is that an important respect in which organizational forms differ is precisely in the information that they give rise to.

In both the M-form and U-form, incentive schemes can depend on $(x_{1A}, x_{2A}, x_{1B}, x_{2B})$. However, the way this set is partitioned into *spheres of influence* of the two middle-level managers differs. In the M-form, the region A and B managers affect (x_{1A}, x_{2A}) and (x_{1B}, x_{2B}) respectively, whereas in the U-form, the industry 1 and 2 managers affect (x_{1A}, x_{1B}) and (x_{2A}, x_{2B}) respectively. In our stripped-down framework, the M-form dominated the U-form from the standpoint of incentives if the M-form's associated conditional variances were smaller than those of the U-form.

Now, in the model of section 2, we must compare *pairs* of random variables, which may seem more complicated than the stripped-down analysis. But it turns out that the comparisons can be reduced to one dimension.

For $i = 1, 2$ and $r = A, B$, we denote

$$\varepsilon_{ir} = \theta_i + \delta_r.$$

Let λ_A solve

$$\min_\lambda \text{Var} (\lambda \varepsilon_{1A} + (1-\lambda)\varepsilon_{2A} \mid \varepsilon_{1B}, \varepsilon_{2B}), \qquad (4)$$

and let λ_1 solve

$$\min_\lambda \text{Var} (\lambda \varepsilon_{1A} + (1-\lambda)\varepsilon_{1B} \mid \varepsilon_{2A}, \varepsilon_{2B}). \qquad (5)$$

Define λ_B and λ_2 analogously. Let

$$\varepsilon_r = \lambda_r \varepsilon_{1r} + (1-\lambda_r)\varepsilon_{2r} \qquad (6)$$

for $r = A, B$, and

$$\varepsilon_i = \lambda_i \varepsilon_{iA} + (1-\lambda_i)\varepsilon_{iB}. \qquad (7)$$

for $i = 1, 2$. We establish that appropriately aggregated information is equivalent to disaggregated information for incentive purposes. Because the shock η plays no role in the subsequent analysis, we henceforth ignore it.

Lemma 1. If $(x_{1A}, x_{1B}, x_{2A}, x_{2B})$ and $(x_{1A}{}^*, x_{2A}{}^*, x_{1B}{}^*, x_{2B}{}^*)$ are the outputs in the U-form and M-form respectively, we can express

$$(x_{1A}, x_{1B}, x_{2A}, x_{2B}) = (x_1, x_1, x_2, x_2) + (u_1, u_2, u_3, u_4)$$

and $(x_{1A}{}^*, x_{2A}{}^*, x_{1B}{}^*, x_{2B}{}^*) = (x_A{}^*, x_A{}^*, x_B{}^*, x_B{}^*) + (v_1, v_2, v_3, v_4)$,

where (x_1, x_1, x_2, x_2) and (u_1, u_2, u_3, u_4) are uncorrelated, $(x_A{}^*, x_A{}^*, x_B{}^*, x_B{}^*)$ and (v_1, v_2, v_3, v_4) are uncorrelated.

Proof: See Appendix.

Lemma 1 can be understood from standard linear regression theory. Vector (x_1, x_1, x_2, x_2) is the fitted regression vector under the "best linear unbiased estimation" procedure for $(x_{1A}, x_{1B}, x_{2A}, x_{2B})$. Therefore, the residual vector (u_1, u_2, u_3, u_4) is uncorrelated (as well as independent due to normality) to (x_1, x_1, x_2, x_2). This decomposition of $(x_{1A}, x_{1B}, x_{2A}, x_{2B})$ essentially makes (x_1, x_2) a sufficient statistic for $(x_{1A}, x_{1B}, x_{2A}, x_{2B})$ under the U-form, and therefore, (x_1, x_2) becomes an appropriate aggregation from the point of view of providing incentives (Holmstrom 1982).

With the help of Lemma 1, we can establish the following lemma, which is the counterpart to our analysis of the stripped-down framework:

Lemma 2. Let $t_1(x_{1A}, x_{1B}, x_{2A}, x_{2B})$ be any transfer scheme for manager 1 in the U-form. Fix the effort levels at e' for all managers but manager A in the M-form and manager 1 in the U-form. There exists an equivalent transfer scheme for manager A in the M-form, i.e., a scheme $t_A(x_{1A}^*, x_{2A}^*, x_{1B}^*, x_{2B}^*)$ such that for all transfer values τ and all effort levels e by manager A or manager 1,

$$\text{Prob } (t_A(x_{1A}^*, x_{2A}^*, x_{1B}^*, x_{2B}^*) = \tau \mid e) = \text{Prob } (t_1(x_{1A}, x_{1B}, x_{2A}, x_{2B}) = \tau \mid e),$$

if and only if

$$\text{Var } (\varepsilon_A \mid \varepsilon_B) \le \text{Var}(\varepsilon_1 \mid \varepsilon_2).$$

Proof: See Appendix.

Finally, because the labels "1," "2," "A," and "B" are arbitrary, applying Lemma 2, we can compare the M-form and U-form straightforwardly as follows:

Proposition 2. Incentives under the M-form are at least as good as those under the U-form (in the sense that any U-form incentive scheme can be replicated by an M-form incentive scheme) provided that

$$\max \{ \text{Var } (\varepsilon_A \mid \varepsilon_B), \text{Var } (\varepsilon_B \mid \varepsilon_A) \} \le \max \{ \text{Var } (\varepsilon_1 \mid \varepsilon_2), \text{Var } (\varepsilon_2 \mid \varepsilon_1) \}, \tag{8}$$

and

$$\min \{ \text{Var } (\varepsilon_A \mid \varepsilon_B), \text{Var } (\varepsilon_B \mid \varepsilon_A) \} \le \min \{ \text{Var } (\varepsilon_1 \mid \varepsilon_2), \text{Var } (\varepsilon_2 \mid \varepsilon_1) \}, \tag{9}$$

where ε_B, ε_A, ε_1, and ε_2 are given by (6) and (7).

Proposition 2 implies an incomplete ranking of the M-form and U-form in terms of managerial incentives. If both (8) and (9) hold, the M-form is at least as good as the U-form; if both fail, the U-form is at least as good as the M-form; and one of them is satisfied and another fails, the result is inclusive.

Notice that our method of argument is to compare two probability distributions of output signals under the alternative organizational forms. The managerial incentive schemes are entirely based on these probability distributions, regardless of particular form of the utility functions of managers. Therefore, our comparison of organizational forms is independent of the utility functions of the managers. Furthermore, it is also independent of the solution concept of the (noncooperative) game played by the managers, such as Nash or dominant strategy equilibrium, or others.

When there is symmetry across regions and across industries and no correlation between industrial and regional shocks, the formulas of Proposition 2 can be simplified into the following intuitive conditions:

Corollary. Assume $\mathrm{Var}(\delta_A) = \mathrm{Var}(\delta_B) = V_R^2$, $\mathrm{Var}(\theta_1) = \mathrm{Var}(\theta_2) = V_I^2$, $\mathrm{Cov}(\theta_i, \delta_r) = 0$ for $i=1,2$ and $r=A,B$. Let $V_{12} = \mathrm{Cov}\,(\theta_1, \theta_2)$ and $V_{AB} = \mathrm{Cov}\,(\delta_A, \delta_B)$. Then, incentives under the M-form are at least as good as those under the U-form if and only if

$$V_R^2 - V_{AB} \le V_I^2 - V_{12}.$$

The corollary demonstrates a linear tradeoff between variances and covariances for the purpose of incentives.

4.   An Application to China

A.   The M-Form Economy of China

Chandler (1966) and Williamson (1975) characterized the two predominant organizational forms of business corporations: the U-form and the M-form. The U-form corporation has a unitary structure and is organized along functional lines. It was popular in the late 1800s and early 1900s. The M-form corporation, by contrast, consists of reasonably self-contained divisions and emerged in the 1920s. Recently, Qian and Xu (1993) proposed comparing the transition paths of economies in Eastern Europe and the former Soviet Union (EEFSU) with that of China from the standpoint of organizational structures. They observed that the economies of EEFSU resembled U-forms (also known as "branch organizations"), whereas the Chinese hierarchy has taken an M-form structure, in which divisions correspond to regions.[8]

It is well documented that enterprises in EEFSU were grouped by industry, each of which was supervised by a ministry (Gregory and Stuart 1989). In order to fully exploit scale economies and avoid conflicting operations, there was little overlap of functions across ministries. Enterprises were highly specialized. Because of the strong interdependence between enterprises in different regions, comprehensive planning and administrative coordination between ministries at the top level of government were crucial for the normal operation of the economy.

China's planning system began by imitating the U-form Soviet model in its first five-year plan between 1953 and 1957, which was formulated with the help of the Soviets. However, China started to deviate from the Soviet scheme and moved toward an M-form economy in the late 1950s. In the process, "blocks" (*kuaikuai*), i.e., regions, replaced "branches" (*tiaotiao*), i.e., specialized ministries, as the foundation of the planning system. In fact, there are now six regional levels for administration: central, provincial, prefecture, county, township, and village (a municipality can have the rank of province, prefecture or county). Regions at the county level and above are relatively self-contained; indeed, they are nearly self-sufficient in function. Hence, the Chinese M-form is "deep" and differs from the U-form of the Soviet Union and Eastern Europe in a thorough going way.[9]

B. Evidence on Conditional Variances of Industrial and Regional Shocks

We now investigate whether the conditional variance condition of Proposition 3 holds empirically. Implicitly, we are comparing the Chinese organizational form (M-form) with a hypothetical U-form. In this U-form, all firms would be organized into hypothetical industrial ministries (although some industrial ministries actually exist in China, most state firms are under the control of regional governments). We will compare conditional variances of regional and industrial shocks under M-form and U-form arrangements.

Our data set consists of 520 Chinese state-owned enterprise from 1986 to 1991.[10] The enterprises sampled are drawn from more than thirty manufacturing industries, located in major cities in 20 different provinces. The data set contains industry classification codes and location codes for each firm.

In our regressions, we group the data by region and by industry so that a proper sample size is maintained. Moreover, as much as possible, we try to reflect actual organization. For industries, we group the data into units similar to Eastern European-style ministries, with headings such as "machinery," "chemicals," and "textiles." Indeed, because of data limitations, we concentrate on these three industries in particular, since they have the largest sample sizes. Because sample sizes in individual cities are too small, our regional exercises are carried out in two ways. In the first scheme (Table 11.1), the cities are grouped into provinces. We select the five provinces with the largest sample sizes. These are Liaoning, Hubei, Hunan, Jiangsu (which includes Shanghai), and Hebei (which includes Beijing and Tianjin). In the second scheme (Table 11.2), we organize cities into "large regions," where each region contains three to six neighboring provinces. We choose the four regions with the largest sample sizes. These are "East" (Jiangsu, Anhui, Zhejiang, and Shanghai), "North" (Hebei, Henan, Shandong, Shanxi, Beijing, Tianjin), "Northeast" (Heilongjiang, Jilin, Liaoning), and "Central South" (Hubei, Hunan, Guangdong, Guangxi, and Fujian), which comprise a total of 18 provinces.

We use the log-linear Cobb-Douglas production function as our regression model to estimate industry-specific shocks (θ) and region-specific shocks (δ). For every industry i, region r, and period t, we include dummy variables D_{it}^I and D_{rt}^R. The coefficients of these dummies serve as proxies for the industry-specific and region-specific shocks in the given period. Formally, we have

$$E(y \mid L, k)$$

$$= (\beta + \Sigma_{i=1}^I \beta_i D_i^I)L + (\gamma + \Sigma_{i=1}^I \gamma_i D_i^I)K$$
$$+ \Sigma_{t=1}^T D_t \eta_t + \Sigma_{t=1}^T \Sigma_{r=1}^R D_{rt}^R \delta_{rt} + \Sigma_{t=1}^T \Sigma_{i=1}^I D_{it}^I \theta_{it}$$

$$= (\beta + \Sigma_{i=1}^I \beta_i D_i^I)L + (\gamma + \Sigma_{i=1}^I \gamma_i D_i^I)K + \Sigma_{t=1}^T D_t \eta_t$$
$$+ \Sigma_{t=1}^T [D_{Rt}^R \delta_{Rt} + \Sigma_{r=1}^{R-1} D_{rt}^R \delta_{rt}] + \Sigma_{t=1}^T [D_{It}^I \theta_{It} + \Sigma_{i=1}^{I-1} D_{it}^I \theta_{it}]$$

$$= (\beta + \Sigma_{i=1}^I \beta_i D_i^I)L + (\gamma + \Sigma_{i=1}^I \gamma_i D_i^I)K$$
$$+ \Sigma_{t=1}^T D_t \eta_t + \Sigma_{t=1}^T \{(D_t^T - \Sigma_{r=1}^{R-1} D_{rt}^R)\delta_{Rt} + \Sigma_{r=1}^{R-1} D_{rt}^R \delta_{rt}\}$$
$$+ \Sigma_{t=1}^T \{(D_t^T - \Sigma_{i=1}^{I-1} D_{it}^I)\theta_{It} + \Sigma_{i=1}^{I-1} D_{it}^I \theta_{it}\}$$

$$= (\beta + \Sigma_{i=1}^I \beta_i D_i^I)L + (\gamma + \Sigma_{i=1}^I \gamma_i D_i^I)K$$
$$+ \Sigma_{t=1}^T D_t^T \zeta_t + \Sigma_{t=1}^T \Sigma_{r=1}^{R-1} D_{rt}^R \delta_{rt}' + \Sigma_{t=1}^T \Sigma_{i=1}^{I-1} D_{it}^I \theta_{it}',$$

where

$$\zeta_t = \eta_t + \delta_{Rt} + \theta_{It},$$

$$\delta_{rt}' = \delta_{rt} - \delta_{Rt}, \text{ and}$$

$$\theta_{it}' = \theta_{it} - \theta_{It},$$

for $t = 1, \ldots, T$; $r = 1, 2, \ldots, R-1$; and $i = 1, 2, \ldots, I-1$.

Because of an identification problem,[11] we cannot estimate (θ_{it}, δ_{rt}) directly. Instead, we drop the dummy variables of one region and

Table 11.1
Comparing Industrial and Regional Variance and Conditional Variance (by Province)

	(1) $V(\varepsilon_A \mid \varepsilon_B)$	(2) $V(\varepsilon_B \mid \varepsilon_A)$	(3) $V(\varepsilon_1 \mid \varepsilon_2)$	(4) $V(\varepsilon_2 \mid \varepsilon_1)$	(5) Comparison
PR11	0.0008187	0.0007571	0.0030142	0.0024633	Both $V^M < V^U$
PR12	0.0009656	0.0013551	0.0028583	0.0100515	Both $V^M < V^U$
PR13	0.0009623	0.0021445	0.0040004	0.0016873	One $V^M < V^U$
PR14	0.0003254	0.0009305	0.0038165	0.0011762	Both $V^M < V^U$
PR15	0.0007978	0.0003191	0.0045005	0.0016317	Both $V^M < V^U$
PR16	0.0015251	0.0019038	0.0028962	0.0022384	Both $V^M < V^U$
PR17	0.0019566	0.0010847	0.0024202	0.0015482	Both $V^M < V^U$
PR18	0.0006965	0.0005134	0.0019411	0.0011535	Both $V^M < V^U$
PR19	0.0036261	0.0010941	0.0027306	0.0027949	One $V^M < V^U$
PR21	0.0035188	0.0075737	0.004532	0.0014271	One $V^M < V^U$
PR22	0.0125974	0.0033652	0.0064482	0.0027321	One $V^M < V^U$
PR23	0.0007243	0.0005763	0.0032571	0.0019396	Both $V^M < V^U$
PR24	0.0035512	0.0017348	0.0083718	0.0076624	Both $V^M < V^U$
PR25	0.0008053	0.0056084	0.0031696	0.0041095	One $V^M < V^U$
PR26	0.0011198	0.0012982	0.0280702	0.0043337	Both $V^M < V^U$
PR27	0.0035219	0.0014758	0.0014134	0.0045301	One $V^M < V^U$
PR28	0.0032017	0.0036066	0.0022232	0.0039406	One $V^M < V^U$
PR29	0.0009339	0.0006265	0.0059682	0.0121066	Both $V^M < V^U$
PR31	0.0041727	0.0043189	0.0086372	0.0023456	One $V^M < V^U$
PR32	0.0116553	0.00325	0.0114781	0.0047748	Both $V^M < V^U$
PR33	0.0003516	0.0002477	0.0032018	0.0012271	Both $V^M < V^U$
PR34	0.0022851	0.0012984	0.0096523	0.0044628	Both $V^M < V^U$
PR35	0.0014829	0.0069914	0.0063509	0.0042792	One $V^M < V^U$
PR36	0.001434	0.0013309	0.0381816	0.0041133	Both $V^M < V^U$
PR37	0.0017801	0.0006927	0.0026892	0.0043122	Both $V^M < V^U$
PR38	0.0039548	0.0055769	0.0033635	0.0040625	One $V^M < V^U$
PR39	0.0002523	0.000138	0.0012346	0.0083788	Both $V^M < V^U$
PR41	0.0022107	0.0042633	0.0063843	0.0044466	Both $V^M < V^U$
PR42	0.0045825	0.0036649	0.009163	0.0031834	One $V^M < V^U$
PR43	0.0042087	0.0078392	0.0067047	0.0037866	One $V^M < V^U$
PR44	0.0026567	0.0021724	0.0101624	0.0078117	Both $V^M < V^U$
PR45	0.0048027	0.0033586	0.0066146	0.0599119	Both $V^M < V^U$
PR46	0.0052495	0.0025457	0.0174984	0.0066967	Both $V^M < V^U$
PR47	0.0028687	0.002188	0.0051838	0.0071966	Both $V^M < V^U$
PR48	0.0044801	0.0044515	0.0031598	0.0106808	One $V^M < V^U$
PR49	0.0047402	0.003174	0.0051034	0.0113329	Both $V^M < V^U$

Table 11.1 (continued)

	(1) $V(\varepsilon_A \mid \varepsilon_B)$	(2) $V(\varepsilon_B \mid \varepsilon_A)$	(3) $V(\varepsilon_1 \mid \varepsilon_2)$	(4) $V(\varepsilon_2 \mid \varepsilon_1)$	(5) Comparison
PR51	0.0019198	0.00453	0.0024876	0.0018453	One $V^M < V^U$
PR52	0.002041	0.0014745	0.00241	0.0018914	Both $V^M < V^U$
PR53	0.0005682	0.0008727	0.0025407	0.0024924	Both $V^M < V^U$
PR54	0.0040096	0.001339	0.003392	0.0067175	One $V^M < V^U$
PR55	0.0006512	0.0012565	0.0028805	0.0143283	Both $V^M < V^U$
PR56	0.0008774	0.001117	0.0029163	0.0067734	Both $V^M < V^U$
PR57	0.0019528	0.0024209	0.0020744	0.0072606	Both $V^M < V^U$
PR58	0.0011385	0.0013931	0.0018707	0.0102239	Both $V^M < V^U$
PR59	0.0006934	0.0008906	0.0039924	0.0069858	Both $V^M < V^U$
PR61	0.0021139	0.0058389	0.0051549	0.0041415	One $V^M < V^U$
PR62	0.0038292	0.0020893	0.0047473	0.0045516	Both $V^M < V^U$
PR63	0.0011121	0.0016206	0.0049029	0.0046627	Both $V^M < V^U$
PR64	0.0021749	0.0014442	0.0044179	0.0027746	Both $V^M < V^U$
PR65	0.0018646	0.0028379	0.0040928	0.012857	Both $V^M < V^U$
PR66	0.001113	0.0010564	0.0062856	0.0031007	Both $V^M < V^U$
PR67	0.0030414	0.0009696	0.0041567	0.0027338	Both $V^M < V^U$
PR68	0.0022042	0.0028437	0.0041358	0.0069915	Both $V^M < V^U$
PR69	0.001927	0.0008932	0.0063637	0.002802	Both $V^M < V^U$
PR71	0.0024754	0.0050791	0.0102891	0.0083058	Both $V^M < V^U$
PR72	0.0033104	0.002966	0.0083431	0.0060816	Both $V^M < V^U$
PR73	0.0033779	0.0083795	0.0154754	0.0061027	One $V^M < V^U$
PR74	0.002703	0.001844	0.0066952	0.0023344	Both $V^M < V^U$
PR75	0.0047986	0.003487	0.0113504	0.0428088	Both $V^M < V^U$
PR76	0.0041169	0.0020171	0.0082085	0.0022948	Both $V^M < V^U$
PR77	0.0055198	0.0018183	0.0048365	0.0022892	One $V^M < V^U$
PR78	0.0043981	0.0047133	0.0047888	0.0067743	Both $V^M < V^U$
PR79	0.0058755	0.0018537	0.0043716	0.0023171	One $V^M < V^U$

Notes: In the comparison, 'Both $V^M < V^U$' means that the estimated means of both conditional variances under the M-form are smaller than their counterparts under the U-form; and 'One $V^M < V^U$' means that at least one of the estimated means conditional variances under the M-form is smaller than its counterparts under the U-form.

Each line of Tables 11.1 and 11.2 corresponds to one set of results corresponding to a specific three regions and three industries with one of them taken as a benchmark. All 63 lines in Table 11.1 are divided into seven groups. The seven groups are the following: group 1: Jiangsu, Hebei, Liaoning; group 2: Jiangsu, Liaoning, Hubei; group 3: Jiangsu, Liaoning, Hunan; group 4: Hubei, Liaoning, Hunan; group 5: Hebei, Liaoning, Hubei; group 6: Hebei, Liaoning, Hunan; and group 7: Hubei, Jiangsu, Hunan. In Table 11.2, the 36 lines are divided into four groups: group 1: East, North, Northeast; group 2: East, North, Central South; group 3: Northeast, North, Central South; and group 4: Northeast, East, Central South. Within each group, we have nine comparison results by rotating the benchmark region and the benchmark industry among the three regions and three industries within the group.

Table 11.2
Comparing Industrial and Regional Variance and Conditional Variance (by Large Region)

	$V(\varepsilon_A \mid \varepsilon_B)$	$V(\varepsilon_B \mid \varepsilon_A)$	$V(\varepsilon_1 \mid \varepsilon_2)$	$V(\varepsilon_2 \mid \varepsilon_1)$	Comparison
LR11	0.0009876	0.000717	0.0025903	0.0014356	Both $V^M < V^U$
LR12	0.0008853	0.0005627	0.0061475	0.0015846	Both $V^M < V^U$
LR13	0.0020441	0.0007281	0.0026581	0.0040902	Both $V^M < V^U$
LR14	0.0008268	0.0007193	0.0024435	0.0027816	Both $V^M < V^U$
LR15	0.0006873	0.0011279	0.0092834	0.0012659	Both $V^M < V^U$
LR16	0.0007685	0.0011829	0.0033395	0.0015871	Both $V^M < V^U$
LR17	0.0005151	0.0011678	0.0016032	0.0024889	Both $V^M < V^U$
LR18	0.0007956	0.000601	0.0014715	0.0018291	Both $V^M < V^U$
LR19	0.0008224	0.0015445	0.0018787	0.0012828	One $V^M < V^U$
LR21	0.0005335	0.001472	0.000835	0.0095962	Both $V^M < V^U$
LR22	0.0016437	0.0005659	0.0014412	0.0060323	One $V^M < V^U$
LR23	0.0012722	0.0007375	0.007627	0.0068863	Both $V^M < V^U$
LR24	0.0009478	0.0012606	0.003262	0.0062783	Both $V^M < V^U$
LR25	0.0004361	0.0003698	0.0005611	0.0006254	Both $V^M < V^U$
LR26	0.000618	0.0006669	0.0020611	0.0013201	Both $V^M < V^U$
LR27	0.0015519	0.0010175	0.0072856	0.0062593	Both $V^M < V^U$
LR28	0.0002648	0.0016529	0.0072931	0.000737	One $V^M < V^U$
LR29	0.0002031	0.0021522	0.0058771	0.000439	One $V^M < V^U$
LR31	0.0005775	0.0012875	0.001453	0.0040046	Both $V^M < V^U$
LR32	0.0017089	0.0005776	0.0013437	0.0021527	One $V^M < V^U$
LR33	0.0011759	0.0008448	0.0035925	0.0021431	Both $V^M < V^U$
LR34	0.0007168	0.0007843	0.0016867	0.0047914	Both $V^M < V^U$
LR35	0.000916	0.0006686	0.0011856	0.0015126	Both $V^M < V^U$
LR36	0.0010723	0.0008347	0.0053094	0.0019045	Both $V^M < V^U$
LR37	0.0011079	0.000722	0.0025876	0.0029192	Both $V^M < V^U$
LR38	0.0007325	0.0034549	0.0022474	0.002	One $V^M < V^U$
LR39	0.0007093	0.0028758	0.0023074	0.0017212	One $V^M < V^U$
LR41	0.0010433	0.0040568	0.0016852	0.0015885	One $V^M < V^U$
LR42	0.0050836	0.0011803	0.0015829	0.0036032	One $V^M < V^U$
LR43	0.0008049	0.0006459	0.0027002	0.0015179	Both $V^M < V^U$
LR44	0.0012797	0.0016134	0.0015776	0.0027378	Both $V^M < V^U$
LR45	0.0005507	0.0011771	0.0016617	0.0014342	Both $V^M < V^U$
LR46	0.0004704	0.0009846	0.0167323	0.001396	Both $V^M < V^U$
LR47	0.0031506	0.0007645	0.0014811	0.0039824	One $V^M < V^U$
LR48	0.0006126	0.001314	0.0022435	0.0013026	One $V^M < V^U$
LR49	0.0010576	0.0007848	0.0040202	0.0029437	Both $V^M < V^U$

one industry, and estimate the coefficients of the dummy variables for the remaining regions and industries. This can be interpreted as using the shocks in one region and one industry as a benchmark to estimate relative industry-specific and relative region-specific shocks (θ_{it}', δ_{rt}').

For any three regions and three industries, $R = I = 3$, and $T = 6$, we take region 3 (or region C) and industry 3 as benchmarks. From the regressions we obtain a time series (θ_{1t}', θ_{2t}', δ_{At}', δ_{Bt}'), which, for notational simplicity, we denote by $\xi_t = (\theta_{1t}, \theta_{2t}, \delta_{At}, \delta_{Bt})$. Then we treat these estimated shocks as if they were real shocks that are uncorrelated over time.

Given the limitation of the data, i.e., the too short time series ($T=6$), we are not able to perform a formal test.[12] In the following, we compare the conditional variances under the M-form with those under the U-form in a descriptive way. The results are reported in Tables 11.1 and 11.2. Columns (1)–(4) report estimated conditional variances of regional shocks and industrial shocks, and column (5) summarizes the comparison.

Of the 63 results in Table 11.1, there are 44 cases in which the estimated means of both conditional variances under the M-form are smaller than their counterparts under the U-form. In the remaining 29 cases where at least one of the conditional variances under the M-form is smaller than its counterparts under the U-form. There is no case where both conditional variances under the M-form are larger than their counterparts under the U-form. The results in Table 11.2 show that out of 36 possible pairs of comparisons, in 25 pairs both conditional variances under the M-form are smaller than their counterparts under the U-form. In the remaining 11 pairs our test statistic at least one estimated mean conditional variance under the M-form is greater than its counterpart under the U-form. Again, there is no case where both conditional variances under the M-form are larger than their counterparts under the U-form. Therefore, in view of Proposition 2, these results suggest that, for the case of Chinese enterprises, the M-form provides better information than the U-form on relative performance.

C.   Evidence on Regional Yardstick Competition
The findings of section 4B suggest that the M-form facilitates yardstick competition, but one may ask whether such relative performance eval-

uations are actually used in China. We now provide some evidence that they are.

We next provide some evidence on promotions of regional government officials based on relative performance evaluation. The Chinese political system is still under one-party rule, and so the representation of a region in the Party Central Committee indicates the status and power of the regional government officials. Reflecting the increased importance of regions in government, regional representation in the Party's Congress and Central Committee as a whole has increased significantly over the reform period. For example, in the 14th Party Congress, more than 70% of delegates were from provinces, whereas only about 16% were from the central government and central Party organs (Saich 1992).

We use a province's representation in the Party's Central Committee as a proxy for the promotion chances of officials in that province. We normalize the representation by the province's population so as to use the "per capita number of Central Committee members" as an index. This is the ratio between the number of Central Committee members from that region and the region's population. We measure economic performance of a province by its growth rate in "national income" (the rough equivalent of GDP).

Table 11.3 lists the ranking of provincial per capita number of Central Committee members in the 11th Party Congress in 1977 (prank77$_r$) and in the 13th Party Congress in 1987 (prank87$_r$), and the ranking of provincial economic performance in growth rate one year before the Party Congress, that is, in 1976 (erank76$_r$) and in 1986 (erank86$_r$) respectively (data for Ningxia and Tibet are not available). The 11th Central Committee was formed before reform started, and at that time promotion criteria were mostly political. It could, therefore, be viewed as a benchmark. The 13th Central Committee was formed in 1987 when reform had been ongoing for almost a decade, and improving economic performance was officially stated as the central task of the Party. Table 11.3 shows that some provinces (e.g., Fujian, Jiangsu, Xinjiang, Zhejiang) improved their relative growth rankings, and their relative rankings of representation in the Central Committee also increased significantly. In contrast, the relative growth rankings of some provinces (e.g., Anhui, Guangxi, and Qinghai) deteriorated, and so did their rankings in representation in the Central Committee.[13]

To investigate the use of relative performance incentives, we focus on how the change of relative ranking in economic performance is

Table 11.3
Provincial Ranking in Economic Performance and Political Position

	1976	1977	1986	1987
Province	Rank in Economic Growth[a] (erank76)	Rank in Party Central Committee Membership[b] (prank77)	Rank in Economic Growth[a] (erank86)	Rank in Party Central Committee Membership[b] (prank87)
Anhui	24	15	27	21
Beijing	1	27	1	1
Fujian	21	6	10	5
Gansu	8	23	20	15
Guangdong	12	21	12	9
Guangxi	11	16	25	26
Guizhou	27	24	24	22
Hebei	18	10	21	11
Heilongjiang	7	26	16	23
Henan	20	20	17	25
Hubei	22	5	14	17
Hunan	19	2	23	19
Jiangsu	16	12	7	4
Jiangxi	25	1	26	24
Jilin	14	22	18	10
Liaoning	4	17	6	7
NeiMongolia	9	14	15	14
Qinghai	3	9	5	27
Shaanxi	6	7	8	20
Shandong	10	13	11	6
Shanghai	2	4	2	2
Shanxi	23	3	19	13
Sichuan	26	18	22	18
Tianjin	5	11	4	12
Xinjiang	13	8	9	3
Yunnan	15	25	13	16
Zhejiang	17	19	3	8

Sources: (a) State Statistic Bureau 1990; and (b) Bartke 1990, p. 374.

related to the change of relative ranking in per capita number of Central Committee members. A simple regression model using the data in Table 11.3 shows the following result (standard error of the estimated coefficient is in parentheses):

$PINDEX_r = -0.453 + 1.76\ EINDEX_r, R^2 = 0.671,$

$$(0.246)$$

where

$EINDEX_r = 10^*\{(1/erank86_r) - (1/erank76_r) + (1/erank86_r)^2\},$

and

$PINDEX_r = 10^*\{(1/prank87_r) - (1/prank77_r) + (1/prank87_r)^2\}.$

For province r, $EINDEX_r$ is the index that measures the change in rank in economic performance between 1976 and 1986, while $PINDEX_r$ is the index that measures the change in rank in political position between 1977 and 1987. Note that we work with inverses. The third terms in EINDEX and PINDEX, $(1/erank86_r)^2\}$ and $(1/prank87_r)^2\}$ respectively, are incorporated into the indices of change in order to capture the feature that staying at the top requires more effort—and thus requires greater reward—than staying at the bottom.[14]

The significant positive correlation between the change of relative economic performance and the change of relative political position of a region suggests the use of regional yardstick competition.

5. Concluding Remarks

Our work is complementary to some other comparative studies of organizations. Arrow (1974) argues, as we do, that the information structures to which organizations give rise constitute an important characteristic by which they should be compared. Cremer (1980) studies how activities should be optimally grouped into shops in a resource allocation problem. Aoki (1986) investigates how Japanese firms are organized differently from those in the U.S. and what implications these differences have for comparative performance. Holmstrom and Milgrom (1991, 1994) study how tasks should be allocated to firms and managers when managers may perform more than one task.

On the literature of the U-form vs. M-form, Williamson (1975) suggests that in a U-form organization, the CEO may be overloaded with daily operational decisions, and therefore cannot concentrate on strategic decisions. An M-form organization helps to mitigate the overload by decentralizing decision-making. Milgrom and Roberts (1992) emphasize the advantage of the M-form corporation in coordinating finance and investment decisions. Aghion and Tirole (1995) compare the M-form and U-form from the standpoint of encouraging managerial initiative. Qian, Roland and Xu (1997) focus on organizational coordination issues, which they model as the problem of getting attributes suitably matched. They compare the M-form and U-form's efficacy in coordinating changes such as reform and innovation.

Appendix: Proofs of Propositions

Proof of Lemma 1: We take

$$\xi = (\theta_1, \theta_2, \delta_A, \delta_B)', \qquad \Sigma = \mathrm{var}(\xi),$$

$$\varepsilon_u = (\varepsilon_{1A}, \varepsilon_{1B}, \varepsilon_{2A}, \varepsilon_{2B})', \qquad \Sigma_u = \mathrm{var}(\varepsilon_u),$$

$$\varepsilon_m = (\varepsilon_{1A}, \varepsilon_{2A}, \varepsilon_{1B}, \varepsilon_{2B})', \qquad \Sigma_m = \mathrm{var}(\varepsilon_m),$$

where

$$(\varepsilon_{1A}, \varepsilon_{1B}, \varepsilon_{2A}, \varepsilon_{2B})' = A_u \xi, \qquad \Sigma_u = A_u \Sigma A_u',$$

$$(\varepsilon_{1A}, \varepsilon_{2A}, \varepsilon_{1B}, \varepsilon_{2B})' = A_m \xi, \qquad \Sigma_m = A_m \Sigma A_m'$$

and

$$A_u = \begin{pmatrix} 1 & 0 & 1 & 0 \\ 1 & 0 & 0 & 1 \\ 0 & 1 & 1 & 0 \\ 0 & 1 & 0 & 1 \end{pmatrix}, \quad A_m = \begin{pmatrix} 1 & 0 & 1 & 0 \\ 0 & 1 & 1 & 0 \\ 1 & 0 & 0 & 1 \\ 0 & 1 & 0 & 1 \end{pmatrix}$$

Note that both A_u and A_m are singular, and so are Σ_u and Σ_m. However, one can verify that Rank(A_u)=Rank(A_m)=3, and $A_u'R=0$ and $A_m'R=0$ for $R=(1,-1,-1,1)'$.

We prove the case for the U-form (the case for the M-form is similar). Let

$$(x_1, x_2)' = (C_u'(C_{u1}\Sigma C_{u1}')^{-1} C_u)^{-1} C_u'(C_{u1}\Sigma C_{u1}')^{-1} Q_u'(x_{1A}, x_{1B}, x_{2A}, x_{2B})'$$

$$(x_A{}^*, x_B{}^*)' = (C_m'(C_{m1}\Sigma C_{m1}')^{-1} C_m)^{-1} C_m'(C_{m1}\Sigma C_{m1}')^{-1} Q_m'(x_{1A}{}^*, x_{2A}{}^*, x_{1B}{}^*, x_{2B}{}^*)'$$

$$C_u = Q_u'A, \qquad C_{u1} = Q_u'A_u, \qquad C_m = Q_m'A, \qquad C_{m1} = Q_m'A_m,$$

$$A = \begin{pmatrix} 1 & 0 \\ 1 & 0 \\ 0 & 1 \\ 0 & 1 \end{pmatrix}, \ Q_u = \begin{pmatrix} 1 & 0 & 1 \\ 1 & 0 & 0 \\ 0 & 1 & 1 \\ 0 & 1 & 0 \end{pmatrix}, \ Q_m = \begin{pmatrix} 1 & 0 & 1 \\ 0 & 1 & 1 \\ 1 & 0 & 0 \\ 0 & 1 & 0 \end{pmatrix},$$

and $(C_{u1}\Sigma C_{u1}')$ and $(C_{m1}\Sigma C_{m1}')$ are non-singular 3x3 matrices.

Let $x = (x_{1A}, x_{1B}, x_{2A}, x_{2B})'$ and $\beta=(e_1,e_2)'$. Then under the U-form:

$$x = A\beta + A_u\xi.$$

Let $\underline{x} = A(x_1, x_2)' = (x_1, x_1, x_2, x_2)'$ and $u = (u_1, u_2, u_3, u_4) = x-\underline{x}$. Because $Eu=Ex-E\underline{x}=A\beta-A\beta=0$, to show $\underline{x}$ and u are uncorrelated, we need only show that $E\underline{x}u'=0$. In fact,

$$E\underline{x}u' = Ex(x-\underline{x})'$$

$$= E\{A(C_u'(C_{u1}\Sigma C_{u1}')^{-1} C_u)^{-1} C_u'(C_{u1}\Sigma C_{u1}')^{-1} Q_u'(A\beta+A_u\xi)\}$$
$$\{(I-A(C_u'(C_{u1}\Sigma C_{u1}')^{-1} C_u)^{-1} C_u'(C_{u1}\Sigma C_{u1}')^{-1} Q_u')(A\beta+A_u\xi)\}'$$

$$= E\{A(C_u'(C_{u1}\Sigma C_{u1}')^{-1} C_u)^{-1} C_u'(C_{u1}\Sigma C_{u1}')^{-1} Q_u'(A\beta+A_u\xi)\}$$
$$(A_u\xi)'\{I-A(C_u'(C_{u1}\Sigma C_{u1}')^{-1} C_u)^{-1} C_u'(C_{u1}\Sigma C_{u1}')^{-1} Q_u'\}'$$

$$= E\{A\beta + A(C_u'(C_{u1}\Sigma C_{u1}')^{-1} C_u)^{-1} C_u'(C_{u1}\Sigma C_{u1}')^{-1} C_{u1} \xi\}$$
$$\xi'A_u'\{I-Q_u'(C_{u1}\Sigma C_{u1}')^{-1} C_u (C_u'(C_{u1}\Sigma C_{u1}')^{-1} C_u)^{-1} A'\}$$

$$= A(C_u'(C_{u1}\Sigma C_{u1}')^{-1} C_u)^{-1} C_u'(C_{u1}\Sigma C_{u1}')^{-1} C_{u1} E(\xi\xi') A_u'$$
$$- A(C_u'(C_{u1}\Sigma C_{u1}')^{-1} C_u)^{-1} C_u'(C_{u1}\Sigma C_{u1}')^{-1} C_{u1} E(\xi\xi')C_{u1}'(C_{u1}\Sigma C_{u1}')^{-1} C_u$$
$$(C_u'(C_{u1}\Sigma C_{u1}')^{-1} C_u)^{-1} A'$$

$$= A(C_u'(C_{u1}\Sigma C_{u1}')^{-1} C_u)^{-1} C_u'(C_{u1}\Sigma C_{u1}')^{-1} C_{u1} \Sigma A_u' - A(C_u'(C_{u1}\Sigma C_{u1}')^{-1}$$
$$C_u)^{-1} A'$$

We multiply $E\underline{x}u'$ from the right a non-singular matrix $[Q_u, R]$, we have,

$$[A(C_u'(C_{u1}\Sigma C_{u1}')^{-1} C_u)^{-1} C_u'(C_{u1}\Sigma C_{u1}')^{-1} C_{u1} \Sigma A_u' - A(C_u'(C_{u1}\Sigma C_{u1}')^{-1} C_u)^{-1} A']Q_u$$

$$= A(C_u'(C_{u1}\Sigma C_{u1}')^{-1} C_u)^{-1} C_u' - A(C_u'(C_{u1}\Sigma C_{u1}')^{-1} C_u)^{-1} C_u'$$

$$= 0.$$

We also have

$$[A(C_u'(C_{u1}\Sigma C_{u1}')^{-1} C_u)^{-1} C_u'(C_{u1}\Sigma C_{u1}')^{-1} C_{u1} \Sigma A_u' - A(C_u'(C_{u1}\Sigma C_{u1}')^{-1} C_u)^{-1}$$
$$A']R = 0$$

because $A_u'R=0$ and $A'R = 0$.

Therefore, $E\underline{x}u' = 0$, that is, $\underline{x}$ and u are uncorrelated and $x = \underline{x} + u$.

Finally, one can show x_1 and x_A as defined above are just $\lambda_1 x_{1A} + (1-\lambda_1)x_{1B}$ and

$$\lambda_A x_{1A}{}^* +(1-\lambda_A)x_{2A}{}^*,$$

where λ_1 and λ_A are given by (4) and (5), respectively. Similarly for x_2 and x_B. Q.E.D.

Proof of Lemma 2: Let

$$(\varepsilon_1, \varepsilon_2)' = (C_u'(C_{u1}\Sigma C_{u1}')^{-1} C_u)^{-1} C_u'(C_{u1}\Sigma C_{u1}')^{-1} C_{u1} \xi,$$

and

$$(\varepsilon_A, \varepsilon_B)' = (C_m'(C_{m1}\Sigma C_{m1}')^{-1} C_m)^{-1} C_m'(C_{m1}\Sigma C_{m1}')^{-1} C_{m1} \xi.$$

From our analysis of the stripped-down framework, Var $(\varepsilon_A \mid \varepsilon_B) \le$ Var$(\varepsilon_1 \mid \varepsilon_2)$ implies that there exist constant α, β, γ and random noise z uncorrelated with (x_A, x_B) such that for all $e_1=e_A$,

$$(x_1, x_1, x_2, x_2) = (x_A{}^* - \alpha x_B{}^*, x_A{}^* - \alpha x_B{}^*, \beta x_B{}^*, \beta x_B{}^*) + (z, z, \gamma, \gamma)$$

in distribution. By Lemma 1, we can choose a random vector (w_1, w_2, w_3, w_4) such that

$$\text{Var}(w_1, w_2, w_3, w_4) = \text{Var}(u_1, u_2, u_3, u_4) = \text{Var}(x_{1A}, x_{1B}, x_{2A}, x_{2B}) -$$
$$\text{Var}(x_1, x_1, x_2, x_2); \tag{i}$$

and

$$(w_1, w_2, w_3, w_4) \text{ is independent of } (x_1, x_2), (x_A{}^*, x_B{}^*), \text{ and } z. \tag{ii}$$

Then we obtain,

Var$(x_{1A}, x_{1B}, x_{2A}, x_{2B})$

$$= \text{Var}(x_1, x_1, x_2, x_2) + [\text{Var}(x_{1A}, x_{1B}, x_{2A}, x_{2B}) - \text{Var}(x_1, x_1, x_2, x_2)]$$

$$= \text{Var}(x_A{}^* - \alpha x_B{}^*, x_A{}^* - \alpha x_B{}^*, \beta x_B{}^*, \beta x_B{}^*) + \text{Var}(z, z, \gamma, \gamma) + \text{Var}(w_1, w_2, w_3, w_4)$$

$$= \text{Var}(x_A{}^* - \alpha x_B{}^* + z + w_1, x_A{}^* - \alpha x_B{}^* + z + w_2, \beta x_B{}^* + \gamma + w_3, \beta x_B{}^* + \gamma + w_4).$$

Furthermore,

$E(x_{1A}, x_{1B}, x_{2A}, x_{2B})$

$= E(x_1, x_1, x_2, x_2)$

$= E(x_A{}^* - \alpha x_B{}^* + z + w_1, x_A{}^* - \alpha x_B{}^* + z + w_2, \beta x_B{}^* + \gamma + w_3, \beta x_B{}^* + \gamma + w_4)$.

Therefore we obtain

$(x_{1A}, x_{1B}, x_{2A}, x_{2B}) = (x_A{}^*-\alpha x_B{}^*+z+w_1, x_A{}^*-\alpha x_B{}^*+z+w_2, \beta x_B{}^*+\gamma+w_3, \beta x_B{}^*+\gamma+w_4)$

in distribution.
Finally, we define

$t_A(x_{1A}{}^*, x_{2A}{}^*, x_{1B}{}^*, x_{2B}{}^*) = t_1(x_A{}^*-\alpha x_B{}^*+z+w_1, x_A{}^*-\alpha x_B{}^*+z+w_2, \beta x_B{}^*+\gamma+w_3, \beta x_B{}^*+\gamma+w_4)$,

which is the same as $t_1(x_{1A}, x_{1B}, x_{2A}, x_{2B})$ in distribution.

Q.E.D.

Notes

* We are grateful to Takeshi Amemiya, Masahiko Aoki, Patrick Bolton, Gary Chamberlain, Javier Hidalgo, Bengt Holmstrom, Jan Magnus, and Frank Wolak for helpful discussions, and to three referees and participants in seminars and conferences in Gerzensee, California Institute of Technology, Harvard, MIT, LSE, CEPR (Brussels), and the Chinese Academy of Social Sciences (Beijing) for useful comments. We thank Juzhong Zhuang for his help with the data; Nancy Hearst for her help with the literature; Angela Lee and Ying Qian for their research assistance. Maskin's research is supported by the NSF, Qian's research by a McNamara Fellowship at Stanford, and Xu's research by STICERD and CEP at LSE (CEP is sponsored by the ESRC).

1. The current Russian economy, including privatized firms, is still deeply affected by their U-form legacy. Data from field work show that Russian firms are still strongly influenced by industrial ministries (Earle and Ross 1996).

2. The Chinese central government has pursued an explicit policy during reform to stimulate regional competition, such as encouraging regions to "get rich first." Indeed, relative performance criteria are sometimes formally incorporated in the procedures for determining government officials' promotions and bonuses. For example, some county governments use the annual ranking of townships (by profit rate on total capital) as a primary criterion to evaluate township government officials (Chapter 2, Whiting 1995). Moreover, government statistical reports and the mass media regularly publish rankings of regions in terms of their performances in growth, profit, foreign investment, etc. Most authoritative national or regional statistical books publish national or regional rankings of provinces, cities and/or counties every year.

3. With this specification, we rule out the possibility that all plants from a given industry be located in the same region, although this was roughly the case for some industries in the Soviet economy. The reason for ruling it out is that it implies that organization by region is identical to organization by industry, whereas we are interested in the contrast between the two.

4. There is another—and perhaps more "standard"—interpretation of our model. Instead of an entire economy, think of the organization as a corporation, say, an automobile manufacturer. The "regions" would then correspond to two different car models, whereas the two "industries" would become two different specialized departments, e.g., production and purchasing. Shocks to "regions" (models) could then be interpreted as shifts in demand for these models, whereas shocks to "industries" (departments) might reflect changes in the cost of labor or parts.

5. We have been speaking of shocks as though they are necessarily a bad thing. But, in the case of a favorable shock, we can reinterpret d as the maximum possible average increase in output that the shock permits. Thus, if the manager does nothing in response to the shock, average output is lower by d relative to what it would have been had the manager taken full advantage of the shock.

6. For simplicity, we are limiting our attention to normal distributions. However, using the methods of Kim (1995) we could obtain generalizations of Propositions 1 and 2 for general distributions.

7. Here, as in the remainder of the paper, we must impose an exogenous upper bound on penalties or else, as a referee pointed out, there would exist incentive schemes approximating the first-best arbitrarily closely (à la Mirrlees (1974)).

8. Qian and Xu (1993) discussed the overall costs and benefits of U-forms and M-forms in terms of scale economies, incentives, and coordination, and also the implications of these costs and benefits for alternative approaches to reform.

9. China's M-form economy is not mere decentralization at the national level due to its large size. Compare Hungary and Guangdong province. The former was organized in a U-form hierarchy with specialized ministries managing all firms, while the latter itself is also organized in an M-form with multiple regions consisting of prefectures, counties, townships and villages, all of them being self-contained economic units.

10. The data were collected by the China System Reform Research Institute, Beijing, China.

11. Dummy variables here have the following property:
$D_t^T = \Sigma_{r=1}^R D_{rt}^R = \Sigma_{i=1}^I D_{it}^I = 1$, in period t
$= 0$, otherwise,
that is, the sum of the regional dummies is the same as that of the industrial dummies creating a collinearity problem.

12. We have derived a formal asymptotic test statistics which could allow us to perform a rigorous test if we had a better data set (see Maskin, Qian and Xu 1997).

13. There are of course important political factors that also had influence on the selection of the Central Committee members. Before reform, provinces such as Hunan, Hubei, and Jiangxi provinces were over-represented in the Central Committee because these were the home provinces of many revolutionary leaders (e.g., Mao Zedong was from Hunan), and other provinces such as Beijing were under-represented because of the purge in the

Cultural Revolution, which ended just before the 11th Party Congress. Furthermore, some provinces such as Xinjiang have always been over-represented because of their political significance.

14. We have run many more regressions with alternative data sets and have obtained qualitatively similar results. Those results are available upon request.

References

Aghion, Philippe and Jean Tirole, "Some Implications of Growth for Organizational Form and Ownership Structure," *European Economic Review*, 1995.

Aoki, Masahiko, "Horizontal vs. Vertical Information Structure of the Firm," *American Economic Review*, 76(5): 971–83, December 1986.

Arrow, Kenneth, *The Limits of Organization*, New York: Norton, 1974.

Bartke, Wolfgang, *Biographical Dictionary and Analysis of China's Party Leadership, 1922–1988*, NY: K. G. Saur, 1990.

Bolton, Patrick, and Joseph Farrell, "Decentralization, Duplication and Delay," *Journal of Political Economy*, 98(4), August, 1990.

Chandler, Alfred Jr., *Strategy and Structure*, New York: Doubleday & Company, Inc., 1962.

Cremer, Jacques, "A Partial Theory of the Optimal Organization of Bureaucracy," *Bell Journal of Economics*, 11, 683–693, 1980.

Earle, John, and R. Ross, "Ownership Transformation, Economic Behavior, and Political Attitudes in Russia," mimeo, 1996.

Gregory, Paul R., and Robert C. Stuart, *Soviet Economic Structure and Performance*, New York: Harper & Row, Publishers, 1981.

Holmstrom, Bengt, "Moral Hazard in Teams," *Bell Journal of Economics*, 13:324–340, 1982.

Holmstrom, Bengt and Paul Milgrom, "Multi-task Principal-Agent Analysis: Incentive Contracts, Asset Ownership and Job Design," *Journal of Law, Economics, and Organization*, 7:24–52, 1991.

Holmstrom, Bengt and Paul Milgrom, "The Firm as an Incentive System," *American Economic Review*, 84:972–991, 1994.

Kim, Son Ku, "Efficiency of an Information System in an Agency Model," *Econometrica*, 63(1):89–102, 1995.

Kornai, Janos, *The Socialist System*, Princeton University Press, 1992.

Lazear, Edward P. and Sherwin Rosen, "Rank-Order Tournaments as Optimum Labor Contracts," *Journal of Political Economy*, 89(5), October, 1981.

Maskin, Eric, Yingyi Qian, and Chenggang Xu, "Incentives, Information, and Organizational Form," HIID Development Discussion Papers 618, Harvard University; CEP Discussion Paper 371, LSE, 1997.

Milgrom, Paul, and John Roberts, *Economics, Organization, and Management*, Prentice Hall, 1992.

Mirrlees, James A., "Notes on Welfare Economics, Information and Uncertainty," in M. Balch, D. McFadden and S. Wu (eds.), *Essays in Economic Behavior under Uncertainty*, pp. 243–58, 1974.

Nalebuff, Barry, and Joseph Stiglitz, "Prizes and Incentives: Towards a General Theory of Compensation and Competition," *Bell Journal of Economics*, 1983.

Qian, Yingyi, Gerard Roland, and Chenggang Xu, "Coordinating Changes in M-form and U-form Organizations," mimeo, Stanford University, ECARE, and LSE, 1997.

Qian, Yingyi, and Chenggang Xu, "Why China's Economic Reform Differ: The M-form Hierarchy and Entry/Expansion of the Non-state Sector," *Economics of Transition*, 1(2), pp. 135–170, June, 1993.

Saich, Tony, "The Fourteenth Party Congress: A Program for Authoritarian Rule," *China Quarterly*, 132:1136–1160, December, 1992.

Shleifer, Andrei, "A Theory of Yardstick Competition," *RAND Journal of Economics*, 16(3):319–27, Autumn, 1985.

State Statistical Bureau, *Quanguo gesheng, zizhiqu, zhixiashi tongji ziliao huibian, 1949–1989* (*Collections of Historical Statistical Materials of All Provinces, Autonomous Regions, and Provincial Level Municipalities, 1949–1989*), Beijing: National Statistics Press, 1990.

Weitzman, Martin, "Price vs. Quantity," *Review of Economic Studies*, 1974.

Whiting, Susan, *The Micro-Foundations of Institutional Change in Reform China: Property Rights and Revenue Extraction in the Rural Industrial Sector*, Ph.D. dissertation, University of Michigan, 1995.

Williamson, Oliver, *Markets and Hierarchies*, New York: Free Press, 1975.

12 Coordinating Reforms in Transition Economies

1. Introduction

The comparison between reforms in China and Eastern Europe is often done in terms of the gradualist and experimental approach vs. the big-bang and comprehensive approach. China's reforms first started with experiments in agriculture followed by experiments in special economic zones in cities.[1] However, one often forgets that some experimental reforms were introduced in Eastern Europe and the Soviet Union in the 1980s, but they failed. Those failures led to the discrediting of the experimental approach to reform, and to the adoption of a comprehensive approach. Ironically, to a large extent, China followed many of the Eastern European gradual reforms in earlier stages of its reforms. In fact, the gradualist Hungarian reform started in 1968 with some initial success, but then ran into difficulties in the 1980s. Gradual reforms in the 1980s were associated with economic stagnation. According to official statistics, the average growth rate of GDP in Hungary was 1.8% between 1981 and 1985 and almost zero in 1988 and 1989. In Poland, the average GDP growth rate was less than 2% between 1981 and 1989.[2] The question is thus raised of why the experimental approach was very successful in China but not in Eastern Europe.

In this paper, we propose a theory, which opens new perspectives on understanding how the differences in organizational forms of centralized economies in the Soviet Union and China affected their reforms and transition paths. It allows us to understand what made China succeed in applying the experimental approaches, whereas Eastern Europe and the former Soviet Union economies failed. Our theory allows us to address more general questions: how do organizational forms of a centralized

With Gerard Roland and Chenggang Xu; originally published in Erik Berglof and Gerard Roland, editors, *The Economics of Transition: The Fifth Nobel Symposium in Economics*, 2007, Palgrave Macmillan.

economy or of government hierarchy affect reforms or institutional change? What is the difference between coordinating changes in a unitary (centralized) state with specialized ministries and in a federal state with coordinating powers delegated to regions?

The central point of our theory is that coordination is among the most important functions for any government organization and various organizational forms differ in their coordination capacity. We introduce the concept of task coordination inside an organization as matching the attributes of specialized tasks in a stochastic environment. This concept is inspired by Milgrom and Roberts' (1992) discussion on "design attributes". An implementation of reform can be viewed as assembling complementary parts. Each part is characterized by its attributes: time, location, technical specifications, legal and administrative terms, etc. A reform is completed successfully only if the characteristics of each attribute of the various parts are matched. Failure in the matching of attributes often implies a breakdown.

In a world without uncertainty, as long as an organization has a perfect plan in which all the attributes are matched by design, all the tasks can be implemented without problems. Alternatively, as long as all agents are able to communicate perfectly, matching attributes will not be a problem either, even when there is uncertainty. However, when there are exogenous random shocks, which we will call "attribute shocks," and when communication between agents is imperfect, the coordination problem becomes non-trivial, and having a perfect plan alone is insufficient. This is because when there is a shock affecting an attribute of one task, any change of this attribute will affect its matching with attributes of other tasks. Thus, the corresponding attributes of other tasks must be adjusted to make them match. But the quality of the adjustment of attributes depends itself on the quality of communication inside an organization. The communication problem arises because only a manager directly and frequently engaging in a particular task has first-hand information and knowledge about that task. Communication is necessary for others to use such information and knowledge, but communication is likely to be imperfect because message transmission, due to the bounded capabilities of human information processing (such as misunderstanding in talking to each other) as well as technical bugs, can go wrong.

However, the communication problem depends on how tasks and decision-making power are assigned within an organization; that is, it depends on the organizational form. We define an M-form organization as one that consists of self-contained units where complementary tasks are grouped together. In contrast, a U-form organization is decomposed into specialized units where similar tasks are grouped together. Because the M-form and the U-form organizations assign tasks differently, the communication problems they face are different.[3]

This definition of M-form and U-form organizations helps us to characterize the striking differences between the organization of the Soviet and the Chinese planning administration (Qian and Xu 1993). We may regard a centrally planned economy as a huge "firm" with the national government as the headquarters, and ministries or subnational governments, such as regional governments, as subunits of the firm. From this perspective, each of the economies in Eastern Europe and the former Soviet Union was organized as a gigantic U-form (also known as a "branch organization"), where state-owned enterprises were subordinated to specialized or functional ministries (e.g., mining, machinery, textile, etc.). This central planning structure makes central coordination essential: in the late 1970s the *Gosplan*, which supervised all specialized ministries, was responsible for 48,000 plan "positions" and 12 million products (Nove 1980).

In contrast, the Chinese economy has been organized mainly on a geographical principle (provinces, prefectures, counties, townships and villages). This corresponds to an M-form organization (also known as a "regional organization"), where most state-owned enterprises were under the control of regional governments. Typically, the production of each region was relatively self-contained. With regional governments taking major responsibilities for coordination, the central government's role of coordination was greatly reduced compared to that in the Eastern Europe and the former Soviet Union. The Chinese State Planning Commission was never responsible for more than 1,000 products (Qian and Xu 1993), and the central statistical agency in China had a total staff of only 280 (in 1981), compared to 41,000 in the Soviet Union (in 1987) (Huang 1994).[4]

According to our theoretical analysis, the introduction of reforms (be they reforms within the central planning system or market-oriented reforms) in Eastern Europe and the former Soviet Union requires a comprehensive approach with coordination from the center. On the other hand, in China, reforms can proceed with local experiments, or even parallel experiments, because coordination is established locally.

Indeed, plagued by many coordination problems, many previous reform experiments in Eastern Europe and the former Soviet Union were not successful. In contrast, China repeatedly adopted successfully an experimental approach to reforms.

In order to focus on the coordination problem, we assume away the incentive problem and take the team theoretical approach. Elsewhere, Maskin, Qian, and Xu (1999) provide an analysis of incentive problems in M-form and U-form organizations in a similar setup. They have demonstrated that different organizational forms give rise to different information about managers' performance and therefore differ according to how incentives encourage good performance. In particular, they have shown that the M-form may provide better incentives than the U-form because it promotes yardstick competition—that is, relative performance evaluation—more effectively. In this paper, we assume that managers under either organizational form have the same incentives to pursue the goal of economic efficiency. That is, there is no intrinsic advantage of one organizational form over another from the point of view of incentives. Therefore, all results are driven by coordination considerations.

In our theoretical model we make a symmetry assumption with two industries in each region. However, in reality, China and the Soviet Union had different patterns of industrial centralization on top of the organizational form. In the Soviet Union, the initial U-form organization led to extreme industrial concentration where one region had only one industry.[5] In that case, regions cannot be self-contained any longer, which means that the properties of the M-form cannot be obtained simply by devolution of powers to the regions. The initial choice of organizational form thus had an impact on location and size of industry. In the Soviet Union, these choices represented a "lock-in" of the U-form, making a change towards the M-form impossible without major industrial investment. This consideration also clarifies the confusion arising frequently in studying the Soviet Union and Russia. It is often thought that the devolution of authority to regional governments under Yeltsin in Russia after 1992 represents a shift from a U-form to an M-form. This is not true. In fact, such a change represents a shift from a U-form, as we have studied, to a "collapsed" U-form, which is equivalent to a U-form where the communication between local and central managers has completely broken down. This is because when industries are regionally concentrated and cannot be moved around easily, regions cannot be self-contained units, as in the case of China.

Beyond transition economies, our theory is also useful in understanding the organization of government in general, specifically the comparison between the unitary and federal state. The unitary state can be viewed as a U-form organization and federalism as an M-form. The organization of the French and Japanese governments are examples of the former and that of the United States is the most prominent example of the latter. The French and Japanese government organizations are much more centralized, in Paris and Tokyo, respectively, with specialized ministries having large powers and regional governments having little. Major changes in government programs, such as education and banking reforms, require initialization by the responsible ministries and coordination by the central government. In contrast, American federalism is known as a "laboratory of the states," in the famous words of the American Supreme Court Justice Louis Brandeis from 1932. Indeed, many government policy changes in the U.S. are experiments by some states and the successful results are imitated later by others. The contrast between the unitary and federal states fits well in our theoretical analysis of organizational forms.

The organization of the rest of the paper is as follows. Section 2 sets up the model and introduces the concept of task coordination as "attribute matching." Section 3 derives the basic results of the U-form and the M-form organizations in coordinating reforms. Section 4 extends the model to include the possibility of parallel reform experiments. Section 5 applies our theory to explain reform strategies in China and the former Soviet Union. Section 6 concludes with a discussion of the application to federalism. The Appendix contains the proofs of the propositions.

2. The Model

The coordination concept in this paper relates to the adjustment of the organization to exogenous disturbances and random contingencies. This concept expresses the idea that a need for coordination arises in response to exogenous disturbances to pre-set plans. We look at task-coordination decisions. There are usually many attributes of a set of tasks required to produce a product or to provide a service: time, location, technical specifications such as size, weight and form, etc. A product or a service is completed only if characteristics of each attribute among a set of tasks are matched ("attribute fit," as referred to by Milgrom and Roberts 1992). When there is a shock affecting an attribute in one task, the attribute in other tasks must be adjusted to achieve "attribute matching."

Consider an economy with two regions, "A" and "B," and two functions, "1" and "2." The technology of the economy can be described fully by four tasks: 1A, 2A, 1B, and 2B, where task ir involves function i for region r. With this specification, we assume that the two regions are symmetric in the sense that each region has two functions.

We suppose that a reform program is designed so that all attributes are matched perfectly *ex ante* in the blueprints. However, in implementing a program, there are always "attribute shocks" which are unexpected contingencies not taken care of in the blueprints. At the implementation stage of a reform program, attributes of subprograms must be mutually adjusted to observed attribute shocks. We assume that attribute matching must take place between tasks $1r$ and $2r$ ($r = A, B$).

We consider an infinite horizon with discount factor δ. We first assume that one and only one blueprint for reform is available in each period to the top manager of the economy. Later we allow the possibility of two independent blueprints in each period. With probability p the blueprint is a good one and with probability $1-p$ it is bad. Blueprints available over time are stochastically independent. We assume that if a blueprint is known to be good, then it will be good in the same region in the future, and it can be good in another region. In contrast, good coordination (i.e., attribute matching) in one region cannot be "copied" in another region, because of differences in local conditions. Therefore, if a blueprint tried in one region is found to be good and coordination has been successful, then the same blueprint can be used successfully elsewhere, but coordination is still necessary in order to adjust to local conditions before a successful outcome can be achieved. We assume that the organization will try new reform programs until success, and then it stays with the successful program forever.[6]

We assume that the manager of a unit has better "local" information about his unit than others. Thus, the effectiveness of corresponding adjustments will be determined by the quality of communication among the managers who are responsible for the related tasks. Moreover, we assume that communication within a unit is perfect, but cross-unit communication is imperfect. This is because when activities are shared by members of a unit they share local information and they communicate extensively with a common language (it can take many formats such as jargon, graphs, body language, etc.) which reduces misunderstandings. However, communication across units is imperfect. This is because when agents are in separate units, they have different idiosyncratic knowledge and different interpretations of the same message. They may speak different languages (e.g., engineering language differs from marketing language and the language of economists may differ from that of sociologists). Moreover, their communication may be restricted to short messages (such as messages carried by phone calls, faxes, memos, meetings, etc.), which may be subject to ambiguous interpretations.

A superior is specialized in supervising subordinate units and communicates with the units more often. However, units are not specialized in communicating with each other. We assume that the center receives imperfect information about shocks in all units but there is no horizontal communication between units. In this sense, a superior has better "global" information about all units than his subordinates do.

We model these differences in information in reduced form by assuming that in each period, if needed, a manager collects information about the attribute shocks and, if required, sends a message to another manager. Each message contains information about all the attributes in one task. We assume that the probability of each message being correct is λ with $0 \leq \lambda \leq 1$. We assume that noises in information transmission are independent across tasks as well as over time. Based on the information received, the manager carries out his main job: attribute matching.

Consider the payoffs for region A (payoffs for region B are defined symmetrically). Let the status quo (without change) payoff in tasks 1A and 2A be $1/2$. The benefits from change are defined as follows. Suppose the reform program is good, then (i) with reform in task 1A but not in task 2A (or reform in task 2A but not in task 1A), the payoff is $(R+1)/4$ if the attributes between 1A and 2A are matched, otherwise 0; and (ii) with reform in both tasks 1A and 2A, the payoff is $R/2$ if the attributes between 1A and 2A are matched, otherwise 0. If the reform program is bad, then the payoff is always 0 when reform is implemented.

Assumption 1. $pR > 1$: the expected per-period benefit from reform is larger than the status quo.

We assume that all blueprints are made available for free, but for each manager there is a setup cost C associated with coordinating reform. This cost can be interpreted as a training cost, that is, to implement a reform program the managers need to be trained on how to match attributes of the reform program. Because blueprints are free and the setup costs for coordination are not, when a failure occurs in the previous period (either due to a bad program or bad coordination), the organization always prefers to use a new blueprint in the next period rather than retry the old one.

Assumption 2. $R/2(1-\delta) - C > 1/2(1-\delta)$, that is, the net benefit from reform is better than the status quo for $p = 1$.

We can now define U-form and M-form organizations. A U-form organization is set up along "functional lines." Two middle managers i ($i = 1, 2$) are responsible for collecting information about shocks in tasks iA and iB. Because the two tasks that need attribute matching are not assigned to the same middle manager, the two middle manager have to report the information to the top manager, who, after receiving information from the two managers, matches attributes between tasks $1r$ and $2r$ ($r = A, B$). This type of organization can be represented by Figure 12.1.

An M-form organization is set up along "regional lines." The middle manager r ($r = A, B$) is responsible for collecting information about shocks in tasks $1r$ and $2r$. Because the two tasks which require attribute matching are assigned to the same manager, the middle manager can match attributes between tasks $1r$ and $2r$ locally by themselves. The top manager provides a blueprint for reform. This type of organization can be represented by Figure 12.2.

Under the M-form, setup costs must be incurred in each unit since attribute matching is done separately in each region unit. This leads to higher setup costs. For example, both managers need to be trained to coordinate the reform. In contrast, under the U-form, only the top manager matches attributes in a centralized way. Therefore, the setup

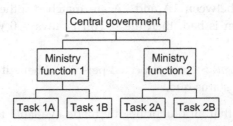

Figure 12.1
A U-form Organization

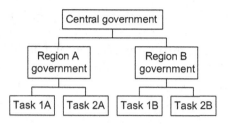

Figure 12.2
An M-form Organization

cost is correspondingly smaller. For simplicity, we will assume that only one setup cost is required when only one manager coordinates.

We provide an example to illustrate the concept. Suppose an economic reform consists of two components: enterprise restructuring (laying off excess workers) and creation of a social safety net. Task 1r is layoffs in region r and task 2r is paying unemployment benefits through the social safety net in region r, where r = A and B. If the reform is organized by specialized ministries, then each ministry is responsible for either enterprise restructuring or the social safety net, and the national government is responsible for matching the attributes between enterprise restructuring and the social safety net (the U-form). If the reform is organized by the regions, each regional government is responsible for matching the attributes between enterprise restructuring and the social safety net in its own region (the M-form).

The attributes of enterprise restructuring are the number and individual characteristics of the laid-off workers, such as age, seniority, family composition, length of residence, sex, type of contract, current wage, history of employment, etc. The attributes of compensation from the social safety net are rules of eligibility, such as length of employment, special circumstances (veteran or not), status of enterprises, rules of benefits such as size and length, types of benefits (monetary or not), technical support of computers, administration, budget, etc. If some attributes of the two tasks are not matched, some laid-off workers may not be compensated appropriately. It is possible that there will be bad coordination between layoff policies and the creation of the social safety net, leading to riots. For example, the rules for eligibility set at the national level may be completely inappropriate in some important regions which have a concentration of older workers, if the national rule for pension eligibility does not make workers close to pension age eligible for any benefits.

3. Coordination, Experimentation, and Organizational Flexibility

In this section, we compare the M-form and the U-form assuming that only one blueprint is available in each time period. Under both organizational forms, the payoff from the status quo (i.e., no reform) is 1 for each period, and thus the status quo discounted payoff is $1/(1-\delta)$.

Consider first the situation in which an organization starts a reform in both of its units and continues in that way afterwards. Under the M-form, every unit manager will be responsible for matching the attributes of the two tasks within his unit. With perfect local information, attribute matching under the M-form will be performed perfectly. If a reform program is good, which happens with probability p, the total payoff from the two units is $R/(1-\delta)$. If a reform program is bad, which happens with probability $1-p$, the current payoff is zero, and a new program will be tried in the next period. Therefore, the expected payoff of continued reform in an M-form is

$$\pi_{m2} = pR/(1-\delta) + (1-p)\delta\pi_{m2},$$

from which we obtain

$$\pi_{m2} = pR/\{(1-\delta)[1-(1-p)\delta]\}.$$

On the cost side, in period 1, $2C$ is paid because two managers are involved in coordination. With probability p, the reform program is good, so no more costs need to be paid afterwards. But with a probability $1-p$ the reform program is bad, which is discovered after one period of change. Then a new reform program is tried in the next period. Because the managers need to be retrained for matching attributes, an additional cost of $2C$ is paid in the next period, and so on. Therefore, we should have

$$c_{m2} = 2C + \delta(1-p)c_{m2},$$

from which we derive

$$c_{m2} = 2C/[1-(1-p)\delta].$$

Under the U-form, the top manager is responsible for coordinating the four tasks. He thus receives four messages through noisy communication, each corresponding to one of the four tasks. When the reform program is bad (with probability $1-p$), the reform fails, and a new reform program will be tried in the next period. If the reform program is good (with probability p), there are three possibilities: (i) With probability λ^4, coordination is successful for both regions A and B. (ii) With probability $(1-\lambda^2)^2$, coordination fails in both A and B. This will give the same outcome as a bad program. (iii) With probability $2\lambda^2(1-\lambda^2)$, coordination for one of the two regions is successful. In this case, knowing that the reform program is good, the top manager will use the same program for the region for which the coordination failed and solve only the attribute matching problem in the next period. Hence, the payoff of reform under the U-form is

$$\pi_{u2} = p\{\lambda^4 R/(1-\delta) + 2\lambda^2(1-\lambda^2)[R/[2(1-\delta)] + \delta\pi] + (1-\lambda^2)^2\delta\pi_{u2}\} + (1-p)\delta\pi_{u2},$$

where π is the expected payoff of change for one region for a good program:

$$\pi = \lambda^2 R/[2(1-\delta)] + (1-\lambda^2)\delta\pi,$$

which implies that

$$\pi = \lambda^2 R/\{2(1-\delta)[1-(1-\lambda^2)\delta]\}.$$

Using the above recursive formula of π, we obtain

$$\pi_{u2} = p\{2\lambda^2[\lambda^2 R/2(1-\delta) + (1-\lambda^2)R/2(1-\delta) + (1-\lambda^2)\delta\pi + (1-\lambda^2)\delta\pi -$$
$$(1-\lambda^2)\delta\pi]/\{1-\delta[p(1-\lambda^2)^2+(1-p)]\}$$

$$= 2p[\lambda^2 R/2(1-\delta) + \lambda^2(1-\lambda^2)\delta\pi + (1-\lambda^2)\delta\pi - (1-\lambda^2)\delta\pi]/$$
$$\{1-\delta[p(1-\lambda^2)^2+(1-p)]\}$$

$$= 2p\pi[1 - (1-\lambda^2)^2\delta]/\{1-\delta[p(1-\lambda^2)^2+(1-p)]\}$$

$$= \lambda^2 pR[1-(1-\lambda^2)^2\delta]/\{((1-\delta)[1-(1-\lambda^2)\delta][1-\delta[p(1-\lambda^2)^2+(1-p)]]\}.$$

On the cost side, when a reform is introduced in period 1, only a setup cost C is paid (instead of $2C$ in the M-form) because only the top manager matches attribute. With probability $1-p$ the reform program is bad, which is discovered after one period. With probability $p(1-\lambda^2)^2$ the reform program is good but coordination fails in both regions. In both cases, a new reform program is tried in the next period. When the reform program is good and coordination is successful for at least one of the two regions, the program will be known to be good. In such a case, no new setup cost needs to be paid in the next period. Indeed, the top manager has already been trained for that program and he has been able to successfully coordinate attribute matching for one region. Under this assumption, we have:

$c_{u2} = C + \delta[p(1-\lambda^2)^2 + (1-p)]c_{u2},$

from which we obtain

$c_{u2} = C/\{1-[p(1-\lambda^2)^2+1-p]\delta\}.$

Lemma 1. (1) $\pi_{u2} \leq \pi_{m2}$, and π_{u2} increases in λ and reaches π_{m2} at $\lambda = 1$.
(2) c_{u2} decreases in λ, and $c_{u2} < c_{m2}$ if and only if $\delta(1-p+2p(1-\lambda^2)^2) < 1$.

When communication between the middle managers and the top manager is perfect, the two organizational forms are equivalent in the expected payoffs. However, when communication is not perfect and because there is no communication problem under the M-form, M_2 always has a higher expected benefit than U_2. Under U_2, costs decrease with λ because better communication decreases the probability of failure with reform, thereby lowering the probability of drawing new experiments and incurring repeated setup costs. The trade-off between costs under M_2 and U_2 is also related to the quality of communication under U_2. The latter avoids the costs of duplication but bad communication leads to a higher failure rate, possibly leading to higher total costs because of the need to draw more experiments before achieving success.

We define the expected net payoff under the M-form and U-form, respectively,

$M_2 = \pi_{m2} - c_{m2},$

and

$U_2 = \pi_{u2} - c_{u2}.$

Proposition 1. Comparing the M-form and the U-form:

(1) the M-form has a higher expected net benefit than the U-form if communication quality (λ) is low enough: for p and C given, there exists $\lambda \in (0,1)$ for which $M_2 > U_2$ if and only if $\lambda < \lambda$.
(2) the U-form has a higher expected net benefit than the M-form if the setup cost (C) is high enough: when $c_{u2} < c_{m2}$ and for p and λ given, there exists $C > 0$ such that $U_2 > M_2$ and if only if $C > C$.

Proposition 1 formulates the basic tradeoff between coordination and scale economies in implementing reform under the M-form and the U-form. The U-form has an advantage in scale economies because the top manager is responsible for coordination in the entire organization. The organization thus saves on setup costs, but the U-form has disadvantages in coordination because local information is communicated imperfectly from the local managers to the top manager. In contrast, the M-form has better coordination because managers can make better use of local information for coordination purposes, but it suffers from disadvantages in scale economies: it pays twice the setup costs because two local managers are responsible for attribute matching instead of one top manager. In view of this trade-off, the M-form will be more efficient than the U-form when communication quality is relatively low, or when the setup cost is relatively small.

We next introduce the possibility that an organization starts a reform program in one of its two units and later extends it to another unit, conditional on successful implementation in the first unit. In other words, we look at the possibility of experimentation in implementing changes.

Under the M-form, suppose at first that a reform program is introduced in region A whereas the status quo is maintained in region B. If the reform program is a good one, the first period payoff is $(R+1)/2$. In the second period, the same program is then used in region B. From then on, the payoff is always R per period. However, if the reform program is bad, the experimenting region A will get 0 payoff and the non-experimenting region B will get $1/2$. In this case, a new experiment in region A will take place again in the next period. Therefore, the expected payoff of the M-form with experimentation is given by

$$\pi_{m1} = p\{R/2(1-\delta) + 1/2 + \delta R/2(1-\delta)\} + (1-p)\{1/2 + \delta\pi_{m1}\},$$

that is,

$$\pi_{m1} = p[R+(1-\delta)+\delta R]/2(1-\delta) + (1-p)\{1/2+\delta\pi_{m1}\}.$$

Therefore, we obtain

$$\pi_{m1} = [pR(1+\delta)+(1-\delta)]/\{2(1-\delta)[1-(1-p)\delta]\}.$$

The setup cost in the first period is C because only region A's manager does attribute matching. If the reform program is good, region B will use the same program in period 2 and another cost C will be paid in period 2 because region B's manager needs to match attributes according to local conditions. Region B thus imitates region A's success, but does not copy it, since local coordination is still required to introduce the successful blueprint. With probability $1-p$, the reform program is bad and a new blueprint must be tried. We are then back to the situation of period 1. Hence we get,

$$c_{m1} = C + \delta[pC + (1-p)c_{m1}],$$

which implies that

$$c_{m1} = (1+p\delta)C/[1-(1-p)\delta].$$

We define the net expected payoff under the M-form with an experimentation strategy as

$$M_1 = \pi_{m1} - c_{m1}.$$

Because of Assumption 1, $pR > 1$, we have:

Lemma 2. (1) $\pi_{m1} < \pi_{m2}$, and $c_{m1} < c_{m2}$.

(2) $dM_2/dp > dM_1/dp > 0$.

Both the expected net benefits under M_1 and M_2 increase monotonically with p. By Lemma 2, we can define p_{m2}^* as the probability such that $M_2 = 1/(1-\delta)$ and p_{m1}^* as the probability such that $M_1 = 1/(1-\delta)$, where $1/(1-\delta)$ is the status quo payoff. Then, for all $p > p_{m1}^*$, M_1 has higher expected net payment than the status quo; and for all $p > p_{m2}^*$, M_2 has higher expected net payment than the status quo. Let $\underline{p}$ be the probability such that $M_1 = M_2$. The following proposition compares two reform strategies in the M-form: experimentation versus immediate full reform (reform introduced in both regions simultaneously).

Proposition 2. (1) $p_{m1}^* < p_{m2}^* < \underline{p} < 1$. That is, $M_1 > M_2$ if and only if the uncertainty $p < \underline{p}$, and experimentation dominates the status quo while immediate full change does not for $p \,\varepsilon\, (p_{m1}^*, p_{m2}^*)$.
(2) for p given, experimentation yields a higher expected net benefit if and only if setup cost $C > \underline{C} = (pR-1)/2(1-p\delta)$.

Proposition 2 demonstrates the following tradeoff. Experimentation provides an option value of waiting to learn about the quality of the blueprint before implementing the reform program in full, but it comes at the cost of delaying a successful reform in the whole organization. The difference in the expected net benefits between experimentation and immediate full change under the M-form is given by

$$M_1 - M_2 = \{C(1-p\delta)-(pR-1)/2\}/[1-\delta(1-p)].$$

The first term $C(1-p\delta)$ in the numerator indicates the option value of waiting to learn about p before sinking C in an additional unit. This option value of waiting increases as p decreases, that is, when there is greater uncertainty about the value of the blueprint. Therefore, experimentation can save on setup costs because of the option value of early reversal of a bad blueprint (Dewatripont and Roland 1995). The second term in the numerator $(pR-1)/2$ (which is positive by Assumption 1) shows the cost of delaying experimentation in one unit under M_1. This cost increases with p. Clearly, when $p = 1$, $M_2 > M_1$ since the numerator becomes $C(1-\delta)-(R-1)/2$, which is smaller than zero by Assumption 2. M_2 continues to dominate M_1 until p falls below $\underline{p}$. In particular, when p falls further into the region of $[p_{m1}{}^*, p_{m2}{}^*]$, M_1 is greater than the status quo but M_2 is not.

We now analyze the possibility of experimentation under the U-form. Without loss of generality, we assume that at first a blueprint is implemented in unit 1 whereas unit 2 maintains the status quo. In line with our assumptions, the top manager does the attribute matching for regions A and B.

We assume that the quality of the reform program (good or bad) can be discovered even when the reform is implemented for only one task. We further assume that in order to match attributes of two tasks, whenever there is a reform in at least one task, information (and thus communication) about the attributes of both tasks is needed. This is because even if a reform is introduced in one task, attribute matching always involves another task. Therefore, under U-form with change in only one unit, all messages corresponding to the four tasks must be communicated by the two middle managers to the top manager.

After one period of experimentation in one unit, if the program is bad, the reform fails, and in the next period a new reform program will be tried. If the program is good, there are three possible outcomes: (i) with probability λ^4 attribute matching is achieved for both regions A and B. Then in the next period, the same program is used in both units and the final payoff will only depend on the outcome of attribute matching. (ii) With probability $(1-\lambda^2)^2$, coordination is bad for both A and B. This will give the same outcome as a bad program and a new reform program will be tried in the next period. (iii) With probability $2\lambda^2(1-\lambda^2)$, coordination for A or B is successful which will reveal that the program is good. In the next period, the two units will use the same program and the payoff for the earlier failed region will depend on the outcome of attribute matching. Hence, the expected payoff of the U-form with experimentation is

$$\pi_{u1} = p\{\lambda^4[(R+1)/2 + \delta 2\pi] + 2\lambda^2(1-\lambda^2)[(R+1)/4 + \delta 2\pi] + (1-\lambda^2)^2\delta\pi_{u1}\} + (1-p)\delta\pi_{u1},$$

where π is, as above, the expected payoff of reform in one region when the program is good, as defined above. Hence, we obtain

$$\pi_{u1} = p\{\lambda^4[(R+1)/2 + \delta 2\pi] + 2\lambda^2(1-\lambda^2)[(R+1)/4 + \delta 2\pi]\}/ \{1-\delta[p(1-\lambda^2)^2+(1-p)]\}.$$

Under the U-form, the setup cost is the same as reform without experimentation. This is because coordination is done at the top and always requires four messages to be sent to the top manager who must be trained to do the appropriate coordination. We also assume that the setup cost C enables the manager to implement both partial and full change.[7] Therefore,

$$c_{u1} = c_{u2} = C/\{1-[p(1-\lambda^2)^2+1-p]\delta\}.$$

We define the net expected payoff under a U-form with experimentation as

$$U_1 = \pi_{u1} - c_{u1}.$$

Proposition 3. Under the U-form, experimentation is always dominated by immediate full change:

$$\pi_{u1} < \pi_{u2}, c_{u1} = c_{u2}, \text{ and } U_1 < U_2.$$

The U-form organization does not benefit from experimentation because of the complications involved in coordinating activities. While the setup cost is not lower, as with full change, there is no additional benefit in coordination and there are only costs in delaying expected benefits.

The flexibility of the M-form yields an advantage over the U-form:

Proposition 4. (1) the U-form has higher expected net benefits than the M-form if the quality of communication λ is close enough to 1. (2) Experimentation under the M-form yields higher expected net benefits than immediate full change under either M-form or U-form if the quality of communication λ is small enough and either $p < \underline{p}$ or $C > \overline{C} = (pA-1)/2(1-p\delta)$.

When communication quality is high, the U-form will dominate because of its advantages in scale economies. The more interesting results are those on the flexibility of the M-form. From Propositions 2 and 3 we know that when the probability of success is low or the setup cost is high, the M-form has the option of experimentation while experimentation has no value to the U-form. In such a case, the M-form can do better than the U-form, provided communication quality is low enough.

4. Coordination and Parallel Experimentation

In this section we assume that two independent blueprints are available at a given time. This introduces a possibility that both blueprints are tried simultaneously in two regions in the M-form, yielding net benefits denoted M_{11}. If there is one successful experiment in one region, it can be copied costlessly in the other region, as in the previous section. Under this strategy:

$$\pi_{m11} = p^2 R/(1-\delta) + 2(1-p)p\{R/2(1-\delta) + \delta R/2(1-\delta)\} + (1-p)^2 \delta \pi_{m11},$$

from which we obtain:

$$\pi_{m11} = \{R(p^2+p(1-p)(1+\delta))\}/(1-\delta)[1-\delta(1-p)^2].$$

Similarly for the cost:

$$c_{m11} = 2C + 2(1-p)p\delta C + (1-p)^2 \delta c_{m11},$$

from which we obtain:

$$c_{m11} = 2C[1+\delta p(1-p)]/[1-\delta(1-p)^2].$$

Lemma 3. Under the M-form, parallel experimentation always yields higher expected benefits and lower expected costs than immediate full change:

$$\pi_{m11} > \pi_{m2} \text{ and } c_{m11} < c_{m2}.$$

If two independent blueprints are available, then it is always better to try one in each region rather than one in both regions. Why do two independent experiments always give higher expected benefits than two perfectly correlated experiments? In the first period, the two will give the same expected outcome, but since two independent experiments have a higher probability of at least one success, success will tend to be implemented earlier with independent experiments. Similarly, the reason for the lower costs with two independent experiments is that under the latter, the probability that no further cost will be paid next period is $1-(1-p)^2$, whereas it is only $1-p$ under two perfectly correlated experiments.

Lemma 4. Under the M-form: (1) parallel experimentation has both higher expected benefits and expected costs than experimentation in one region:

$\pi_{m11} > \pi_{m1}$ and $c_{m11} > c_{m1}$.

(2) parallel experimentation has higher net expected benefits than experimentation in one region if and only if

$$C < C^1 = pA(1+\delta(1-p)^2)/2[1-\delta+\delta p(1-p)(1-\delta(1-p))]+(1-\delta(1-p)^2).$$

The higher benefit of parallel experimentation compared to experimentation in one region is for two reasons. First, it has a higher first-period expected benefit ($pR > pR/2 + 1/2$ because $pR > 1$ by Assumption 1). Second, the former has a higher probability (that is, $1-(1-p)^2$) than the latter (that is, $1-p$) to have a known good blueprint from the second period onward.

The reason why parallel experimentation has higher costs than experimentation in one region is that under the former at least $2C$ always has to be paid out up front. Note that both c_{m11} and c_{m1} decline with p. The former declines faster than the latter as under M_{11} learning about a success is faster. Nevertheless, when p approaches 1, c_{m11} approaches $2C$ while c_{m1} approaches $C(1+\delta)$, which still remains smaller.

Looking at the difference ($M_{11} - M_1$), we have:

$$d(M_{11} - M_1)/dp = R(1+\delta(1-p)^2)-2pR\delta(1-p)-2C[\delta(1-2p)$$
$$(1-\delta(1-p))+\delta^2 p(1-p)]-2\delta(1-p)$$

$$= R(1+\delta(1-p)(1-3p))-2C\delta[1-2p-\delta(1-p)(1-3p)]-2\delta(1-p)$$

$$= \delta(1-p)(1-3p)(R+2C\delta)+R-2C\delta(1-2p)-2\delta(1-p).$$

There is thus a non-linear relationship between p and ($M_{11} - M_1$). Comparing the net benefits in M_{11} and M_1 is therefore complicated. But one sees intuitively that the lower C is relative to A, the higher the advantage of M_{11} over M_1, and vice versa.

We can now summarize the comparison between various organizational forms:

Proposition 5. (1) the U-form has higher expected net benefits than all other organizational forms if $\lambda = 1$ and either $p = 1$ or $C > C^2 = pR\delta(1-p)^2/[1-\delta(1-p)^2(1+2\delta p)]$.

(2) experimentation in one region under the M-form dominates if λ is low enough and $C > C^1$.

(3) parallel experimentation under the M-form dominates if either $\lambda = 1$ but $C < C_1$ or if λ is low enough, $p > \underline{p}$ or $C < C^1$.

The U-form dominates when communication quality is high and either setup costs are high or there is no uncertainty about the experiment. The M-form with experimentation in one region dominates when communication quality is low and setup costs are high; it dominates with parallel experimentation either when costs are low enough (in which case it dominates the U-form) or when communication quality is low enough but setup costs are sufficiently low and the probability of success sufficiently high (in which case it dominates partial experimentation). A major difference between Propositions 4 and 5 is as follows. When parallel experimentation is not available, the flexibility advantage of the M-form can be achieved when setup costs are high and the probability of success is low, whereas when parallel experimentation is available an additional flexibility advantage of the M-form can be achieved when setup costs are low and the probability of success is high.

5. Reforms in Transition Economies

We use the agricultural reform in China and the former Soviet Union to illustrate our theory on how organizational forms of governments affect reforms strategy and outcomes. The Chinese reforms started in the late 1970s and early 1980s within a M-form planning system. The success of agricultural reform is closely related to the roles of regional governments in solving coordination problems. With the deepening of the reform, planning was gradually abandoned. However, the inherited M-form structure of the government organization still played an important part in further reforms. In contrast, the Soviet Union started their agricultural reform in the 1980s within a U-form planning system, which failed to coordinate reform-related activities. This contributed to the failure of the agricultural reform. Moreover, problems inherited from U-form structure continued to hamper transition after the collapse of the Soviet Union.

Agricultural reforms in both countries aimed at replacing collective farming by household farming. There were many "blueprints" for farming reform. Control rights of land may be partly delegated to households for a short time period, or may be leased to households for a longer period of time. Alternatively, ownership of land may be transferred completely to households. These reforms faced blueprint uncertainty and implementation (attribute matching) problems. First, it was not clear *ex ante* how households would respond to incentives under different reform blueprints.[8] Second, coordination problems arise in introducing household farming. Household farming allows households to choose new crops/products for profit—say, to change from grain to vegetables, fruits, aquatic products, dairy products, etc. Producing and harvesting new products involve interactions with other sectors. For example, when farmers change production from grain to fishery, compared with grain production, aquatic production/harvesting may interfere with water traffic and irrigation; moreover, transport and storage of aquatic products have substantially different requirements than those of grain. Only when related attribute matching problems are solved, can an agriculture reform succeed.

Under the M-form planning structure, Chinese regional governments, such as county governments, have the responsibility of coordinating activities in agricultural production, transport, storage, and processing etc. It is in this institutional context that the agricultural household responsibility system was introduced/experimented with through initiatives of some regional governments. Together with the redistribution of land rights, regional governments' coordination over economic activities across sectors and across households has played a critical role in making reform successful.

Before the reform, Chinese agriculture was over-concentrated on grain production. A major feature of the successful Chinese agricultural reform is the change of production (made by household farms with the help of regional governments), from grain to other crops/products, such as aquatic products, animal husbandry, and fruits etc. Taking the fishery sector as an example, at the national level the total output of aquatic products increased from 4.6 million tons in 1978 to 41.2 million tons in 1999, while total output of grain increased from 304.8 million tons in 1978 to 508.4 million tons in 1999. As a result, the share of fishery in the value of agricultural gross output increased from 1.4% in 1978 to 10.3% in 1999.

When farmers choose to shift from grain production to fish farming, the physical and informational infrastructure requirements must be adapted. These involve a substantial amount of coordination across sectors/industries, which household farms usually cannot do by themselves. Attribute matching problems may occur in the following dimensions:

(1) Conditions required for raising fish or fishing may be in conflict with requirements for water transport and irrigation of grain fields in terms of quality, quantity, location, and timing of the use of water;
(2) Fish species may be region-specific; moreover, the selection of fish species and grain species are different in different areas;
(3) Transport and storage required for harvesting fish differ from those for harvesting grain; and
(4) Disease control is different for fish and plants.

In the following, we use the example of aquatic production in Xinhui county in Guangdong Province to illustrate how regional governments under a M-form structure solved these problems. All the materials about this county are from Xinhui Xianzhi Editorial Committee (1995, 1997).

Under the M-form structure, Xinhui County government successfully made attribute matching in the growing fishery sector during the reform, which ensured a smooth transition to household farming along all four dimensions listed above:

First, a key factor in the growth of aquatic industry is the increase in the aquatic production area. The total aquatic production area can be increased by using rivers, ponds, and reservoirs. The coordination role of local government is important here. Attributes to be matched in order to increase the aquatic production area include timing, origination/destination/route, quality/quantity of water transmission to match demands in aquatic production, irrigation and transport. If too much water is diverted from a river into fishing ponds at the wrong time, the water level of the river may decrease too much, making transport difficult or leaving too little water for the irrigation of rice fields. Water-sharing for the purposes of irrigation and aquatic ponds has been coordinated by the county government. Part of the coordination is done by building new reservoirs to ensure a regular water supply. It would be much more difficult to coordinate transport, irrigation, and aquatic activities if these were controlled separately by different specialized ministries.

Second, the selection of species best suitable to the county is also important. Some species take better than others to a particular region's weather, water quality, water plants, plankton, etc. The county government's Aquatic Bureau took the initiative in coordinating technological changes in aquatic production, such as helping select aquatic species best suited for the county and giving technical support to aquatic farmers. For example, in 1979 the Aquatic Bureau helped to coordinate an enlargement of production of fingerling and fry. By 1985, the area of fish ponds for growing fingerling and fry had increased by 65.8% compared with 1976; and the output of fingerling and fry increased by 130% over the same time period.

Third, the supply of fish feed and cold storage for harvested fish are other important factors that affect aquatic production. There are important attribute matching problems involved in fish feed supply (and similarly in cold storage services). When a new species of fish is introduced or whenever there is a substantial change in weather conditions, requirements for fish feed (or for storage) must be adjusted accordingly, which in turn requires adjustments in raw materials used by fish feed plants. When markets were not well developed enough to take care of these problems, the county government again played an important coordination role. In 1979, the county government built a cold storage plant—the Xinhui County Yamen Cold Storage Plant, which has provided ice, cold storage and processing (e.g., quick freezing) for the aquatic industry in the county. In 1983 and 1984, jointly with some township governments, the county government built two fish feed plants (Tangxia Fish Feed Plant and Hetang State-Township Joint Fish Feed Plant).

Fourth, disease control, in particular prevention of contagious fish diseases, is another critical factor and often requires an emergency response. Diseases may indeed spread via different waterways at a considerable speed. Disease control requires coordination between aquatic production, supply of drugs/disinfectants, transport, irrigation, R&D for the region, and solutions specific to the local fish species. Controlling aquatic diseases is an emergency matter, requiring quick action to specify drugs/disinfectants and appropriate methods of using them, so time is of overriding importance. This is similar to dispatching an ambulance to meet particular requests in a medical emergency (Milgrom and Roberts 1992). In this situation, markets may not be able to coordinate in time. The capacity of county government in coordinating all affected sectors is then critical for implementing disease control measures. In Xinhui, the Disease Prevention and

Vaccination Department under the County Aquatic Bureau has played such a coordination role, taking into account various ecological problems. The Department provided fish immunization services and other medicines for fish. For example, in 1985, it provided vaccination for 4.3 million Buffalo fish, which increased the survival rate of these fish substantially.

As a result of the coordination role of local government, Xinhui aquatic production has increased rapidly since the reform. Total aquatic production in Xinhui in 1985 increased by 2.3 times over that of 1978. The success of Chinese local governments like Xinhui illustrates the strong capacity of the M-form structure in coordinating attribute matching. The local government has a good knowledge of local conditions and can respond efficiently given its authority in achieving attribute matching at the local level.

In sharp contrast to the Chinese experience, in the Soviet Union, it appears that regional governments were not able to solve coordination problems arising in their agricultural reforms. Total agricultural production in Russia declined by 29% between 1990 and 1994 (Laird 1997). Under the Soviet system, farming was subordinated to many different ministries. In the 1980s, tasks related to the agro-food industry were shared by eleven or more ministries: the Ministry of Agriculture, Trade, Cereal and Grain Production, Fruit and Vegetable Farming, Machine Building for Animal Husbandry and Feed Production, Tractors and Farm Machinery, Land Reclamation and Water Resources, Meat and Dairy Industry, Food Industry, Rural Construction, and Fertilizer Production (Wegren 1998, p. 62). Regional authorities had no control over farming and played only a role of "expediters, throwing themselves in the search for batteries, belts and harvester blades, undoing complex knots in the supply system" (van Atta 1993b). Tractors were provided centrally by the so-called MTS stations. The tasks of providing inputs to the farmers, of managing their operations, storage, processing, transport, and road infrastructure were all allocated to separate agencies over which collective farms had no control. Warehouses and processing plants were more likely to be located hundreds of kilometers away from farms (van Atta 1993a). Under this structure it is very hard to solve coordination problems. For example, within this structure, any change in grain production involved five ministries: Ministry of Agriculture, Trade, Cereal and Grain Production, Tractors and Farm Machinery, Food Industry, Rural Construction, and Fertilizer Production. When any farm (private or collective) changed from grain to vegetable production, it had to deal with these ministries plus another two ministries: Land Reclamation and Water Resources, and Fruit and Vegetable Farming.

Before any reform measure was introduced, serious coordination problems created by this structure led to substantial waste at the storage, transport, and processing stages. Coordination failure was so important that at the end of the 1980s, there was a consensus among experts of Soviet agriculture that the biggest problem in that sector was at the distribution stage (Wädekin 1992). In Russia, about a quarter of total grain products (average of 49 million tons of grain in 1986–1990) was wasted due to bad storage conditions, the rotting of bread; and 30–40% of potatoes were lost to rot in storage. Of the 40% loss in potatoes and vegetables, a third was lost in bad transport and storage, and 20% because of poor coordination (inadequate transport capacity, not enough gas, oil, or spare parts).

In the Soviet period, some reform attempts were introduced to change organizational forms partially to mitigate these problems in agriculture. In the 1980s, organizations called RAPO (*raïonnoe agropromyshlennoe obyedinenie*) were created to coordinate activities locally between the various ministries. However, this led to a conflict of authority between the functional ministries and the new regional coordination structure. The RAPOs did not have any power over resources controlled by the ministries[9] and they were generally ignored by the latter. Other attempts at reforms such as the introduction of an overarching ministry called the *Gosagroprom*, the introduction of agrofirms on a smaller scale, and even the introduction of leasing contracts (*arenda*) failed similarly because of lack of control over the overall farming process (Butterfield 1990).

In March 1989, the Central Committee of the Soviet Communist Party decided under pressure from Gorbachev to launch a reform in agriculture whereby peasants could lease land with long-term contracts up to fifty years. This may seem similar to the Chinese reform in the early 1980s but it left coordination problems to the farmers. Although leasing gave incentives to the peasants, farmers were dependent on the infrastructure and machinery, and on the feed, fodder, and seeds provided by agents under different ministries, and technical support and mechanized assistance from the collective farm. Input supplies were not guaranteed.

After the collapse of the Soviet Union, although central planning was abandoned, the problems inherited from the U-form structure continued to cause great trouble for reforms aimed at establishing household farms. In general, serious coordination problems inherited from the Soviet system appeared to be a major factor hampering Russia's privatization in farming. Wehrheim et al. (2000) argue that underdeveloped institutions and infrastructure, such as a lack of a system of market information (where to buy and sell, and at what price), are the main problems plaguing Russian agriculture. There is even evidence that the post-harvest waste was increasing in the 1990s (Laird 1997). Indeed, in many regions, the cost of shipping agricultural goods exceeds the producer prices (Liefert-Swinnen 2002). Without proper solutions to the coordination problems, Russian private farmers have to work under very primitive conditions which discourage collective farm employees from becoming private farmers. Wegren (1998) cites an article about how coordination problems hamper privatization in agriculture in Moscow *oblast*: once becoming private farmers "they immediately encountered massive problems—no machinery, nowhere to obtain gas, nowhere to sell produce, and so on. People saw this and did not want to follow their example." A survey by the World Bank in 1994 showed that 92% of collectively-owned or state-owned farm employees did not want to become private farmers. The main reasons invoked were difficulties with the purchase of farm inputs (60% of respondents) and insufficient capital (74%) (Brooks et al. 1994). A 1994 World Bank-sponsored survey on agriculture found that in two-thirds of state farms, only fewer than 10 people left (Wegren 1998, p. 83). Moreover, for similar reasons land leasing also remained very limited and did not enjoy popularity among peasants (Wegren 1998, p. 68).

6.   Concluding Remarks: The Organization of Government and Foundation of Federalism

Our theory on coordinating reforms in transition economies opens new perspectives on understanding how the differences in organizational forms in Eastern Europe and the former Soviet Union and China affected their reform strategies. For the first time, we formally address the following questions: Why is China special in its use of experimental approaches? Why is the U-form not suitable for doing local experiments? In Eastern Europe, some experimental reforms were introduced before the transition but failed. On this basis, the regional experimental approach to reforming a planned economy has been discredited and abandoned during later transitions in these economies.

Our analysis has the potential to go beyond transition economies and to address a more general question of the organization of government. Two organizational forms of government have received much attention: the unitary state and the federal state. Our analysis starts to provide a theoretical foundation of both, especially federalism. France and Japan, among others, have a unitary state, and their governments are mainly organized along functional lines where specialized ministries concentrate most powers, leaving regional governments with relatively little authority[10]. The organizational form of the U.S. government is a primary example of federalism. The fifty states have the constitutional rights and responsibilities for coordinating government activities inside their jurisdictions. This spawns an environment encouraging them to try innovative policies for themselves.

It has been perceived a long time ago that the American federal system may facilitate experimenting with innovative policies. It was argued in 1888 that "federalism enables people to try experiments which could not safely be tried in a large centralized country" (Bryce 1901). A few decades later, the American Supreme Court Justice, Louis Brandeis, characterized American federalism famously as the "laboratory of the states." By laboratories, he meant that the states could experiment with new solutions to social and economic problems. Those that worked could be applied nationally; those that failed could be discarded. He said in 1932, "it is one of the happy incidents of the federal system that a single courageous state may... serve as a laboratory; and try novel societal and economic experiments without risk to the rest of the country" (Osborne 1988). Indeed, many changes of legal rules and government policies in America were initiated by states, usually richer or liberal ones, such as Massachusetts, California, and New York. And these experiments were later imitated by other states.

Policy experimentation has attracted attention in political science and sociology and there is a large literature that looks at the timing of policy imitation across states in the U.S. That literature takes state-level policy experimentation/imitation as given and focuses on the time path of new policies, such as policies on education, welfare, civil rights, etc., from their first experiments in one state to general imitation or adoption by a large number of states. The records date back to the late 18th century.

The first example involves the origin of the New Deal policies—state policy experimentation. Facing the challenges and risks associated with the rapid industrialization of the American economy early in the twentieth century, a few states initiated innovative policies within their jurisdictions, such as unemployment compensation schemes, massive public programs, and schemes related to deposit insurance and social security. Most of these programs were complementary to each other, and state government coordination was critical to the implementation. Later, many of the successful ones were institutionalized at the federal level, which sped up the adoption of the policies. In fact, a large number of Roosevelt's New Deal policies were inspired by or precisely copied from successful state-level experiments. Roosevelt acknowledged that, "practically all the things we've done [about the New Deal] in the federal government are like things Al Smith did as governor of New York" (Osborne 1988).

The second example involves state coordinated policy experiments to deal with challenges associated with the replacement of traditional industries by high-tech business since the 1980s. Since the late 1970s there has been a trend in the U.S. toward adopting new policies, such as reform of public education systems; creating public venture capital funds; setting up programs to match local academia and business to advance technological innovation etc. This trend began with 'experiments' in Massachusetts and California. With the help of the federal government's agents, successful policies were developed by the Midwest, and these spread out to the rest of the nation. For example, heavily subsidized community colleges were rare before the mid-1970s. However, following the successful models of Massachusetts and California, they have become standard public education institutions in most states.

Appendix: Mathematical Proofs

Proof of Lemma 1: (1) Because

$$\pi_{u2} = 2p\pi[1 - (1-\lambda^2)^2\delta]/\{1-\delta[p(1-\lambda^2)^2+(1-p)]\},$$

where both $\pi = \lambda^2 R/\{2(1-\delta)[1-(1-\lambda^2)\delta]\}$ and $[1-(1-\lambda^2)^2\delta]/\{1-\delta[p(1-\lambda^2)^2+(1-p)]\}$ increases in λ (the latter because $[1-x\delta]/\{1-\delta[px+(1-p)]\}$ decreases in x), then π_{u2} increases in λ.

(2) $c_{u2} = C/\{1-[p(1-\lambda^2)^2+(1-p)]\delta\}$ decreases in λ.

$c_{u2} < c_{m2}$ if and only if

$$1 - \delta(1-p) < 2[1-\delta(p(1-\lambda^2)^2+1-p)]$$

if and only if

$$2\delta p(1-\lambda^2)^2 + \delta(1-p) < 1,$$

which is valid for all λ provided $\delta < 1/(1+p)$.∎

Proof of Proposition 1: (1) By Lemma 1, at $\lambda = 1$, $\pi_{u2} = \pi_{m2}$; but $c_{u2} = C/(1-\delta(1-p)) < c_{m2} = 2C/(1-\delta(1-p))$, then $U_2 > M_2$. Also by Lemma 1, π_{u2} increases in λ and c_{u2} decreases in λ, then $U_2 = \pi_{u2} - c_{u2}$ increases in λ. Because M_2 is independent of λ and because U_2 goes to 0 as λ decreases, then for p and C given there exists $\underline{\lambda} > 0$ such that $M_2 > U_2$ if and only if $\lambda < \underline{\lambda}$.

(2) For any $\lambda < 1$, $M_2 > U_2$ at $C = 0$. When $c_{u2} < c_{m2}$, c_{m2} also increases faster than c_{u2} as C increases, therefore, for p and λ given, such a C exists. (U_2 could be the same as M_2 if both have the same value as the status quo at C.)

Proof of Lemma 2: (1) Note that $pR(1+\delta)/2+(1-\delta)/2$ is a weighted sum of pR and 1. Therefore, because $pR > 1$ by Assumption 1, then the sum is less than pR, or $\pi_{m1} < \pi_{m2}$.

(2) Because $d\pi_{m1}/dp = [R(1+\delta)/2 - \delta/2]/[1-(1-p)\delta]^2$ and $dc_{m1}/dp = -\delta^2 C/[1-(1-p)\delta]^2$, we have:

$$dM_1/dp = [R(1+\delta)/2 - \delta/2 + \delta^2 C]/[1-(1-p)\delta]^2 > 0.$$

Also because $d\pi_{m2}/dp = R/[1-(1-p)\delta]^2$ and $dc_{m2}/dp = -2C\delta/[1-(1-p)\delta]^2$, then we have

$$dM_2/dp = \{R + 2C\delta\}/[1-(1-p)\delta]^2 > 0.$$

Therefore, by $R(1+\delta)/2 < R$, $\delta C - 1/2 < 2C$, we have $R(1+\delta)/2 - \delta/2 + \delta^2 C < R + 2C\delta$, then, $dM_2/dp > dM_1/dp > 0$.∎

Proof of Proposition 2: (1) Because

$$M_1 - M_2 = \{pR/2(1+\delta) + (1-\delta)/2 - pR - (1-\delta)C(1+p\delta) + 2C(1-\delta)\}/(1-\delta)$$
$$[1-\delta(1-p)]$$

$$= [C(1-p\delta)-(pR-1)/2]/[1-\delta(1-p)],$$

then $M_1 > M_2$ if and only if $p < \underline{p}$. Furthermore, $\underline{p} < 1$ if and only if $R/2(1-\delta) - C > 1/2(1-\delta)$.

From $M_1 = 1/(1-\delta)$ we obtain:

$$p_{m1}^* = (2C+1)(1-\delta)/\{R(1+\delta)-2\delta(C(1-\delta)+1)\},$$

and from $M_2 = 1/(1-\delta)$ we obtain:

$p_{m2}{}^* = (2C+1)(1-\delta)/(R-\delta)$.

Then $p_{m1}{}^* < p_{m2}{}^*$ if and only if $R/2(1-\delta) - C > 1/2(1-\delta)$.

By Lemma 2, $p_{m1}{}^* < p_{m2}{}^*$ must imply that $p_{m1}{}^* < p_{m2}{}^* < \underline{p}$.

(2) follows directly from the expression for $M_1 - M_2$.■

Proof of Proposition 3: We note that

$\pi_{u2} = p\{\lambda^4[R/(1-\delta)] + 2\lambda^2(1-\lambda^2)[R/2(1-\delta) +\delta\pi]\}/\{1-\delta[p(1-\lambda^2)^2+(1-p)]\}$

$= p\{\lambda^4[R + \delta R/(1-\delta)] + 2\lambda^2(1-\lambda^2)[R/2 + \delta[\pi + R/2(1-\delta)]]/$
$\{1-\delta[p(1-\lambda^2)^2+(1-p)]\}$.

Comparing π_{u2} with π_{u1}, because $R > (R+1)/2$ and $R/2(1-\delta) \geq \pi$, then
$\pi_{u2} > \pi_{u1}$.■

Proof of Proposition 4: (1) For $\lambda = 1$, $\pi_{u2} = \pi_{m2} > \pi_{m1}$ and $c_{u2} < c_{m1} < c_{m2}$.
Therefore, for λ large enough, by continuity, $U_2 > M_2$ and $U_2 > M_1$.

(2) If λ is small enough, U_2 will always be dominated by M_1 or M_2. The
rest of the proposition follows directly from Proposition 2.■

Proof of Lemma 3: $\pi_{m11} > \pi_{m2}$ if and only if

$\{R(p^2+p(1-p)(1+\delta))\}/(1-\delta)[1-\delta(1-p)^2] > pR/\{(1-\delta)[1-(1-p)\delta]\}$,

if and only if

$[1-\delta(1-p)](p^2+p(1-p)(1+\delta)) > p(1-\delta(1-p)^2)$,

if and only if

$[1-\delta(1-p)](1+\delta(1-p)) > 1-\delta(1-p)^2$,

if and only if

$1-\delta^2(1-p)^2 > 1-\delta(1-p)^2$,

which is verified since $\delta < 1$.

Similarly, $c_{m11} < c_{m2}$ if and only if

$2C[1+\delta p(1-p)]/[1-\delta(1-p)^2] < 2C/[1-(1-p)\delta]$,

if and only if

$(1-\delta(1-p))(1+\delta p(1-p)) < 1-\delta(1-p)^2$

if and only if

$\delta^2 p(1-p)^2 > 0,$

which is verified.∎

Proof of Lemma 4: (1) $\pi_{m11} > \pi_{m1}$ if and only if

$\{R(p^2+p(1-p)(1+\delta))\}/(1-\delta)[1-\delta(1-p)^2] > [pR(1+\delta)+(1-\delta)]/2(1-\delta)[1-(1-p)\delta],$

if and only if

$2\{R(p^2+p(1-p)(1+\delta))\}[1-(1-p)\delta] > [pR(1+\delta)+(1-\delta)][1-\delta(1-p)^2],$

if and only if

$[2pR][1-\delta^2(1-p)^2] > [pR(1+\delta)+(1-\delta)][1-\delta(1-p)^2].$

Because $pR > 1$ if and only if $2pR > pR(1+\delta)+(1-\delta)$, furthermore, $1-\delta^2(1-p)^2 > 1-\delta(1-p)^2$, then the above inequality holds.

Similarly, $c_{m11} > c_{m1}$ if and only if

$2C[1+\delta p(1-p)]/[1-\delta(1-p)^2] > C(1+p\delta)/[1-(1-p)\delta],$

if and only if

$2-2\delta(1-p)^2 - 2\delta^2 p(1-p)^2 > 1 - \delta(1-p)^2 + p\delta - \delta^2 p(1-p)^2,$

if and only if

$1 > \delta[p + (1-p)^2 + \delta p(1-p)^2],$

if and only if

$1 - \delta > -\delta p(1-p)(1-\delta(1-p)),$

which is always valid since $1 > \delta(1-p)$.

(2) $M_{11} > M_1$ if and only if

$\{R(p^2+p(1-p)(1+\delta))-2C(1-\delta)(1+\delta p(1-p))\}[1-\delta(1-p)]$

$> \{pR(1+\delta)/2+(1-\delta)/2-C(1-\delta)(1+p\delta)\}[1-\delta(1-p)^2]$

if and only if

$R(p^2+p(1-p)(1+\delta)-pR(1+\delta)/2-(1-\delta)/2+C(1-\delta)(1+p\delta)-2C(1-\delta)(1+\delta p(1-p))$

$> \delta(1-p)\{R(p^2+p(1-p)(1+\delta))-2C(1-\delta)(1+\delta p(1-p))-(1-p)[pR(1+\delta)/$
$2+(1-\delta)/2-C(1-\delta)(1+p\delta)]\}$

if and only if

$$(pR-1)(1-\delta)/2+pR\delta(1-p)-C(1-\delta)[1-p\delta(2p-1)]$$

$$> \delta(1-p)\{pR[1+\delta(1-p)+p]/2-(1-p)(1-\delta)/2-C(1-\delta)(1+p+\delta p(1-p))\}$$

if and only if

$$(pR-1)(1-\delta)/2+pR\delta(1-p)-\delta(1-p)[pR(1+\delta(1-p)+p)/2-(1-p)(1-\delta)/2]$$

$$> C(1-\delta)[1-p\delta(2p-1)]-\delta(1-p)C(1-\delta)(1+p+\delta p(1-p))$$

if and only if

$$(pR/2)[1-\delta+2\delta(1-p)-\delta(1-p)(1+p+\delta(1-p))]-(1-\delta)(1-\delta(1-p)^2)/2$$

$$> C(1-\delta)[1-p\delta(2p-1)-\delta(1-p)(1+p+\delta p(1-p))]$$

if and only if

$$(pR/2)[1-\delta+\delta(1-p)(1-p-\delta(1-p))]-(1-\delta)(1-\delta(1-p)^2)/2$$

$$> C(1-\delta)[1-\delta+\delta p(1-p)(1-\delta(1-p))]$$

if and only if

$$pR(1+\delta(1-p)^2) > 2C[1-\delta+\delta p(1-p)(1-\delta(1-p))]+(1-\delta(1-p)^2). \blacksquare$$

Proof of Proposition 5: (1) If $p=1$, we know from proposition 2 that M_2 dominates M_1. It is easy to check that M_{11} and M_2 are equivalent and equal to $R/(1-\delta) - 2C$. If $\lambda = 1$, then $U_2 = R/(1-\delta) - C$ which clearly dominates. If $p < 1$ but $\lambda = 1$, $U_2 > M_1$, because $\pi_{u2} = \pi_{m2} > \pi_{m1}$ and $c_{u2} < c_{m1}$. At $\lambda = 1$, $U_2 > M_{11}$ if and only if

$$[pR-C(1-\delta)]/(1-\delta)[1-\delta(1-p)] > \{pR(1+\delta(1-p))-2C(1-\delta)(1+\delta p(1-p))\}/(1-\delta)$$
$$[1-\delta(1-p)^2]$$

if and only if

$$(1-\delta(1-p)^2)(pR-C(1-\delta)) > [1-\delta(1-p)]\{pR(1+\delta(1-p))-2C(1-\delta)(1+\delta p(1-p))\}$$

if and only if

$$pR\{(1-\delta(1-p)^2)-[1-\delta^2(1-p)^2]\} > C(1-\delta)\{(1-\delta(1-p)^2)-2(1+\delta p(1-p))(1-\delta(1-p))\}$$

if and only if

$$-pR\delta(1-p)^2 > -C[1-\delta(1-p)^2(1+2\delta p)]$$

if and only if

$$pR\delta(1-p)^2 < C[1-\delta(1-p)^2(1+2\delta p)].$$

We verify that $1 > \delta(1-p)^2(1+2\delta p)$ for all p and $\delta < 1$. Therefore, when $C > C^2 = pR\delta(1-p)^2/[1-\delta(1-p)^2(1+2\delta p)]$, $U_2 > M_{11}$ at $\lambda = 1$.

(2) If λ is low enough, then U_2 is dominated. By Lemma 4, M_1 dominates if and only if $C > C^1$.

(3) By Lemma 3, M_{11} always dominates M_2. By Proposition 2, $M_2 > M_1$ for $p > \underline{p}$. Therefore, $M_{11} > M_1$ for $p > \underline{p}$. Again if λ is low enough, U_2 is dominated. The rest follows from Lemma 4. Because M_{11}, M_1 and M_2 are independent of λ, for such p, $M_{11} > U_2$ for low enough values of λ. Similarly, because both M_{11} and M_1 are independent of λ and, by Lemma 4, M_{11} dominates M_1 for $C < C^1$. For any such C, U_2 goes to 0 when λ becomes small, then M_{11} also dominates U_2 for λ low enough. From the proof of (1), we know that $M_{11} > U_2$ if $\lambda = 1$ and $C < C^2$.

Notes

* We are grateful to Wei Li, Paul Milgrom, Dani Rodrik, Oliver Williamson and the participants at the Fifth Nobel Symposium in Economics for helpful discussions and comments. Gerard Roland and Chenggang Xu benefited from an ACE grant, and Roland benefited from a fellowship at the Center for Advanced Studies in Behavioral Sciences at Stanford in 1998–1999.

1. For related literature, see McMillan and Naughton (1992), Dewatripont and Roland (1997), Sachs and Woo (1997).

2. Data source for Hungary and Poland is from Table 9.1 of Kornai (1992).

3. Chandler (1962, 1977) and Williamson (1975, 1985) are among the first to study the M-form and U-form organizations in the context of large American business corporations.

4. We further note that the different organizational forms between China and Eastern Europe and the former Soviet Union is not due to the different sizes of the corresponding economies. In fact, China's central statistical agency was even smaller than that in Hungary, which is about 100 times smaller than China in terms of population. A comparison between Hungary and a small Chinese province, Hainan, may further illustrate the point. Hungarian ministries controlled most of the firms before the transition. However, the control of firms in Hainan is distributed at different levels of hierarchy, although Hainan is smaller than Hungary, in terms of both population and GDP.

5. In the Soviet Union, for example, a large number of consumer goods and producer goods (e.g., sewing machines, freezers, hydraulic turbines, and 87 percent of all the 5,885 products in machine building industry) had only a single producer located in one geographic area. In 1988, about two thirds of all the products had no more than three producers (IMF et al. 1991, Vol. II, pp. 39–40).

6. The model in Qian, Roland and Xu (2006) is a more general version of the present model. It models continuous adoption of new programs over time and also models another type of coordination called "attribute compatibility." It also allows an organization to have n regions and m functions.

7. It would be reasonable to assume that the setup cost should be incurred twice, a first time when partial innovation is tried and a second time when the full innovation is implemented since the nature of the coordination is different in both cases. This assumption would however only reinforce the result of proposition 3.

8. Households may doubt that the reform will continue. Such concerns were well-founded. Indeed a policy reversal did happen in the late 1960s in China and those hard working farmers who became richer suffered politically and economically.

9. Due to the U-form structure, production infrastructures remained geographically dispersed which made regional coordination more difficult.

10. It is interesting to note that France introduced some decentralization of power in 1981.

References

Brooks, Karen, Elmira Krylatykh, Zvi Lerman, Aleksandr Petrikov and Vasilii Uzun. "Agricultural Reform in Russia: A view from the Farm Level" World Bank Discussion Paper Number 327, 1996.

Bryce, James (1901), *The American Commonwealth*, London: Macmillan (first published 1888).

Butterfield, John. "Devolution in Decision-Making and Organizational Change in Soviet Agriculture," in W. Moskoff (ed.), *Perestroika in the Countryside*. Sharpe, pp. 19–46, 1990.

Chandler, Alfred Jr. *Strategy and Structure*. New York: Doubleday & Company, Inc., 1962.

Chandler, Alfred Jr. *The Visible Hand: The Managerial Revolution in American Business*. Cambridge: Belknap Press of Harvard University Press, 1977.

Dewatripont, Mathias, and Gérard Roland. "The Design of Reform Packages under Uncertainty." *American Economic Review*, December 1995, *85*(5), pp. 1207–1223.

Dewatripont, Mathias, and Gérard Roland. "Transition as a Process of Large-Scale Institutional Change," in Kreps, David, and Kenneth Wallis (ed.), *Advances in Economic Theory*, Cambridge University Press 1997, vol. II, pp. 240–278.

Huang, Yasheng. "Information, Bureaucracy and Economic Reforms in China and the Soviet Union." *World Politics*, 1994, vol. 47, pp. 102–134.

IMF, World Bank, OECD and EBRD. *A Study of the Soviet Economy*, vol. II & III, Paris: OECD, 1991.

Kornai, Janos. The Socialist System. Princeton University Press and Oxford University Press, 1992.

Laird, Roy. "Kolkhozy, the Russian Achilles Heel: Failed Agrarian Reform." *Europe-Asia Studies*, 1997, vol. 49, no. 3, pp. 469–478.

Liefert, William and Johan Swinnen. "Changes in Agricultural Markets in Transition Economies," United States Department of Agriculture, Agricultural Economic Report Number 806, 2002.

Maskin, Eric, Yingyi Qian, and Chenggang Xu. "Incentives, Information, and Organizational Form." *Review of Economic Studies*, forthcoming, 1999.

McMillan, John, and Barry Naughton. "How to Reform a Planned Economy: Lessons from China." *Oxford Review of Economic Policy*, Spring 1992, 8, pp. 130–143.

Milgrom, Paul, and John Roberts. *Economics, Organization, and Management*. Prentice Hall, 1992.

Nove, Alec. *The Soviet Economic System*, second edition. Boston: Allen & Unwin. 1980.

Osborne, David. *Laboratories of Democracy*. Boston: Harvard Business School Press, 1988.

Qian, Yingyi, and Chenggang Xu. "Why China's Economic Reform Differ: The M-form Hierarchy and Entry/Expansion of the Non-state Sector." *Economics of Transition*, June 1993, 1(2), pp. 135–170.

Qian, Yingyi, Gérard Roland, and Chenggang Xu. "Coordination and Experimentation in M-form and U-form Organizations." *Journal of Political Economy*, April 2006, vol. 114, no. 2.

Sachs, Jeffrey, and Wing T. Woo. "Understanding China's Economic Performance," mimeo, Harvard University, 1997.

Van Atta, D. "Russian Agriculture between Plan and Market," in van Atta (ed.), *The "Farmer Threat,"* Westview Press, Boulder Colorado, 1993a, pp. 9–24.

Van Atta, D. "The Return of Individual Farming in Russia," in van Atta (ed.), *The "Farmer Threat,"* Westview Press, Boulder Colorado, 1993b, pp. 71–95.

Wädekin, Karl-Eugen. "Verlustminderung als zentrale Aufgabe der Nahrungswirtschaft in Russland und der GUS (SNG). Osteuropa, November 1992, pp. 938-950.

Wegren, Stephen. *Agriculture and the State in Soviet and Post-Soviet Russia*, University of Pittsburgh Press, Pittsburgh 1998.

Wehrheim, P., K. Frohberg, E. Serova and J. von Braun, editors, *Russia's Agro-food sector: Towards Truly Functioning Markets*, Dordrecht Netherlands, Kluwer, 2000.

Williamson, Oliver. *Markets and Hierarchies*, New York: Free Press, 1975.

Williamson, Oliver. *The Economic Institutions of Capitalism*, New York: Free Press, 1985.

Xinhui Xianzhi Editorial Committee, Xinhui Xianzhi (Annals of Xinhui County: http://www.xinhuinet.gov.cn/Xhsz/sz/xhsz.htm), 1995.

Xinhui Xianzhi Editorial Committee, Xinhui Xianzhi Xubian (Annals of Xinhui County—Continuation: http://www.xinhuinet.gov.cn/Xhsz/szxp/SZXP.htm), 1997.

Index

Printed in the United States
By Bookmasters